Raspberry Pi 5 System Administration Basics

This book covers Raspberry Pi 5 OS concepts and commands that allow a beginner to perform essential system administration and other operations. This is a mandatory set of commands that even an ordinary, non-administrative user would need to know to work efficiently in a character text-based interface (CUI) or in a graphical interface (GUI) to the operating system. Each chapter contains sequential, in-line exercises that reinforce the material that comes before them. The code for the book and solutions to the in-chapter exercises can be found at the following link: www.github.com/bobk48/Raspberry-Pi-5-OS.

The first introductory chapter illustrates a basic set of text-based commands which are the predominant means that a system administrator uses to maintain the integrity of the system. User account control is an example of the fundamental integrity aspect of administration, requiring the addition of users and groups while maintaining secure access. Storage solutions involve integrating persistent media such as USB3 SSDs and NVMe drives, ensuring proper file system classification based on physical or virtual media, including NFSv4 and iSCSI setups.

The second chapter, which is the core of the book, covers many critical and pertinent system administration commands and facilities. For example, how to attach additional media to the Raspberry Pi 5 and how to install and boot the Raspberry Pi 5 from an NVMe SSD, rather than from the traditional microSD card medium. This chapter also covers many advanced topics to expand the beginner's knowledge of system maintenance and control.

The third chapter shows how system administration is streamlined with systemd, which allows efficient service management. The systemd "superkernel" is a powerful initialization and service management framework that has revolutionized Linux system administration. It introduces a structured approach to system control through sub-commands and applications, enhancing system efficiency. At its core, systemd units and unit files serve as essential building blocks, defining system behavior.

The fourth chapter gives a basic introduction to the Python 3 programming language, with a complete explication of the syntax of the language, and many illustrative examples.

Robert M. Koretsky is a retired lecturer in mechanical engineering, formerly of the University of Portland School of Engineering. He now writes books on UNIX and Linux, particularly for the Raspberry Pi SOC. His hobbies include woodworking and playing early 80s synth pop music.

Raspberry Pi OS System Administration with systemd

A Practical Approach

Series Editor: Robert M. Koretsky

Raspberry Pi OS System Administration with systemd: A Practical Approach
Robert M. Koretsky

Raspberry Pi OS System Administration with systemd and Python: A Practical Approach
Robert M. Koretsky

Raspberry Pi OS Text Editors, git, and LXC: A Practical Approach
Robert M. Koretsky

Raspberry Pi OS System Administration: Ancillary Topics
Robert M. Koretsky

Raspberry Pi 5 System Administration Basics
Robert M. Koretsky

www.routledge.com/Raspberry-Pi-OS-System-Administration-withsystemd/book-series/123

Raspberry Pi 5 System Administration Basics

Robert M. Koretsky

CRC Press
Taylor & Francis Group
Boca Raton London New York

CRC Press is an imprint of the
Taylor & Francis Group, an **informa** business

A CHAPMAN & HALL BOOK

First edition published 2026
by CRC Press
2385 NW Executive Center Drive, Suite 320, Boca Raton FL 33431

and by CRC Press
4 Park Square, Milton Park, Abingdon, Oxon, OX14 4RN

CRC Press is an imprint of Taylor & Francis Group, LLC

ISBN: 978-1-041-09904-8 (hbk)
ISBN: 978-1-041-09903-1 (pbk)
ISBN: 978-1-003-65242-7 (ebk)

DOI: 10.1201/9781003652427

Typeset in Palatino
by KnowledgeWorks Global Ltd.

Contents

Preface

The hallmarks of computer science systems, in general, are change and constant evolution. And that applies to both operating systems and to the hardware they run on. Certainly, the Linux kernel itself has gone through constant evolution since its inception in the 1990s. Since the last volumes of this Raspberry Pi OS System Administration Fundamentals were published, there have been a few adjustments and corrections to the upstream Debian OS that the Raspberry Pi OS is based upon, and to the downstream Raspberry Pi OS itself. And no doubt that will continue into the future.

Most significant, and perhaps critically, are the ongoing hardware changes to the Raspberry Pi platform itself. And the addition of a PCIe 2.0 × 1 interface connector to the main board, which then allows auxiliary NVMe adapters, or "hats", to be added to the hardware, is the most exciting and vital change between the Raspberry Pi 4b/ 400 and the Raspberry Pi 5b/500. This ups the game for the Raspberry Pi, and brings it out of the perceived hobbyist class of SoC systems, and into the wider and more competitive world of laptop and desktop computers. Even if in reality it's always already been there!

This book is a compendium of easy-to-use and essential Raspberry Pi 5 OS system administration tasks for the beginner. The Raspberry Pi 5 OS is derived from the Debian branch of Linux, and as of this writing, Debian Bookworm was the most current and stable version of that operating system. To present the system administration topics and commands here, I have selected some very basic stuff, and a few more advanced concepts, topics, commands, and details that might not appear in a more complete system administration book.

The overriding idea behind system administration of a modern, 21st-century Linux system, such as the Raspberry Pi 5 OS, is the use of systemd to ensure that the Linux kernel works efficiently and effectively to provide these three foundation stones of computer operation and management:

P.1 Computer System Concurrency, Virtualization, and Secure Persistence

And this control of the kernel by a "super-kernel", which is what systemd essentially is, must also promote the highest level of system performance and speed, given the use case(s) your Raspberry Pi 5 computer might be put to, and the perceived needs of the target user base that the computer serves. Unless that novice user, or even a more seasoned system professional, has not only a basic, but also a more complete knowledge of how systemd controls, administrates, and oversees every process operation of a modern Linux system, they will never be able to master implementing the kind of functionality that their use case(s) might ultimately require. Particularly for the user base on the system, and the demands that user base makes.

Everything illustrated in all chapters of the book, in the specific form (and the syntax of commands) found there, is explicitly applicable to all Debian-family distributions, including the Raspberry Pi 5 OS, and also to all other versions of Debian, including Ubuntu, and Linux Mint; it's also applicable to RedHat-family CentOS, and Slackware distros, such as SuSE. The major areas of development of Linux over the last several years, and into the future as well, have been and will be the expansion of the role that systemd plays in every aspect of Linux operating system use.

Certainly, out of the multitude of possible topics we could have presented, the ones you find detailed here have basically been selected in somewhat of a subjective way. That selective way was mainly guided by these concerns:

a. The secure maintenance, in terms of concurrency, virtualization, and persistence, of a single Raspberry Pi 5 computer system that an ordinary novice user can install on her own personal computer.

b. How important the topics are in a perceived ranking of essential Linux system administration tasks.

c. How systemd plays into the maintenance regimen chosen by that ordinary user.

d. The overall pedagogic integration of the selected topics presented on system administration with each other.

e. How well these topics serve to prepare a student for entry into any chosen information technology or computer science profession, or how someone already in those professions can use this book to better their practice of that profession. In other words, for educational and continuing education audiences.

f. To some degree, making it possible to extrapolate these topics (for audiences in e.) from a single computer system environment to a broader and larger-scaled computing environment, such as is found on small-to-medium sized servers, or to cloud-based, virtual computing.

The fundamental prerequisites of all the chapters are (1) knowledge of how to type a syntactically-correct Linux command on the command line (as detailed explicitly in Chapter 0,) (2) having access to a dedicated Raspberry Pi 5 computer with the latest Raspberry Pi 5 Operating System available to you to install and run on it, and (3) for many operations, being a privileged user on the system that is able to execute the **sudo** command to assume superuser status.

An online Github site, with further materials and updates, program code, and solutions to in-chapter exercises, is provided for this book. It can be found at www.github.com/bobk48/Raspberry-Pi-5-OS

All command line instructions in this volume were tested on a Raspberry Pi 5, with 4GB of memory, and the latest version of the Raspberry Pi OS at the time.

P.2 Routes through This Book

- Browse the Contents.
- Select a topic that interests you.
- Do the Examples or all the command-line materials presented for that topic.
- Maybe pick another topic that interests you and do the examples and all the command-line materials there.
- Finally, go back to the beginning of each chapter. Do everything from start to finish.
- Rinse and repeat the above as necessary.
- Refer as much as possible to the systemd materials in Chapter 2, using them as an encyclopedic source for the material you select out of the other chapters.
- Have fun!

Robert M. Koretsky
Portland, Oregon

0

"Quick Start" into Sysadmin for the Raspberry Pi 5 OS

cat cd cp exit hostname -I ip login lp lpr ls man mesg mkdir more mv passwd PATH
pwd rm rmdir telnet unalias uname whatis whereis who whoami

0.1 Objectives and Introduction

- To explain how to manage and maintain files and directories
- To show where to get system-wide help for Raspberry Pi 5 OS commands
- To demonstrate the use of a beginner's set of utility commands
- To cover the basic commands and operators

cat cd cp exit hostname -I ip login lp lpr ls man mesg mkdir more mv passwd PATH
pwd rm rmdir telnet unalias uname whatis whereis who whoami

To start working productively with system administration on the Raspberry Pi 5 OS, the beginner needs to have some familiarity with these sequential topics, as follows:

a. How to maintain and organize files in the file structure of the operating system. Creating a tree-like structure of folders (also called directories) and storing files in a logical fashion in these folders is critical to working efficiently in the Raspberry Pi 5 OS.

b. How to get help on text-based commands and their usage. With keyboard entry, in a command-based, Character User Interface(CUI) environment, being able to find out, in a quick and easy way, how to use a command, its options, and arguments by typing it on the keyboard correctly, is imperative to working efficiently.

c. How to execute a small set of essential utility commands to set up or customize your working environment. Once a beginner is familiar with the right way to construct file maintenance commands, adding a set of utility commands makes each session more productive.

To use this chapter successfully as a springboard into the remainder of the book, you should carefully read, follow, and execute the instructions and command line sessions we provide, in the order presented. Each section in this chapter, and every subsequent chapter as well, builds on the information that precedes it. They will give you the concepts, command tools, and methods that will enable you to do system administration using the Raspberry Pi 5 OS.

Throughout this book, we illustrate everything using the following version of the Raspberry Pi 5 OS, on the hardware listed:

System:
  Host: raspberrypi Kernel: 6.12.34+rpt-rpi-2712 arch: aarch64 bits: 64
    compiler: N/A Desktop: LXDE v: 0.10.1 Distro: Debian GNU/Linux 12 (bookworm)
Machine:
  Type: ARM System: Raspberry Pi 5 Model B Rev 1.0 details: N/A rev: c04170
    serial: a5b3f4f94c31353d

In this chapter, and all of the others in this book, the major commands we want to illustrate are first defined with an abbreviated syntax description, which will clarify general components of those commands. The syntax description format is as follows:

Syntax: The exact syntax of how a command, its options, and its arguments are correctly typed on the command line

Purpose: The specific purpose of the command

Output: A short description of the results of executing the command

Commonly used options/features: A listing of the most popular and useful options and option arguments

In addition, the following web link is to a site that allows you to type in a single or multiple Raspberry Pi 5 OS command, and get a verbose explanation of the components of that command:

https://explainshell.com/

****Note****

The Raspberry Pi 5 OS is a Linux operating system!

The premise and prerequisite of this book is that you know what the correct form, or structure, of a Linux command is, and how to type one in on the console or terminal command line!

The general syntax, or structure of a single Linux command (often referred to as a *simple command*) as it is typed on the command line, is as follows:

$ command [[-]option(s)] [option argument(s)] [command argument(s)]

where:

$ is the command line, or shell prompt, from the Raspberry Pi OS (in our case, the Bash shell);

anything enclosed in [] is not always needed;

command is the name of the valid Linux command for that shell in lowercase letters;

[-option(s)] is one or more modifiers that change the behavior of command;

[option argument(s)] is one or more modifiers that change the behavior of **[-option(s)]**; and

[command argument(s)] is one or more objects that are affected by **command**.

Note the following seven essential characteristics of a Linux command:

- A space separates command, options, option arguments, and command arguments, but no space is necessary between multiple option(s) or multiple option arguments.
- The order of multiple options or option arguments is irrelevant.
- A space character is optional between the option and the option argument.
- Always press the **<Enter>** key to submit the command for interpretation and execution.
- Options may be preceded by a single hyphen - or two hyphens, --, depending on the form of the option. The short form of the option is preceded by a single hyphen, the long form of the option is preceded by two hyphens. No space character should be placed between hyphen(s) and option(s).
- A small percentage of commands (like **whoami**) take <u>no</u> options, option arguments, or command arguments.

Everything on the command line is case sensitive!

Also, it is possible and <u>very</u> common to type *multiple* Linux commands (sometimes called *compound* commands, to differentiate them from simple commands) on the same command line, before pressing the **<Enter>** key. The components of a multiple Linux command are separated with input and output redirection characters, to channel the output of one into the input of another.

In-Chapter Exercises

1. Type the following commands on your Raspberry Pi 5 OS's command line, and note the results. Which ones are syntactically incorrect?

Why? (The Bash prompt is shown as the $character in each, and we assume that **file1** and **file2** exist.)
$ la -ls
$ cat
$ more -q file1
$ more file2
$ time
$ lsblk-a

2. How can you differentiate a Raspberry Pi 5 OS command from its options, option arguments, and command arguments?
3. What is the difference between a single Raspberry Pi 5 OS command and a multiple Raspberry Pi 5 OS command, as typed on the command line before pressing **<Enter>**?
4. If you get no error message after you enter a Raspberry Pi 5 OS command, how do you know that it actually accomplished what you wanted it to?

0.2 File Maintenance Commands and Help on Raspberry Pi 5 OS Command Usage

After successful installation on your hardware and your first-time login to a new Raspberry Pi 5 OS system, one of your first actions will be to construct and organize your workspace environment, and the files that will be contained in it. The operation of organizing your files according to some logical scheme is known as *file maintenance*. A logical scheme used to organize your files might consist of creating *bins* for storing files according to their subject matter or dates of their creation. In the following sections, you will type file creation and maintenance commands that produce a structure similar to what is shown in Figure 0.1. Complete the operations in the following sections in the order they are presented to get a better overview of what file maintenance really is. Also, it is critical that you review what was presented in Section 0.1 regarding the structure of a Raspberry Pi 5 OS command, so that when you begin to type commands for file maintenance, you understand how the syntax of what you are typing conforms to the general syntax of any Raspberry Pi 5 OS command.

0.2.1 File and Directory Structure

When you first open a terminal, or console, window, you are working in the *home directory*, or folder, of the autonomous user associated with the username and password you used to log into the system with. Whatever

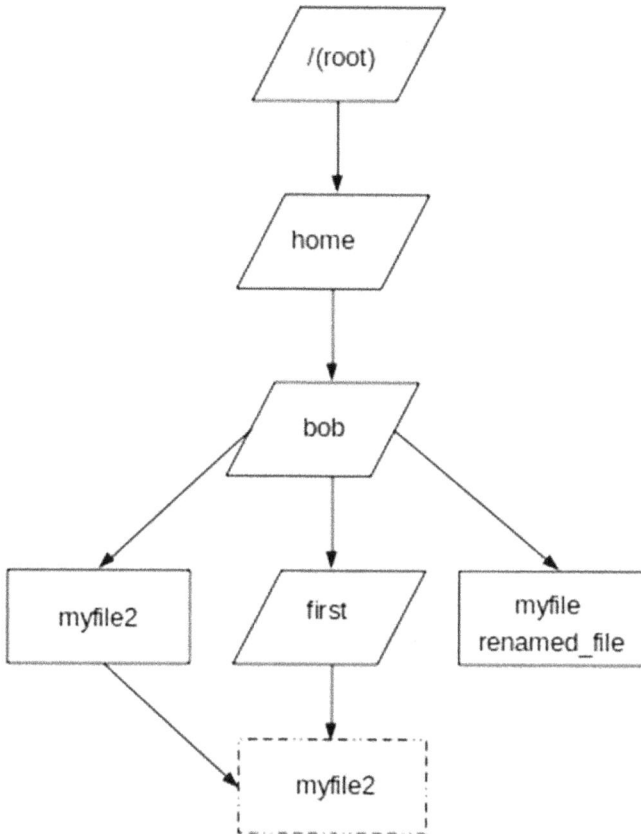

FIGURE 0.1
Example directory structure.

directory you are presently in is known as the *current working directory*, and there is only one current working directory active at any given time. It is helpful to visualize the structure of your files and directories using a diagram. Figure 0.1 is an example of a home directory and file structure for a user named **bob**. In this figure, directories are represented as parallelograms, and plain files (e.g., files that contain text or binary instructions) are represented as rectangles. A *pathname*, or path, is simply a textual way of designating the location of a directory or file in the complete file structure of the Raspberry Pi 5 system you are working on. For example, the path to the file **myfile2** in Figure 0.1 is **/home/bob/myfile2**. The designation of the path begins at the root (/) of the entire file system, descends to the folder named **home**, and then descends again to the home directory of the user named **bob**.

As shown in Figure 0.1, the files named **myfile**, **myfile2**, and **renamed_file** are stored under or in the directory **bob**. Beneath **bob** is a *subdirectory* named **first**. In the following sections, you will create these files and the subdirectory structure in the home directory of the username that you have logged into your Raspberry Pi 5 OS system with.

In-Chapter Exercise

5. Type the following two commands on your Raspberry Pi 5 OS system:

    $ cd /
    $ ls

Similar to Figure 0.1, sketch a diagram of the directories and files whose names you see listed as the output of the second command. Save this diagram for use later.

0.2.2 Viewing the Contents of Files

To begin working with files, you can easily create a new text file by using the **cat** command. The syntax of the **cat** command is as follows:

cat [options] [file-list]
Purpose: Join one or more files sequentially or display them in the console window
Output: Contents of the files in **file-list** displayed on the screen, one file at a time
Commonly used options/features:
+E   Display $ at the end of each line
-n   Put line numbers on the displayed lines
-- help   Display the purpose of the command and a brief explanation of each option

The **cat** command, short for concatenate, allows you to join files. In the example, you will join what you type on the keyboard to a new file being created in the current working directory. This is achieved by the redirect character >, which takes what you type at the *standard input* (in this case, the keyboard) and directs it into the file named **myfile**. You can consider the keyboard, and the stream of information it provides, as a file. As stated in the Introduction above, this usage is an example of a command, **cat** with no options, option arguments, or command arguments. It simply uses the command, a redirect character, and a target, or destination, named **myfile**, where the redirection will go.

The following is a very simple example of a *multiple command* typed on the command line, as opposed to a single command, as briefly described in the Introduction. In a multiple command, you can string together single Raspberry Pi 5 OS commands in a chain with connecting operators, such as the redirect character shown here.

****Note****

Combinations of key presses on the keyboard are denoted as **<Key+Key>**, where the first **Key** is <u>pressed and held down</u>, and then the second **Key** is pressed.

$ cat > myfile

This is an example of how to use the cat command to add plain text to a file

<Ctrl+D>
$

You can type as many lines of text, pressing **<Enter>** on the keyboard to distinguish between lines in the file, as you want. Then, on a new line, when you hold down **<Ctrl+D>**, the file is created in the current working directory, using the command you typed.

You can view the contents of this file, since it is a plain text file that was created using the keyboard, by doing the following:

$ more myfile

This is an example of how to use the cat command to add plain text to a file

$

This is a simple example of the syntax of a single Raspberry Pi 5 OS command.

The general syntax of the **more** command is as follows:

more [options] [file-list]
Purpose: Concatenate/display the files in **file-list** on the screen, one screen at a time
Output: Contents of the files in **file-list** displayed on the screen, one page at a time
Commonly used options/features:
+E/str   Start two lines before the first line containing **str**
-nN   Display N lines per screen/page
+N   Start displaying the contents of the file at line number N

The **more** command shows one screenful of a file at a time by default. If the file is several pages long, you can proceed to view subsequent pages by pressing the **<Space>** key on the keyboard, or by pressing the **Q** key on the keyboard to quit viewing the output.

In-Chapter Exercise

6. Use the **cat** command to produce another text file named testfile. Then join the contents of myfile and testfile into one text file, named myfile3, with the **cat** command.

0.2.3 Creating, Deleting, and Managing Files

To copy the contents of one file into another file, use the **cp** command. The general syntax of the **cp** command is as follows:

cp [options] file1 file2
Purpose: Copy **file1** to **file2**; if **file2** is a directory, make a copy of **file1** in this directory
Output: Copied files
Commonly used options/features:
-i   If destination exists, prompt before overwriting
-p   Preserve file access modes and modification times on copied files
-r   Recursively copy files and subdirectories

For example, to make an exact duplicate of the file named **myfile**, with the new name **myfile2**, type the following:

$ cp myfile myfile2
$

This usage of the **cp** command has two required command arguments. The first argument is the source file that already exists and which you want to copy. The second argument is the destination file, or the name of the file that will be the copy. Be aware that many Raspberry Pi 5 OS commands can take plain, ordinary, or regular files as arguments, or can take directory files as arguments. This can change the basic task accomplished by the command. It is also worth noting that not only can file names be arguments, but *pathnames* as well. A pathname is the route to any particular place in the file system structure of the operating system. This changes the site or location, in the path structure of the file system, of the operation of the command.

In order to change the name of a file or directory, you can use the **mv** command. The general syntax of the **mv** command is as follows:

mv [options] file1 file2
mv [options] file-list directory
Purpose: First syntax: Rename file1 to file2
              Second syntax: Move all the files in file-list to directory
Output: Renamed or relocated files
Commonly used options/features:
-f   Force the move regardless of the file access modes of the destination file
-i   Prompt the user before overwriting the destination

In the following usage, the first argument to the **mv** command is the source file name, and the second argument is the destination name.

$ mv myfile2 renamed_file
$

****Note****

In programming and text processing, there are two common types of single (') and double (") quotes:

1. Straight Quotes (also called ASCII quotes or Typewriter Quotes):
   - Single: ' (ASCII code: 0x27)
   - Double: " (ASCII code: 0x22)
   - These are plain and commonly used in Linux commands, programming languages like Python, JavaScript, and shell scripting.
2. Curly Quotes (also called Smart Quotes or Typographic Quotes):
   - Left Single: ' (Unicode: U+2018), Right Single: ' (Unicode: U+2019)
   - Left Double: " (Unicode: U+201C), Right Double: " (Unicode: U+201D)
   - These are used in typography, word processors, and proper typesetting for books and articles. They are rarely found in Linux commands!

It is important at this point to notice the use of spaces in Raspberry Pi 5 OS commands. What if you obtain a file from a Windows system that has one or more spaces in one of the file names? How can you work with this file in Raspberry Pi 5 OS? The answer is simple. Whenever you need to use that file name in a command as an argument, enclose the file name in straight double quotes ("). For example, you might obtain a file that you have "detached" from an e-mail message from someone on a Windows system, such as **latest revisions october.txt**.

In order to work with this file on a Raspberry Pi 5 OS system – that is, to use the file name as an argument in a Raspberry Pi 5 OS command – enclose the whole name in straight double quotes. The correct command to rename that file to something shorter would be:

```
$ mv "latest revisions october.txt" laterevs.txt
$
```

In order to delete a file, you can use the **rm** command. The general syntax of the **rm** command is as follows:

rm [options] file-list
Purpose: Removes files in **file-list** from the file structure (and disk)
Output: Deleted files
Commonly used options/features:
-f   Remove regardless of the file access modes of **file-list**
-i   Prompt the user before removing files in **file-list**
-r   Recursively remove the files in **file-list** if **file-list** is a directory; use with caution!

To delete the file **renamed_file** from the current working directory, type:

```
$ rm renamed_file
$
```

In-Chapter Exercise

   7. Use the **rm** command to delete the files testfile and myfile3.

The most important command you will execute to do file maintenance is the **ls** command. The general syntax for the **ls** command is as follows:

ls [options] [pathname-list]
Purpose: Sends the names of the files and directories in the directory specified by **pathname-list** to the display screen
Output: Names of the files and directories in the directory specified by **pathname-list**, or the names only if **pathname-list** contains file names only
Commonly used options/features:
-F   Display a slash character (/) after directory names, an asterisk (*) after binary
       executables, and an "at" character (@) after symbolic links
-a   Display names of all the files, including hidden files
-i   Display inode numbers
-l   Display long list that includes file access modes, link count, owner, group, file size
       (in bytes), and modification time

The **ls** command will list the names of files or folders in your current working directory or folder. In addition, as with the other commands we have used so far, if you include a complete pathname specification for the **pathname-list** argument to the command, then you can list the names of files and folders along that pathname list. To see the names of the files now in your current working directory, type the following:

```
$ ls
Desktop Documents Downloads Dropbox Music Pictures Public Templates Videos
$
```

Please note that you will probably not get a listing of the same file names as we showed above here, because your system will have placed some files automatically in your home directory, as in the example we used, aside from the ones we created together, named **myfile** and **myfile2**. Also note that this file name listing does <u>not</u> include the name **renamed_file**, because we deleted that file.

The next command you will execute is actually just an alternate or modified way of executing the **ls** command, one that includes the command name and options. As shown in the Introduction, a Raspberry Pi 5 OS command has options that can be typed on the command line along with the command to change the behavior of the basic command. In the case of the **ls** command, the options **l** and **a** produce a longer listing of all ordinary and system (dot) files, as well as providing other attendant information about the files.

Don't forget to put the space character between the **s** and the - (dash). Remember again that spaces delimit, or partition, the components of a Raspberry Pi 5 OS command as it is typed on the command line!

Now, type the following command:

```
$ ls -la
total 152
drwx------      18    bob  bob    4096   Mar  5   11:04   .
drwxr-xr-x       3    root root   4096   Mar  1   14:52   ..
-rw-------        1    bob  bob    1734   Mar  5   11:07   .bash_history
-rw-r--r--        1    bob  bob     220   Nov 19   05:32   .bash_logout
-rw-r--r--        1    bob  bob    3523   Nov 19   05:32   .bashrc
drwxr-xr-x       2    bob  bob    4096   Nov 19   05:36   Bookshelf
```

Output truncated...

As you see in this screen display (which shows the listing of files in our home directory and will most likely not be the same as the listing of files in your home directory!), the information about each file in the current working directory is displayed in eight columns. The first column shows the type of file, where **d** stands for directory, l stands for symbolic link, and – stands for ordinary or regular file. Also in the first column, the access modes to that file for user, group, and others are shown as **r**, **w**, or **x**. In the second column, the number of links to that file is displayed. In the third column, the username of the owner of that file is displayed. In the fourth column, the name of the group for that file is displayed. In the fifth column, the number of bytes that the file occupies on disk is displayed. In the sixth column, the date that the file was last modified is displayed. In the seventh column, the time that the file was last modified is displayed. In the eighth and final column, the name of the file is displayed. This way of executing the command is a good way to list more complete information about the file. Examples of using the more complete information are (1) so that you can know the byte size and be able to fit the file on some portable storage medium, or (2) to display the access modes, so that you can alter the access modes to a particular file or directory.

In-Chapter Exercise

8. Use the **ls -la** command to list all of the filenames in your home directory on your Raspberry Pi 5 OS system. How does the listing you obtain compare with the listing shown above? Remember that our listing was done on a Raspberry Pi 5 OS system.

You can also get a file listing for a single file in the current working directory by using another variation of the **ls** command, as follows:

```
$ ls -la myfile
-rw-r--r-- 1 bob  bob  797 Jan 16 10:00 myfile
$
```

This variation shows you a long listing with attendant information for the specific file named **myfile**. A breakdown of what you typed on the command line is 1) **ls**, the command name, 2) **-la**, the options, and 3) **myfile**, the command argument.

What if you make a mistake in your typing, and misspell a command name or one of the other parts of a command? Type the following on the command line:

```
$ lx -la myfile
lx: not found
$
```

The lx: not found reply from Raspberry Pi 5 OS is an error message. There is no **lx** command in the Raspberry Pi 5 OS, so an error message is displayed. If you had typed an option that did not exist, you would also get an error message. If you supplied a file name that was not in the current working directory, you would get an error message, too. This makes an important point about the execution of Raspberry Pi 5 OS commands. If no error message is displayed, then the command executed correctly, and the results might or might not appear on screen, depending on what the command actually does. If you get an error message displayed, you must correct the error before Raspberry Pi 5 OS will execute the command as you type it.

****Note****

Typographic mistakes account for the largest percentage of the errors that beginners make when using typed commands!

0.2.4 Creating, Deleting, and Managing Directories

Another critical aspect of file maintenance is the set of procedures and the related Raspberry Pi 5 OS commands you use to create, delete, and organize directories in your Raspberry Pi 5 OS account on a computer. When moving through the file system, you are either ascending or descending to reach the directory you want to use. The directory directly above the current working directory is referred to as the *parent* of the current working directory. The directory or directories immediately under the current working directory are referred to as the *children* of the current working directory. The most common mistake for beginners is misplacing files. They cannot find the file names listed with the **ls** command because they have placed or created the files in a directory either above or below the current working directory in the file structure. When you create a file, if you have also created a logically organized set of directories beneath your own home directory, you will know where to store the file. In the following set of commands, we create a directory beneath the home directory and use that new directory to store a file.

To create a new directory beneath the current working directory, you use the **mkdir** command. The general syntax for the **mkdir** command is as follows:

mkdir [options] dirnames
Purpose: Creates directory or directories specified in **dirnames**
Output: New directory or directories
Commonly used options/features:
-m MODE   Create a directory with given access modes
-p   Create parent directories that don't exist in the pathnames
                     specified in **dirnames**

To create a child, or subdirectory, named **first** under the current working directory, type the following:

$ mkdir first
$

This command has now created a new subdirectory named **first** under, or as a child of, the current working directory. Refer back to Figure 0.1 for a graphical description of the directory location of this new subdirectory.

In order to change the current working directory to make it this new subdirectory, you use the **cd** command. The general syntax for the **cd** command is as follows:

cd [directory]
Purpose: Change the current working directory to **directory** or return to the home directory when **directory** is omitted
Output: New current working directory

To change the current working directory to **first** by descending down the path structure to the specified directory named **first**, type the following:

$ cd first
$

You can always verify what the current working directory is by using the **pwd** command. The general syntax of the **pwd** command is as follows:

pwd
Purpose: Displays the current working directory on screen
Output: Pathname of current working directory

You can verify that **first** is now the current working directory by typing the following:

$ pwd
/home/bob/first
$

The output from the Raspberry Pi 5 OS on the command line shows the pathname to the current working directory or folder. As previously stated, this path is a textual route through the complete file structure of the computer that Raspberry Pi 5 OS is running on, ending in the current working directory. In this example of the output, the path starts at /, the root of the file system. Then it descends to the directory **home**, a major branch of the file system on the computer running Raspberry Pi 5 OS. Then it descends to the directory **bob**, another branch, which is the home directory name for the user. Finally, it descends to the branch named **first**, the current working directory.

On some systems, depending on the default settings, another way of determining what the current working directory is can be done by simply looking at the command line prompt. This prompt may be prefaced with the complete path to the current working directory, ending in the current working directory.

You can ascend back up to the home directory, or the parent of the subdirectory **first**, by typing the following:

```
$ cd
$
```

An alternate way of doing this is to type the following, where the tilde character (~) resolves to, or is a substitute for, the specification of the complete path to the home directory:

```
$ cd ~
$
```

To verify that you have now ascended up to the home directory, type the following:

```
$ pwd
/home/bob
$
```

You can also ascend to a directory above your home directory, sometimes called the parent of your current working directory, by typing the following:

```
$ cd ..
$
```

In this command, the two periods (..) represent the parent, or branch above the current working directory. Don't forget to type a space character between the **d** and the first period. To verify that you have ascended to the parent of your home directory, type the following:

```
$ pwd
/home
$
```

To descend to your home directory, type the following:

```
$ cd
$
```

To verify that there are two files in the home directory that begin with the letters my, type the following command:

```
$ ls my*
myfile   myfile2
$
```

The asterisk following the **y** on the command line is known as a *metacharacter*, or a character that represents a pattern; in this case, the pattern is any set of characters. When Raspberry Pi 5 OS interprets the command after you press the **<Enter>** key on the keyboard, it searches for all files in the current working directory that begin with the letters **my** and end with anything else.

In-Chapter Exercise

9. Use the **cd** command to ascend to the root (/) of your Raspberry Pi 5 file system, and then use it to descend down each sub-directory from the root recursively to a depth of 2 sub-directories, sketching a diagram of the component files found on your system. Make the named entries in the diagram as complete as possible, listing as many files as you think necessary. Retain this diagram as a useful map of your particular Raspberry Pi 5 OS distribution's file system.

Another aspect of organizing your directories is the movement of files between directories, or changing the location of files in your directories. For example, you now have the file **myfile2** in your home directory, but you would like to move it into the subdirectory named **first**. See Figure 0.1 for a graphic description to change the organization of your files at this point. To accomplish this, you can use the second syntax method illustrated for the **mv file-list directory** command to move the file **myfile2** down into the subdirectory named **first**. To achieve this, type the following:

```
$ mv myfile2 first
$
```

To verify that **myfile2** is indeed in the subdirectory named first, type the following:

```
$ cd first
$ ls
myfile2
$
```

You will now ascend to the home directory and attempt to remove or delete a file with the **rm** command.

Caution: You should be very careful when using this command, because once a file has been deleted, the only way to recover it is from archival backups that you or the system administrator have made of the file system.

```
$ cd
$ rm myfile2
rm: myfile2: No such file or directory
$
```

You get the error message because in the home directory, the file named **myfile2** does not exist. It was moved down into the subdirectory named first.

Directory organization also includes the ability to delete empty or nonempty directories. The command that accomplishes the removal of empty directories is **rmdir**. The general syntax of the **rmdir** command is as follows:

rmdir [options] dirnames
Purpose: Removes the empty directories specified in **dirnames**
Output: Removes directories
Commonly used options/features:
-p   Remove empty parent directories as well
-r   Recursively delete files and subdirectories beneath the current directory

To delete an entire directory below the current working directory, type the following:

```
$ rmdir first
rmdir: first: Directory not empty
$
```

Since the file **myfile2** is still in the subdirectory named **first**, **first** is not an empty directory, and you get the error message that the **rmdir** command will not delete the directory. If the directory was empty, **rmdir** would have accomplished the deletion. One way to delete a nonempty directory is by using the **rm** command with the **-r** option. The **-r** option recursively descends down into the subdirectory and deletes any files in it before actually deleting the directory itself. Be cautious with this command also, since you may inadvertently delete directories and files with it that you don't really intend to delete. To see how this command deletes a nonempty directory, type the following:

```
$ rm -r first
$
```

The directory **first** and the file **myfile2** are now removed from the file structure.

0.2.5 Obtaining Help with the man Command

A very convenient utility available on Raspberry Pi 5 OS systems is the online help feature, achieved via the use of the **man** command. The general syntax of the **man** command is as follows:

man [options][-s section] command-list
man -k keyword-list
Purpose: First syntax: Display Raspberry Pi 5 OS Reference Manual pages for commands in **command-list** one screen at a time
Second syntax: Display summaries of commands related to keywords in **keyword-list**
Output: Manual pages one screen at a time
Commonly used options/features:
-k keyword-list   Search for summaries of keywords in **keyword-list** in a database and display them
-s sec-num   Search section number **sec-num** for manual pages and display them

To get help by using the **man** command, on usage and options of the **ls** command, for example, type the following:

```
$ man ls
```

```
LS(1)              User Commands              LS(1)

NAME
       ls - list directory contents

SYNOPSIS
       ls [OPTION]... [FILE]...

DESCRIPTION
       List information about the FILEs (the current directory
       by default).
       Sort entries alphabetically if none of -cftuvSUX nor –sort
       is specified.

       Mandatory arguments to long options are mandatory for
       short options too.

       -a, --all
              do not ignore entries starting with .

       -A, --almost-all
              do not list implied . and ..

       --author
Manual page ls(1) line 1 (press h for help or q to quit)
```

This output from Raspberry Pi 5 OS is a Raspberry Pi 5 OS *manual page*, or *man page*, which gives a synopsis of the command usage showing the options, and a brief description that helps you understand how the command should be used. Typing **q** after one page has been displayed, as seen in the example, returns you to the command line prompt. Pressing the **<Space>** key on the keyboard would have shown you more of the content of the manual pages, one screen at a time, related to the **ls** command.

To get help in using all the Raspberry Pi 5 OS commands and their options, use the **man man** command to go to the Raspberry Pi 5 OS reference manual pages.

The pages themselves are organized into eight sections, depending on the topic described, and the topics that are applicable to the particular system. Table 0.1 lists the sections of the manual and what they contain. Most users find the pages they need in Section 1. Software developers mostly use library and system calls and thus find the pages they need in Sections 2 and 3. Users who work on document preparation get the most help from Section 7. Administrators mostly need to refer to pages in Sections 1, 2, 5, and 8.

The manual pages comprise multi-page, specially formatted, descriptive documentation for every command, system call, and library call in Raspberry Pi 5 OS. This format consists of seven general parts: name, synopsis, description, list of files, related information, errors, warnings, and known bugs. You can use the **man** command to view the manual page for a command. Because of the name of this command, the manual pages are normally referred to as Raspberry Pi 5 OS man pages. When you display a manual page on the screen, the top-left corner of the page has the command name with the section it belongs to in parentheses, as with LS(1), seen at the top of the output manual page.

TABLE 0.1

Sections of the Raspberry Pi 5 OS Manual

Section	Description
1	User commands (executable programs or shell commands)
2	System calls (functions provided by the kernel)
3	Library calls (functions within program libraries)
4	Special files (usually found in /dev)
5	File formats and conventions (e.g., /etc/passwd)
6	Games and screensavers
7	Miscellaneous (e.g., macro packages, conventions, and standards)
8	System administration commands (usually only for root)
9	Kernel routines (non-standard, often for kernel developers)

The command used to display the manual page for the **passwd** command is:

$ **man passwd**

The manual page for the **passwd** command now appears on the screen, but we do not show its output. Because they are multi-page text documents, the manual pages for each topic take up more than one screen of text to display their entire contents. To see one screen of the manual page at a time, press the **<Space>** key on the keyboard. To quit viewing the manual page, press the **Q** key on the keyboard.

Now type this command:

$ **man pwd**

If more than one section of the man pages has information on the same word and you are interested in the man page for a particular section, you can use the **-S** option. The following command line therefore displays the man page for the read system call, and not the man page for the shell command read.

$ **man -S2 read**

The command **man -S3 fopen fread strcmp** sequentially displays man pages for three C library calls: **fopen**, **fread**, and **strcmp**.

To exit from the display of these system calls, type **<Ctrl+C>**.

Using the **man** command and typing the command with the **-k** option allows specifying a keyword that limits the search. It is equivalent to using the **apropos** command. The search then yields useful man page headers from all the man pages on the system that contain just the keyword reference. For example, the following command yields the on-screen output on our Raspberry Pi 5 system:

```
$ man -k passwd
chgpasswd (8)      - update group passwords in batch mode
chpasswd (8)       - update passwords in batch mode
exim4_passwd (5)    - Files in use by the Debian exim4 packages
exim4_passwd_client (5) - Files in use by the Debian exim4 packages
fgetpwent_r (3)     - get passwd file entry reentrantly
getpwent_r (3)      - get passwd file entry reentrantly
gpasswd (1)        - administer /etc/group and /etc/gshadow
openssl-passwd (1ssl) - compute password hashes
pam_localuser (8)    - require users to be listed in /etc/passwd
passwd (1)         - change user password
passwd (1ssl)       - compute password hashes
passwd (5)         - the password file
passwd2des (3)      - RFS password encryption
update-passwd (8)    - safely update /etc/passwd, /etc/shadow and /etc/group
vncpasswd (1)       - VNC Server password utility
Output truncated...
```

0.2.6 Other Methods of Obtaining Help

To get a short description of what any particular Raspberry Pi 5 OS command does, you can use the **whatis** command. This is similar to the command **man -f**. The general syntax of the **whatis** command is as follows:

whatis keywords
Purpose: Search the whatis database for abbreviated descriptions of each keyword
Output: Prints a one-line description of each keyword to the screen

The following is an illustration of how to use **whatis-**

The output of the two commands are truncated.

```
$ whatis man
man (7)         - macros to format man pages
man (1)         - an interface to the on-line
                  reference manuals
$
```

You can also obtain short descriptions of more than one command by entering multiple arguments to the **whatis** command on the same command line, with spaces between each argument. The following is an illustration of this method:

```
$ whatis login set setenv
login (1)       - begin session on the system
login (3)       - write utmp and wtmp entries
setenv (3)      - change or add an environment variable
set: nothing appropriate.
$
```

The following In-Chapter exercises ask you to use the **man** and **whatis** commands to find information about the **passwd** command. After completing the exercises, you can use what you have learned to change your login password on the Raspberry Pi 5 OS system that you use.

In-Chapter Exercises

10. Use the **man** command with the **-k** option to display abbreviated help on the **passwd** command. Doing so will give you a screen display similar to that obtained with the **whatis** command, but it will show all apropos command names that contain the characters p a s w d.

11. Use the **whatis** command to get a brief description of the **passwd** command shown above, and then note the difference between the commands **whatis passwd** and **man -k passwd**.

0.3 Utility Commands

There are several major commands that allow the beginner to be more productive when using a Raspberry Pi 5 OS system. A sampling of these kinds of utility commands is given in the following sections and is organized as system setups, general utilities, and communications commands.

0.3.1 Examining System Setups

The **whereis** command allows you to search along certain prescribed paths to locate utility programs and commands, such as shell programs. The general syntax of the **whereis** command is as follows:

whereis [options] filename
Purpose: Locate the binary, source, and man page files for a command
Output: The supplied names are first stripped of leading pathname components and extensions, then pathnames are displayed on screen
Commonly used options/features:
-b   Search only for binaries
-s   Search only for source code

For example, if you type the command **whereis bash** on the command line, you will see a list of the paths to the Bash shell program files themselves, as follows:

$ whereis bash

bash: /bin/bash /etc/bash.bashrc /usr/share/man/man1/bash.1.gz

Note that the paths to a "built-in", or internal, command cannot be found with the **whereis** command.

When you first log on, it is useful to be able to view a display of information about your **userid**, the computer or system you have logged on to, and the operating system on that computer. These tasks can be accomplished with the **whoami** command, which displays your **userid** on the screen. The general syntax of the **whoami** command is as follows:

whoami
Purpose: Displays the effective user id
Output: Displays your effective user id as a name on standard

The following shows how our system responded to this command when we typed it on the command line.

$ whoami
bob
$

The following In-Chapter Exercises give you the chance to use **whereis**, **whoami**, and two other important utility commands, **who** and **hostname** to obtain important information about your system.

To find out the IP address of the Raspberry Pi you are working on, you can use the ip command. The general syntax of the **ip** command is as follows:

ip [OPTIONS] OBJECT { COMMAND | help }
Purpose: Show / manipulate routing, network devices, interfaces and tunnels.
Output: Information about your LAN.

To find out the IP address of the computer you are working on, type the following command in a terminal, or console window:

```
$ ip addr show
1: lo: <LOOPBACK,UP,LOWER_UP> mtu 65536 qdisc noqueue state UNKNOWN group
default qlen 1000
    link/loopback 00:00:00:00:00:00 brd 00:00:00:00:00:00
    inet 127.0.0.1/8 scope host lo
      valid_lft forever preferred_lft forever
    inet6 ::1/128 scope host
      valid_lft forever preferred_lft forever
2: eth0: <BROADCAST,MULTICAST,UP,LOWER_UP> mtu 1500 qdisc mq state UP group
default qlen 1000
    link/ether dc:a6:32:ee:c6:6b brd ff:ff:ff:ff:ff:ff
    inet 192.168.1.2/24 brd 192.168.1.255 scope global dynamic noprefixroute eth0
      valid_lft 65558sec preferred_lft 54758sec
    inet6 fe80::78d9:c72e:75e2:82c/64 scope link
      valid_lft forever preferred_lft forever
3: wlan0: <BROADCAST,MULTICAST> mtu 1500 qdisc noop state DOWN group default
qlen 1000
    link/ether dc:a6:32:ee:c6:6c brd ff:ff:ff:ff:ff:ff
$
```

In the above output, the IP address 192.168.1.2 is the address on the Local Area Network (LAN) of this computer.

In-Chapter Exercises

12. Use the **whereis** command to locate binary files for the Korn shell, the Bourne shell, the Bourne Again shell, the C shell, and the Z shell. Are any of these shell programs not available on your system?

13. Use the **whoami** command to find your username on the system that you're using. Then use the **who** command to see how your username is listed, along with other users of the same system. What is the on-screen format of each user's listing that you

obtained with the **who** command? Try to identify the information in each field on the same line as your username.

14.   Use the **hostname -I** command to find out the IP address of host computer you are logged on to, on your LAN. Compare this to the output of the **ip addr** command on that same system.

0.4 Printing Commands

A very useful and common task performed by every user of a computer system is the printing of text files at a printer. This is accomplished using the configured printer(s) on the local or a remote system. Printers are controlled and managed with the Common UNIX Printing System (CUPS). We show this utility in detail in Chapter 1.

The common commands that perform printing on a Raspberry Pi 5 OS system are **lpr** and **lp**. The general syntax of the **lpr** command is as follows:

lpr [options] filename
Purpose: Send files to the printer
Output: Files sent to the printer queue as print jobs
Commonly used options/features:
-P printer   Send output to the named printer
-# copies   Produce the number of copies indicated for each named file

The following **lpr** command accomplishes the printing of the file named **order.pdf** at the printer designated on our system as **spr**. Remember that no space is necessary between the option (in this case **-P**) and the option argument (in this case **spr**).

```
$ lpr -Pspr order.pdf
$
```

The following **lpr** command accomplishes the printing of the file named **memo1** at the default printer.

```
$ lpr memo1
$
```

The following multiple command combines the **man** command and the **lpr** command, and ties them together with the Raspberry Pi 5 OS pipe | redirection character, to print the man pages describing the **ls** command at the printer named **hp1200**.

```
$ man ls | lpr -Php1200
$
```

The following shows how to perform printing tasks using the **lp** command. The general syntax of the **lp** command is as follows:

lp [options][option arguments] file(s)
Purpose: Submit files for printing on a designated system printer, or alter pending print jobs
Output: Printed files or altered print queue
Commonly used options/features:
-d destination   Print to the specified destination
-n copies   Sets the number of copies to print.

In the first command, the file to be printed is named **file1**. In the second command, the files to be printed are named **sample** and **phones**. Note that the **-d** option is used to specify which printer to use. The option to specify the number of copies is **-n** for the **lp** command.

$ lp -d spr file1
request id is spr-983 (1 file(s))
$ lp -d spr -n 3 sample phones
request id is spr-984 (2 file(s))
$

0.5 Chapter Summary

In this introductory chapter, we covered essential Raspberry Pi 5 OS commands that allow a system administrator to do file maintenance and perform other useful operations. This is a mandatory set of essentials that even an ordinary, non-administrative user would need to know to work efficiently in a character, or text-based interface to the operating system. Text-based commands are the predominant means that a system administrator uses to maintain the integrity of the system. Table 0.2 provides a compendium of useful

TABLE 0.2

Useful Commands for the Beginner

Command	What It Does
<Ctrl+D>	Terminates a process or command
alias	Allows you to create pseudonyms for commands
biff	Notifies you of new e-mail
cal	Displays a calendar on screen
cat	Allows joining of files
cd	Allows you to change the current working directory
cp	Allows you to copy files

(Continued)

TABLE 0.2 (*Continued*)

Useful Commands for the Beginner

Command	What It Does
exit	Ends a shell that you have started
hostname	Displays the name of the host computer that you are logged on to
ip	Displays IP information of the current host
login	Allows you to log on to the computer with a valid username/ password pair
lpr or lp	Allows printing of text files
ls	Allows you to display names of files and directories in the current working directory
man	Allows you to view a manual page for a command or topic
mesg	Allows or disallows writing messages to the screen
mkdir	Allows you to create a new directory
more	Allows viewing of the contents of a file one screen at a time
mv	Allows you to move the path location of, or rename, files
passwd	Allows you to change your password on the computer
pg	Solaris command that displays one screen of a file at a time
pwd	Allows you to see the name of the current working directory
rm	Allows you to delete a file from the file structure
rmdir	Allows deletion of directories
talk	Allows you to send real-time messages to other users
telnet	Allows you to log on to a computer on a network or the Internet
unalias	Allows you to undefine pseudonyms for commands
uname	Displays information about the operating system running the computer
whatis	Allows you to view a brief description of a command
whereis	Displays the path(s) to commands and utilities in certain key directories
who	Allows you to find out login names of users currently on the system
whoami	Displays your username
write	Allows real-time messaging between users on the system

commands for the beginner. We gave examples and showed the basic format of the following commands and primitives-

cat cd cp exit hostname -I ip login lp lpr ls man mesg mkdir more mv passwd PATH pwd rm rmdir telnet unalias uname whatis whereis who whoami

1

Raspberry Pi 5 OS System Administration Fundamentals

ACL addgroup adduser APT apt apt-get BIOS capabilities cgroups chgrp chmod chown cipher text clone Clonezilla cpio CUI DAC dd delgroup deluser df Docker du ext4 fail2ban fdisk Filezilla find firewalld free GID git GitHub GParted GRUB2 GUI gunzip gzip halt IDS ifdown ifup inxi ip IPS iSCSI journalctl LIO ls lsblk LVM LXC LXD MAC MBR mdadm mirror mkfs newusers NFSv4 nice NIDS NVMe openssh passwd passwd persistent cgroup pgrep plain text POSIX1.e ACL ps RAID RBAC renice repositories rsync SAN shutdown SSD ssh su sudo system.slice systemctl systemd systemd-cgls systemd-run tar top transient cgroup UEFI ufw UID umount untar update upgrade usermod vdev Webmin zfs zpool

1.0 Objectives and Introduction

1. Do an installation of a 64-bit Raspberry Pi 5 OS onto a microSD card, and do a preliminary configuration of the system and the OS.

2. Illustrate booting strategies and how to gracefully bring the system down.

3. Detail the basics of using systemd to manage system services.

4. Add additional users and groups to the system, and show how to design and maintain user accounts.

5. Add persistent media to the system, in particular an NVMe SSD. Outline a strategy of traditionally maintaining the Raspberry Pi 5 OS on a microSD card as the system, or boot disk, and user data files on secondary media. Establish a framework for connecting and maintaining the file system on that media, which classifies it as either existing on a physical device that is connected to the computer or a virtual medium (NFSv4, iSCSI).

   And non-traditionally, connecting and booting from an NVMe SSD while storing the entire file system there.

6. Provide strategies using traditional Command Line Interface(CLI) generic commands to back up and archive the system files and user files.

DOI: 10.1201/9781003652427-2

7. Update and maintain the operating system, and add/upgrade/ remove user application package repository software to both increase functionality and upgrade existing packages.

8. Monitor the performance of the system and tune it for optimal performance characteristics.

9. Give a brief but important exposure to the Zettabyte File System(ZFS).

10. Provide strategies for system security to harden the individual Internet-connected Raspberry Pi 5 system.

11. Provide network connectivity strategies, both on a LAN and the Internet.

12. Give an overview of system virtualization, using LXD/LXC.

13. Cover the following commands and primitives-

ACL addgroup adduser APT apt apt-get BIOS capabilities cgroups chgrp chmod chown cipher text clone Clonezilla cpio CUI DAC dd delgroup deluser df Docker du ext4 fail2ban fdisk Filezilla find firewalld free GID git GitHub GParted GRUB2 GUI gunzip gzip halt IDS ifdown ifup inxi ip IPS iSCSI journalctl LIO ls lsblk LVM LXC LXD MAC MBR mdadm mirror mkfs newusers NFSv4 nice NIDS NVMe openssh passwd passwd persistent cgroup pgrep plain text POSIX1.e ACL ps RAID RBAC renice repositories rsync SAN shutdown SSD ssh su sudo system.slice systemctl systemd systemd-cgls systemd-run tar top transient cgroup UEFI ufw UID umount untar update upgrade usermod vdev Webmin zfs zpool

The fundamental prerequisite of this chapter are (1) having knowledge of how to type a syntactically-correct Linux command on the command line (as detailed in Chapter 0), (2) having access to a dedicated Raspberry Pi 5 computer with the latest Raspberry Pi 5 Operating System available to you to install and run on it, and (3) being a privileged user on the system that is able to execute the **sudo** command to assume superuser status.

An online GitHub site, with further materials and updates, program code, solutions to both In-Chapter and End-of-Chapter Problems, Questions, and Projects, and other supplements, is provided for this book. It can be found at:

www.github.com/bobk48/Raspberry-Pi-5-OS

All command line instructions in this volume were tested on a Raspberry Pi 5, with 4GB of memory, and the latest version of the Raspberry Pi 5 OS at the time.

This chapter is central to a major component of Raspberry Pi 5 OS use: system administration.

In order to install, maintain, and effectively use a Raspberry Pi 5 system composed of both hardware and software components, it is often necessary to perform the set of common tasks shown in the following sections.

In this chapter, we target an individual, novice user, who performs these tasks exclusively for her own use, on her own personal desktop/laptop computer. The common tasks may also be performed by an appointed administrator for a more complex system used by many people. It is possible to divide these common tasks into those performed by an administrator and those performed by a single user or a group of ordinary, autonomous users.

Even though we show the basics of those common tasks, it is possible to extrapolate from what is presented to the wider context of much larger-scale computer systems, run by a system administrator.

Additionally, on the book website at www.github.com/bobk48/Raspberry-Pi-5-OS, we provide other materials that supplement our presentation of these tasks here in the printed book.

In order to do many of the system administration tasks in this chapter, it is absolutely necessary to either have superuser or root user privileges on the system. That means you need to know the superuser password, which you (or a designated system administrator) can establish at the installation of your Raspberry Pi 5 system.

Both the **su** and **sudo** commands are used to execute programs and other commands with root permissions. The root user has maximum permissions and can do anything to the system that a system administrator can. Normal users execute programs and commands with reduced permissions.

To execute something that requires maximum permissions, you must first execute the **su** or **sudo** commands. Using the **su** command makes you the super user—or root user—when you execute it with no additional options. You are prompted to enter the root account's password. Also, the **su** command allows you to switch to any user account. If you execute the command **su**, you'll be prompted to enter the password, and the command shell's current working directory will be your home directory. Once you're done running commands in the root shell, you should type **exit** to leave the root shell and go back to limited-privileges mode.

Note

The root shell is <u>not</u> the login shell.

In contrast, **sudo** runs a single command with root privileges. When you execute

```
$ sudo command
```

the system prompts you for your current user account's password before running the **command,** whatever it happens to be, as the root user. In order to use the **sudo** command, you must be part of the sudoers group. More information on the **sudo** command and its details can be found in section 1.15.3.

In our "learning-by-doing" approach, we have selected a common set of system administration tasks aimed specifically at an individual novice Raspberry Pi 5 OS user, as stated above in section 1.0.

Besides these common tasks we have selected to present, there are numerous extensions, and also many additional tasks that the Raspberry Pi 5 system administration encompasses.

You must realize that we have listed all of the tasks in section 1.0 based on the use cases we target.

To extend some of the system administration topics covered in this book so that they are reflective of modern Linux systems, and to anticipate other use cases you might have, we provide some additional materials and references in this volume as follows-

The three major functions performed by the modern Linux kernel (or the Linux super-kernel, systemd), which are the core of the Raspberry Pi 5 OS, are:

Concurrency, Virtualization, and Secure Persistence.

1.1 System Administration the Easy Way

How can you do the majority of what is shown in this chapter in an easy way?

Use Webmin.

Webmin is a modern Linux web browser-based GUI system administration tool that allows you to do many of the system administration tasks shown in this chapter in a very intuitive, fast, and simple way. We strongly encourage you to first download and install Webmin on your Linux system, following the instructions we give here. Then you can explore the Webmin facilities before you begin the rest of this chapter, and even go back to Webmin to find out how something which we show in the rest of this chapter can be done (or can't be done!) in Webmin.

This section details how to install and do a very basic configuration of Webmin on the Raspberry Pi 5 OS. Webmin has a GUI control Panel for doing many system administration tasks, and most importantly, it is a web-based interface, which can be used very effectively to manage your system. Webmin can set up user and group accounts, install web servers, initialize file sharing, and perform other common system administration activities. Webmin is time-effective for beginners who do not know much about the Linux command line or who just want a simpler, more intuitive graphical interface to the system.

Example 1.1 will lead you through the step-by-step download, installation, and initial minimal but critical configuration of Webmin on the Raspberry Pi 5 OS. The instructions given here were executed on a Raspberry Pi 5.

Example 1.1 Webmin Installation on Raspberry Pi 5 OS

1. Update Your System
    Before installing Webmin, update your package list and upgrade installed packages:

    $ sudo apt update && sudo apt upgrade -y
    Output truncated...

2. Install Required Dependencies
    Ensure that required dependencies are installed:

    $ sudo apt install -y wget curl apt-transport-https
    Output truncated...

3. Download and Run the Webmin Repository Setup Script
    Run the following commands to add the Webmin repository to your system:

    $ curl -o webmin-setup-repo.sh https://raw.githubusercontent.com/webmin/webmin/master/webmin-setup-repo.sh
    Output truncated...
    $ sudo sh webmin-setup-repo.sh
    Output truncated...

    This script will configure the repository and install the necessary GPG keys.

4a. Install Webmin:
    Once the repository is set up, install Webmin using:

    $ sudo apt install -y webmin --install-recommends
    Output truncated...

4b. (Optional) If ufw is installed and active on your system (which by default it is <u>not</u> on the Raspberry Pi 5 OS), allow Webmin through the firewall with the following command:

    $ sudo ufw allow 10000

5. Webmin uses 10000 as its default port into the system. To access the Webmin panel using your favorite web browser from anywhere on your LAN (or for that matter, from the same machine you installed Webmin on), type this into your URL bar on your web browser.

    https://your-ip-address:10000

    where **your-ip-address** is the IP address of the machine you just installed Webmin on.

6. A warning appears in the browser window the first time you try to access Webmin, reading
    "Your connection is not private".

Make the Advanced choice in the dialog box that appears on-screen, and Add Exception button choice in the subsequent box. Then choose Proceed to your_ip_address (unsafe).

7. The Webmin sign-in screen appears in your browser window. Login to your account on the system with your username and password pair, making sure you put an x in the box for *Remember me*, and click on Sign in.

   The Webmin System Information panel appears on screen, showing a very extensive display of the state of your Raspberry Pi 5 OS.

8. Play with Webmin in a non-destructive way. In other words, if you encounter a Webmin function or activity that asks you to change the basic configuration of the system, do not proceed at this point. Once you learn more about Linux configuration from the sections in this chapter, you will be better prepared to use Webmin to change them. When you are done, make the Logout choice from the Webmin panel on the left of your web browser display.

In the sections below, you can go back into Webmin at any time, and experiment with Webmin to find out how relatively efficient and effective Webmin is in handling the tasks we detail in those sections!

1.1.1 inxi

How can you get a quick, informational snapshot of how your Raspberry Pi 5 OS system is configured, particularly the hardware?

Use these two commands (When we did this on our Raspberry Pi 5 OS, with the latest operating system version on it, we got the following output to the 2nd command):

```
$ sudo apt install inxi
Output truncated …
$ sudo inxi -GSCMm -t c -P -x
System:
  Host: raspberrypi Kernel: 6.12.34+rpt-rpi-2712 arch: aarch64 bits: 64
    compiler: N/A Desktop: LXDE v: 0.10.1 Distro: Debian GNU/Linux 12 (bookworm)
Machine:
  Type: ARM System: Raspberry Pi 5 Model B Rev 1.0 details: N/A rev: c04170
    serial: a5b3f4f94c31353d

Memory:
  RAM: total: 3.96 GiB used: 939.4 MiB (23.2%) gpu: 8 MiB
  RAM Report: smbios: No SMBIOS data for dmidecode to process
CPU:
  Info: quad core model: N/A variant: cortex-a76 bits: 64 type: MCP
    arch: ARMv8 rev: 1 cache: L1: 512 KiB L2: 2 MiB L3: 2 MiB
```

```
 Speed (MHz): avg: 2400 min/max: 1500/2400 cores: 1: 2400 2: 2400 3: 2400
   4: 2400 bogomips: 432
 Features: Use -f option to see features
Graphics:
 Device-1: bcm2712-hdmi0 driver: vc4_hdmi v: N/A bus-ID: N/A
 Device-2: bcm2712-hdmi1 driver: vc4_hdmi v: N/A bus-ID: N/A
 Display: wayland server: X.Org v: 1.22.1.9 with: Xwayland v: 22.1.9
   compositor: wayfire v: 0.7.5 driver: dri: vc4
   gpu: vc4-drm,vc4_crtc,vc4_dpi,vc4_dsi,vc4_firmware_kms,vc4_hdmi,vc4_hvs,vc4_txp,vc4_
v3d,vc4_vec
   resolution: 1920x1080~60Hz
 API: OpenGL v: 3.1 Mesa 23.2.1-1~bpo12+rpt3 renderer: V3D 7.1
   direct-render: Yes
Partition:
 ID-1: / size: 27.84 GiB used: 6.64 GiB (23.9%) fs: ext4 dev: /dev/mmcblk0p2
Processes:
 CPU top: 5 of 223
 1: cpu: 2.4% command: lxterminal pid: 2416 mem: 44.5 MiB (1.0%)
 2: cpu: 2.3% command: xwayland pid: 1548 mem: 93.8 MiB (2.3%)
 3: cpu: 2.3% command: soffice.bin pid: 1581 mem: 351.7 MiB (8.6%)
 4: cpu: 0.8% command: wayfire pid: 955 mem: 127.9 MiB (3.1%)
 5: cpu: 0.2% command: pcmanfm pid: 1121 mem: 97.4 MiB (2.4%)
$
```

See the man page on your Raspberry Pi 5 OS for more information about the **inxi** command.

1.1.2 FileZilla

FileZilla is nominally a graphics-based ftp client and server program that can use ssh as the tunnel, or conduit between systems. It has a number of useful functions and menu choices that allow the system administrator to successfully, confidentially, and efficiently backup and restore single files or directories, globally via a network. It is most useful for backing up and restoring single-user files and directories.

It is not a replacement or substitute for the command line facilities shown in the following sections.

Both client and server, in our case a local machine running the Raspberry Pi 5 OS system, and a remote machine running the same OS, must have ssh communications protocol enabled between them. To see more about establishing ssh between Raspberry Pi 5 OS systems, see section 1.1.3. You can have login access to an account on the remote server, or you can anonymously log in as well if that is enabled.

After launching FileZilla on the client, to log in to a remote host server, you need to supply the IP address of the server, the login name and password, and the port number (22 for ssh). Once you have successfully logged in, the local machine's directory and file structure is shown on the left side of the figure. The remote machine's directory structure is shown on the right side of the figure. To transfer files or directories between machines, you simply drag and drop between the appropriate panes on the left or right. If you are overwriting previously transferred files or directories, the FileZilla default is to give you the chance to overwrite or rename the files being transferred.

There are a number of other menu choices at the top of the FileZilla screen that allow you to affect preferences, set bookmarks, etc. For example, via the menu choice Manage Bookmarks and the Site Manager, you can automatically make multiple local directories and remote directories available for ssh transfer as soon as you log in to the remote server sites.

1.1.3 SSH and System Service Management Using systemd: VSFTP

Secure Shell (SSH) is a cryptographic network protocol used for securely accessing and managing remote systems over an unsecured network. It enables encrypted communication between a client and a server, protecting sensitive data such as login credentials and command executions. SSH is widely used for remote administration, secure file transfers (via SCP or SFTP), and tunneling services. It supports authentication methods like passwords, public keys, and multi-factor authentication. SSH runs on port 22 by default and is essential for securely managing servers, especially in the Raspberry Pi OS environment, preventing unauthorized access through strong encryption and integrity verification.

Very Secure FTP (VSFTP) is an FTP server designed for security, performance, and stability. It is widely used for transferring files between clients and servers in Unix and Linux environments. Unlike traditional FTP, VSFTP enhances security by supporting encrypted connections via FTPS (FTP over SSL/TLS) and integrating system-level user authentication. It is lightweight, scalable, and configurable, making it suitable for high-traffic environments. With features like chroot jailing, anonymous login control, and bandwidth limitation, VSFTP ensures secure and efficient file transfers while minimizing vulnerabilities associated with legacy FTP servers. It is a preferred choice for hosting secure FTP services.

1.1.3.1 Connecting via an SSH Client between Raspberry Pi 5 OS Machines

The basic methodology and the techniques we show below allow a user on one Raspberry Pi 5 OS computer to remotely log in and log out of another computer using the SSH protocol. The computer you are using to log into another computer with is known as the SSH *client*. The computer you want to log into with SSH is known as the *server* or the *host* system.

Before this methodology can be used, both client and server systems must be able to talk to each other over the SSH channel. In other words, the server system must have the SSH server-side software package installed and enabled on it. This is usually not the default on most Linux systems, so you have to follow the installation and/or enabling instructions given for your particular flavor of Linux to accomplish this.

There are a few approaches to enabling SSH server-side software on the latest Raspberry Pi 5 OS, as follows:

1. Starting from scratch, you could directly enable it when the system is flashed to the microSD card you might be running the system from. At installation, a convenient graphical dialog box allows you to do this.

2. On an already-installed system, in a terminal window, you can use the command **sudo raspi-config**, to descend through the Raspberry Pi Software Configuration Tool menu choices Interface Options>SSH, and enable it.

****OR****

Launch the Raspberry Pi Configuration Tool from the Preferences Menu, and do the same thing by using the slider button to the right of the SSH: choice.

3. By default, the SSH server-side package was <u>not</u> installed on our Raspberry Pi 5 OS systems, but in a terminal window, we were able to install it with the following command:

$ sudo apt-get install openssh-server

After the above command is executed successfully, the SSH server-side "service" is installed, started, and enabled. Being "enabled" means being able to start at subsequent reboots of the Raspberry Pi 5 OS system.

The client-side SSH software is installed by default on most Linux system implementations, including on our Raspberry Pi 5 OS system.

****Note****

The user must know a valid username/password pair on the remote server system to be able to log in to the remote system!

1.1.3.2 Login and Logout Procedures

We show three possible methods that can be used in this two-way communications dialog, once server-side software is installed.

First, if the user has already logged into the host successfully from the client before, and the authentication keys have not changed. Second, if the user has <u>never</u> logged into the host successfully before from the client. And third, if the user has logged into the host before, but the authentication key on the host has changed since the last successful login. These are practical situations one might encounter anytime when you are using this remote login method.

What the user types are shown in **bold** text.

Method 1. Having logged in before successfully:

$ **ssh bob@192.168.1.15**
bob@192.168.1.15's password: **www**
Linux raspberrypi 6.1.21-v8+ #1642 SMP PREEMPT Mon Apr 3 17:24:16 BST 2023 aarch64

The programs included with the Debian GNU/Linux system are free software;
the exact distribution terms for each program are described in the
individual files in /usr/share/doc/*/copyright.

Debian GNU/Linux comes with ABSOLUTELY NO WARRANTY, to the extent
permitted by applicable law.
Last login: Fri May 5 07:17:44 2023 from 192.168.1.11
$ **Execute Command Line Linux Commands**
$ **logout**
Connection to 192.168.1.15 closed.
$

Method 2. Having never logged in before:

$ **ssh bob@192.168.1.15**
The authenticity of host '192.168.1.15 (192.168.1.15)' can't be established. ECDSA key
fingerprint is SHA256:uZpqi4U6uBN5SOBVFRbqbl5HspmV3eZAw/nUvPBTS5I.
Are you sure you want to continue connecting (yes/no)?**yes**
Warning: Permanently added '192.168.1.15' (ECDSA) to the list of known hosts.
Bob@192.168.1.15's password: **www**
Linux raspberrypi 6.1.21-v8+ #1642 SMP PREEMPT Mon Apr 3 17:24:16 BST 2023 aarch64

The programs included with the Debian GNU/Linux system are free software;
the exact distribution terms for each program are described in the
individual files in /usr/share/doc/*/copyright.

Debian GNU/Linux comes with ABSOLUTELY NO WARRANTY, to the extent
permitted by applicable law.
Last login: Fri May 5 07:17:44 2023 from 192.168.1.2
$ **Execute Command Line Linux Commands**
$ **logout**
Connection to 192.168.1.15 closed.
$

Method 3. Logged in before, but host key has changed:

$ **ssh bob@192.168.1.15**
@@@
@@@@@@@@@@@@@@@@@@@@@@@

@   WARNING: REMOTE HOST IDENTIFICATION HAS CHANGED!   @
@@
@@@@@@@@@@@@@@@@@@@@@@
IT IS POSSIBLE THAT SOMEONE IS DOING SOMETHING NASTY!
Someone could be eavesdropping on you right now (man-in-the-middle attack)!
It is also possible that a host key has just been changed.
The fingerprint for the ECDSA key sent by the remote host is
SHA256:hNGE725MKYvuOrAHkTX7nwLYP8GKqutPJG3pAKJmvzw.
Please contact your system administrator.
Add correct host key in /home/bob/.ssh/known_hosts to get rid of this message.
Offending ECDSA key in /home/bob/.ssh/known_hosts:2
  remove with:
  ssh-keygen -f "/home/bob/.ssh/known_hosts" -R "192.168.1.15"
ECDSA host key for 192.168.1.15 has changed and you have requested strict checking.
Host key verification failed.
rsync: connection unexpectedly closed (0 bytes received so far) [sender]
rsync error: unexplained error (code 255) at io.c(228) [sender=3.2.3]
$ ssh-keygen -f "/home/bob/.ssh/known_hosts" -R "192.168.1.15"
Output truncated...
$ ssh bob@192.168.1.15
The authenticity of host '192.168.1.15 (192.168.1.15)' can't be established.
ECDSA key fingerprint is 43:e8:cf:33:d5:ed:dd:05:d9:e9:a5:9d:d3:18:1d:2b.
No matching host key fingerprint found in DNS.
Are you sure you want to continue connecting (yes/no)? **yes**
Warning: Permanently added '192.168.1.15' (ECDSA) to the list of known hosts.
Bob@192.168.1.15's password: **www**
Last login: Sat Dec 24 16:54:10 2016 from 192.168.1.2
Output truncated...
$ Execute Command Line Linux Commands...
$ logout
Connection to 192.168.1.15 closed.
$

In all three methods, the user is assumed to have an account with the same username, and possibly password, on both client and host systems.

In method 2, the keys are generated on the host and client after the user types in **yes** and presses <Enter>.

In method 3, after the first failed attempt to establish an SSH connection, the error message indicates that the authentication key has changed on the host. A very helpful component of the error message is the instruction-

Add correct host key in /home/bob/.ssh/known_hosts to get rid of this message.
Offending ECDSA key in /usr/home/bob/.ssh/known_hosts:2

So, a removal of the offending key in the file **/home/bob/.ssh/known_hosts** on the client machine is done by using the command-

$ ssh-keygen -f "/home/bob/.ssh/known_hosts" -R "192.168.1.15"

Then a new key is generated, an exchange can take place, and the login can proceed.

The line in all three methods above that reads "**Execute Command Line Linux Commands...**" is where the user types in any of the valid Linux commands we show in this chapter and throughout the rest of this book. Finally, after typing **logout**, the user cuts the SSH channel connection and is returned to the command line prompt of the local client system.

Example 1.2 VSFTPD

Objectives: To install and start a system service for a secure form of ftp, using systemd

Prerequisites: Knowledge of basic Linux commands, having SSH enabled on your Raspberry Pi 5 OS.

Background: One of the most important uses of systemd for system administration is the management of essential system services. Very Secure File Transfer Protocol Daemon (VSFTPD) is a secure ftp server that can be used by client machines on your network, or the Internet, to log into a host machine, and exchange files. We show our session below on both the host machine (the Raspberry Pi 5 you're trying to gain access to,) and the client machine (the Linux or Raspberry Pi 5 machine you're trying to connect to the host from).

Requirements: Do the following steps, in the order presented, to meet the requirements of this example:

1. Download and install the VSFTPD server on the host and client machines with the following commands:

```
host$ sudo apt install vsftpd
Output truncated...
client# sudo install ftp
Output truncated...
```

2. Use the systemd systemctl command to check the status of the VSFTPD service, using the following command:

```
host$ systemctl status vsftpd.service
• vsftpd.service - vsftpd FTP server
   Loaded: loaded (/lib/systemd/system/vsftpd.service; enabled; preset: enabled)
   Active: active (running) since Sun 2025-03-02 07:30:34 PST; 35s ago
   Process: 5684 ExecStartPre=/bin/mkdir -p /var/run/vsftpd/empty
(code=exited, status=0/SUCCESS)
  Main PID: 5685 (vsftpd)
    Tasks: 1 (limit: 4758)
     CPU: 5ms
   CGroup: /system.slice/vsftpd.service
           └─5685 /usr/sbin/vsftpd /etc/vsftpd.conf
```

Mar 02 07:30:34 raspberrypi systemd[1]: Starting vsftpd.service - vsftpd FTP server...
Mar 02 07:30:34 raspberrypi systemd[1]: Started vsftpd.service - vsftpd FTP server.

Notice from the above output that the command from step 1 not only downloaded but also installed and started the vsftpd service.

3. From the client machine on your network, use the ftp command to connect to the vsftpd server on your host Raspberry Pi 5 machine. Substitute the IP address of the machine you want to ftp into for the IP 192.168.0.14 shown in this command:

client# **ftp 192.168.1.14**
Connected to 192.168.1.14.
220 (vsFTPd 3.0.3)
Name (192.168.1.14:bob): **bob**

331 Please specify the password.
Password: **QQQ**
230 Login successful.
Remote system type is UNIX.
Using binary mode to transfer files.

4. Get a directory listing of the files on the machine you are connected to:

ftp> **ls**

Here is a directory listing on the machine you connected to-

200 PORT command successful. Consider using PASV.
150 Here comes the directory listing.

```
-rw-r--r--    1 1000    1000              0 Jun 10 08:01 32m
drwxr-xr-x    2 1000    1000           4096 Jul 02 12:13 Desktop
drwxr-xr-x    2 1000    1000           4096 Jun 09 16:51 Documents
drwxr-xr-x    2 1000    1000           4096 Jun 09 16:51 Downloads
drwx------   23 1000    1000           4096 Jul 02 11:51 Dropbox
drwxr-xr-x    2 1000    1000           4096 Jun 09 16:51 Music
drwxr-xr-x    2 1000    1000           4096 Jun 09 16:51 Pictures
drwxr-xr-x    2 1000    1000           4096 Jun 09 16:51 Public
drwxr-xr-x    2 1000    1000           4096 Jun 09 16:51 Templates
drwxr-xr-x    2 1000    1000           4096 Jun 09 16:51 Videos
-rw-r--r--    1 1000    1000      134217728 Jun 10 08:14 disk1
226 Directory send OK.
```

5. Terminate the connection with the following ftp command:

ftp> **exit**
221 Goodbye.
client#

6. In order to stop the vsftpd service, use the following command:

host$ **sudo systemctl stop vsftpd.service**
host$

7. Check the status of the vsftpd service with the following command:

host$ systemctl status vsftpd.service

8. To restart the vsftpd service, use the following command:

host$ sudo systemctl restart vsftpd.service

9. To make sure a service starts automatically at boot time, use the following command:

host$ sudo systemctl enable vsftpd.service
Synchronizing state of vsftpd.service with SysV init with /lib/systemd/systemd-sysv-install...
Executing /lib/systemd/systemd-sysv-install enable vsftpd
host$

10. To disable a service from starting at boot, use the following command:

host$ sudo systemctl disable vsftpd.service
Synchronizing state of vsftpd.service with SysV service script with /lib/systemd/systemd-sysv-install.
Executing: /lib/systemd/systemd-sysv-install disable vsftpd
Removed /etc/systemd/system/multi-user.target.wants/vsftpd.service.
host$

Conclusion: This example allowed you to download, install, and start a system service known as VSFTPD on a host Raspberry Pi 5 computer. You were then able to connect to and use the computer as a secure VSFTP server. Additionally, we showed some basic systemd service management commands applied to the vsftpd service.

1.2 Installation of the Raspberry Pi 5 OS onto Various Media, and Preliminary System Configuration

****Note****

We do not show how to do a "bare metal", or brand new install of the Raspberry Pi 5 OS, when there was no operating system on your hardware to begin with. That's because many new users purchase their hardware with the necessary operating system already loaded on a microSD card that comes along with the computer itself. The instructions for doing a bare metal install are freely and easily available to you at the Raspberry Pi Foundation website at:

https://www.raspberrypi.com/documentation/computers/getting-started.html

The following sub-sections contain these operations:

section 1.2.1 – this shows how to download and install a 64-bit version
  of the Raspberry Pi 5 OS onto a microSD card, so that you can insert
  that card into the Raspberry Pi 5 hardware card slot, and operate that
  hardware with it. The Raspberry Pi 5 officially supports microSD
  cards up to 1TB in capacity, provided they are formatted correctly
  (typically exFAT for cards over 32GB). However, larger microSD
  cards above 1TB may work if they are formatted to FAT32 or exFAT,
  but compatibility is not guaranteed.

****Note****

For best performance, use a UHS-I (U3) or A2-rated microSD card to ensure
faster read/write speeds.

section 1.2.2 – Gives some performance criteria comparisons between
  microSD, USB 3.0-mounted SSDs, and NVMe SSDs.
Sections 1.2.3, 1.2.4, 1.2.5 – Show how to install an externally-mounted
  NVMe SSD medium on the PCIe bus., how to boot from the NVMw
  SSD medium instead of from the microSD card, and how to boot
  from and run a Raspberry Pi 5 OS from a USB3-mounted SSD.

The following sub-sections assume that you will be using the most current
release of the software system that is designed for the 64-bit ARM-architecture
Raspberry Pi 5 hardware. Be aware that some of the systems administration
tasks illustrated in this book are, or may be, done in a different way in earlier (or
later) releases of the operating system software! And, this section assumes that
you will be running the Raspberry Pi 5 OS system from persistent media (either
a microSD card mounted in the provided slot on the Raspberry Pi hardware, or
from an NVMe or USB3-mounted SSD drive.)

1.2.1 Imager Download and Install of 64-bit Version of
Raspberry Pi 5 OS onto a microSD Card

Objectives:
To detail how to create, boot from, and run your Raspberry Pi 5 system from
a mounted microSD card.

Pre-Requisites:
We do the operations in this Example on the following Raspberry Pi 5 system:

System:
  Host: raspberrypi Kernel: 6.12.34+rpt-rpi-2712 arch: aarch64 bits: 64
    compiler: N/A Desktop: LXDE v: 0.10.1 Distro: Debian GNU/Linux 12 (bookworm)

Machine:
  Type: ARM System: Raspberry Pi 5 Model B Rev 1.0 details: N/A rev: c04170
    serial: a5b3f4f94c31353d

Background:
The Raspberry Pi 5 OS is traditionally booted from and run from a microSD card mounted on the hardware.

Requirements:
Do the steps below, in the order shown, to complete the requirements for this example.

This section is probably the easiest and most often used means of getting the Raspberry Pi 5 OS onto your hardware. At the time this book was written, specific instructions for doing this were found at the following website:

https://www.raspberrypi.com/documentation/computers/getting-started. html

They are presented here as follows:

1. From a Raspberry Pi 5 that's already working with an installed operating system on it, and is connected to the Internet, type the following at the command prompt:

   $ sudo apt install rpi-imager

2. Connect a USB-SD card reader to that computer with an adequately-sized microSD card in it. We did this step with a 32 GB microSD card.

3. From the Pi menu, make the choice **Accessories > Raspberry Pi Imager**, to run the Raspberry Pi Imager, and choose:
   a. Select Raspberry Pi 5 as the Raspberry Pi Device.
   b. Select Raspberry Pi OS (64-bit) as the Operating System.
   c. Choose the microSD card from step 2 as Storage.
   d. Click Write and wait for the installation to complete.

5. At this point, while running the Imager, if you so desire, choose "Advanced Options", and enable things like SSH and hostname.

6. The Imager runs. When finished with the Imager, quit it, take the microSD card out of the card reader (not the microSD card running your Raspberry Pi 5!), and place it into the Raspberry Pi 5 hardware you want the operating system to run on. Boot into that microSD card, and follow the instructions presented.

1.2.2 Comparison of Various Raspberry Pi 5 OS Media

If you need faster storage and performance, consider using a USB 3.0 SSD with the Raspberry Pi 5 instead of a microSD card.

What would be the performance advantage to using a USB 3.0 SSD over a microSD card, especially in terms of speed?

Using a USB 3.0 SSD instead of a microSD card on a Raspberry Pi 5 can provide significant performance advantages, particularly in terms of speed, reliability, and longevity. Here's how they compare:

1. Speed: Read and Write Performance

Storage Type	Read Speed	Write Speed
MicroSD (UHS-I, A2)	~100 MB/s	~80 MB/s
USB 3.0 SATA SSD	~400–500 MB/s	~300–500 MB/s
USB 3.0 NVMe SSD	~800–1000 MB/s	~700–900 MB/s

The Raspberry Pi 5's microSD card interface is limited by UHS-I speeds, so even high-end microSD cards will be much slower than an SSD.

The USB 3.0 ports on the Raspberry Pi 5 support up to 5 Gbps (~625 MB/s), making an SSD significantly faster.

2. Boot Time and System Performance
   - Booting from an SSD can cut boot times by half or more compared to a microSD card.
   - Application launch times and general system responsiveness improve dramatically.
   - Compiling software, database operations, and file transfers are much faster.

3. Reliability and Endurance
   - MicroSD cards wear out faster due to limited write cycles (especially with heavy logging or database usage).
   - SSDs have better endurance and error correction, making them less prone to corruption.

4. Thermal Considerations
   - MicroSD cards generate minimal heat.
   - SSDs can get warm under heavy load, especially NVMe SSDs, but a heatsink or thermal pad can help.

5. Best Use Cases for an SSD
   - Running an OS (like Raspberry Pi OS, Ubuntu, or Home Assistant).
   - Hosting a database, web server, or file server.
   - Compiling code or running Docker containers.
   - Media storage for a NAS or Plex server

Conclusion: Is It Worth Upgrading?

- If you're just doing basic tasks (web browsing, light scripting, GPIO control), a high-quality A2-rated microSD card is fine.
- If you need faster boot times, reliability, and better performance for heavy workloads, an SSD is a *major upgrade*.

1.2.2.1 Comparing USB 3.0 SSD vs. NVMe SSD (PCIe) on Raspberry Pi 5

The Raspberry Pi 5 introduced a PCIe 2.0 x1 interface, allowing NVMe SSDs to be connected via an adapter. This can significantly improve performance compared to USB 3.0-mounted SSDs. Below is a detailed comparison of speed, boot time, endurance, and thermal considerations.

1. Speed: Read and Write Performance

Storage Type	Interface	Theoretical Max Speed	Real-World Read Speed	Real-World Write Speed
MicroSD (UHS-I, A2)	SD Card Slot	**104 MB/s**	~100 MB/s	~80 MB/s
USB 3.0 SATA SSD	USB 3.0 (5 Gbps)	**500–550 MB/s**	~400–500 MB/s	~300–500 MB/s
USB 3.0 NVMe SSD	USB 3.0 (5 Gbps)	**500–550 MB/s**	~400–500 MB/s	~300–500 MB/s
PCIe NVMe SSD	PCIe 2.0 x1 (4 Gbps)	**400 MB/s**	~350–390 MB/s	~300–380 MB/s

Key Observations:
- **USB 3.0 SATA SSDs and USB 3.0 NVMe SSDs** max out at around **400–500 MB/s**.
- **PCIe NVMe SSDs on the Pi 5** are **limited by the PCIe 2.0 x1 interface**, which has a theoretical max of **500 MB/s** (realistically closer to 350–400 MB/s).
- **USB and PCIe NVMe SSDs have similar speeds**, but **PCIe avoids USB bottlenecks** and latency.

2. Boot Time and System Performance

Storage Type	Boot Time (Raspberry Pi OS)
MicroSD Card (A2)	**~30–40s**
USB 3.0 SATA SSD	**~15–20s**
USB 3.0 NVMe SSD	**~12–18s**
PCIe NVMe SSD	**~10–15s**

- **PCIe NVMe SSDs boot the fastest**, as they bypass USB controller overhead.

- **USB 3.0 NVMe SSDs** are slightly slower due to the **USB proto-col overhead**.

3. Reliability and Endurance

Storage Type	Lifespan (TBW- Terabytes Written)	Data Corruption Risk
MicroSD Card (A2)	**150–300 TBW** (consumer-grade)	**High (limited write cycles, corruption issues with power loss)**
USB 3.0 SATA SSD	**300–600 TBW** (typical SATA)	Low
USB 3.0 NVMe SSD	**400–1000 TBW** (consumer NVMe)	Low
PCIe NVMe SSD	**400–1000+ TBW** (consumer NVMe)	**Lowest (direct PCIe access, no USB overhead)**

- **PCIe NVMe SSDs offer the best endurance and lowest failure rate**, as they avoid USB bottlenecks and potential power issues.
- **MicroSD cards are the worst in terms of reliability** due to their limited write cycles.

4. Thermal Considerations

Storage Type	Heat Output (Under Load)	Cooling Required?
MicroSD Card	**Low (<40°C)**	✖ No
USB 3.0 SATA SSD	**Moderate (~45°C–50°C)**	✖ No
USB 3.0 NVMe SSD	**High (~50°C–60°C)**	⚠ Maybe (heatsink recommended)
PCIe NVMe SSD	**Higher (~55°C–70°C)**	✅ Yes (passive heatsink advised)

- **PCIe NVMe SSDs generate the most heat**, especially in enclosed cases. A **heatsink or thermal pad is highly recommended.**
- **USB 3.0 NVMe SSDs also get hot**, but external USB enclosures often have some cooling.

5. Latency and System Responsiveness

Storage Type	Random Read Latency	System Responsiveness
MicroSD Card (A2)	**High (~150 µs)**	Slowest
USB 3.0 SATA SSD	**Medium (~50–100 µs)**	Good
USB 3.0 NVMe SSD	**Lower (~30–70 µs)**	Better
PCIe NVMe SSD	**Lowest (~10–30 µs)**	Best

- **PCIe NVMe SSDs have the lowest latency**, making them the most responsive for OS tasks and databases.

- **USB 3.0 NVMe SSDs are slightly slower due to USB protocol overhead**.

Final Verdict: Which One Should You Choose?

Use Case	Recommended Storage
General OS use, basic tasks	Fast microSD (A2-rated, 128GB+)
Better performance, but low cost	USB 3.0 SATA SSD
Best value (balance of speed and cost)	USB 3.0 NVMe SSD
Maximum speed and lowest latency	PCIe NVMe SSD (with heatsink)

Best Overall Choice for Performance:
PCIe NVMe SSD, if you want the fastest experience, can handle more power draw, and are comfortable using a PCIe adapter.
Best Plug-and-Play Choice:
USB 3.0 NVMe SSD – almost as fast as PCIe, and simpler to set up.

1.2.3 How to attach an NVMe SSD to a Raspberry Pi 5

Objectives:
To detail how to attach a USB3-mounted SSD to your Raspberry Pi OS system.

Pre-Requisites: We do the operations in this Example on the following Raspberry Pi 5 system:

```
System:
  Host: raspberrypi Kernel: 6.12.34+rpt-rpi-271  arch: aarch64 bits: 64
    compiler: gcc v: 12.2.0 Desktop: wayfire v: 0.7.5 Distro: Debian GNU/Linux
    12 (bookworm)
Machine:
  Type: ARM System: Raspberry Pi 5 Model B Rev 1.0 details: N/A rev: c04170
    serial: a5b3f4f94c31353d
```

Background:
As recommended in our storage model in the next section, the Raspberry Pi 5 OS is traditionally booted from and run from a microSD card mounted on the hardware. With the operating system kernel at release 6.12.34+rpt-rpi-271, as shown in the above system description, it is possible, and highly advantageous, to boot and run the system from a USB3-mounted SSD, or other external device, such as the NVMe SSDs we illustrated this with in the sections below.

Requirements:
Do the steps below, in the order shown, to complete the requirements for this example.

Step 0: Install a viable NVMe adapter and an adequately-sized NVMe SSD of your choice onto your Raspberry Pi 5. I recommend the Geekworm X1001 "Shield" adapter and a KingSpec 1 TB M.2 NVMe SSD, because at the time this book was written, both of those worked out of the box for me.

Also, to test the viability and functionality of my candidate NVMe SSD, I used an Eluteng NVMe M.2 NVMe SSD to USB adapter with my candidate NVMe SSD attached correctly to it, and inserted the adapter into one of the USB 3.0 ports on my Raspberry Pi 5. When the Pi 5 OS detected the NVMe SSD in /dev, I mounted it and formatted it to the ext4 filesystem using GParted.

****Note****

If the candidate NVMe SSD doesn't show up as /dev/nvme0n0 and nvme0n1, the most expeditious action you can take is to get and use another NVMe SSD. Essentially, Step 0 allows you to test the NVMe SSD that you chose to use on your system and see that it's functional!

Step 1: If you haven't done this recently, update the Raspberry Pi 5 firmware before anything else, to ensure your Raspberry Pi 5 is running the latest firmware.

   a. Boot the Pi 5 from a microSD card with the latest Raspberry Pi 5 OS already installed and successfully running on it.

   b. Open a terminal and type the following:

```
$ sudo apt update && sudo apt full-upgrade -y
Output truncated...
$ sudo rpi-eeprom-update -a
 Output truncated...
```

   c. Shut the system down. Attach your NVMe adapter and SSD according to the manufacturer's instructions. Be careful to attach the cabling between adapter and Raspberry Pi 5 correctly, as indicated in the instructions!

   d. Reboot:

```
$ sudo reboot
```

Step 2: Check again to see if the NVMe SSD is detected

   a. After rebooting, check if the Pi 5 detects it:

```
$ lsblk
```

   ◦ You should see an entry like **/dev/nvme0n0 and /dev/nvme0,1**.

   b. If it is not detected, check PCIe status:

$ lspci

○ You should see something like the following if it is detected:

0000:00:00.0 PCI bridge: Broadcom Inc. and subsidiaries BCM2712 PCIe Bridge (rev 21)
0000:01:00.0 Non-Volatile memory controller: Realtek Semiconductor Co., Ltd. RTS5765DL NVMe SSD Controller (DRAM-less) (rev 01)
0001:00:00.0 PCI bridge: Broadcom Inc. and subsidiaries BCM2712 PCIe Bridge (rev 21)
0001:01:00.0 Ethernet controller: Raspberry Pi Ltd RP1 PCIe 2.0 South Bridge

Step 3. After reboot, give the following commands to mount the NVMe SSD at a specific directory under your home directory, if you so desire, files on it to reside there:

$ sudo mkdir somename
$ sudo mount /dev/nvme0n1 /home/bob/somename

where:

/dev/nvme0n1 is the name your system assigns to the NVMe SSD in /dev
/home/bob/somename is the directory you want the NVMe SSD files to be found in. Of course, your home directory will have a different name.

1.2.4 How to Boot a Raspberry Pi 5 from an NVMe SSD

Objectives:
To detail how to boot from and run your Raspberry Pi 5 OS system from an NVMe SSD.

Pre-Requisites:
We do the operations in this Example on the following Raspberry Pi 5 system:

System:
  Host: raspberrypi Kernel: 6.12.34+rpt-rpi-271 arch: aarch64 bits: 64
    compiler: gcc v: 12.2.0 Desktop: wayfire v: 0.7.5 Distro: Debian GNU/Linux
    12 (bookworm)
Machine:
  Type: ARM System: Raspberry Pi 5 Model B Rev 1.0 details: N/A rev: c04170
    serial: a5b3f4f94c31353d

Background:
As recommended in our storage model in the next section, the Raspberry Pi 5 OS is traditionally booted from and run from a microSD card mounted on the hardware. With the operating system kernel at release 6.12.34+rpt-rpi-271, as shown in the above system description, it is possible, and highly advantageous, to boot and run the system from a USB3-mounted SSD, or

other external device, such as the NVMe SSDs we illustrated this with in the previous sections.

Requirements: Do the steps below, in the order shown, to complete the requirements for this example.

As shown in section 1.2.3, since the Raspberry Pi 5 has a PCIe 2.0 x1 interface, you can boot directly from an NVMe SSD connected via a viable NVMe adapter. Here's a step-by-step guide to get it set up.

> Step 0: As in section 1.2.3, install a viable NVMe adapter and an adequately-sized NVMe SSD of your choice. I recommend the Geekworm X1001 "Shield" and a KingSpec 1 TB M.2 NVMe SSD, because at the time this book was written, both of those worked out of the box for me. Also, to test the viability of my candidate NVMe SSD, I used an Eluteng NVMe M.2 NVMe SSD to USB adapter with my candidate NVMe SSD attached correctly to it, and inserted it into one of the USB 3.0 ports on my Raspberry Pi 5; when the Pi 5 OS detected the NVMe SSD in /dev, I mounted it and formatted it to ext4 with GParted.
>
> ****Note****
>
> If the candidate NVMe doesn't show up in /dev/nvme0n0 and nvme0n1, get another one. Essentially, Step 0 allows you to test the NVMe SSD that you chose to use on your system and see that it's functional!
>
> Step 1: If you haven't done this recently, update the Raspberry Pi 5 firmware before anything else, to ensure your Raspberry Pi 5 is running the latest firmware.
>
> > a. Boot the Pi 5 from a microSD card with the latest Raspberry Pi 5 OS already installed and successfully running on it.
> >
> > b. Open a terminal and type the following:
> >
> > ```
> > $ sudo apt update && sudo apt full-upgrade -y
> > Output truncated...
> > $ sudo rpi-eeprom-update -a
> >  Output truncated...
> > ```
> >
> > c. Shut the system down. Attach your NVMe adapter and SSD according to the manufacturer's instructions. Be careful to attach the cabling between adapter and Raspberry Pi 5 correctly, as indicated in the instructions!
> >
> > d. Reboot:
> >
> > ```
> > $ sudo reboot
> > ```

Step 2: Check again to see if the NVMe SSD is detected

    a. After rebooting, check if the Pi 5 detects it:

```
$ lsblk
```

    b. ◦ You should see an entry like **/dev/nvme0n0 and /dev/nvme0,1**.

    c. If it's not detected, check PCIe status:

```
$ lspci
```

◦ You should see something like the following if it is detected:

> 0000:00:00.0 PCI bridge: Broadcom Inc. and subsidiaries BCM2712 PCIe
> Bridge (rev 21)
> 0000:01:00.0 Non-Volatile memory controller: Realtek Semiconductor Co.,
> Ltd. RTS5765DL NVMe SSD Controller (DRAM-less) (rev 01)
> 0001:00:00.0 PCI bridge: Broadcom Inc. and subsidiaries BCM2712 PCIe
> Bridge (rev 21)
> 0001:01:00.0 Ethernet controller: Raspberry Pi Ltd RP1 PCIe 2.0 South
> Bridge

Additionally, if the NVMe SSD does <u>not</u> appear in /dev, you can check the following:

    a. The PCIe adapter and its cabling are correctly installed.

    b. The SSD is firmly seated in the adapter.

    c. The power supply is strong enough (5V 5A or 27 W is recommended).

Step 3: Install Raspberry Pi OS on the NVMe SSD

    a. Use Raspberry Pi Imager on your Raspberry Pi 5, as shown in section 1.2.1.

    b. Select Raspberry Pi 5 as the Raspberry Pi Device.

    c. Select Raspberry Pi OS (64-bit) as the Operating System.

    d. Choose the NVMe SSD as Storage.

    e. Click Write and wait for the installation to complete.

****Note****

We had to <u>uncheck</u> the box displaying Exclude System Drives to be able to select our NVMe SSD in step 3.d.

Let the Pi imager proceed to write the image to your NVMe SSD.

Step 4: Enable Booting from NVMe

    a. Open a terminal and enter the bootloader configuration:

```
$ sudo raspi-config
```

b. Navigate to:

Advanced Options → Boot Order → NVMe Boot

c. Select NVMe first, then reboot:

d. Exit raspi-config using the Tab key on your keyboard. Then use the final choice in raspi-config to reboot.

Step 5: Verify Boot from NVMe

a. Once the Pi 5 reboots, check the boot device:

$ lsblk
If it shows /dev/nvme0n1 as the root (/), you have successfully booted from NVMe!

b. You can now remove the microSD card (if used initially).

At this point, if you have booted from the NVMe SSD, you can remove the microSD card from its slot under the Raspberry Pi 5 system board.

Step 6. *Troubleshooting*
NVMe Not Booting?
Try setting the boot order manually:

$ sudo nano /boot/firmware/config.txt

Add this line:

program_usb_boot_mode=1

Then reboot:

$ sudo reboot

If the SSD is not detected, update the bootloader manually:

$ sudo rpi-eeprom-config --edit

Change the BOOT_ORDER line to:

BOOT_ORDER=0xf216

Save and exit, then reboot.

******Note****

a. Raspberry Pi 5 supports native NVMe booting, so no extra configurations are needed.

    b. PCIe NVMe booting is much faster than microSD (faster boot times and better performance). See section 1.2.2.1!

    c. If using an NVMe with high power draw, ensure your power supply is at least 5V 5A 27W.

1.2.5 How to Boot from and Run a Raspberry Pi OS System from a USB3-mounted SSD

Objectives:
To detail how to boot from and run your Raspberry Pi OS system from a USB3-mounted SSD.

Pre-Requisites:
We do the operations in this Example on the following Raspberry Pi 5 system:

System:
  Host: raspberrypi Kernel: 6.12.34+rpt-rpi-2712 arch: aarch64 bits: 64
   compiler: gcc v: 12.2.0 Desktop: wayfire v: 0.7.5 Distro: Debian GNU/Linux
   12 (bookworm)
Machine:
  Type: ARM System: Raspberry Pi 5 Model B Rev 1.0 details: N/A rev: c04170
   serial: a5b3f4f94c31353d

Background:
As recommended in our storage model in the next section, the Raspberry Pi 5 OS is traditionally booted from and run from a microSD card mounted on the hardware. With the operating system kernel at release 6.12.34+rpt-rpi-2712, as shown in the above system description, it is possible, and highly advantageous, to boot and run the system from a USB3-mounted SSD, or other external device, such as the NVMe SSDs we illustrated this with in the previous sections.

Requirements:
Do the steps below, in the order shown, to complete the requirements for this example.

1. Update your package manager on your system, using the following commands:

   $ sudo apt update
   Output truncated...

   $ sudo apt upgrade
   Output truncated...

2. Insert an SSD, or other suitable device that has a SATA-to-USB3 cable connection capability, into a USB3 port on your Raspberry Pi 5

hardware. On our Raspberry Pi 5, the USB3 ports had a blue-colored tab inside them, visible from the outside. We connected a 512GB Silicon Power SSD, which was inside an Orico SATA-to-USB tool less enclosure. We previously had formatted the SSD in GParted, with an ext4 partition on it.

3. The SSD mounts automatically. We then used the Raspberry Pi Accessories Menu > SD Card Copier to copy the microSD Raspberry Pi OS system to the USB3-mounted SSD.

****Note****

In the SD Card Copier, make sure that you copy the system from the microSD card to the SSD!

4. When the copying is done, shut down the system, and remove the microSD card from its slot in the hardware.

5. Disconnect the power, and then reconnect it to reboot the system.

6. The Raspberry Pi OS now boots from and runs on the USB3-mounted SSD. That SSD is an exact clone of what was on the microSD card, as you did the above steps.

Conclusion:
At the time of the writing of this book, the Raspberry Pi 5 OS is able to boot from and run from an external USB3 SSD. To gauge the performance speed advantages of using an SSD, we encourage you to use the Accessories Menu> Raspberry Pi Diagnostics program to gauge the relative performance speed advantages of an SSD over a microSD card, whether that SSD has been attached via a USB3 cable or is in an NVMe adapter. The log readings of SSD versus microSD card provide that information.

1.3 Pre-and-Post Installation Considerations and Choices

Once you've determined exactly what you want to use your Raspberry Pi 5 hardware and software for, you need to carefully consider the following listing of questions, which suggest very important aspects of your envisioned usage. These are considerations you can make over and above the default installation choices presented to you by the operating system, as you proceed with the installation. Viewing these as suggestions rather than as highly formal constraints, you should really consider them as informally-presented guides as to how you can choose certain aspects of a prospective purchase of hardware, for example, that the installation will serve on, in the very subjective light of how you actually will use your Raspberry Pi 5. For example, should you buy the Raspberry Pi 5 with the larger available main memory?

1.3.1 Pre-Installation Considerations

1. Where will the system boot from? There are several options here, as shown in section 1.2, especially if you are going to add additional equipment to your base Raspberry Pi 5 hardware on the General Purpose Input/Output(GPIO) 40-pin header, HATS like an NVMe adapter, etc. Are you always going to boot from a microSD card that you used the Imager to create, from a USB3-connected SSD, from a network connection or from some connected NVMe M.2 device? All of these things affect performance and boot speed as illustrated in section 1.2.2. And booting the system using one of these options usually dictates that that medium becomes the primary *system disk*, where the operating system resides and runs from there.

2. Are you going to be a casual user of a Raspberry Pi 5, making only light demands on it in terms of computational tasks, or graphics? Are you going to be a gamer who needs not only heavy computational power but also extreme graphics capabilities? Or are you going to cluster Raspberry Pi hardware together in a server array, and rely upon free or commercial NAS software to service your customer and user base, or use it as a home media server?

    Given the way that you want to use your Raspberry Pi 5, does the hardware that you already have, or intend to purchase, have an adequate amount of physical memory, or RAM, for your intended use case? This consideration is basically a performance concern. For example, the Raspberry Pi 5 comes with 4, 8, or 16GB of RAM. The Raspberry Pi 5 we do all of our work on only comes with 4 GB of RAM, which is adequate for what we do. Which one are you going to buy, or which one do you have? In any situation, you should always first consider whether you have, or will have, an adequate amount or size of physical memory installed on the Raspberry Pi hardware, if that is a viable option.

    How would you know that? Read reviews online, look at benchmark tests performed by reputable sources, and talk to other Raspberry Pi 5 users that would have similar use cases as yourself. The Raspberry Pi Forums are a good place to start.

    https://forums.raspberrypi.com/

3. Two of the most integral and important considerations you must make are a) what persistent media data storage model are you going to use given your use case, and b) how much, and what type of externally-mounted media can or does your computer have physically connected to it?

    a. With regard to the first consideration, are you going to need to attach virtual storage media, via protocols such as NFSv4 or iSCSI? Are you going to connect and work within the contexts of Network Attached Storage(NAS) or a Storage Area Network(SAN)?

b. With regard to the second consideration, if you are only going to use the microSD card, or one external NVMe-mounted SSD as the system disk, that microSD card or NVMe-mounted SSD will most likely be the bootable system disk and the user file system data disk. If it is foreseeable that you will have additional USB3-mounted disk media installed on the system, what strategies will you use to backup or "clone" the bootable system disk, and perhaps "mirror" all other user data on the multiple data SSDs, with some dependable and robust strategy of backup?

****Note****

Our Data Storage Model Recommendation:

We recommend that you install the operating system on one medium (traditionally, a microSD card, or preferably an NVMe SSD, or a USB3-adaptor-connected device), and store all of the user data on another single medium, or an array of external media. That way, if the operating system and its bootable medium become corrupted or unusable for some reason, your user data is on a separate medium or array of media. This technique, or storage model, dovetails very well with the most practical methods of operating system upgrades. Using it, you can then simply replace the operating system medium and reinstall either the current version of the operating system or a newer version, without significantly impacting your user data storage. This will allow you to reattach the data media to the new operating system and its medium, whatever that might be. This is highly valuable not only for single-user desktops but also for NAS server-class systems as well. The way that your data is deployed on your media is a critical design consideration when you are building your system and is highly dependent on the particular use case that is guiding it.

One caveat you must consider when using the above recommended storage model is that some application software, most prominently LXC/LXD containers, store required files in both the system area and in the data storage area.

4. Do you want to have a wireless connection to a local area network and the Internet? A wired connection through DHCP is not automatically done on installation by the Raspberry Pi 5 OS 64-bit Desktop version, so you must configure the network settings during the default installation procedure. What is the IP address of your Raspberry Pi, and is it automatically assigned by the DHCP server on your network?

5. How many users are you going to initially establish at installation, and what are their user profiles going to be? For example, what users will have administrative privileges other than yourself, and what kind of security will each profile have? Integral with these questions are the considerations of the storage model you will establish after the initial installation of the operating system on a single medium, as defined in 1)b). For example, will all users home directories be on separate media from the system medium? Also, what user groups are you going to establish at installation, and how are you going to manage groups in a post-installation environment?

6. Who will be responsible for the items of systems administration tasks listed above? For example, that will influence your media management tasks concerning file systems for users and projects, according to the data storage model you employ.

7. What kind of software tools do you want to include, given the version of the Raspberry Pi 5 OS you are going to install, for the kinds of tasks you and your user base will be doing? For example, during installation, you are able to add packages on top of the default package installation to help accomplish those tasks. How are the user groups established in item 5) going to have access privileges to this software? What are your policies with respect to group access to software tools, and how do you enforce these policies?

8. Will you have a GUI windowing system after you install your system? You have a choice of installing either a GUI Desktop version, or one with a Command Line Interface (CUI) only, no graphical or desktop environment, a minimal set of application packages, and is the equivalent of a server operating system. Your previous experience and preferences with a particular style of computer environment can be implemented at installation, and dictated by your use case. Will you need a server install, based on your use case? A server install and the management of a server system involve another whole universe of considerations and design decisions.

In-Chapter Exercise

1. Make a detailed listing on paper of your answers to the above eight sets of questions before you begin to install your operating system. Then, read through the sections below referencing the procedures for actual installation, and for each of your answers, determine ahead of time how you will proceed through the procedures. This exercise is meant to serve as a "dry run" through any particular path you might take through the purchase, installation, and usage procedures.

1.3.2 Post-Installation Choices and Actions

The highly practical things you do to your Raspberry Pi 5 OS after it is installed successfully are <u>very</u> dependent upon your individual pre-installation considerations, as outlined in section 1.3.1, and how you implemented those considerations in detail. As presented in the pre-installation considerations, you should view the suggested post-installation considerations here as informally presented guides to how you can choose certain post-installation aspects of your operating system.

Our minimal set of recommendations for post-installation tasks are specific to our Raspberry Pi 5 and their hardware configurations. They follow directly from pre-installation considerations we made in section 1.3.1.

1. Our initial boot/system medium for our Raspberry Pi 5 is a 32 GB microSD card SSD.

2. Since we installed a desktop system on our Pi 5, which was going to rely heavily on a very convenient and easy to use GUI environment, it wasn't possible on those particular models of the hardware to increase the amount of installed physical memory, to speed up this kind of usage. See the output of the **inxi** commands shown in section 1.1.1 and In-Chapter Exercise 2 to gain more information and insight into how to view physical memory size on your Raspberry Pi 5 system.

   As stated above, your particular physical memory needs depend upon how you use your Raspberry Pi 5 system. We had to go with the defaults affecting the size of virtual memory, paging, and swap space, although these may be important considerations for you, depending on the model of Raspberry Pi 5 you have.

3. Use the Pi Menu Preferences > Add/Remove Software to install absolutely essential applications that you need to use that are not already pre-installed. For us, the required software was the Chromium Web Browser, the LibreOffice suite on our version of the operating system, in priority order, FileZilla, GParted, Webmin, and the GNU Image Manipulation Program. We also put desktop icons on our desktop for all of our important applications.

4. Our highly-recommended storage model dictates the use of **mdadm**, so we installed that package. Our Raspberry Pi 5 OS was originally built on 32 GB microSD cards, but then we rebuilt it to boot from a 1 TB capacity NVMe SSD. We then added additional USB3-mounted media later, in order to conform to our recommended storage model.

5. Since printing documents was an essential operation that our system needed to perform, we attached and set up (via CUPS) a laser

printer directly to the hardware of the Raspberry Pi 5, with a USB connection.

6. We used the Raspberry Pi Configuration tool, selecting the "System" tab, to configure our network settings and connect to a wired intranet network. We then exposed our system on the local intranet as a basic ssh server, so we immediately modified the sshd configuration file, and constructed ufw firewall rules, according to what we show below in this chapter, to secure the system.

7. We minimally exposed our system as a web server using nginx, and our custom web programs, but went with the default security measures for those applications.

8. We needed only a very sparse set of additional users and groups on the system, so we immediately set those up using the method shown in the sections below, and added to them as necessary. This method of adding new users and groups is shown below. The primary advantage this confers is that users, and their data files, which for us are on their own redundant pair of hard drives, are discreet and maintained separately from the operating system installation. We feel that this model is useful for a single-user computer desktop system, a shared multi-user computer, or low-to-midlevel enterprise-level servers as well.

There are various text-based Raspberry Pi 5 OS commands that survey system hardware, in order to provide you with a basis for doing performance tuning and post-installation modification of the system. Some of these are lscpu, lshw, hwinfo, lspci, lspci, lsusb, inxi, lsblk, df, fdisk, mount, free, hdparm, and examining the relevant contents of the /proc directories.

But, in order to get a very useful summary of the actual post-installation configuration of their system, we have found that the **inxi** command is the most useful and expedient way for beginners.

In-Chapter Exercise

2. Following up on your answer to In-Chapter Exercise 1, completely list and detail how you implemented your pre-installation considerations on the system you have installed. Or, if you did not implement them because you didn't do an installation, how would you implement them on an actual hardware platform of your choice? Use our set of minimal recommendations for post-installation tasks as a guide for how to fulfill the requirements of this exercise. In addition, you could consult with the person who actually installed your system on the hardware, if that person is available.

1.4 System Services Administration, Startup, and Shutdown Procedures

What you have to think about first, in terms of system "booting" as it's generally called, is:

"How do you want the system to boot?"

As stated in section 1.3, that is one of the most important pre-installation considerations you have to make. There are a few options, and the details of them, especially for an ARM-architecture machine, are complex

This section gives an overview of the general procedures for booting, managing the startup process, and gracefully shutting down the Raspberry Pi 5 OS, given how you've answered the above question. It gives a brief summary overview of the steps that the operating system and hardware go through in successfully starting up and shutting down. It then gives some further references to the basic but important systemd services administration utilities available to a system administrator. In those further references, we give examples of commands for manipulating and changing system services by enabling and running new services.

1.4.1 The Boot and Startup Processes

Here are the general steps that the Raspberry Pi 5 OS goes through to boot up:

1. When the Raspberry Pi 5 is first turned on, the ARM core is off, and the GPU core is on. At this point, the SDRAM is disabled.
2. The ROM on the SoC initiates the first stage of booting.
3. The boot behavior for a microSD or USB boot is controlled by a configuration file in the EEPROM, and can be edited via the **rpi-eeprom-config** tool, with the command

   ```
   $ sudo -E rpi-eeprom-config –edit
   ```

   The EEPROM second stage consists of the following steps:
   a. Initialize clocks and SDRAM.
   b. Read the EEPROM configuration file.
   c. Determine if booting should be a restart/stop, or from a microSD card, the network, a USB device, or an PCIe NVME device.

The Raspberry Pi 5 boot process, for example, is similar to other Linux-based computers, with the main differences being that:

a. it traditionally, by default, uses a microSD card as its primary storage device, and boot medium, or alternate sources, and

b. is controlled by an EEPROM.

The term "booting" is used here to mean bringing the operating system from a complete power-off condition to a point where systemd can take over. Then in "startup", systemd brings the computer to a steady-state, fully normal operating condition.

When a system hangs up during the shutdown procedure, a contemporary way of diagnosing the problem is to examine the systemd journal with the **journalctl** command. This way, if some process or program is preventing the system from reaching a powered-off condition, the journal logs will allow you to see what that process or program that's causing the problem. On shutdown, systemd attempts to stop all services, and unmount all file systems. The system is finally powered down. We give more details of how a Raspberry Pi 5 system using systemd shuts down in the next section.

In-Chapter Exercises

3. How can you boot into an alternative environment found on another boot medium on your Raspberry Pi5, and in which phase of the bootup process shown in Figure 1.1 might this alternative method be presented to you? Why would you want to do this? Make note of exactly how this might be done on the Raspberry Pi 5 OS. Also, draw an arrow, or arrows, in Figure 1.1 that would specify what path would be followed if the system were to be rebooted rather than powered off.

4. Which methodology of booting (from a traditional microSD, from a USB3-mounted SSD/ NMVe M.2 device, or a network) would allow you to test drive different Raspberry Pi 5 OS versions in the quickest and easiest way on the same piece of hardware? **And not necessarily on Raspberry Pi 5 hardware**. Sketch exactly how this would be accomplished, given your choice. (Note: Not simultaneously, but sequentially!)

1.4.2 systemd and Traditional System Reboot or Shutdown

systemd is in charge of taking the system from the normal operating condition to a power-off state, or to reboot the system. The relevant systemd **systemctl** commands, with their options, that achieve shutting the system down

```
┌─────────────────┐        ┌─────────────────┐
│    Power On     │ ┄┄┄▶   │      POST       │
└─────────────────┘        └─────────────────┘
         ▲                          │
         │                          ▼
         │                 ┌─────────────────┐
         │                 │    BIOS/UEFI    │
         │                 └─────────────────┘
         │                          │
         │                          ▼
         │                 ┌─────────────────┐
         │                 │ Device Selection│
         │                 └─────────────────┘
         │                          │
         │                          ▼
         │                 ┌─────────────────┐
         │                 │    Load & Run   │
         │                 │     GRUB2       │
         │                 └─────────────────┘
         │                          │
         │                          ▼
┌─────────────────┐        ┌─────────────────┐
│ System Powered  │        │  Select, Load, &│
│      Off        │        │   Run kernel    │
└─────────────────┘        └─────────────────┘
         ▲                          │
         │                          ▼
         │                 ┌─────────────────┐
         │                 │Initiate kernel File│
         │                 │ Systems & Data  │
         │                 └─────────────────┘
         │                          │
         │                          ▼
         │                 ┌─────────────────┐
         │                 │   Run systemd   │
         │                 └─────────────────┘
         │                          │
         │                          ▼
         │                 ┌─────────────────┐
         │                 │ Invoke Default  │
         │                 │     Target      │
         │                 └─────────────────┘
         │                          │
         │                          ▼
┌─────────────────┐        ┌─────────────────┐
│    Shutdown     │ ◀┄┄┄   │ Running System  │
└─────────────────┘        └─────────────────┘
```

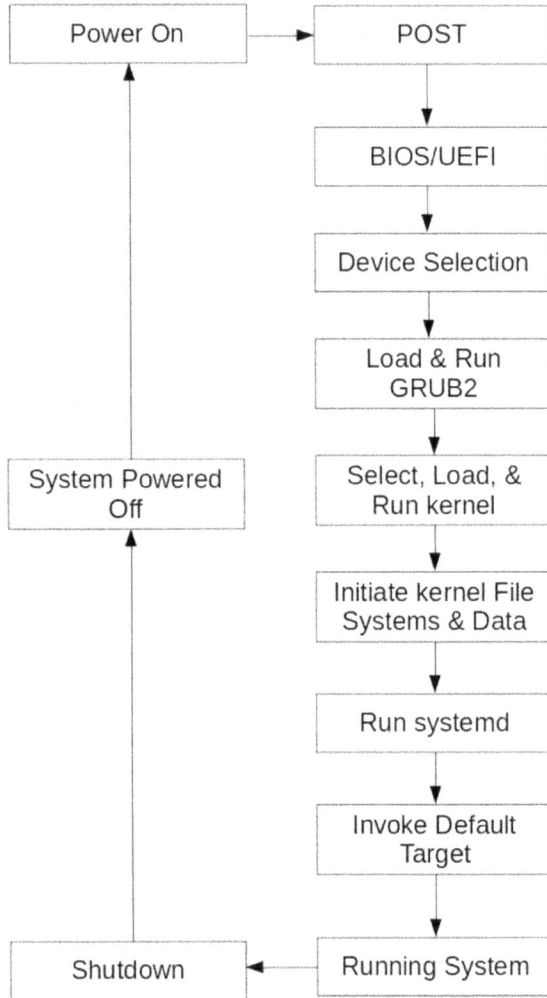

FIGURE 1.1
Traditional Linux boot process steps.

or rebooting it, and briefly what they accomplish, are shown in Table 1.1. The systemd shutdown path through possible target states, from a normal operating condition to a powered-off state, is described in Figure 1.2.

Traditionally, the graceful shutdown or reboot procedures can be done graphically (with the Raspberry Pi Menu > Logout choice) from the active window system, or from the command line or console window, using the **halt** or **shutdown** commands and their options. The **shutdown** command has the advantage of allowing you to specify a time when shutdown processes are initiated.

TABLE 1.1

systemd systemctl Shutdown Commands

Command	Description
systemctl halt	Halts the system.
systemctl poweroff	Powers off the system.
systemctl reboot	Restarts the system.
systemctl suspend	Suspends the system.
systemctl hibernate	Hibernates the system.
systemctl hybrid-sleep	Hibernates and suspends the system.

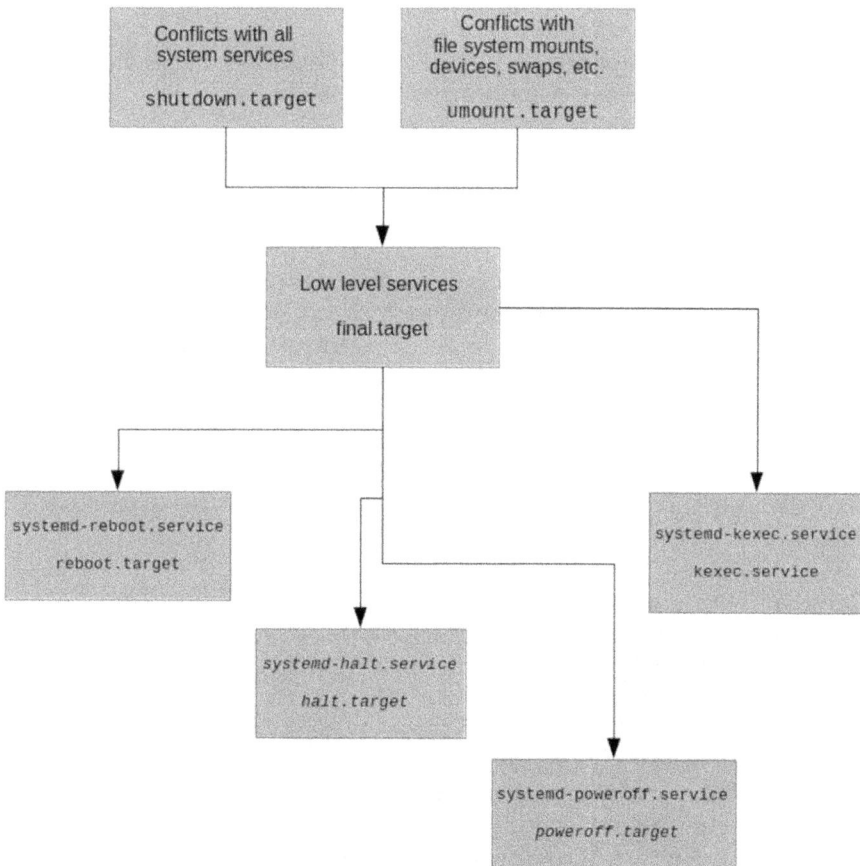

FIGURE 1.2
systemd shutdown path.

Graceful shutdown procedures are generally done as follows:

1. Shutdown system and user processes
2. Flush system memory to disk
3. Unmount file systems
4. Power off

An example of using the **shutdown** command on a Raspberry Pi 5 system is as follows:

$ shutdown –h now

where:

h means halt the processor, and **now** is the time option, which means immediately.

To get a more complete description of the **shutdown** command, particularly the format of the time option, see the man page on your Raspberry Pi system.

1.4.3 Preliminary Considerations When Managing System Services with systemd

The system service manager that is available in our base Raspberry Pi 5 system is systemd. In fact, systemd is the system service manager for all distributions in the three major branches of Linux, and all important downstream Linux distributions as well, including Raspberry Pi 5 OS.

We detail system service management with systemd in Chapter 2, and provide several examples there of how to effectively control operating system services in a modern systemd-controlled Linux system.

We first pose a couple of preliminary questions about "system services" on the Raspberry Pi 5 OS.

Question: What is a daemon?

Answer: Basically, a daemon is a background, ongoing process that is not linked or controlled by a terminal. Particularly, it's not connected in the usual way to standard output or stand error.

Question: Is a "service" a daemon?

Answer: Sometimes. More accurately and generally, a service can be a process or collection of processes, the overall state of the system, or the state of a physical device, a virtual device, a dataset, etc. And as a provider of resources, or a collection of an application's capabilities, it can have more than one instance. For example, the many-layered file systems present on the system, or the multiple means of remote login to the system.

1.4.4 Further References for System Service Management Using systemd

In this section, we provided some preliminary references for the use of systemd for service management. Our primary reference is the example detailed above of how to enable server-side host services for a secure ftp daemon, known as vsftpd. That is a complete primary, basic example of using systemd to manage system services.

Here are some references that provide descriptions and explanations of systemd:

1. Freedesktop.org—systemd Documentation
   Official documentation covering systemd concepts, unit files, journal logging, and administration.
   URL: https://www.freedesktop.org/wiki/Software/systemd/

2. systemd man pages.
   Detailed documentation on systemd commands and unit configuration.
   Run locally with:

   $ man systemd

   Or view online: https://man7.org/linux/man-pages/man1/systemd.1.html

3. Arch Linux Wiki—systemd
   Comprehensive guide explaining systemd services, unit files, troubleshooting, and practical usage.
   URL: https://wiki.archlinux.org/title/systemd

4. Red Hat Documentation—Managing Services with systemd
   Enterprise-focused guide on using systemd for service and process management.
   URL: https://access.redhat.com/documentation/en-us/red_hat_enterprise_linux/8/html/configuring_basic_system_settings/managing-services-with-systemd_configuring-basic-system-settings

5. Linux Handbook—systemd Basics
   A beginner-friendly tutorial on systemd and its common commands.
   URL: https://linuxhandbook.com/systemd/

Chapter 2 provides a more complete description of service management with systemd. You should be cautious when executing the examples found there when you are on an insecure network connected to the Internet. You must have root privileges on the computer to execute the examples we show in the above references as well.

In-Chapter Exercise

5. What is the danger of using ftp, telnet, rlogin, or rsh from a remote site on the Internet into your home computer?

1.5 User Administration

The two most important objectives of user administration are service and security. First, providing service to ensure that the user base has access to and can fully take advantage of the resources that the Raspberry Pi 5 OS can provide. Second, securing the files and processes that the user base needs to utilize those resources. Later in this chapter, we go over some of the security methodologies that a system administrator can deploy to keep the system secure.

The traditional Linux technique for providing service and security to users is through read, write, and execute (**rwx**) access privileges, for the individual user, the group, or all others (**u,g,o**) on the system, to specific objects on the system, such as directories, or folders, and most importantly, to the files contained in them. Designing and implementing user groups and access privileges for user groups are the most important parts of this technique.

Certainly, user account and group creation and configuration are the first steps in providing maximum service and security to the user base. That is true even if you are the only user of the system!

A very integral part of designing user accounts and groups is the detailed consideration given to the recommended user data storage model we showed in section 1.3.1, Item 3.

****Note****

This is done by securing user files on a second, possibly redundant, storage medium, so that they can be kept separate from the operating system boot medium itself. It can be practically achieved by properly creating user accounts so that they have their home directories on that second hard drive. As we show in section 1.8, various ways of adding redundant persistent media very easily and effectively implement the model.

We concentrate here on how to manage user accounts and groups on the Raspberry Pi 5 OS with the **adduser, addgroup, deluser, delgroup, newusers, passwd,** and **usermod** commands. These activities are usually done a significant time after the initial installation of your Raspberry Pi 5 system, but can be done during installation and initialization of the system as well. Table 1.2 shows brief descriptions of these commands:

TABLE 1.2

Basic User Administration Commands

Command	Description
adduser	Add a new user account
deluser	Delete a user account
addgroup	Add a new group
delgroup	Delete a group
newusers	Update and create new users in batch mode
passwd	Manage user passwords
usermod	Modifies user accounts

The examples in this section illustrate:

- simple cases of text-based user account creation and configuration,
- text-based group creation and configuration, and
- text-based deletion of a user account and a group.

In-Chapter Exercise

6. Make a table or chart of what users and groups need to be added to your system, and what their default account parameters and group memberships should be. What command can you use to identify all existing groups on the system?

1.5.1 Adding a User and Group in a Text-Based Interface

The commands **adduser** and **addgroup**, by default, add a "normal" (non-system) user or group to the system, using command line options and option arguments. They take default configuration information from /etc/adduser. conf. They are a more developed front-end for the older, low-level commands, such as **useradd**, **groupadd**, and **usermod**. **Adduser**, and utilize patented UID and GID values for creation of new accounts and groups. By default, they create a home directory from a skeletal configuration file, etc.

adduser itself is a script file that interfaces to the following commands and their functionality:

useradd, groupadd, passwd, gpasswd, usermod, chfn, chage, edquota.

An abbreviated listing of the syntax of the **adduser** and **addgroup** commands, taken from the man page for adduser, is as follows:

```
*************************************************************************
adduser, addgroup - add a user or group to the system
Syntax:
    adduser [options] [--home DIR] [--shell SHELL] [--no-create-home]
```

[--uid ID] [--firstuid ID] [--lastuid ID] [--ingroup GROUP | --gid ID]
[--disabled-password]   [--disabled-login]   [--gecos   GECOS]
[--add_extra_groups] [--encrypt-home] user

adduser --system [options] [--home DIR] [--shell SHELL] [--no-create-
home] [--uid ID] [--group | --ingroup GROUP | --gid ID] [--disabled-
password] [--disabled-login] [--gecos GECOS] user

addgroup [options] [--gid ID] group

addgroup --system [options] [--gid ID] group

adduser [options] user group

Purpose:
>   adduser and addgroup add users and groups to the system according to
>   command line options and configuration information in
>   /etc/adduser.conf. They are friendlier front ends to the low level
>   tools like useradd, groupadd and usermod programs, by default choosing
>   Debian policy conformant UID and GID values, creating a home directory
>   with skeletal configuration, running a custom script, and other fea-
>   tures. adduser and addgroup can be run in one of five modes:

Output: New or modified user accounts or groups.

Commonly Used Options:
>   [--quiet] [--debug] [--force-badname] [--help|-h] [--version] [--conf
>   FILE]

****

The basic, simple usage as superuser of the following **adduser** command,
does the following 5 things:

$ sudo adduser username

1. Create the user named username.
2. Create the user's home directory (the default is /home/username), and copy the files
   from /etc/skel into it.
3. Create a group with the same name as the user, and place the user in it.
4. Prompt for a password for the user (by default not shown on-screen), and its
   confirmation.
5. Prompt for personal information about the user, such as telephone, office contact, etc..

Below are two simple examples of how to add a new user in a text-based,
command-line interface. The first example illustrates how to interactively create a single user account from the command line as a superuser. If you make a
mistake in creating a user account, you can always remove the account immediately by using the **deluser** command, as shown in section 1.5.3.

Example 1.3 adduser Command for a Single User Account

$ sudo adduser sarwar
[sudo] password for bob: **qqq**
Adding user `sarwar` ...
Adding new group `sarwar` (1002) ...
Adding new user `sarwar` (1002) with group `sarwar` ...
Creating home directory `/home/sarwar` ...
Copying files from `/etc/skel` ...
Enter new UNIX password: **www**
Retype new UNIX password: **www**
passwd: password updated successfully
Enter the new value, or press ENTER for the default
      Full Name []: ENTER
      Room Number []: ENTER
      Work Phone []: ENTER
      Home Phone []: ENTER
      Other []: ENTER
Is the information correct? [Y/n] **Y**
$

In-Chapter Exercise

7. Create a single new account on your Raspberry Pi system, with the **adduser** command as shown above. Be sure to use the entries you made in your answer to In-Chapter Exercise 6 to override the defaults for user account configurations on your system!

The second example uses the command **newusers**, which allows "batch" mode creation of new users, in conjunction with a file that contains a listing of several user accounts that can be added all at one time. A brief description of the **newusers** command, taken from the man page, is as follows:

****

newusers - update and create new users in batch mode

Syntax: newusers [options] [file]

Purpose: The newusers command reads a file (or the standard input by default) and uses this information to update a set of existing users or to create new users. Each line is in the same format as the standard password file, as follows:
pw_name:pw_passwd:pw_uid:pw_gid:pw_gecos:pw_dir:pw_shell
  where pw_name is the name of the user you want to create,
  pw_passwd is the password,
  pw_uid is the UID,
  pw_gid is the GID,
  pw_gecos is an identifying comment,
  pw_dir is the home directory path,
  pw_shell is the new users default shell.

Common Options:
  -h, --help
    Display help message and exit.
  -r, --system
    Create a system account.
****

Example 1.4 Creating Several New Users in "Batch" Mode

  1. Use your favorite text editor to create the following file, named "dev_grp.txt" in your home directory. Feel free to add more lines similar to the one shown to add more new users to the listing.

hassan:QQQ:2001:2001:CFO of Accounting:/home/hassan:/bin/bash

The seven fields of the above line, separated by colons (:), are the new user accounts name, password, UID, GID, GECOS commentary, default home directory, and default shell.

  2. Use the following command to create the user(s) encoded in the file dev_grp.txt:

```
$ sudo newusers dev_grp.txt
[sudo] password for bob: qqq
$
```

  3. Check the addition of the new user(s) using the following command:

```
$ more /etc/group
Output truncated…
hassan:x:2001:
$
```

In-Chapter Exercise

  8. According to the table or chart of user accounts and their configuration requirements you did for In-Chapter Exercise 6, create a file of new user accounts. <u>Don't recreate the user account you added in In-Chapter Exercise 7!</u> For each user account, you must have a single line in the file with seven colon-delimited fields that contain the configuration for each user. The table, or chart design with its entries, determines what is in the file.

1.5.2 Adding and Maintaining Groups in a Text-Based Interface

The easiest and most efficient way to create and manage user accounts and groups is by using Webmin. From Webmin's main menu, you can make the System > Users and Groups choice to view, create, and delete both. We certainly recommend that, but for text-based interaction in a console or terminal window, you can use the **addgroup** and **adduser** commands to manage groups.

The following is an example of how to add and manage groups.

> **Example 1.5 Adding and Managing Groups and Users from the Command Line**
>
> Objectives: To add a new group and manage those users that are in that group.
>
> Pre-Requisites: Having completed all previous Examples, having default groups available on your system.
>
> Background: Text-based management of groups is accomplished with the **addgroup** command and its options.
>
> Requirements: Do the following steps, in the order presented, to complete the requirements of this example:
>
> 1. Create a group named "development", using the **addgroup** command as follows:
>
> ```
> $ sudo addgroup development
> [sudo] password for bob:
> Adding group `development' (GID 1003) ...
> Done.
> $
> ```
>
> 2. Add the user sarwar to the group named "development" using the **adduser** command as follows:
>
> ```
> $ sudo adduser sarwar development
> Adding user `sarwar' to group `development' ...
> Adding user sarwar to group development
> Done.
> $
> ```
>
> 3. List the groups on the system, and verify sarwar as a member of the group named
>
> ```
> $ cd /etc
> /etc$ more group
> Output truncated...
> sarwar:x:1002:
> development:x:1003:sarwar
> /etc $
> ```
>
> 4. Remove the user sarwar from the group named "development":
>
> ```
> /etc $ sudo deluser sarwar development
> Removing user `sarwar' from group `development' ...
> Done.
> /etc $
> ```

5. Verify that sarwar has been removed from the group named "development":

/etc $ **more group**
Output truncated...
sarwar:x:1002:
development:x:1003:

In-Chapter Exercises

9. You have an air-gapped Raspberry Pi 5 in a room. You want only certain users in a defined group named "proj" to be able to access files in a directory named "proj1" in your account on the file system of that computer. Use the above command line commands to add those certain users, and yourself, to the group "proj". Create the "proj1" directory. Then, set the permission bits appropriately on your home directory, the "proj1" directory, and any files put in that directory, so that only those certain users can read, write, and execute the files in it. The room is open to the public, but to login to the computer, each individual user has to use her own password.

1.5.3 Modifying and Deleting a User Account and Group from the Command Line

To effectively delete a user account or a group from the system using the command line, use the **deluser** or **delgroup** commands. A brief description of those commands, taken from the man pages on the Raspberry Pi 5 OS, is as follows:

****
deluser, delgroup - remove a user or group from the system

Syntax:
deluser [options][--force][--remove-home] [--remove-all-files]
        [--backup] [--backup-to DIR] user
deluser --group [options] group
delgroup [options] [--only-if-empty] group
deluser [options] user group

Purpose: deluser and **delgroup** remove users and groups from the system according to command line options and configuration information in /etc/deluser.conf and /etc/adduser.conf.

Common Options:
    [--conf FILE]   Use FILE instead of /etc/deluser.conf
    --version   Display version and copyright information.
****

To modify an existing user account from the command line, you can use the **usermod** command. A brief description of that command, taken from the man page on the Raspberry Pi 5 OS, is as follows:

****

usermod - modify a user account

Syntax:
  usermod [options] LOGIN

Purpose: usermod modifies the system account files to reflect the changes that are
  specified on the command line, for LOGIN name.

Common Options:
  -a, --append
  Add the user to the supplementary group(s). Use only with the -G option.
  -d, --home HOME_DIR
  The user's new login directory.
  -G, --groups GROUP1[,GROUP2,...[,GROUPN]]]
  A list of supplementary groups which the user is also a member of. Each group is
  separated from the next by a comma, with no intervening whitespace.
  -l, --login NEW_LOGIN
  The name of the user will be changed from LOGIN to NEW_LOGIN.
  Nothing else is changed. In particular, the user's home directory
  should probably be renamed manually to reflect the new login name.
  -m, --move-home
  Move the content of the user's home directory to the new location.
  -s, --shell SHELL
  The name of the user's new login shell. Setting this field to blank causes the system
  to select the default login shell.
****

Following is an example of deleting a user account named sarwar from the system, using the **deluser** command:

Example 1.6 User Account Deletion with deluser

Objectives: To delete a user account from the command line.

Pre-requisites: Having completed all previous Examples, or having a user account on your system that you want to permanently delete.

Background: Similar to the **adduser** command, **deluser** deletes a user account from the system.

Requirements: Do the following steps, in the order shown, to complete the requirements of this Example:

1. To delete the user account sarwar, type the following command:

```
$ sudo deluser sarwar
[sudo] password for bob: XXX
Removing user `sarwar' ...
Warning: group `sarwar' has no more members.
Done.
$
```

1.5.4 A Method of User and Group Creation on a Second Storage Medium

According to our recommended storage model from section 1.3.1, Item 3, it would be advantageous to install the operating system on one bootable medium (preferably a fast, but not necessarily large capacity USB3 Solid State Drive [SSD], or a NVMe-adaptor-connected M.2 PCIe device), and store all of the user data on <u>another</u> single medium of a similar type, but with much larger capacity, or even some kind of array of external media. In this section, we show a simple way of conforming to that model when new users are created on your Raspbeery Pi 5 OS.

Note that this technique does <u>not</u> show how to transfer an already-existing user, with their entire home directory, over to a newly added medium. Although we do leave that as an In-Chapter Exercise for you to accomplish within the scope of this section.

The prerequisites and the steps we took to accomplish this technique are as follows:

0. You have a USB3-mountable medium, formatted to ext4, that you want to use for the new user's home directory, it is mountable and recognized by your Raspberry Pi 5 system (shows up in /dev), and is not currently mounted.

1. The new user in our case is named sarwar.

2. The home directory of the administrative user that will execute this technique, in our case, is */home/*bob

3. The home directory of the new user, in our case, will be */media/sarwar*

4. The pathname to the external medium, in our case a USB3 thumb drive, is **/media/bob/04fd2202-8879-46f2-8040-446753ed077c**

5. We will be putting the new user's login directory on an ext4 file system.

Follow these steps sequentially to achieve the desired result:

0. Add the external medium to the system. Find out its device name and UUID with the **blkid** command, and then unmount it (if it is mounted!) with this command:

```
$ sudo umount /media/bob/04fd2202-8879-46f2-8040-446753ed077c
```

1. Show the results of the command in step 0.(in /dev) of unmounting the external medium, with the following command:

```
$ sudo blkid -o list
device              fs_type    label     mount point            UUID
--------------------------------------------------------------------------------
/dev/sda1           vfat       boot      /boot         5EA1-EC88
/dev/sda2           ext4       rootfs    /             f0702b0a-e54b-4c34-bd2d-6e52a561898c
/dev/sdb1           ext4                 (not mounted) 04fd2202-8879-46f2-8040-446753ed077c
$
```

On our system, it was /dev/sdb1 with UUID of **04fd2202-8879-46f2-8040-446753ed077c**, and in the output showed as being (not mounted).

2. Create a new directory on the system in /media for the new user.

$ sudo mkdir /media/sarwar

3. Add the new user with the **adduser** command.

```
$ sudo adduser sarwar
Adding user `sarwar' ...
Adding new group `sarwar' (1001) ...
Adding new user `sarwar' (1001) with group `sarwar' ...
Creating home directory `/home/sarwar' ...
Copying files from `/etc/skel' ...
New password: www
Retype new password: www
passwd: password updated successfully
Changing the user information for sarwar
Enter the new value, or press ENTER for the default
        Full Name []:
        Room Number []:
        Work Phone []:
        Home Phone []:
        Other []:
Is the information correct? [Y/n] y
$
```

Note that we've gone with all of the defaults, except supplying a new password for the new user.

4. Mount the external medium as an ext4 file system, at /media/sarwar

$ sudo mount -t ext4 -o defaults /dev/sdb1 /media/sarwar

5. Use the **usermod** command to change the new user's home/login directory to /media/sarwar

$ sudo usermod --home /media/sarwar sarwar
$

6. Use the **chown** and **chgrp** commands to change the access privileges of the directory */media*/sarwar so that the new user can work in that directory when logging in.

```
$ sudo chown sarwar /media/sarwar
$ sudo chgrp sarwar /media/sarwar
$
```

7. Log in to the system with the new user's login name and password. Verify that the current working directory upon login is */media*/sarwar. Add files to Sarwar's home directory, and note their access privileges.

Conclusion:
The new user now has their home directory, or login directory, on the external medium and on the boot/system medium. At this point, you can safely delete the new user's home/login directory on the boot/system medium.

Followup: Unmounting and Mount on boot
To unmount the external medium, while in the administrative account, use the following command:

```
$ sudo umount /dev/sdb1
```

If you want this user's home/login directory to mount and be available after reboots of the system, you need the information from the column UUID from Step 1's output above, to be able to have this exact medium device mount on subsequent reboots of the system. Edit the file /etc/fstab with any editor, for example **nano**.

```
$ sudo nano /etc/fstab
```

Add the following line at the end of the file. Make sure to replace the UUID and the path of the mounted device with what is on your system, <u>not</u> what shows on ours here in this Example!

```
UUID=04fd2202-8879-46f2-8040-446753ed077c    /media/sarwar  ext4   defaults 0
```

It's possible to use /dev/sdb1 instead of UUID=… in the above line in the file, but using the UUID ensures that you are mounting this <u>exact</u> external medium, and not another one that you could put in the same USB slot on the Raspberry Pi upon reboot.

In-Chapter Exercise

10. Using a hybrid version of the above technique, move the home/ login directory of another user you have previously added to the

system, from the boot/system medium to another post-installation medium. How would this affect the file system parameters of the files of the existing user?

1.6 Basic Password Management

It is often necessary for the person responsible for user and group account management, and for obvious security reasons, to make changes to passwords. This is accomplished most easily with the **passwd** command. We give a few basic examples of the use of this command in this section. For a more complete description of the **passwd** command, see the man page for the command on your Raspberry Pi 5 system.

To reset the password for a user account, use the following command:

```
$ sudo passwd mansoor
[sudo] password for bob: QQQ
Enter new UNIX password: ZZZ
Retype new UNIX password: ZZZ
passwd: password updated successfully
$
```

To obtain a brief listing of the options available with the **passwd** command, use the following command:

```
$ sudo passwd -h mansoor
Usage: passwd [options] [LOGIN]

Options:
 -a, --all              report password status on all accounts
 -d, --delete            delete the password for the named account
 -e, --expire            force expire the password for the named account
 -h, --help            display this help message and exit
 -k, --keep-tokens        change password only if expired
 -i, --inactive INACTIVE     set password inactive after expiration to INACTIVE
 -l, --lock            lock the password of the named account
 -n, --mindays MIN_DAYS      set minimum number of days before password
                  change to MIN_DAYS
 -q, --quiet          quiet mode
 -r, --repository REPOSITORY  change password in REPOSITORY repository
 -R, --root CHROOT_DIR      directory to chroot into
 -S, --status          report password status on the named account
 -u, --unlock          unlock the password of the named account
 -w, --warndays WARN_DAYS     set expiration warning days to WARN_DAYS
 -x, --maxdays MAX_DAYS      set maximum number of days before password
                  change to MAX_DAYS
$
```

To see the status of a particular user's password, use the following command:

```
$ sudo passwd -S mansoor
mansoor P 11/15/2016 0 99999 7 -1
$
```

The output of the above command is described in the man page for **passwd** as follows:

1. Username – The user's login name.

2. Encrypted Password – The hashed password (or special values like !, *, or !! to indicate no password or locked account).

3. Last Password Change – The number of days since January 1, 1970, when the password was last changed.

4. Minimum Days – The minimum number of days required before a password can be changed.

5. Maximum Days – The maximum number of days before a password must be changed.

6. Warning Days – The number of days before password expiration when the user is warned.

7. Inactive Days – The number of days after password expiration before the account is disabled.

1.7 Determining and Changing File Access Privileges

Once a user or group account has been added to the system, the next concern of a system administrator is how to maintain file access security, in terms of that user or group accounts' permissions to access and utilize system services, and all files in general.

Traditional UNIX and Linux permissions, which define secure access to file objects, such as regular files or directories, are the permissions of *read(r), write(w), and execute(x)*.

Additionally, there are other advanced techniques for setting permissions, such as setting the setuid, setgid, and sticky bit. Beyond these, the POSIX ACL model gives users finer-grained control over file and directory object security. Every file object can be thought of as having associated with it an access ACL that controls the discretionary access to that object. For a directory, this ACL is referred to as a default ACL. The Raspberry Pi 5 OS, by default, uses what is known as the POSIX.1e ACLs model. We discuss system security, in general, in section 1.15, and follow that up with specific details of it in the sub-sections of that section.

1.7.1 How to Reveal File Access Privileges

The **ls** command, with the **-l** or **-la,** and **-ld**, options can display access permissions for an individual named file, or a list of files or directories. A brief description of the **ls** command with the three options, taken from the man page on our Raspberry Pi 5 OS, are as follows:

```
********************************************************************
ls [options][file-list][directory-list]
```

Syntax
ls -l, ls -la [file-list]
ls -ld [directory-list]

Purpose   First syntax: Display the long list of files and/or directories in the
             space-separated file-list on the display screen; in the case where file-list
             contains directories, display long list of all the files in these directories
             Second syntax: Display the long list of directories in directory-list on the
             display screen.

Common Options
-a, --all   Display a long listing.
-d, --directory   List directories themselves, not their contents.
-g   Similar to -l, but do not list the owner of the file(s) or directories.
-l   Use a long listing format.
```
********************************************************************
```

If no **file-list** is given, the **ls** command gives long lists for all the files (except hidden files, sometimes known as "dot" files) in the current working directory. If you include the **-l** and **-a** options on the command line, hidden files are displayed as follows:

```
$ ls -la
total 532
drwx------    16    bob bob   4096   Mar   2   13:49. .
drwxr-xr-x     3    root root  4096   Mar   1   14:52. .
-rw-------     1    bob bob    530   Mar   2   13:09. bash_history
-rw-r--r--     1    bob bob    220   Nov  19   05:32. bash_logout
-rw-r--r--     1    bob bob   3523   Nov  19   05:32.bashrc
drwxr-xr-x     2    bob bob   4096   Nov  19   05:36 Bookshelf
drwx------    11    bob bob   4096   Mar   2   13:49. cache
drwxr-xr-x    16    bob bob   4096   Mar   2   13:49. config
drwxr-xr-x     3    bob bob   4096   Mar   1   15:01 Desktop
Output truncated...

$
```

TABLE 1.3

Permissions of the Files for the Three Kinds of Users

File Name	User	Group	Other
17_3_4.bash	Read, write, execute	Read	Read
17_3_4.docx	Read, write	Read	Read
Blandedmic.txt	Read, write	Read	Read
Bookshelf	Read, write, execute	Read, execute	Read, execute

Following is a description of the fields in the output:

1. The leftmost character in the first field of the output is the file type (**d** for a directory and **-** (hyphen) for an ordinary file). The rest of the nine characters in the first field show the file access privileges for user, group, and others.
2. The second field shows the number of hard links to the file.
3. The third field shows the owner's login name.
4. The fourth field shows the file's group owner.
5. The fifth field displays the file's size (in bytes).
6,7. The sixth and seventh fields display the date and time of file's creation (or last update).
8. The last field is the file's name.

Table 1.3 shows what constituent file in the displayed output has what type of access privileges, for the files in the truncated output.

In the current working directory, where the **ls -l** command is executed from, the command displays the long listing of all the files and directories in it, without showing hidden files. You can use the **ls -ld** command to display the long listing of only directories. When executed without an argument, this command displays the long listing for the current working directory, as shown in the first command below. The second and third commands show that when the **ls -ld** command is executed with a list of directories as its arguments, it displays the long listing for those directories only. If an argument to the **ls -ld** command is a file, the command displays the long listing for the file, as shown in the display after the fourth command below. The fifth command below, **ls -ld Bookshelf/***, displays the long listing for all the files and directories in the Bookshelf directory.

```
$ ls -ld
drwxr-xr-x   25  bob bob   4096   May   18   05:40   .
$ ls -ld remzi
drwxr-xr-x   2   bob bob   4096   Nov   5    2022   remzi
```

$ ls -ld ~/Downloads remzi

drwxr-xr-x	2	bob bob	4096	May	14	10:23	/home/bob/Downloads
drwxr-xr-x	2	bob bob	4096	Nov	5	2022	remzi

$ ls -ld test.py

-rw-r--r--	1	bob bob	106	Jun	5	07:00	test.py

$ ls -ld Bookshelf/*

-rw-r--r--	1	bob bob	35954684	Apr	4	2022	Bookshelf/

BeginnersGuide

$

1.7.2 Changing File Access Privileges

The **chmod** command changes access privileges for files and directories, <u>if you have the permissions and system privilege to do so</u>. The following description is taken from the man page on our Raspberry Pi 5 OS for the **chmod** command:

****

chmod [options][file(s)][directory]

Syntax
      chmod [OPTION]... MODE[,MODE]... FILE...
      chmod [OPTION]... OCTAL-MODE FILE...
      chmod [OPTION]... --reference=RFILE FILE...

Purpose   Change/set permissions for files in file-list

Common Options
-R   Recursively descend through directories changing/setting permissions for all the files and subdirectories under each directory
-f   Force specified access permissions; no error messages are produced if you are the owner of the file
****

Symbolic mode, also known as "mode control", has the form [who][operator] [privilege], with possible values for "who," "operator," and "privilege", as shown in Table 1.4. This table shows the use of the + and – operators for the **chmod** command, to respectively add, and remove designated permissions.

Note that u, g, or o can be used as a privilege with the = operator only. Multiple values can be used for "who" and "privilege," such as ug for the "who" field, and rx for the "privilege" field. Some useful examples of the **chmod** command, and their purposes, are listed in Table 1.5.

Also, the permission bits can be set as octal numbers, according to Table 1.6.

The text explanations of the following commands (that are in Tables 1.3–1.6, as well as typed on the command line below) are provided here to illustrate how access privileges for files can be interrogated and set.

TABLE 1.4

Values for Symbolic Mode Components

Who	Operator	Privilege
u User	+ Add privilege	r Read bit
g Group	− Remove privilege	w Write bit
o Other	= Set privilege	x Execute/search bit
a All		u User's current privileges
ugo All		g Group's current privileges
		o Others' current privileges
		l Locking Set-group-ID privilege bit
		s Sets user or group ID mode bit
		t Sticky bit

The **chmod** command is used to modify or initially set access privileges. The **ls -l** (or the **ls -ld** and **ls -la**) commands are used to show the results of the applied **chmod** command. After the **chmod 700 Bookshelf** command has been executed, the owner of the Bookshelf file has read, write, and execute access privileges for it, and no other user has any privileges. The

TABLE 1.5

Examples of the **chmod** Command and Their Meanings

Command	Meaning
chmod 700 *	Sets access privileges for all files, including directories, in the current directory to read, write, and execute for the owner, and provides no access privilege to anyone else
chmod 740 Bookshelf	Sets access privileges for Bookshelf to read, write, and execute for the owner and read-only for the group, and provides no access for others
chmod 751 ~/Bookshelf	Sets access privileges for ~/Bookshelf to read, write, and execute for the owner, read and execute for the group, and execute-only permission for others
chmod 700 ~	Sets access privileges for the home directory to read, write, and execute (i.e., search) for the owner, and no privileges for anyone else
chmod u=rwx Bookshelf	Sets owner's access privileges for Bookshelf to read, write, and execute and keeps the privileges of group and others at their present values
chmod ugo-rw test or chmod a-rw test	Does not let anyone read or write test
chmod a+x test	Gives everyone execute permission for test
chmod g=u test	Makes test's group privileges match its user (owner) privileges
chmod go= test	Removes all access privileges to test for group and others

TABLE 1.6

Access Permissions for a File and Their Octal Equivalents, and Meanings

r	w	x	Octal Digit	Meaning
0	0	0	0	No permission
0	0	1	1	Execute-only permission
0	1	0	2	Write-only permission
0	1	1	3	Write and execute permissions
1	0	0	4	Read-only permission
1	0	1	5	Read and execute permissions
1	1	0	6	Read and write permissions
1	1	1	7	Read, write, and execute permissions

chmod g+rx Bookshelf command adds read and execute access privileges to the Bookshelf file for the group. The privileges of the owner and others remain exactly the same. The **chmod o+r Bookshelf** command adds read access privilege to the Bookshelf file for others. The **chmod a-w *** command takes away the write access privilege from all users for all the files in the current working directory. The **chmod go+x, o+r *** command enables the execute permission for group and others, and read permission to others to all the files in the current working directory. The **chmod 700 [l-t] *** command sets the access permissions to 700 for all the files that start with letters "l" through "t," as illustrated by the output of the last **ls -l** command, which shows access privileges for the files labs and temp changed to 700.

```
$ ls -l
drwxr-x---   2   bob   bob   512   Apr   23   09:37   Bookshelf
-rwxrwxrwx   1   bob   bob   12    May   01   13:22   labs
-rwxr--r--   1   bob   bob   163   May   05   23:13   temp
$ chmod 700 Bookshelf
$ ls -ld Bookshelf
drwx------   2   bob   bob   512   Apr   23   09:37   Bookshelf
$ chmod g+rx Bookshelf
$ ls -ld Bookshelf
drwxr-x---   2   bob   bob   512   Apr   23   09:37   Bookshelf
$ chmod o+r Bookshelf
$ ls -ld Bookshelf
drwxr-xr--   2   bob   bob   512   Apr   23   09:37   Bookshelf
$ chmod a-w *
$ ls -l
dr-xr-x---   2   bob   bob   512   Apr   23   09:37   Bookshelf
-r-xr-xr-x   1   bob   bob   12    May   01   13:22   labs
-r-xr--r--   1   bob   bob   163   May   05   23:13   temp
```

```
$ chmod go+x, o+r *
$ ls -l
dr-xr-xr--    2      bob    bob    512    Apr    23       09:37  Bookshelf
-r-xr-xr-x    1      bob    bob    12     May    01       13:22  labs
-r-xr—xr--    1      bob    bob    163    May    05       23:13  temp
$ chmod 700 [l-t] *
$ ls -l
dr-xr-x---    2      bob    bob    512    Apr    23       09:37  Bookshelf
-rwx------    1      bob    bob    12     May    01       13:22  labs
-rwx------    1      bob    bob    163    May    05       23:13  temp
$ chmod +x *
$ ls -l
dr-xr-x--x    2      bob    bob    512    Apr    23       09:37  Bookshelf
-rwx--x--x    1      bob    bob    12     May    01       13:22  labs
-rwx--x--x    1      bob    bob    163    May    05       23:13  temp
$
```

The access permissions for the files and directories nested beneath one or more upper-level directories can be set by using the **chmod** command with the **-R** option. In the following commands, the first command sets access permissions for all the files and directories under the directory called Bookshelf to 711, <u>recursively</u>. The second command sets the permissions for all the files and directories under ~/temp/motions to 700, recursively. "Recursively" means by descending downward to all subdirectories under the specified directories, i.e., Bookshelf and ~/temp/motions on these two command lines.

```
$ chmod -R 711 Bookshelf
$ chmod -R 700 ~/temp/motions
$
```

If you set access privileges with a single octal digit in a **chmod** command, it is used by the command to set the access privileges for "others"; the access privileges for "user" and "group" are both set to 0 (i.e., no access privileges). If you specify two octal digits in a **chmod** command, the command uses them to set access privileges for "group" and "others". The access privileges for "user" are set to 0.

In the following two commands, the first **chmod** command sets "others" access privileges for the Bookshelf directory to 7 (rwx) and 0 (---) for owner and group. The second **chmod** command sets "group" and "others" access privileges for the temp directory to 7 (rwx) and 0 (---), respectively, and no access rights for the file owner. The **ls -l** command shows the results of these commands.

```
$ chmod 7 Bookshelf
$ chmod 70 temp
$ ls –l Bookshelf temp
d------rwx   2   bob bob   512   Nov   10   09:43   Bookshelf
d---rwx---   2   bob bob   512   Nov   10   09:43   temp
$
```

1.7.3 Access Privileges for Directories

The read permission on a directory lets you read the contents of the directory (the contents of a directory are the names of ordinary files and directories under it), the write permission allows you to create a file in the directory, or delete an existing file or sub-directory from it, and the execute permission for a directory allows searching the contents of the directory.

****Note****

Read and write permissions on directories are <u>not</u> meaningful without the search permission. You must have both read and execute permissions on a directory to be able to list the names of files under it. You must have both write and execute permissions on a directory to be able to create a file in it.

In the following commands, the write permission for the directory Bookshelf has been turned off. Thus, you cannot create a subdirectory ee345 in this directory by using the **mkdir** command or copy a file foo into it. Similarly, as you do not have search permission for the directory personal, you cannot use the **cd** command to enter (change directory to) this directory. If the directory test had a subdirectory, say foobar, for which the execute permission was turned on, you still could not change directory to foobar, because search permission for test is turned off. Finally, as the read permission for the directory personal is turned off, you cannot display the names of files and directories in it by using the **ls** command, even though the search permission on it is turned on.

```
$ chmod 600 sample
$ chmod 500 Bookshelf
$ chmod 300 personal
$ ls -ld Bookshelf personal sample
dr-x------     2     bob bob     512     Aug  4 06:36     Bookshelf
d-wx------     2     bob bob     62      Aug  4 06:36     personal
drw-------     2     bob bob     88      Aug  4 06:36     sample
$ mkdir Bookshelf/Salinger
mkdir: Bookshelf/Salinger: Permission denied
$ cp foo Bookshelf
cp: Bookshelf/foo: Permission denied
$ cd sample
cd: sample: Permission denied
$ ls -l personal
total 0
ls: personal: Permission denied
$
```

The next set of commands shows that having read or write permission on a directory is <u>not</u> adequate to read its contents (e.g., display them with the **ls** command) or create a file or sub-directory in it. For example, the directory dirtest has the write permission turned on, but you cannot copy the morsel. txt file into it, because the search permission on it is turned off. Similarly, you cannot remove the file steak.txt from dirtest2. After you turn on its search permission with the **chmod u+x dirtest2** command, you can remove the file steak.txt.

```
$ ls -ld dir?
d-w-------     2     bob  bob     2 Aug  4 06:59     dirtest
d-w-------     2     bob  bob     3 Aug  4 06:59     dirtest2
$ cp morsel.txt dirtest
cp: dirtest/morsel.txt: Permission denied
$ rm dirtest2/steak.txt
rm: dirtest2/steak.txt: Permission denied
$ chmod u+x dirtest2
$ ls -ld dirtest2
d-wx------     2     bob  bob     3 Aug  4 06:59     dirtest2
$ rm dirtest2/steak.txt
$
```

1.8 File Systems, Connections to Persistent Media, and Adding Media to Your System

Question: What is a computer file system?

Answer: A way of logically ordering data, so that it is persistent, can be securely and easily located very quickly, and then accessed in a consistent way for use.

Providing data persistence, which is the third primary objective of an operating system, in large part involves establishing and maintaining connections to persistent media, such as the NMVe SSD that may be the system/ boot disk on your hardware. Alternative forms of this media, and the file systems found on them, can be physically connected via the USB3 ports on the Raspberry Pi itself, such as with SATA SSDs inside external enclosures, or USB3 thumb drives. They can also be some form of remote virtual drive, such as network-available, and mounted NFSv4 shares, or remote volumes and complements of drives.

And in some cases, a file system may <u>not</u> make use of a persistent storage device or medium at all!

At this higher level of abstraction, the file system can access, use, organize, and represent <u>any</u> form of data, whether it is persistent or volatile. We use the word volatile here to mean during the transient lifetime of some process or service. Of course, systemd and the Linux kernel control all processes and services running on the Raspberry Pi 5 OS. *Pseudo* and special-purpose file systems (sometimes called *synthetic file systems*), which can be thought of as virtual file systems, have this kind of characteristic.

There are also established protocols for connecting to and accessing either physical, virtual, or pseudo file systems, in the locations where they may reside. Two examples of access protocols that establish and maintain connections to virtual, network-available media and file systems are the Network File System, version 4 (NFSv4), and the Internet Small Computer System Interface (iSCSI).

In this section, we first present an organizing scheme that you can use to think about types of media and file systems. A file system may be nominally assigned according to what medium it exists on: a directly-connected physical medium (such as an NMVe SSD), a virtual medium (such as Network-Attached Storage or Storage Area Networks that use NFSv4 or iSCSI), or as a specialized pseudo-file system that is not on a persistent medium at all (such as the cgroups or proc file systems we discuss below).

We then go on to give some particular examples of adding directly-connected, physical media to the Raspberry Pi 5 OS hardware.

Additionally, we suggest a traditional approach, when using the recommended storage model we give in section 1.3.1, to adding persistent media to your system. This is as follows:

Where you first properly connect the device to the Raspberry Pi 5 via attaching it to a USB3 port, partition that medium, manually add a file system to it (typically the ext4 file system), and then finally create directories and files in the partition(s) on the media. The sections below detail this more traditional approach.

According to our organizing scheme, a file system can be separated into three hierarchically-arranged layers that perform very particular functions. These layers, arranged from farthest-to-nearest to the actual hardware of the physical medium in question, are as follows:

The Logical Layer
This layer is used for interaction with user application programs, and the processes they consist of, via Linux system calls. It provides the application programming interface (API) for file operations, for example, system calls to **OPEN, CLOSE, READ**, etc., and connects with the layer below it for processing. The Logical Layer achieves efficient file access, logically-organized directory operations, and provides user-autonomy and security. In Figure 1.3, this layer is represented by the ISCSI and Process Inputs blocks at the top of the figure.

The Virtual Layer
This layer provides the interface mechanisms for maintaining multiple, simultaneously-existing implementations of physical and virtual file systems on the same computer. For example, it makes it possible to mount and transparently use NFSv4, btrfs, ext3, ext4, fat32, or ZFS at the same time on the same system, and operate with files from all of those implementations as if they were all of the same type.

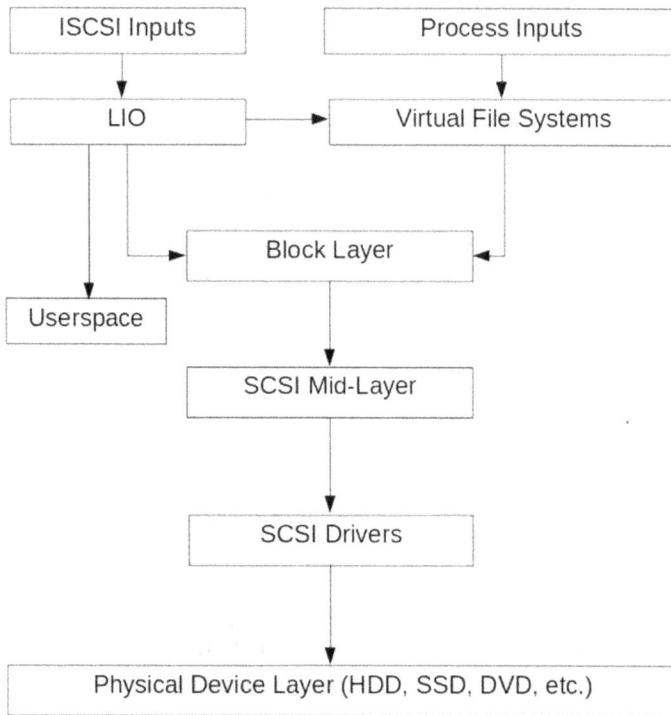

FIGURE 1.3
Raspberry Pi 5 OS file system storage layers.

The Linux IO (LIO) block shown in Figure 1.3 is known as an iSCSI "target", and represents Virtual Layer connectivity to persistent media from various network connections. These connections traditionally use high-speed Fibre Channel technology to create a Storage Area Network (SAN), but most importantly, can also be achieved using Ethernet and TCP/IP.

A more detailed architectural scheme of classifying Virtual Layer file systems further separates that layer into block-based, network, stackable, pseudo, and special-purpose categories. In Figure 1.3, many of the different implementations of file systems, such as NFSv4, ext4, xfs, btrfs, initramfs, and the procfs, would be situated within the Virtual file systems block shown in that diagram. Two very contemporary and extremely important virtual file systems are the cgroups file system (cgroupsfs) used by systemd, and the userland, block-based file system, ZFS.

The Physical Layer
This layer is concerned with the physical operation of the persistent storage device. It processes physical blocks being read or written. It handles buffering and memory management and is responsible for the physical placement

of blocks in specific locations on the storage medium. The physical file system interacts with the device drivers or with the channels that physical devices communicate over. At a certain level of simplification, this layer can be schematically represented in Figure 1.3 by the integrated grouping of Block Layer, SCSI Layers, and the Physical Device Layer.

1.8.1 Types of File System and ext4

Furthermore, and as a very integral part of the operation of the Linux kernel as it exists in a transient and volatile state as we have defined it, the pseudo and special purpose file systems can be viewed as a series of conduits through which the entire system itself "flows". Thinking along these lines, when the kernel is in the CPU and attendant RAM, the kernel code itself is organized as a file system. The kernel (or systemd super-kernel) can be viewed as a file system of transitory data structures, that maintains the steady state of the hardware and software using these conduits exclusively; this achieves the important controlling goals of virtualization, concurrency, user-autonomy, security, and the necessary archival, long-term data persistence on the file systems that are there to serve the user base.

Over the history of Linux, various file systems have been used to provide speed, efficiency, security, and utility to the ordinary user. The most contemporary and universal of these, across the three major branches of Linux, is the Linux Extended File System (ext). All of the representative downstream releases of Linux use it as the default file system.

The 4th version of ext, ext4, is the current and most robust version so far. It has several features, such as large scalability, the ability to map to very large disk array sizes, and other very critical features, such as "journaling". Following is a compact listing of some of the features of ext4:

1. It can support volumes with sizes up to 1 exabyte, and files with sizes up to 16 terabytes.
2. It uses an "extents" mapping scheme, which replaces block mapping used by earlier versions of ext. An extent is a range of contiguous physical blocks.
3. It is backward-compatible with ext3 and ext2. Therefore, ext3 and ext2 file systems can be mounted as ext4.
4. It delays block allocation until data is flushed to disk.
5. It has an unlimited number of sub-directories that can be created.
6. It has a multi-block allocator that can make better choices about allocating files contiguously on disk.
7. It provides timestamps, measured in nanoseconds.

****Note****

From the perspective of our Raspberry Pi 5 OS recommended data storage model, adding a second medium, for example, allows you to keep the operating system and the user data on two different physical persistent media. That way, if the operating system fails and the system disk is corrupted and unusable, the data survives on the user data disk and can very easily be recovered!

There are many traditional, legacy methods of achieving the objective of this data storage model, using facilities such as:

1. disk and file maintenance commands.

2. utilities such as mdadm (a software RAID manager), and Linux Volume Management (LVM).

3. But from our perspective, the modern and contemporary way of implementing the recommended data storage model is using the Zettabyte File System (ZFS) on redundant additional persistent media. With ZFS, you get bit-level data integrity, volume management, RAID capabilities at all levels, and a failure-proof backup strategy, all rolled into one utility. See section 1.9 for a brief introduction to ZFS.

1.8.2 Persistent Media and Devices

There are some very important reasons for adding persistent media to your system, aside from conforming to our recommended storage model. Your boot, or system disk, may be running out of space or beginning to show signs of failure. In a traditional legacy scheme, these situations might involve downtime of the system in order to correct the problem. Whereas, with our storage model implementation, and some of the facilities shown in the sections below, that situation can be handled by without bringing the system down.

1.8.2.1 Partitioning Schemes and Strategies

By now, it should be evident to you that the Raspberry Pi 5 OS organizes everything in files and uses a file system to organize those files. A disk partition can be most simply defined as a logical area of the disk that holds a file system.

Once you verify that your Raspberry Pi 5 system can actually recognize and mount the additional media, there are several reasons to adopt a particular partitioning scheme for the newly added media. Creating multiple partitions on a disk avoids full disk problems by segregating directories into those partitions, and gives the system administrator control over access to those directories and partitions. And you can maintain different file system structures simultaneously in different partitions.

When you are adding new media, you have the option of using the traditional method of doing disk partitioning with command line utilities such as **fdisk** or **gdisk**, or the option of using a GUI-based method, with a utility such as the Gnome Partition Editor (GParted). We show the basics of using GParted in section 1.8.4, and you can use it to implement our recommended data storage model with a traditional ext4 file system scheme. We present a GParted example in section 1.8.4 detailing how to do this using the traditional ext4 scheme.

To help the administrator of a Linux system with the task of adding persistent media, the following sections will also address these general concerns:

- The availability of software device drivers for the new hardware to be added.

- How the hardware will be recognized, configured and deployed on the system.

- Identification of possible paths to replacement and upgrading of existing hardware, within the context of using our recommended data storage model.

As discussed in Item 3) of section 1.3.1, our data storage model for a Raspberry Pi 5 OS, used for our deployed models, is capable of mounting and using two or more externally-mounted media, and that implementation is made possible by what we show in the following sub-sections.

The additions in the traditional ext4-based example shown in section 1.8.5 will be done for USB3 thumb drives but can also be easily extended to other persistent media, such as USB3-mounted external SSD(s), or for NVMe SSD devices, for example.

1.8.2.2 External Media Additions

Generally, when you add additional media some significant time after you have installed the operating system on the Raspberry Pi 5 hardware, you will want to partition it. You might even want to create a new partition table on it, create one or more partitions, and format those partitions using a standard file system, such as ext4. We emphasize and encourage the use of the GParted GUI-based application to do this.

When you add an external USB2 or 3 medium, such as a thumb drive, or other form of persistent storage device, it is generally already formatted to the file system type known as FAT32 (in the case of most popular commercially available USB thumb drives), or to some other format depending on the media. Traditionally, you can then partition the disk using the **fdisk** command and add a file system to it with the **mkfs** command. We emphasize and encourage the use of **fdisk**, or its newer sister, **gdisk**, to do the partitioning if you choose this traditional operation.

Note that safe removal of USB media can be done manually, via a graphical means, on the Raspberry Pi 5. For example, on the desktop, left-click on the icon in the upper-right of the menu bar (the icon that looks like an upward-facing arrow with a bar underneath it), choose the available medium, and left-click again on the medium to eject, or unmount it. Unmounting a USB thumb drive, or other USB-bus media, can also be done from the command line with the **umount** command.

When a USB thumb drive, or other external medium, is automatically mounted, the path to it is **/media/your_home_dir/id**, where **your_home_dir** is the name of your home directory on the system, and **id** is the disk id number or identifier of the medium.

For example, when we added a USB thumb drive, and created a single primary partition on it with GParted, along with an ext4 file system automatically added to that partition at the same time, the newly-mounted hard drive was accessed via the path:

/media/bob/04fd2202-8879-46f2-8040-446753ed077c

1.8.3 Preliminary Considerations When Adding New Media

****Note****

If you insert a USB thumb drive, or any other USB-mountable media, that you know is functioning properly into your Raspberry Pi 5, and it is <u>not</u> recognized, the chances are that the operating system does <u>not</u> have a device driver available to enable communication between the Raspberry Pi 5 hardware and the thumb drive. In that case, it might be very prudent to find an alternative medium.

How do you know if a new disk drive is recognized, and most importantly, is usable on your system?

There are at least three quick and easy ways to know if the new disk drive is recognized.

1. If it is a USB thumb drive, and it has previously been formatted to FAT32, the Raspberry Pi 5 OS will auto-mount it, and an icon for it will open on the desktop (along with a prompt asking you if you want to view its contents).

2. In a terminal window, you can use the command **systemctl –f** and watch the screen display as you insert the device. It will show that a new device has been added (of course, given that the system has drivers for it!), even though in the case of a USB thumb drive, it might be formatted to something other than FAT32!

3. Use the before-and-after technique shown in section 1.8.4.

The same is true when you connect another type of USB-mountable external medium properly, but the probability of it <u>not</u> being recognized can be lower. The best and easiest thing to do in a case when the medium is not recognized is to use another device. The Raspberry Pi 5 OS has facilities to find and install device drivers on your system for a device, but this process is time consuming, and may not be fruitful for the particular device in question, particularly for the beginner. Also, it is possible to write a driver for your device, which is even more time consuming, and even less fruitful for the beginner. The important thing here is that perhaps the USB thumb drive, for example, is <u>not</u> formatted to FAT32, but that a manufacturer hasn't supplied the device drivers, or made them available to Linux kernel developers.

In many instances, it is important to know the physical device name, the instance name, and the logical device name of disk drives on your system, but practically speaking, for the Raspberry Pi 5 OS administrator, easily finding out the logical device name of a disk drive is most important.

You may want to add media to your Raspberry Pi 5 system that has been used on another computer operating system previously. In that case, the primary and secondary examples we show can be deployed to re-partition and prepare that hard disk for new use with the Raspberry Pi 5 OS.

1.8.4 Five Quick and Easy Ways to Find Out the Logical Device Names of Media

Before attaching a new medium to your Raspberry Pi system, it is important to know how to determine, in a very quick and easy manner, what the currently installed logical device names of the media actually attached and usable on your system are. What we mean by "attached and usable" is that the medium is properly connected and recognized by the system, and has a device driver that the system can use to communicate with it.

Before and after: If you want to find out the logical device name of a newly-installed medium, use one of the following methods to see what media are on your system <u>before</u> you add the new one, and then use the same method <u>after</u> the new one has been added, and note the difference. The different or new logical name that appears will be the logical device name of the new medium.

The five simple methods that follow show how to determine what media are attached and usable on your system, and what the logical device names of those and any others you might want to add to your system are.

<u>Method 1</u>
Change your current working directory to /dev. Type **ls**. A microSD card, for example, will show up in the **ls** listing as mmcblk*. The full path to the first slice, or partition, on one of these disks is specified as mmcblk0p1. A USB bus device, like a thumb drive, would show up in the **ls** listing as sdb, or

whatever letter designation the system has assigned to it, and the full path to the first slice on it would be sdb1. A USB3-mounted SSD will show up as sda, and the first slice on it would be sda1. These are exactly what designations appeared in /dev on our Raspberry Pi 5.

Method 2
Type **df -hT** on the command line to find out the file system names and paths they are mounted at on your system. On our Raspberry Pi 5 system, when we did this to see if a 256 Gb USB3 thumb drive was recently successfully attached to the system, this is the output-

```
$ df -hT
Filesystem       Type       Size    Used    Avail    Use% Mounted on
udev             devtmpfs   2.0G    0       2.0G     0%   /dev
tmpfs            tmpfs      405M    6.4M    399M     2%   /run
/dev/mmcblk0p2   ext4       28G     6.8G    20G      26%  /
tmpfs            tmpfs      2.0G    0       2.0G     0%   /dev/shm
tmpfs            tmpfs      5.0M    48K     5.0M     1%   /run/lock
/dev/mmcblk0p1   vfat       510M    67M     444M     14%  /boot/firmware
tmpfs            tmpfs      405M    208K    405M     1%   /run/user/1000
/dev/sda1        exfat      954G    8.1G    946G     1%   /media/bob/X31
/dev/sdb1        ext4       227G    5.7G    209G     3%   /media/bob/5874a622-...
$
```

Notice that our root, or system disk (shown as / under the "Mounted on" column), is 28 GB in size. That's because we're running this Raspberry Pi 5 from a 32 GB microSD card with that capacity (6.8GB used). A 1 TB USB3-mounted SSD shows in the **df** listing as /dev/sda1, and a newly-mounted USB3 thumb drive shows as /dev/sdb1. We address more details of the **df** command in section 1.14.3.

Method 3
Very similar to using the **df** command, use the **lsblk -a** command. When we used this command and option on our Raspberry Pi system, after we had attached the 32 Gb USB thumb drive, we got the following output-

```
$ lsblk -a
NAME     MAJ:MIN   RM    SIZE    RO    TYPE MOUNTPOINTS
ram0     1:0       0     4M      0     disk
ram1     1:1       0     4M      0     disk
Output truncated...
ram15    1:15      0     4M      0     disk
loop0    7:0       0     0B      0     loop
loop1    7:1       0     0B      0     loop
Output Truncated...
```

loop7	7:7	0	0B	0	loop	
sda	8:0	0	953.9G	0	disk	
└─sda1	8:1	0	953.9G	0	part	/media/bob/X31
sdb	8:16	1	230.9G	0	disk	
└─sdb1	8:17	1	230.9G	0	part	/media/bob/5874a622...
mmcblk0	179:0	0	28.9G	0	disk	
├─mmcblk0p1 179:1		0	512M	0	part	/boot/firmware
└─mmcblk0p2 179:2		0	28.4G	0	part	/
$						

Method 4
Use the **findmnt** command.

Notice that some of the file system types (FSTYPE) are shown as types such as ext4, sysfs, tmpfs, nfsd, proc, etc.

Method 5
You can also very efficiently use the GUI-based Gnu Partition Editor(GParted), as shown. With GParted, you can easily find out the logical device names of disks on your system. In addition, with GParted you can use graphical editing methods to affect several important characteristics of the media, such as the format and partitioning of the drives.

In-Chapter Exercise

11. a.   Insert a USB thumb drive into your Raspberry Pi, and mount it if necessary. What command would you use to mount it? Use the **findmnt** command to find out its logical device name. What is the logical device name for this thumb drive? Along what path is it mounted on your system? What are the uses and meanings of the other file system types shown, as output to the **findmnt** command? For example, are cgroup, proc, fuse.gvf, and tempfs logical, virtual, or physical file systems, and how exactly do these differ from ext4?

11. b.   What does an MNVe SSD show up as in the **lsblk -a** display on your Raspberry Pi 5? In the **df -hT** display?

1.8.5 Adding New Media to the System

Example 1.7 shows how to add new media to your system and partition it. We chose to use the GUI-based GParted partition editor, primarily because it's easy to use, and can be quickly installed on the Raspberry Pi 5 OS. We also chose it, instead of the **gdisk** utility, or the legacy **fdisk** command, because it has a GUI front-end, and that GUI is easy to use. For example, with it, you don't have to remember command names, options, or arguments to accomplish what you want. This GUI software not only lets you easily find out what the logical device names of media attached to your Raspberry Pi are but also allows you to partition newly added media and put a file system onto them at the same time.

Example 1.7 Adding a New Medium, and Using GParted to "Slice", or Partition It

Objectives: To practice using the GParted Partition Editor to place a disk partition, with an ext4 file system on that partition, onto a USB thumb drive mounted on your Raspberry Pi.

Pre-Requisites: Having a usable USB thumb drive for your system.

****Note****

Your media attached to your Raspberry Pi 5 will probably have different designations than the ones we show in the GParted displays and figures of this example. Depending, of course, on what your boot/system disk is, and what you're attaching to your Raspberry Pi 5.

Requirements: Do the steps below in the sequence presented to complete the requirements of this example.

1. Install the GParted Partition Editor software, if it is not already installed on your system. This is most efficiently done using the GUI-based Raspberry Pi menu Preferences > Add/Remove Software. Also, it would be very efficient to place an icon for this software on your desktop.
2. Properly connect the new media to the system via either the USB2 or USB3 connectors on your Raspberry Pi 5 hardware. USB3 is a faster protocol, and will give you better performance when working with or on the new media.
3. Launch the GParted Partition Editor, either graphically or from the command line with the command **gparted**. Enter your password in the window that appears.
4. The GParted screen opens on screen, as shown in Figure 1.4.
5. The current media attached to the system appear in the pull-down menu bar at the upper right. Make note of all the complete paths to the current disks. For example, the boot or root disk might be designated as /dev/mmcblk0 if you're running your system from a microSD card, /dev/sda as our system is if you're running your system from a USB3-attached and mounted SSD, or /dev/nvme0n1 if you are running your Raspberry Pi 5 from an NVMe SSD. This is seen in Figure 1.4.
6. Click the down-facing arrow shown in the menu bar in the upper right corner of the GParted screen. Scroll in that bar until you reach the medium you just added to the system.

****Note****

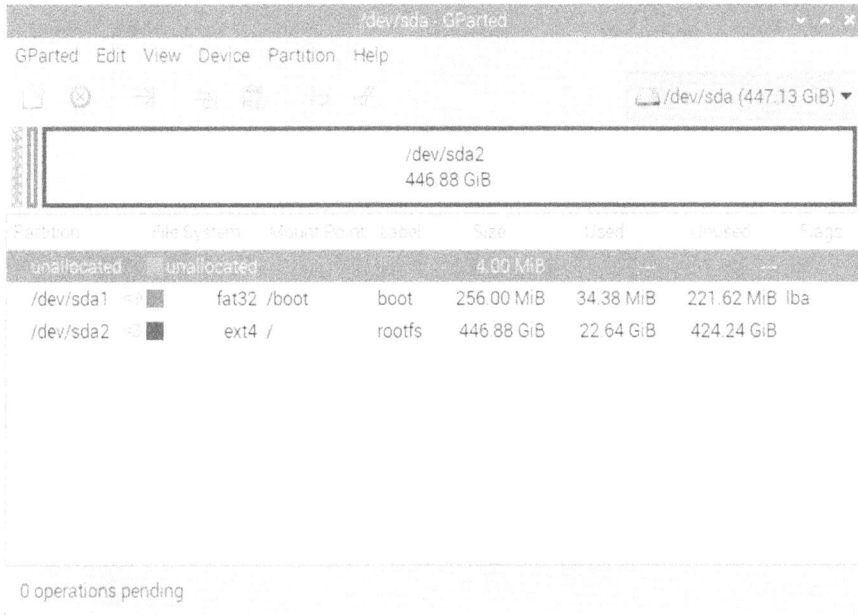

FIGURE 1.4
GParted main window.

If the disk drive you just added <u>doesn't</u> appear in the GParted listing, as a beginner you can't easily use that disk drive.

If it <u>does</u> appear, continue to the next step. On our Raspberry Pi system, the new medium appeared as /dev/sdb.

7. Pick that new medium in the menu bar. It is shown in the main GParted pane. Click on that disk in the main GParted pane. You can now partition and format that new disk. In our example, it is shown as /dev/sdb, a new disk we inserted at step 2. This is shown in Figure 1.5. Notice in that figure that the disk contains a single partition, /dev/sdb1 that has a fat32 file system on it, and no label.

8. From the pull-down menus at the top of the GParted window, make the menu choice Partition > Unmount. Then click on the red X in the icon bar. This will delete the partition information on that disk. It is now a pending operation.

9. In order to execute the pending operation, make the pull-down menu choice Edit > Apply All Operations. In the warning window, click Apply. A window appears showing you the progress, and hopefully successful application, of the pending operation. Click close in that window when the operation is complete.

10. The new disk should now be shown as unallocated. Click on its listing in the main GParted pane. Make the pull-down menu choice Device > Create Partition Table. The new partition table type shows msdos. That's good and useful for us. Click Apply in the warning window. Everything on that disk will be erased!

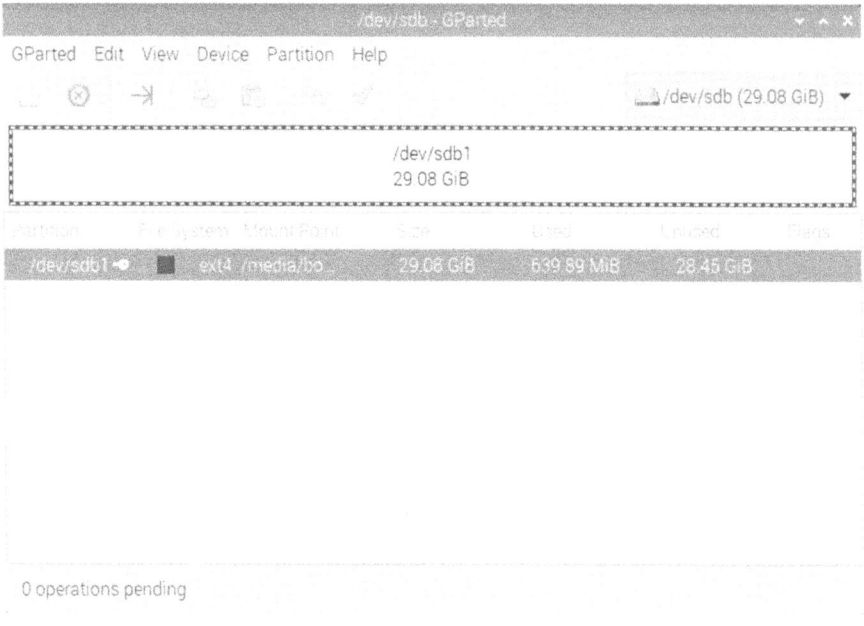

FIGURE 1.5
/dev/sdb Partition 1.

When GParted has created a new partition table, click on that disk again in the main GParted pane. The Partition and File System appear as unallocated.

11. Make the pull-down menu choice Partition > New. The Create New Partition window appears on screen, as shown in Figure 1.6. The defaults for the new partition, as seen in

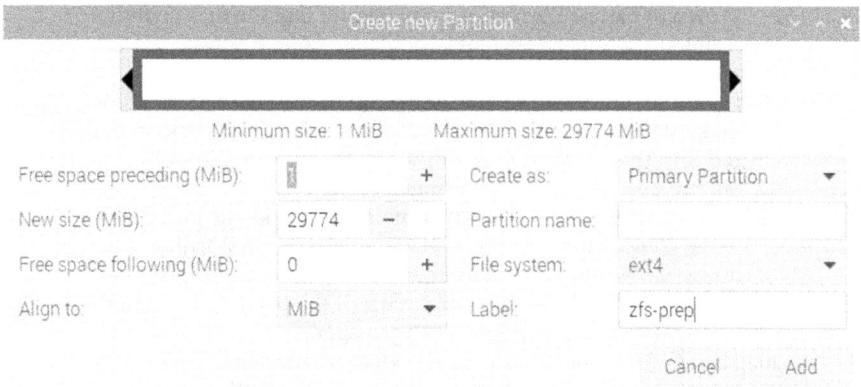

FIGURE 1.6
Create new partition window.

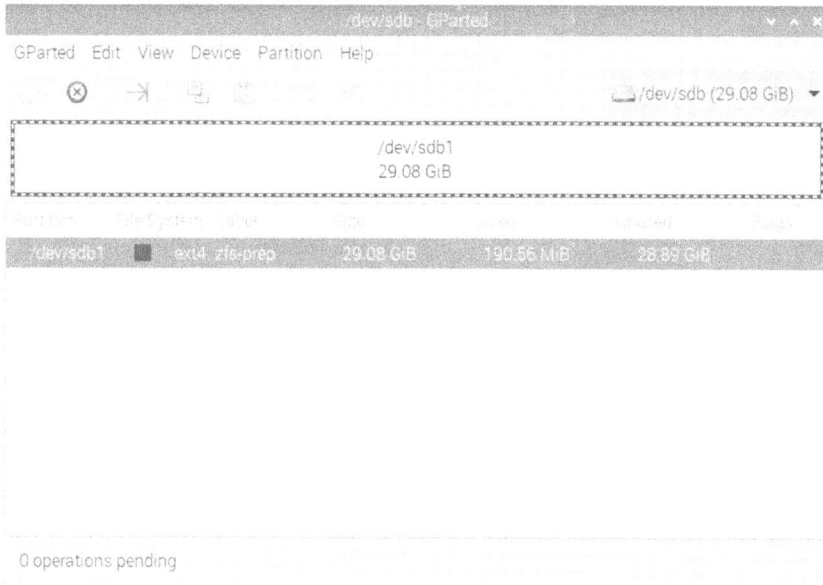

FIGURE 1.7
/dev/sdb1, Partition 1 modified.

Figure 1.6, are to take the whole disk up with this partition, create it as a primary partition, and create the file system on it as ext4.

12. Add any label designation of your choice in the Label field, so that you can more readily identify this medium. We have chosen to label this partition as **zfs-prep**, as seen in Figure 1.6. Leave all of the other defaults in place. Click the Add button. Make the pull-down menu choice Edit > Apply All Operations (It appears as a green check mark in the menu bar at the top of the GParted window). In the warning window, click Apply. Click the Close button when the Applying pending operations message appears, showing the operation has completed successfully.

13. You now have created a partition table on, partitioned, and formatted a usable medium on the system. Congratulations! On our system, it is shown in Figure 1.7 as /dev/sdb1 29.08 GB.

14. Quit GParted, by making the pull-down menu choice GParted>Quit.

Conclusion: We have added a new hard disk to our Raspberry Pi 5 OS hardware, and partitioned it with GParted.

1.8.6 Adding Disks Using fdisk

A more traditional approach to adding media to the system a significant time after installation is covered in this section. We conform to our recommended storage model, as in the previous section where we implemented it for an additional hard disk added using GParted. In this section, we use the **fdisk** command to partition another disk. The example in this section uses an externally-mounted USB thumb drive, which is more easily added because there is a higher likelihood that drivers for it are in the kernel, is cheaper, and is much more available to the ordinary user as an additional storage medium.

This Example can be easily extended to externally-mounted USB3 SATA SSDs, or other forms of media like NVMe SSDs. In section 1.9, we give examples of ZFS-based redundancy to illustrate a similar backup strategy with ZFS.

1.8.6.1 Partitioning a Disk Using fdisk

fdisk is a command line, interactive, dialog-driven program used to create and manage partition tables on Linux. The following is a brief description of **fdisk** syntax and use:

****

fdisk – Create and manages partition tables

Syntax: fdisk [options] device
         fdisk -l [device...]

Output: New or manipulated partitions on the media **device**.

Common Interactive Commands:
n   Create a new partition. You enter a partition number, starting sector, and an ending sector. Both start and end sectors can be specified in absolute terms as sector numbers. Pressing the Enter key with no input specifies the default value, which is the start of the largest available block for the start sector and the end of the same block for the end sector.
p   Display basic partition summary data. This includes partition numbers, starting and ending sector numbers, partition sizes, fdisk's partition types codes, and partition names.
t   Change a single partition's type code. You enter the type code using a two-byte hexadecimal number.
w   Write data. Use this command to save your changes.

Example:
$ sudo fdisk /dev/sdb   As superuser, run fdisk on the disk /dev/sdb

****

> **Example 1.8 Placing a Single Partition on a USB thumb
> Drive Using fdisk**
>
> Objectives: To use the **fdisk** utility to practice placing a disk partition, with an ext4 file system on that partition, on a USB thumb drive mounted on your Raspberry Pi 5.

Pre-Requisites: Having a usable USB thumb drive for your system.

Requirements: Do the steps below in the sequence presented to complete the requirements of this example.

1. Having previously determined that the thumb drive is rec-ognized on your system, and what its logical device name is (ours was /dev/sdb), insert it into a USB port. We used an 8 GB Kingston thumb drive; it's <u>very</u> reliable, and always auto-mounts on Raspberry Pi 5 systems.

   On our Raspberry Pi 5, the thumb drive was auto-mounted. Use the following commands to unmount it:

   $ sudo umount /dev/sdb1

2. Use the **fdisk** command to partition the newly-added USB thumb drive, making sure to first delete any partitions that are on it. For our Kingston USB thumb drive, there was only one default partition on it: a fat32 partition, with a msdos partition table.

   $ sudo fdisk /dev/sdb

   Welcome to fdisk (util-linux 2.38.1).
   Changes will remain in memory only, until you decide to write them.
   Be careful before using the write command.
   The device contains "vfat" signature, and it will be removed by a write command. See fdisk(8) man page and – wipe option for more details.
   Device does not contain a recognized partition table.
   Created a new DOS disklabel with disk identifier 0xa4dcc322.

   ```
   Command (m for help): n
   Partition type
     p   primary (0 primary, 0 extended, 4 free)
     e   extended (container for logical partitions)
   Select (default p): p

   Partition number (1-4, default 1): <Enter>
   First sector (2048-60975103, default 2048): <Enter>
   Last sector, +/-sectors or +/-size{K,M,G,T,P}  (2048-60975103, default
   60975103): <Enter>

   Created a new partition 1 of type 'Linux' and of size 29.1 GiB.

   Command (m for help):

   Command (m for help): p
   Disk /dev/sdb1: 29.08 GiB, 31219253248 bytes, 60975104 sectors
   Units: sectors of 1 * 512 = 512 bytes
   Sector size (logical/physical): 512 bytes / 512 bytes
   ```

```
I/O size (minimum/optimal): 512 bytes / 512 bytes
Disklabel type: dos
Disk identifier: 0xa4dcc322

Device     Boot Start    End Sectors Size Id Type
/dev/sdb1p1     2048 60975103 60973056 29.1G 83 Linux

Command (m for help): l

***A long list of types and codes is displayed; we want type 83- Linux!***

Command (m for help): t
Selected partition 1
Hex code or alias (type L to list all): 83
Changed type of partition 'Linux ' to 'Linux'.

Command (m for help): p
Disk /dev/sdb1: 29.08 GiB, 31219253248 bytes, 60975104 sectors
Units: sectors of 1 * 512 = 512 bytes
Sector size (logical/physical): 512 bytes / 512 bytes
I/O size (minimum/optimal): 512 bytes / 512 bytes
Disklabel type: dos
Disk identifier: 0xa4dcc322

Device     Boot Start    End Sectors Size Id Type
/dev/sdb1p1     2048 60975103 60973056 29.1G 83 Linux

Command (m for help): w
The partition table has been altered.
Calling ioctl() to re-read partition table.
Syncing disks.
$
```

3. In order for this partition to be usable, you must add a file system to it. We would like to add an ext4 file system to the partition. To do this, use the **mkfs** command as follows:

```
$ sudo mkfs -t ext4 /dev/sdb1
mke2fs 1.46.2 (28-Feb-2025)
Found a dos partition table in /dev/sdb1
Proceed anyway? (y,N) y
Creating file system with 7621888 4k blocks and 1908736 inodes
file system UUID: 8946ddbc-b94a-4dc4-9966-66f0a8411b4e
Superblock backups stored on blocks:
        32768, 98304, 163840, 229376, 294912, 819200, 884736, 1605632, 2654208,
        4096000

Allocating group tables: done
Writing inode tables: done
Creating journal (32768 blocks): done
Writing superblocks and file system accounting information: done
$
```

Now, in order to use this partition for data, you can create directories and files in those directories.

Conclusion: Using the **fdisk** utility, and the **mkfs** command, we deleted any existing partitions on a USB thumb drive, and created a Linux partition on it with an ext4 file system.

In-Chapter Exercises

12. Why do you have to remount */dev*/sdb1 in Example 1.8 in order to add directories and files to the disk, and how do you achieve remounting? What is the designation of this thumb drive on your system, and where is it mounted?

13. Do the steps of Example 1.8 to partition a USB thumb drive with a single primary partition, and then add an ext4 file system to it. Create directories on the thumb drive.

14. a. Do the steps of Example 1.8 to partition an externally-mounted SSD in a USB3 enclosure, placing a single primary partition on it, and then add an ext4 file system to it. Create directories on the hard drive.

14. b. Do the steps of Example 1.8 to partition an externally-mounted NVMe SSD, placing a single primary partition on it, and then add an ext4 file system to it. Create directories on the NVMe SSD.

1.9 Installing ZFS, zpool, and zfs Command Syntax

The Zettabyte File System(ZFS) is an advanced journaling file system and volume manager developed at Sun Microsystems, and has many useful functions and facilities for maintaining redundancy and security on server-class computers. But it's also useful for an individual user at home, who wants to ensure the same objectives, but on a smaller scale system, such as one using Raspberry Pi hardware. The following are the instructions for installing ZFS, and the general syntax forms for the **zpool** and **zfs** commands, the two premier ZFS tools. For a more complete description of these two important commands, see the man pages for zfs and zpool (after you have installed ZFS according to the instructions given in section 1.9.1).

****Note****

The history of ZFS installation on the Raspberry Pi is fraught with errors and difficulties, mainly because the Linux kernel, for some inexplicable reason (probably due to legal issues), doesn't play well with ZFS. In some releases of Debian Linux and the Raspberry Pi OS based upon it, ZFS was easy to install, as we show for Debian Bookworm below, and the Raspberry Pi 5 OS that's the downstream release of it. Who knows what the Raspberry Pi 5 OS based upon Debian Trixie will bring to this vital and progressive file system installation on the Raspberry Pi 5 ?

1.9.1 Installing ZFS on the Raspberry Pi 5 OS

Installing ZFS on the Raspberry Pi 5 OS at the time this book was written was a simple, straightforward operation. Use the following commands:

$ sudo apt update
Output truncated...

$ sudo apt install raspberrypi-kernel-headers
Output truncated...

$ sudo apt install zfs-dkms zfsutils-linux
Output truncated...

After a few minutes, the software is installed.

If ZFS is loaded successfully, you can verify that as follows:

$ dmesg | grep ZFS
[4.665181] ZFS: Loaded module v2.2.3-1~bpo12+1~rpt1, ZFS pool version 5000, ZFS filesystem version 5

 You can also use the following commands to verify that ZFS has been installed correctly-

$ zfs - -version
zfs-2.2.3-1~bpo12+1~rpt1
zfs-kmod-2.2.3-1~bpo12+1~rpt1
$ zpool list
no pools available
$

1.9.2 The Syntax of the zpool and zfs Commands

The following are the abbreviated syntax of the **zpool** and **zfs** commands, taken from the man pages on our Raspberry Pi 5 system after we installed ZFS in section 1.9.1:

```
*********************************************************************
zpool
Syntax:
zpool subcommand [options] [option arguments] [command arguments]
Purpose: To create and manage storage pools of virtual devices, such as disk drives
Commonly used options/features:
zpool create name vdev       Creates a new pool with name on the specified vdev
zpool create –o copies=2 name Creates a new pool name with the property copies set to 2
zpool destroy name           Destroys, or removes, a pool name
zpool list name              Lists storage space and health of pool name
zpool scrub name             Verifies that the checksums on pool name are correct
zpool status name            Displays the status of pool name
*********************************************************************
```

```
**************************************************************************
zfs
Syntax:
zfs subcommand [options] [option arguments] [command arguments]
Purpose: To create and manage datasets or file systems mapped to devices such as disk
drives
Commonly used options/features:
zfs create name              Creates a dataset with name
zfs create –o copies=2 name  Creates a dataset name with the property copies set to 2
zfs destroy name             Destroys, or removes, a dataset name
zfs list                     Lists all datasets
zfs rollback name            Returns dataset name to a previous snapshot state
**************************************************************************
```

1.9.3 ZFS Terminology

The following describes the basic terminology used throughout this section, and as it applies to ZFS practice in general as well:

> *Boot environment*: A boot environment is a bootable environment consisting of a ZFS root file system and, optionally, other file systems mounted underneath it. Exactly one boot environment can be active at a time.

****Warning****

This warning applies at the time of the writing of this book, and it is important to realize that if you want to create and use ZFS on any system,   you must have an additional storage device, or devices, attached to your hardware. This could be additional externally-mounted USB3 or NVMe SSDs, or even USB2 or USB3 thumb drives.

We have found that if you attempt to create zpools on your system or boot disk on a Raspberry Pi 5 OS, this will render that disk <u>unbootable</u>!

> *Checksum*: A 256-bit hash of the data in a file system block. The checksum capability can range from the simple and fast fletcher4 (the default) to cryptographically strong hashes such as SHA256.

> *Clone*: A file system whose initial contents are identical to the contents of a ZFS snapshot.

> *Dataset*: A generic name for the following ZFS components: clones, file systems, snapshots, and volumes. Each dataset is identified by a unique name in the ZFS name space. Datasets are identified using the following format:

> **pool/path[@snapshot]**

where:

pool   Identifies the name of the storage pool that contains the dataset

path   A slash-delimited pathname for the dataset component

snapshot An optional component that identifies a snapshot of a dataset

Deduplication: Data deduplication is a method of reducing storage capacity needs by eliminating redundant data. Only one unique instance of the data is actually retained on storage media. Redundant data is replaced with a pointer to the unique data copy.

file system: A ZFS dataset of type file system that is mounted within the standard system namespace and behaves like other file systems.

Mirror: A vdev that stores identical copies of data on two or more disks, in a variety of ways defined by Redundant Array of Independent Disks (RAID) specifications. If any disk in a mirror fails, any other disk in that mirror can provide the same data, according to those RAID specifications.

Pool: A logical group of devices describing the layout and physical characteristics of the available storage. Disk space for datasets is allocated from a pool.

RAIDZ: A virtual device that stores data and parity on multiple disks, using the RAID specifications.

Resilvering: The process of copying data from one device to another device is known as resilvering. For example, if a mirror device is replaced or taken offline, the data from an up-to-date mirror device is copied to the newly restored mirror device. This process is referred to as mirror resynchronization in traditional volume management.

Slice: A disk partition created with partitioning software.

Snapshot: A read-only copy of a file system or volume at a given point in time.

virtual device (vdev): A whole disk, a disk partition, a file, or a collection of the previous, usually all of the same type. There is no performance penalty for using disk partitions rather than entire disks. The write cache is disabled for partitions, thus incurring a performance penalty. Using files as vdevs is discouraged, except for experimenting and testing purposes as we do in this chapter for beginners! A collection of vdevs is a mirror.

Volume: A dataset that represents a block device. For example, you can create a ZFS volume as a swap device.

1.9.4 How ZFS Works

The following simplified statement summarizes the operation of ZFS:

Create zpool mapped to vdev > Create ZFS file system(s) on zpool > Add files

So, simply stated, you create a named zpool first, which at the time it is created is mapped or associated with a vdev, such as an external, USB3 medium. Then you create one or more file systems in that zpool; you add files to those file systems. Finally, you manage the files, file systems, pools, and vdevs using the appropriate ZFS commands.

Working with ZFS is a matter of efficiently and easily managing zpools that have vdevs "mapped" to them, and then managing file systems and their files in those zpools.

Figure 1.8 shows these relationships between files, datasets (file systems), pools, and disks. **Pool 1** has two disks mapped to it, and a dataset with a number of files in it. **Pool 2** has a single disk mapped to it and has a dataset in it. This layering of files and datasets, pools, and disks is the basic structure of ZFS.

1.9.5 Important ZFS Concepts

Some very important points have to be made here:

1. Only one zpool can be mapped or associated with any vdev. So, if you want to create a zpool on a physical hard disk or one of its slices, no other existing active zpool can be mapped to that vdev!

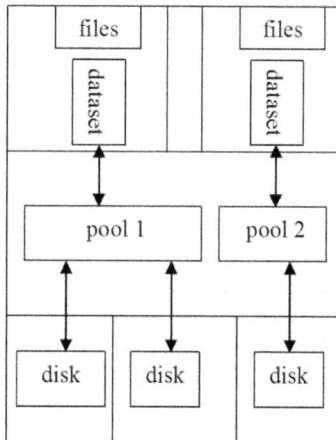

FIGURE 1.8
ZFS components.

2. There are six types of vdev in ZFS:

   a. Disk (default): The physical hard drives in your system, usually the whole drive or primary slice.

   b. File: The absolute path of preallocated files/images.

   c. Raidz1/2/3: Nonstandard distributed parity-based software RAID levels.

   d. Spare: Hard drives marked as a *hot spare* for ZFS software RAID.

   e. Cache: Device used for a level-2 adaptive read cache (L2ARC).

   f. Log: A separate log (SLOG) called the ZFS intent log (ZIL).

3. Unlike a traditional file system, where the mount point of the file system begins at a particular logical drive letter, the default mount point for a zpool is root (/). This is how the path to a file named **test. txt** appears when it is in the zpool named **data1** on the file system **named bobs**:

   /data1/bobs/test.txt

   Here's how the path to a file named **test.txt** appears on a traditional file system:

   C:\Users\bob\Desktop\test.txt

   When you want a ZFS file system to expand onto more than one disk, for example, you add more disks to the zpool.

4. A zpool can be enlarged by adding more devices, but it cannot be shrunk (at least not at this time)!

1.9.6 Basic ZFS Examples

In this section, we present an instructive, introductory example of how to work with ZFS. It is expected that for you to get the full benefit from it, you do it and the attendant In-Chapter Exercises in the order presented.

> **Example 1.9 The zpool Command: Using Files Instead of Disks as Vdevs**
>
> Objective: To introduce the **zpool** command, implemented on files instead of disks, and to show forms of ZFS pool creation and mirroring.
>
> Introduction: A vdev, as defined previously, can be a physical device such as a disk drive, a file, a single slice on a hard disk drive, or a collection of devices. Before beginning to use ZFS on physical devices and to practice using ZFS on an existing file system instead of deploying ZFS

on actual physical media, we will create and manipulate files with the important ZFS commands.

    Also, if you do not have attached USB3 media, you can follow this example to gain an appreciation of what ZFS is.

In case you want to use real disks mounted and partitioned in this preliminary introductory example, make a note of the full path to their device names (e.g., /dev/sdb1). You will be destroying all the partition information and data on these disks, so be sure they're not needed!

Note

If you make a mistake anywhere along the way, you can always start over by executing the cleanup steps shown at the end of the Example and begin again.

Prerequisites: Installation of ZFS on Raspberry Pi 5 system, and running on your Raspberry Pi 5 hardware, as shown in section 1.9.1.

Procedures: Follow the steps in the order shown to complete this example.

1. Become root, and then create four 128 MB files as follows (the files must be a minimum of 64 MB in size):

```
$ sudo -i

root@bob-desktop:~#
root@bob-desktop:~# truncate --size 128m /home/bob/disk1
root@bob-desktop:~# truncate --size 128m /home/bob/disk2
root@bob-desktop:~# truncate --size 128m /home/bob/disk3
root@bob-desktop:~# truncate --size 128m /home/bob/disk4
```

    Check the /home/bob directory with the following command:

```
root@bob-desktop:~# ls -lh /home/bob
total 48K
...
-rw-r--r-- 1 root root 128M May 22 18:47 disk1
-rw-r--r-- 1 root root 128M May 22 18:47 disk2
-rw-r--r-- 1 root root 128M May 22 18:47 disk3
-rw-r--r-- 1 root root 128M May 22 18:48 disk4
Output truncated...
```

    In this example, we initially create and use files to simulate disks on an already existing file system, and we named them **disk1**, **disk2**, **disk3**, and **disk4** to enhance that illusion. Also, it is assumed in the example code that the current working directory is **/home/bob** unless otherwise noted.

2. Before creating new pools, you should check for existing pools, if there are any, to avoid confusing them with the example pools we create here. You can check what pools exist with the **zpool list** command:

    root@bob-desktop:~# **zpool list**
    no pools available
    root@bob-desktop:~#

3. Pools are created using **zpool create**. We can create a single disk pool using a file as follows (you must use the absolute path to the file), and check the zpools that now exist:

    ```
    root@bob-desktop:~# zpool create data /home/bob/disk1
    root@bob-desktop:~# zpool list
    NAME  SIZE ALLOC  FREE CKPOINT EXPANDSZ FRAG  CAP DEDUP  HEALTH ALTROOT
    data  112M 106K   112M    -        -    2%  0% 1.00x    ONLINE -
    ```

4. Now we will create an actual file in the new pool, check its size, and get a zpool listing of it:

    ```
    root@bob-desktop:~# truncate --size 32m /data/data20file
    root@bob-desktop:~# ls -lh /data/data20file
    -rw-r--r-- 1 root root 32M May 22 18:54 /data/data20file
    root@bob-desktop:~# zpool list
    NAME  SIZE ALLOC  FREE CKPOINT EXPANDSZ FRAG  CAP DEDUP  HEALTH ALTROOT
    data  112M 110K  112M     -        -    2%  0% 1.00x    ONLINE  -
    ```

5. We will now destroy the pool data with zpool destroy, and check on zpools now available:

    root@bob-desktop:~# **zpool destroy data**
    root@bob-desktop:~# **zpool list**

    No pools available

6. Creating a Mirrored Pool with Files
    <u>A pool composed of a single disk doesn't offer any redundancy!</u> One way of providing protection against physical disk failure is to use a mirrored pair of disks in a pool:

    ```
    root@bob-desktop:~# zpool create data2 mirror /home/bob/disk1 /home/bob/disk2
    root@bob-desktop:~# zpool list
    NAME   SIZE ALLOC  FREE CKPOINT EXPANDSZ FRAG  CAP DEDUP  HEALTH ALTROOT
    data2  112M 105K  112M     -        -    2%  0% 1.00x    ONLINE  -
    ```

7. To get more information about the pool **data2**, we use **zpool status**:

    root@bob-desktop:~# **zpool status data2**

```
  pool: data2
 state: ONLINE
config:

        NAME              STATE    READ WRITE CKSUM
        data2             ONLINE     0    0     0
          mirror-0        ONLINE     0    0     0
            /home/bob/disk1 ONLINE   0    0     0
            /home/bob/disk2 ONLINE   0    0     0
```

errors: No known data errors

8. Create a file in the **data2** pool.

root@bob-desktop:~# truncate --size 32m /data2/data2file

Note the change in the pool after we have added a file to it, using the following command:

root@bob-desktop:~# zpool list
```
NAME   SIZE ALLOC  FREE CKPOINT EXPANDSZ FRAG  CAP DEDUP  HEALTH ALTROOT
data2  112M  154K  112M    -        -     4%   0% 1.00x   ONLINE -
```

A fraction of the disk has been used, but more importantly, the data is now stored redundantly over two disks.

9. Let's test that redundancy by overwriting the first "disk" label with random data. If you are using real media, like a thumb drive, you could physically remove it from the computer to achieve this next operation.

root@bob-desktop:~# dd if=/dev/random of=/home/bob/disk1 bs=512 count=1
```
1+0 records in
1+0 records out
512 bytes copied, 0.00143395 s, 357 kB/s
```

10. ZFS automatically checks for errors when it reads/writes files, but we can force a check with the **zfs scrub** command.

root@bob-desktop:~# zpool scrub data2

11. Let's check the status of the pool:

root@bob-desktop:~# zpool status
```
  pool: data2
 state: DEGRADED
status: One or more devices could not be used because the label is missing or
        invalid.  Sufficient replicas exist for the pool to continue
        functioning in a degraded state.
```

action: Replace the device using 'zpool replace'.
  see: https://openzfs.github.io/openzfs-docs/msg/ZFS-8000-4J
  scan: scrub repaired 0B in 00:00:01 with 0 errors on Fri May 23 05:56:49 2025
config:

NAME	STATE	READ	WRITE	CKSUM	
data2	DEGRADED	0	0	0	
mirror-0	DEGRADED	0	0	0	
/home/bob/disk1	UNAVAIL	0	0	0	corrupted data
/home/bob/disk2	ONLINE	0	0	0	

errors: No known data errors

12. The disk we used the **dd** command on is showing as UNAVAIL (unavailable) with corrupted data, but no data errors are reported for the pool as a whole, and we can still read and write to the pool as follows:

root@bob-desktop:~# truncate --size 32m /data2/data2file2
root@bob-desktop:~# ls -l /data2/
total 1
-rw-r--r-- 1 root root 33554432 May 23 05:52 data2file
-rw-r--r-- 1 root root 33554432 May 23 06:01 data2file2

13. To maintain redundancy, we should replace the broken disk with another. If you are using real media, you can use the **zpool replace** command (the zpool man page provides details of this command). However, in this file-based example, we simply remove the disk file from the mirror and recreate it.

    Devices can be detached with the **zpool detach** command, as follows:

root@bob-desktop:~# zpool detach data2 /home/bob/disk1

14. Let's check the status of the pool:

root@bob-desktop:~# zpool status data2
  pool: data2
 state: ONLINE
  scan: scrub repaired 0B in 00:00:01 with 0 errors on Fri May 23 05:56:49 2025
config:

NAME	STATE	READ	WRITE	CKSUM
data2	ONLINE	0	0	0
/home/bob/disk2	ONLINE	0	0	0

errors: No known data errors

15. Let's remove the disk and then try to replace it to simulate a failure:

```
root@bob-desktop:~# rm /home/bob/disk1
root@bob-desktop:~# truncate --size 128m /home/bob/disk1
```

16. In order to replace it in the mirror, we need to do the following. To attach another device, we specify an existing device in the mirror to attach it to with **zpool attach**:

```
root@bob-desktop:~# zpool attach data2 /home/bob/disk2 /home/bob/disk1
```

17. Check the status of the pool:

```
root@bob-desktop:~# zpool status data2
  pool: data2
 state: ONLINE
  scan: resilvered 206K in 00:00:00 with 0 errors on Fri May 23 06:23:02 2025
config:
```

NAME	STATE	READ	WRITE	CKSUM
data2	ONLINE	0	0	0
mirror-0	ONLINE	0	0	0
/home/bob/disk2	ONLINE	0	0	0
/home/bob/disk1	ONLINE	0	0	0

```
errors: No known data errors
```

18. Adding to a Mirrored Pool

A very critical system administration procedure accomplished by ZFS is to add media to a pool <u>without taking it offline</u>. Let's double the size of our **data2** pool:

```
root@bob-desktop:~# zpool list
NAME   SIZE ALLOC  FREE CKPOINT EXPANDSZ FRAG  CAP DEDUP  HEALTH ALTROOT
data2  112M  126K  112M       -        -   5%   0%  1.00x  ONLINE -
```

19. We can use the **zpool add** command to add disks to the existing pool.

```
root@bob-desktop:~# zpool add data2 mirror /home/bob/disk3 /home/bob/disk4
root@bob-desktop:~# zpool list
NAME   SIZE ALLOC  FREE CKPOINT EXPANDSZ FRAG  CAP DEDUP  HEALTH ALTROOT
data2  224M  184K  224M       -        -   2%   0%  1.00x  ONLINE -
```

20. The file systems within the pool are always available. If we look at the status now, it shows the pool consists of two mirrors:

```
root@bob-desktop:~# zpool status data2
  pool: data2
 state: ONLINE
```

scan: resilvered 206K in 00:00:00 with 0 errors on Fri May 23 06:23:02 2025
config:

NAME	STATE	READ	WRITE	CKSUM
data2	ONLINE	0	0	0
mirror-0	ONLINE	0	0	0
/home/bob/disk2	ONLINE	0	0	0
/home/bob/disk1	ONLINE	0	0	0
mirror-1	ONLINE	0	0	0
/home/bob/disk3	ONLINE	0	0	0
/home/bob/disk4	ONLINE	0	0	0

errors: No known data errors

21. We can see where the data is currently written in our pool using the **zpool iostat -v** command:

root@bob-desktop:~# zpool iostat -v data2

pool	capacity alloc	free	operations read	write	bandwidth read	write
data2	141K	224M	0	0	23	360
mirror-0	127K	112M	0	2	1.54K	16.8K
/home/bob/disk2	-	-	0	0	21	151
/home/bob/disk1	-	-	0	1	41	6.27K
mirror-1	14K	112M	0	0	152	14.9K
/home/bob/disk3	-	-	0	0	76	7.47K
/home/bob/disk4	-	-	0	0	76	7.47K

22. All the data is currently written on the first mirror pair and none on the second. This is logical, since the second pair of disks was added after the data was written. If we write some new data to the pool, the new mirror will be used:

root@bob-desktop:~# truncate --size 64m /data2/data2file3

root@bob-desktop:~# zpool iostat -v data2

pool	capacity alloc	free	operations read	write	bandwidth read	write
data2	142K	224M	0	0	23	363
mirror-0	119K	112M	0	2	1.28K	14.1K
/home/bob/disk2	-	-	0	0	21	152
/home/bob/disk1	-	-	0	0	34	5.29K
mirror-1	23K	112M	0	0	111	11.1K
/home/bob/disk3	-	-	0	0	55	5.53K
/home/bob/disk4	-	-	0	0	55	5.53K

23. We see how a little more of the data has been written to the new mirror than to the old: ZFS tries to make the best use of all the resources in the pool. Now do these In-Chapter Exercises, and then continue onto the final "cleanup" steps.

In-Chapter Exercises

15. If you have not already done so, execute all of the steps of Example 1.9 using proper commands and pathnames.

16. In Example 1.9, step 4, what is the pathname to **datafile20**?

17. If you were to use a text editor like emacs to create a text file named **text1.txt** in the file system named **data**, how would you designate the complete pathname to that text file?

18. In Example 1.9, after step 6 was executed correctly, and you created a text file with emacs in the **data2** file system, would the pathnames to the two mirrored versions of that text file be different? In other words, could you edit each one of them separately by designating different pathnames to them?

19. In Example 1.9, step 19, could you add a single disk into the mirrored **data2** zpool, instead of the two disks specified?

20. In Example 1.9, step 20, are the mirrors named **mirror-0** and **mirror-1** mirrors of each other?

21. To clean up after doing our work, let's delete everything we created in this example.
    From the root directory, destroy the **data2** file system and its files.

    root@bob-desktop:~# zfs destroy -r data2

22. Next, destroy the **data2** zpool.

    root@bob-desktop:~# zpool destroy data2

23. Finally, destroy the disk simulation files, and leave root.

    root@bob-desktop:~# rm /home/bob/disk*
    root@bob-desktop:~# **exit**
    logout
    $

Conclusion: We can use the **zpool** command and its **create** sub-command to associate or map file systems to vdevs, whether the vdev is a file itself or a disk drive.

Example 1.10 Creating a ZFS Pool on a USB thumb drive

Objectives: To create a zpool, and a ZFS dataset in that pool, on a USB thumb drive mounted and running on your Raspberry Pi 5 hardware.

Introduction:

Question: Where would this example be most useful?

Answer: In preparation for implementing our recommended storage model on a ZFS zpool, and because you want to learn the basics of ZFS.

The following example uses the two most essential commands in ZFS, the **zpool** and **zfs** commands, with the sub-command **create** applied to a USB thumb drive, installed on a Raspberry Pi 5. The real power of ZFS can be harnessed to common, readily available hardware vdevs that are available on that system, by an ordinary user.

Note

If the only thing you want to do is use a USB thumb drive to transfer files (such as text files, C program source code, LibreOffice documents, and so on) to and from your Raspberry Pi 5, you do not have to use the procedures of this example to accomplish that!

If you make a mistake anywhere along the way, you can always start over by executing the cleanup step shown at the end of the example, and then simply begin again.

Prerequisites:

0. You have installed ZFS, as shown in **section 1.9.1**, and are using that system on Raspberry Pi 5 hardware.

1. That you have an expendable USB thumb drive that is usable on that system, and already has only one partition, and no data you want to keep on it. More specifically, if the USB thumb drive is by default formatted to FAT32 (which most commercially-available thumb drives are), then there is a high probability that it will automatically mount and show up as an icon on your desktop in the Raspberry Pi 5 OS.

2. That there is no zpool named **test3** already defined on the primary partition of the USB thumb drive, and there is no zpool named **test3** on your Raspberry Pi 5 system. To find this out, in a terminal window type **zpool list** on the command line, after the USB thumb drive has been inserted and auto-mounts.

3. That you can determine the logical device name and the full path to the thumb drive using any one of the methods in section 1.8.4. The full path to our USB thumb drive is /dev/sdb, and the path to the first

partition on it is /dev/sdb1. This may <u>not</u> be the same designations as the USB thumb drive on your system, but you can substitute your logical device designations for them.

4. That you have done disk partitioning with GParted or the **fdisk** command.

Procedure: All commands are shown in **bold** type, and are typed at the command line, followed by pressing the <Enter> key on the keyboard.

1. Plug the thumb drive into a USB port on your Raspberry Pi 5. If it's a fat32-formatted USB thumb drive, it should automatically mount and appear as an icon on your system desktop. Determine the logical device name of the USB thumb drive, as shown in section 1.8.4.

2. If it is mounted, unmount the thumb drive using the **umount** command:

$ sudo umount /dev/sda1
$

At this point, the desktop icon for the USB thumb drive will disappears on your system, if the thumb drive automounted! Also, it no longer shows in the display of mounted drives at the upper right corner, under the upward facing arrow and dash.

It must still show up in an **ls** listing of /dev to be usable. If the thumb drive is not recognized in /dev after the above step has been done, you need to use another thumb drive!

3. You can now create a zpool named **test3** on the primary partition on the thumb drive you worked on in step 2. To create a zpool on the thumb drive, use the following command:

$ sudo zpool create -f test3 /dev/sda1
$

We included the **-f** option on **zpool create** to force creation of a ZFS file system on partition 1 of the thumb drive, effectively eradicating whatever file system was on it.

4. Check that the zpool has been created:

```
$ zpool list
NAME  SIZE ALLOC  FREE CKPOINT EXPANDSZ FRAG  CAP DEDUP  HEALTH ALTROOT
test3 119G  106K  119G    -        -      0%   0% 1.00x   ONLINE -
$
```

5. You can now create a file system named **newfile system** on the zpool **test3**, using the following command:

```
$ sudo zfs create test3/newfile system
$
```

6. Obtain a listing of the datasets on your computer, using the following command. Several datasets may be listed. Notice in the listing that the mount point of each dataset is given in the last column. This is the path that you designate leading to the datasets' directory. If you put files in that directory, they are part of that file system.

```
$ sudo zfs list
NAME            USED  AVAIL  REFER  MOUNTPOINT
test3           147K  115G   24K    /test3
test3/newfile   24K   115G   24K    /test3/newfile
$
```

To put files in the ZFS dataset *newfile system*, put them in the directory */test3/newfile system*

7. If you want to continue using this thumb drive as an additional ZFS drive on your system, stop here. Be aware that if you remove the thumb drive without taking it offline according to ZFS protocols, unexpected results will occur. If you want to use the thumb drive for other purposes, continue.

The following three steps allow you to undo everything you have done in this example (except, of course, the deletion of any data that was on the thumb drive before you began this example!).

8. To begin, first destroy the file system.

```
$ sudo zfs destroy test3/newfile system
```

9. Then destroy the zpool.

```
$ sudo zpool destroy test3
```

10. Pull the thumb drive out of the USB port. To reuse the thumb drive for non-ZFS, purely data storage purposes, you will need to use GParted, or other facilities such as fdisk, to delete the partition on it, and put a new partition table and partition on it. This effectively destroys the ZFS partition we created in this example.

Conclusion: You have created and destroyed a zpool and a ZFS dataset on a USB thumb drive that you attached to your Raspberry Pi 5 system. If you did not destroy the zpool and dataset on it, you can now create additional datasets on it and place files in those datasets.

All of the ZFS commands in section 1.9 can be used to manage zpools and zfs datasets on this drive. You can also use this drive as a backup for user data files and use all of the ZFS functionality to do backups.

1.10 Configuring a Printer

There are fundamental and modern methods for adding and configuring a local printer on a Raspberry Pi 5 system, and printing documents on it, using the Common UNIX Printing System (CUPS). You can configure and manage a printer for use on your Raspberry Pi 5 system, using three basic methods. These methods are generally applicable to printers that are connected directly to your computer, and this most likely is via a USB connection.

The three basic methods are:

1. A web-based browser CUPS interface,
2. Using the Raspberry Pi 5 OS Menu choice Preferences > Print Settings, and
3. Using the Raspberry Pi 5 OS command line in a terminal.

The configured printer in all three methods is controlled and managed with the Common UNIX Printing System (CUPS).

In method 1, a web-based browser front end to CUPS allows you to manage printers, print jobs, and other configuration settings using intranet connectivity or over the Internet.

In method 2, the built-in graphical front end to CUPS, accessed via the Raspberry Pi Menu > Preferences > Print Settings, which comes with Raspberry Pi 5 OS, achieves much of the same functionality as method 1.

In method 3, there is a completely text-based interface for controlling and managing printers from the Raspberry Pi 5 OS command line.

1.10.1 What the Common UNIX Printing System (CUPS) Accomplishes

Using CUPS is a standard way of printing in both Linux and UNIX. Since it was developed to provide as many printer definitions as possible, it will more than likely enable you to directly connect your model of printer or connect to a print server on your LAN.

It is basically composed of two parts – a scheduler, and a filtering system. The scheduler arranges jobs in print queues and sends them to the filtering system, which translates the print data into device driver information for the particular printer you want your documents to print on.

1.10.2 Managing CUPS Locally with systemd

Using systemd, via the **systemctl** command, allows you to start, stop, reload, or restart the CUPS service. This is a higher level of management for your local printers via a system service.

1.10.2.1 Starting CUPS Service Using systemd

In the Raspberry Pi 5 OS, when you attach a new printer via a USB cable to the hardware, it will generally be automatically recognized and attached via CUPS. If the CUPS service has not already been started, it will be automatically started and run in the process of connecting the new printer. But to start the CUPS service without having any printers attached or powered on, do the following:

To start the CUPS service and check its status, use the following commands in a terminal:

```
$ sudo systemctl start cups
$ sudo systemctl status cups
● cups.service - CUPS Scheduler
    Loaded: loaded (/lib/systemd/system/cups.service; enabled; preset: enabled)
    Active: active (running) since Fri 2025-03-14 07:07:22 PDT; 2h 46min ago
TriggeredBy: ● cups.socket
            ● cups.path
      Docs: man:cupsd(8)
  Main PID: 824 (cupsd)
    Status: "Scheduler is running..."
     Tasks: 2 (limit: 4758)
       CPU: 7.129s
    CGroup: /system.slice/cups.service
            ├─ 824 /usr/sbin/cupsd -l
            └─2211 /usr/lib/cups/notifier/dbus dbus://
```

Mar 14 07:09:27 raspberrypi hpcups[2214]: prnt/hpcups/HPCupsFilter.cpp 813: First raster data plane..
Mar 14 07:09:33 raspberrypi hpcups[2214]: prnt/hpcups/HPCupsFilter.cpp 813: First raster data plane..
Output truncated...

We see from the output that CUPS is running. Press Q to return to the terminal command line.

1.10.2.3 Stopping CUPS Service with systemd

The CUPS service can be stopped using the **systemctl stop cups.service** command, as follows:

```
$ sudo systemctl stop cups.service
```

When you check the status of the CUPS service after stopping the CUPS service, its status is inactive (dead), but still enabled.

Note

"Enabled" is systemd jargon that means it will persistently start every time the system is rebooted.

1.10.2.4 Restarting, Enabling, or Disabling the CUPS Service with systemd

Restarting a service means that a service is stopped and then started again. If the service is not currently running, restarting it simply starts the service. Use the following command to restart the CUPS service:

$ sudo systemctl restart cups.service

You can also perform a conditional restart of a service using systemctl. A conditional restart only restarts a service if it is currently running. Any service in an inactive state is not started.

$ sudo systemctl condrestart cups.service

In the above command example, the CUPS service was in an inactive state before the command was executed. When the conditional restart is accomplished, no error messages appear. The CUPS "daemon" was not started because conditional restarts only affect active services.

It is always a good practice to check the status of a service, after stopping, starting, or conditionally restarting it.

1.10.2.5 Configuring CUPS as a Persistent Service Using systemd

You can use **systemctl** commands to enable or disable the CUPS services on your Raspberry Pi 5 OS system server, whether that is local or remote.

Using the **enable** option on the **systemctl** command sets a service to always start at boot (be persistent). The following shows exactly how to accomplish this:

$ sudo systemctl enable cups.service

1.10.2.6 Disabling a Service with systemd

You can use the disable option of the **systemctl** command to keep a service from starting at boot. However, it does not immediately stop the service. You need to use the **stop** command shown above to stop the service. The following command example shows how to disable a currently enabled service.

$ sudo systemctl disable cups.service

1.11 File System Backup and Recovery

The general necessity of backing up user and system files on a single-user Raspberry Pi 5 system, as a part of an ordinary user's routine operations, should be obvious, even to the beginner. Also, for complex, multi-machine, multi-user systems, it's an absolutely necessary procedure for anyone responsible for the administration of those classes of systems.

According to Linux system administration professionals, there is an easy-to-remember and important set of considerations you must make when backing up the system, as the system administrator. This set of considerations can be posed in simple question form as:

How, What, Why, When, Where, and Who?

Some of the answers to these simple questions can be dovetailed together, and we provide a selected list of example answers as follows :

"How" means, most importantly, using specific commands, utilities, applications, or combinations of hardware and software to accomplish the backup and archival process. These facilities are described in the sub-sections below. It also means incrementally, in a rolling fashion, or across the entire file system structure totally, using various strategies.

"What" means just some of the user files and user account files, all of them, only certain kinds of documents, the whole storage medium or media, multiple media, system files, either all or a selected subset of the system files, etc.

"Why" means deciding on the relative importance of "What" you are backing up.

"When" means hourly, once a day, once a week, once a month, every time you save a particular file, and at what time exactly, like 3 A.M.

"Where" means on a local medium, like automatically to an externally-mounted USB3 SSD or an NMVe SSD, to Dropbox/Google/Amazon cloud storage, to a USB thumb drive manually, to another computer or NAS on your home network via NFSv4, automatically by cron, to another kind of attached medium manually, totally, incrementally, to RAID of various levels using ZFS, or any variant and combination of the previous.

"Who" means by the only user on the system, by the initiator or executor, such as by cron automatically, by the designated system administrator, either manually or semi-automatically, or by an automated process running at Dropbox, Google, or Amazon, for example.

1.11.1 A Strategic Synopsis and Overview of File Backup Facilities

There are several strategies that a single user, or system administrator, can use in confidently and efficiently backing up the file components of a Raspberry Pi 5 system. Table 1.7 presents a basic overview of those strategies and the facilities that implement them on the Raspberry Pi 5 OS. In the sections that follow the table, we briefly give details of these facilities. The man pages on your system give more complete descriptions, along with command options, arguments, and option arguments for all of the Raspberry Pi 5 OS commands listed in Table 1.7.

1.11.2 Linux Gnu tar

A Linux operating system, such as the Raspberry Pi 5 OS, has several utilities that allow you to archive your files and directories in a single file, and the **tar** command is the most popular, widely used, and traditional method that allows you to do this.

Note

Contemporary **tar** on Linux <u>is</u> the Gnu version.

The **tar** (short for *tape archive*) utility was originally designed to save file systems on tape as a backup, so that files could be recovered in the event of a system crash. It is primarily used now to pack a directory hierarchy as an ordinary disk file. That disk file can then be either saved for system backup

TABLE 1.7

Raspberry Pi 5 OS File Backup Facilities

Backup Facility	Description
tar	Command and options to pack a file or a directory hierarchy as an ordinary disk file for backup, archiving, or moving to another location or system. **gtar** is the GNU version.
cpio	Less popular than tar, but with much of the same functionality.
rsync	A disk space-efficient command to copy files and directories.
dd	A simple and abbreviated backup utility.
zfs snapshot	Built-in commands and options in ZFS offer a variety of backup modes.
SD Card Copier	The built-in backup facility of the Raspberry Pi 5 OS
git and GitHub	Online facility, and command repertoire, to archive code, etc.
Script files	Administrator or user-written shell scripts or other programming language backup systems that can use all of the above commands in them.
3rd party software	Many products, both local and online. One very useful example that is most significant for ordinary users is Filezilla.

purposes locally or remotely, or transmitted to someone via the Internet. It is also used commonly with a compression utility, such as **gzip**, via a command line option. Doing so saves disk space and transmission time. The saving in disk space results primarily from the fact that empty space within a cluster is not wasted. A brief description of the **tar** utility follows.

The GNU version of **tar** has some important functional features and incorporates a more friendly syntax, than traditional UNIX **tar**. Therefore, for beginners we only show the "long form" of the Gnu-style syntax because it's more intuitive, and easy to understand. Once you get more familiar with **tar**, you may switch to the UNIX-style short form at your discretion.

System administrators normally use a cost-effective archival medium for archiving complete file system structures as backups, so that when a system crashes for some reason, files can be recovered. Linux-based computer systems normally crash for reasons beyond the operating system's control, such as a hardware failure or failure of the processor itself. The Raspberry Pi 5 OS rarely causes a system to crash, because it's a well-designed, coded, and tested operating system. In a typical commercial installation, backup is done every day during off hours (late night or early morning) when the system is not normally in use, with appreciable demand placed on it.

The general syntax of the **tar** command, shown with Gnu-style syntax as opposed to traditional UNIX-style syntax, is as follows:

```
************************************************************************
```
tar

Syntax: tar [operation mode] [operation mode options] [FILE...]

Purpose: Archive (copy in a particular format) files to or, restore files from, an archival medium (which can be an ordinary file). Directories are by default archived and restored recursively.

Output: Archived or restored files or directory structures.

Main Operations and Operation Options in Gnu-Style Usage:
--append   Append files to the end of an archive.
--concatenate   Append an archive to the end of another archive.
--compare   Find differences between archive and file system.
--create   Create a new tape and record archive files on it
--delete   Delete from the archive.
--extract   Extract files from an archive.
--help   Display a short option summary.
--list   List the contents of an archive.
--show-defaults Show built-in defaults for options.
--test-label   Test the archive volume label and then exit.
--update   Append files which are newer than the versions in an archive.
--usage   Display a list of available options.
--version   Display program version and copyright information.

Common Options:

--preserve-permissions	Extract information about traditional file permissions.
--acls	Enable POSIX.1e ACL support.
--gzip	Filter the archive through gzip.
--verbose	Verbosely list files processed.
--file ARCHIVE.tar	Send archive to file named ARCHIVE.tar.

Command Arguments:

FILE...	Target, either an archive file, or file object to be archived.

****

1.11.2.1 Archiving and Restoring Files Using tar

A normal Raspberry Pi 5 OS user can achieve their own work if they want to. They would normally need to do this with file objects related to a project, so that they can transfer them to someone or somewhere via e-mail, ssh, or via mobile secondary storage media (USB thumb drive, for example). Or perhaps they would want to retain their own file system objects as backups via the same methods. In fact, the backups I do to external media are augmented by daily or semi-daily backups I do to another Raspberry Pi system using FileZilla account.

The primary reason for making an archive is the convenience of dealing with (sending or receiving) a single file instead of a complete directory hierarchy. Without an archive, the sender might have to send several files and directories (a file structure) that the receiver would have to restore in their correct hierarchical structure. Without an archiving facility such as **tar**, depending on the size of the files and directory structure, the task of sending, receiving, and reconstructing the file structure can be very time consuming.

There are other file compression facilities, such as **bzip2**, **gzip**, **gunzip**, **gzexe**, **xz**, **zcat**, and **zmore** commands, and we must point out that compression saves disk space and transmission time. But compressing small files normally does not result in much compression, and storage space. Also, compressing files of one cluster in size (the minimum unit of disk storage, i.e., one or more sectors) or less does not help save storage media space, even if compression does result in smaller files, because the system ends up using one cluster to save the compressed file anyway. But if compression does result in a smaller file, you do save time in transmitting the compressed version. If the disk block size is 512 bytes and a cluster consists of more than two blocks, you can use the **tar** command to pack files together in one file, with a 512-byte tar header at the beginning of each file, as shown in Figure 1.9.

1.11.2.2 Eight Easy tars

In this section, I show eight of the simplest uses of the **tar** command.

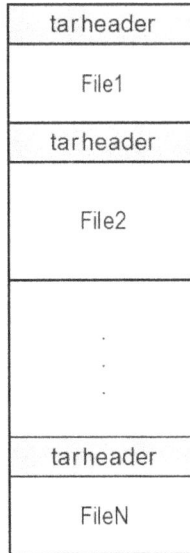

FIGURE 1.9
Tar-Packed file.

1. Creating an archive
   This is the simplest command to create an archive file from a directory.

   $ **tar --create --verbose --file archive_name.tar directory_name**

   where:

   --create is the operation to create a new archive

   --verbose is the operation to list the files being processed

   --file is the operation that specifies that the file **archive_name.tar** is the name of the archive file, and

   directory_name is the directory you want to archive.

2. Creating an archive and preserving its ACL permissions
   A simple variation on creating an archive is using an option to preserve ACLs that the directory has. ACLs are detailed fully in Volume 1, both the POSIX.1e and NFSv4 varieties.

   $ **tar --acls --create --verbose --file archive_name.tar directory_name**

   where:

   --acls is the option to preserve the ACLs that the directory has

   --create is the operation to create a new archive

--**verbose** is the operation to list the files being processed

--**file** is the operation that specifies that the file **archive_name.tar** is the name of the archive file, and

directory_name is the directory you want to archive.

3. Extracting an archive
   This is the simplest command to extract a directory from an archive file.

   `$ tar --extract --verbose --file archive_name.tar`

   where:

   --**extract** is the operation to extract a **directory_name** from an archive file

   --**verbose** is the operation to list the files being processed

   --**file** is the operation that specifies that the file **archive_name.tar** is the name of the archive file.

   In this simplest form, the directory which will be created from the archived file will have the same name as the archive file, minus the .tar extension.

4. Extracting an archive and restoring its ACL entries
   A simple variation on extracting an archive is using an option to restore the preserved ACLs that the archive file has (if any).

   `$ tar --acls --extract --verbose --file  archive_name.tar`

   where:

   --**acls** is the option to restore the preserved the ACLs that the archived file has

   --**extract** is the operation to extract the archived file

   --**verbose** is the operation to list the files being processed

   --**file** is the operation that specifies that the file **archive_name.tar** is the name of the archive file

   In this simplest form variation, the directory which will be created from the archived file will have the same name as the archive file, minus the. tar extension.

5. Listing the contents of an archive
   This procedure allows you to view the contents of an archive file without extracting anything from it

   `$ tar --list --verbose --file archive_name.tar`

where:

--list is the operation that lists the contents of the archive file

--verbose is the operation to list the files being processed

--file is the operation that specifies that the file **archive_name.tar** is the name of the archive file

6. Extracting a single file from an archive file
The following command extracts only a specific file from an archive file.

$ tar --extract --verbose --file archive_file.tar file_pathname

where:

--extract is the operation to extract the single file

--verbose is the operation to list the files being processed

--file is the operation that specifies that the file **archive_name.tar** is the name of the archive file you are extracting from, and

file_pathname is the complete pathname specification to the file you want to extract inside the archive.

7. Extracting a single directory from an archive file
A variation on extracting just a single file from an archive, to extract a single directory, along with recursively extracting any of it's sub-directories and files, specify the directory name that you want to extract as follows:

$ tar --extract --verbose --filef archive_file.tar directory_pathname

where:

--extract is the operation to extract the single file

--verbose is the operation to list the files being processed

--file is the operation that specifies that the file **archive_name.tar** is the name of the archive file you are extracting from, and

directory_pathname is the complete pathname specification to the directory you want to extract inside the archive.

8. Adding a file or directory to an existing archive using – append option
To add files to an existing archive, do the following:

$ tar –append –verbose --file archive_name.tar file_or_directory_name

where:

--append is the operation to add the single file or directory to the archive

--verbose is the operation to list the files or directories being processed

--file is the operation that specifies that the file **archive_name.tar** is the name of the archive file you are adding files or directories to, and

--file_or_directory_name is the complete pathname specification to the file or directory you want to add inside the archive.

In-Chapter Exercise

21.

a. Referring to the abbreviated man page shown above, or to the man page for **tar** on your Raspberry Pi 5 system, give a command that would create a gzipped archive of a directory named ziptest.

b. Give a command that would extract the gzipped archive into another directory named ziptest2.

1.12 rsync

The **rsync** command is a very modern and space-efficient way to backup files and directories, particularly from one machine to another, using **ssh** across a network. Its operation can also be automated via the use of systemd scheduling.

Its most important and defining feature is the data transfer "quick check" algorithm it uses, which reduces the amount of data transmitted. This is done by sending only the differences between the source files and the same existing destination files (if any). If files need to be transferred, because there is a difference between source and destination, they are copied, or "synced", using this algorithm. The algorithm looks for files that have changed in size or modification time. Changes in the other possible preserved file object attributes (such as permissions, or ACLs) are made on the destination file directly when the quick check indicates that the destination file needs to be updated in that way.

An abbreviated summary of the **rsync** man page is as follows:

```
****************************************************************
rsync
Syntax:
Local:  rsync [OPTION...] SRC... [DEST]
Remote:
        via remote shell:
        Pull mode: rsync [OPTION...] [USER@]HOST:SRC... [DEST]
        Push mode: rsync [OPTION...] SRC... [USER@]HOST:DEST
```

via rsync daemon:
Pull mode: rsync [OPTION...] [USER@]HOST::SRC... [DEST]
    rsync [OPTION...] rsync://[USER@]HOST[:PORT]/SRC... [DEST]
Push mode: rsync [OPTION...] SRC... [USER@]HOST::DEST
    rsync [OPTION...] SRC... rsync://[USER@]HOST[:PORT]/DEST

Purpose: To transfer files locally or remotely using an efficient and fast data transfer algorithm. To copy locally, to/from (push/pull) another host over any remote shell, or to/from (push/pull) a remote rsync daemon.

Output: Transferred files, either locally or remotely.

Common Options:

-a, --archive	archive mode
-A, --acls	preserve ACLs (implies -p)
--delete	delete extraneous files from destination dirs
-e, --rsh=COMMAND	specify the remote shell to use
--existing	skip creating new files on receiver
-h, --human-readable	output numbers in a human-readable format
-H, --hard-links	preserve hard links
-k, --copy-dirlinks	transform symlink to dir into referent dir
-K, --keep-dirlinks	treat symlinked dir on receiver as dir
-n, --dry-run	perform a trial run with no changes made
-p, --perms	preserve permissions
-q, --quiet	suppress non-error messages
-r, --recursive	recursively descend into directories
--remove-source-files	sender removes synchronized files (non-directory)
-v, --verbose	increase verbosity
-z, --compress	compress file data during the transfer

Command Arguments:

SRC	the source file or directory.
DEST	the destination path.

****

1.12.1 rsync Examples

One of the basic assumptions we are making in the following set of examples is that the source is generally a file object that is changing over time, such as a directory where you are modifying files by adding or deleting them from it, or from its sub-directories. Also, the destination is a file object that is unchanging, or fixed over time, such as when you do an archival backup. This is usually the case when you are using an archiving utility, although, as you have seen above with the **tar** command, the archive (or destination) can be added to, or extracted from in various ways.

Note

We do not cover more complex or advanced uses of **rsync**.

We have organized the **rsync** Examples based upon whether they apply where both source and destination are on a local machine, or where either the source or destination is on a remote machine. The Examples may also be divided into those that deal with files exclusively, or those that deal with directories and files.

Local Examples

1. Using **rsync** to copy a single file named **rsynctest** from the source current working directory to the local destination directory **/home/bob/USBint**. The files are transferred in "archive" mode, done using the **-a** option of the command.

    This ensures that symbolic links, devices, attributes, permissions, ownerships, etc., are preserved.

    $ **rsync -av rsynctest /home/bob/USBint**

2. Copying a single local file in compressed form, with the operation feedback presented in human-readable form, from the source **backup.tar** (in the current working directory) to the destination directory **/home/bob/backup1,** which you have permissions on.

    $ **rsync -zvh backup.tar /home/bob/backup1**

3. Using **rsync** to copy the entire source directory contents from the directory named **syncdir** locally to a destination directory locally named **/usr/home/bob/USBint**. The slash at the end the designated source means "copy the contents of this directory", <u>not</u> "copy the directory by name".

    $ **rsync -av syncdir/ /usr/home/bob/USBint**

4. Copying a single source directory **/home/bob/backups** in compressed form, with the operation feedback presented in human-readable form, to the destination directory **/home/remote/backups,** which you have permissions on.

    $ **rsync -avzh /home/bob/backups /home/remote/backups/**

5. Copying a single source directory **/home/bob/backups**, and its files and sub-directory structure, in compressed form, to the destination directory **/home/remote/backups,** which you have permissions on.

    $ **rsync -zvr /home/bob/backups /home/remote/backups**

6. Doing a dry-run, where you remove the source files and compress the transmitted file object.

   $ rsync --dry-run --remove-source-files -zvh backup.tar /tmp/backups/backup.tar

Remote Examples-

7. Copying a single directory, named **Music**, from the local machine to a remote machine at **192.168.1.8** into bob's home.

   $ rsync -avz Music bob@192.168.1.8:/home/bob/

8. Copying an entire local directory, named **syncdir2**, using ssh, to a remote machine at **192.168.0.7** and into the OS X-style directory / Users/b/Linux3e.

   $ rsync -av -e ssh syncdir2 bob@192.168.0.7:/Users/b/Linux3e

9. Copying a remote directory to a local directory.

   $ rsync -avzh root@192.168.0.100:/home/bob/backups /home/bob/temp

10. Copying just the contents of the remote directory **/home/bob/Linux2e**, updating (sometimes called "syncing") with the **--existing** option, only the existing files at the destination. If the source has new files, which are not on the destination, these new files are not put on the destination. The destination is signified by the .(period) at the end of the command, which translates to the current working directory.

    $ rsync -avz --existing bob@192.168.1.2:/home/bob/Linux2e/.

11. Copying a single local file, named **backup.tar**, using ssh, to a remote machine at **192.168.0.8**

    $ rsync -avzhe ssh backup.tar bob@192.168.0.8:/home/bob/backups/

12. Copying a single remote file to the current working directory using ssh.

    $ rsync -avzhe ssh bob@192.168.0.100:/usr/home/bob/systemctl.log.

13. Copying only the local files in **/home/bob/files** to a remote machine with an IP address of **192.168.0.8.** With the **--delete** option present, extraneous files on the destination that no longer exist in the source directory, are deleted. The **-v** option ensures that what is being transferred is output. **rsync** using ssh on an ephemeral port 32000.

    $ rsync -av --delete -e 'ssh -p 32000' /home/bob/files/ bob@192.168.0.8:/home/bob/files/

In-Chapter Exercises

22. What is the basic assumption in all of the Examples above where you copy to a remote host?

23. Do all of the above 13 examples locally on your system, and remotely on your LAN, substituting file names, directories, account names, and IP addresses as necessary.

1.12.2 Script Files for Backup and Recovery

User-written script files can be deployed by a Raspberry Pi 5 OS administrator to quickly and efficiently perform backup and archiving. Whether they are coded in Python (or some other scripting language), or in a shell programming language that embeds any of the above command line facilities that we've shown, they can be used to expedite, facilitate, and automate the backup, recovery, and archiving of files, directories, or entire file systems.

Additionally, there are several online sources for commercially available backup and archiving script files available, but there's no need for us to justify the utility for planning, coding, or maintaining your own script file code base, versus using an online, ready-made program.

The following is an example of a Bash shell script file, using a legacy application of **tar**.

Example 1.11 Simple Bash Shell Example for Automating tar Backups

Objective: The following Bash shell script will backup a directory, /home/bob/bashtest, to another directory previously created named simple_backup, in a compressed format.

Procedures: Do the following steps, in the order presented, to complete the requirements of this example.

1. Create a subdirectory of your home directory named **bashtest**.
2. Create another subdirectory of your home directory named **simple_backup**.
3. Copy some files into the directory **bashtest**.
4. Use an editor of your choice, such as nano, to create the following file in your home directory, and name that file **backup.bash**. Be sure to substitute your username for bob in the body of the script file!

```
#!/bin/bash
# To backup additional directories, put more pathnames in the following command,
# separated by spaces, such as /home/bob, /home/bill, etc.
backup_source=/home/bob/bashtest
backup_destination=/home/bob/simple_backup
filename=back1.tgz
```

```
echo "Backing up your bashtest directory"
tar --create --verbose --gzip --file $backup_destination/$filename
$backup_source
echo "Backup Complete"
```

5. Give yourself execute privilege on the file **backup.bash** with the following command:

```
$ chmod u+x backup.bash
$
```

6. Execute the Bash script with the following command:

```
$ ./backup.bash
"Backing up your bashtest directory"
tar: Removing leading `/' from member names
/home/bob/bashtest/
/home/bob/bashtest/nfs_client.txt
"Backup Complete"
$
```

7. Check that the backup was achieved with the following two commands:

```
$ cd simple_backup
$ ls -la
total 12
drwxr-xr-x    2 bob bob   4096    May 24 11:46   .
drwxr-xr-x   27 bob bob   4096    May 24 11:42   ..
-rw-r--r--    1 bob bob    808    May 24 11:46   back1.tgz
$
```

In-Chapter Exercises

24. Give the commands necessary to automate the above script file using systemd, to run the backup.bash script at 3:00 AM every day of the week. Feel free to modify the time, days, and source and destination directories and files, so that you can use the script file to backup information important to you on your Raspberry Pi 5 system.

25. How would you "decompress" the file you created with backup. bash in another directory?

1.12.3 Software for Backup and Recovery: FileZilla, SD Card Copier, and git

There are many commercial software and hardware packages that can be deployed to backup and archive your system. One very easy-to-use commercial product that allows you to clone entire hard disks in a "broadcast" fashion over a network, from a server to one or more machines, is Norton Ghost.

But the most readily available, useful, and free software facility, available through the Pi Menu choice > Preferences > Add/Remove Software on the Raspberry Pi 5 OS, that can do a variety of file system backup and recovery, disk recovery, and disk cloning operations is FileZilla.

Additionally, the Raspberry Pi 5 menu choice Accessories > SD Card Copier allows you to clone the entire microSD card, thus replicating whatever is on your system/boot disk at the time you do the copy. Admittedly, a brute force approach to backup for recovery, it is effective even for copying the microSD card to a USB2 or 3-mounted SSD, or other suitable USB medium.

You can also use the **git** command and GitHub.com to effectively backup user files.

Of course, if you adhere to our recommended storage strategy of keeping user files on media other than the boot/system medium, then whatever strategies you use to back those media up, for recovery or archival purposes, apply. You can mix and match any of the techniques and facilities we show in the following three Sections, to suit your requirements, and the specific needs of your selected data storage model.

1.12.3.1 *FileZilla*

FileZilla is nominally a graphics-based ftp client and server program that can use ssh as the tunnel, or conduit between systems. It has a number of useful functions and menu choices that allow the system administrator to successfully, confidentially, and efficiently backup and restore single files or directories, via a network, locally or globally. It is most useful for backing up and restoring single-user files and directories. It is not a replacement or substitute for the command line facilities shown in the preceding sections.

Figure 1.10 illustrates the screen display and menus available in the "client" version of FileZilla.

Both client and server, in our case a local machine running the Raspberry Pi 5 OS, and a remote Linux machine, must have ssh communications protocol enabled between them. You can have login access to an account on the remote server, or you can log in anonymously as well if that is enabled.

After launching FileZilla on the client, to log in to a remote host server, you need to supply the IP address of the server, the login name and password, and the port number (22 for ssh). Once you have successfully logged in by making the Quickconnect menu button choice, the local machine's directory and file structure are shown on the left side of the figure. The remote machine's directory structure is shown on the right side of the figure. To transfer files or directories between machines, you simply drag and drop between the appropriate panes on the left or right. If you are overwriting previously transferred files or directories, the FileZilla default is to give you the chance to overwrite or rename the files being transferred.

There are a number of other menu choices at the top of the FileZilla screen that allow you to affect preferences, set bookmarks, etc. For example, via the

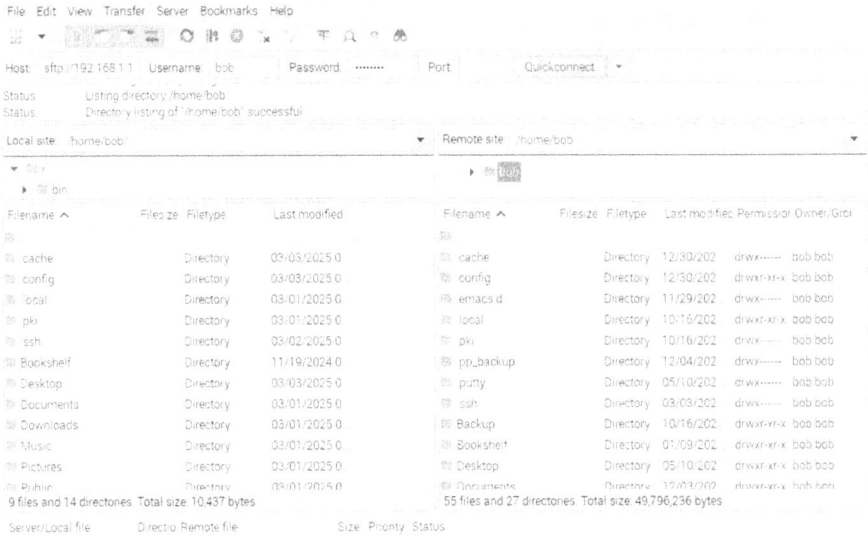

FIGURE 1.10
FileZilla main window.

menu choice Manage Bookmarks and the Site Manager, you can automatically make multiple local directories and remote directories available for ssh transfer as soon as you log in to the remote server sites.

There are some limitations to using FileZilla, however. It's primarily designed as an ftp client and server software, rather than as a dedicated backup tool. While it can be used to transfer files between systems, it lacks built-in functionality for automated backups. However, you can achieve automatic file backups by utilizing external tools in conjunction with FileZilla. Here's a general approach you can consider:

1. Set up a backup tool: Choose a backup software or script that suits your needs. There are numerous options available, such as **rsync** triggered by systemd systemctl timers. Ensure that your chosen tool supports automatic scheduling.

2. Configure the backup software: Set up the backup software to include the specific files and folders you want to back up. Configure the backup destination (e.g., local storage, network drive, cloud storage) and establish the backup schedule (e.g., hourly, daily, weekly).

3. Integrate FileZilla: Use FileZilla to transfer the files to the designated backup location. You can manually initiate the transfers or create a bash script file, for example, that executes the transfers automatically. FileZilla Pro and FileZilla Pro CLI provide a command-line interface (CLI) that allows you to do script file transfers, but they're not free!

4. Schedule the backup process: Depending on the backup tool you've chosen, use its scheduling capabilities to automatically trigger the backup process at regular intervals. This ensures that the specified files are backed up periodically.

By combining a backup tool with FileZilla and scheduling functionality, you can create an automated backup system for your specific files. Remember to consult the documentation and resources of your chosen backup software for detailed instructions on configuration and automation.

1.12.3.2 SD Card Copier

There's system cloning software built right into the Raspberry Pi 5 OS!

If you deployed the system installation technique shown in section 1.2.3, you can use a hybrid form of that method to archive your entire operating system, including the boot partition. If the system/boot disk is a microSD card, then you can simply add another blank(or not) microSD card into a suitable microSD-to-USB adapter, mount it in one of the USB ports on your Raspberry Pi hardware, and then use the Pi Menu choice Accessories > SD Card Copier menu choice to clone the current system/boot disk to the blank one.

And if you followed the technique in section 1.2.3, and your boot/system medium is an externally-mounted USB2 or 3 device, like an NMVe SSD, you can use the SD Card Copier to clone that original SSD onto another one of at least the same, or greater, capacity than the original.

Provided, of course, that you have an appliance, such as a multi-port adapter for NMVe SSDs, to mount more than one NMVe SSD into it.

A couple of words of caution are in order here.

First, when using the SD Card Copier, make sure you specify the "Copy from Device", and the "Copy to Device" **correctly**. The "Copy from Device" must be the original boot/system medium, and the "Copy to Device" can be another equal-or-larger capacity medium that is mounted inside of an enclosure, and connected via another USB port on the Raspberry Pi hardware. Don't confuse the two media, or else you'll end up with no usable clone and no bootable system! When we cloned a boot/system SSD, the original and the clone were the exact same SSDs, made by Silicon Power, mounted in Orico USB3 External Hard Drive enclosures. And we were very careful to specify them correctly to the SD Card Copier!

Second, some manufacturers' products, even though they're nominally the same capacity, are, in fact, different. So you should try to ensure this ahead of time.

The drawback to using this approach is, of course, that the cloning takes a snapshot of the entire system as it exists at <u>one particular moment in time</u>. This is unlike using the **rsync** command, automated by either cron or a systemctl timer, where the snapshots can be taken <u>regularly</u> and automatically, according to some timed schedule.

1.12.3.3 Using git and github to Backup File Systems

The **git** command and Github.com are useful, efficient, and powerful means you can use to create a distributed version-control system for your software projects. They can also be used as a cloud-based storage and archiving facility, particularly if you follow the storage model we recommend in this chapter. That is, if your Raspberry Pi 5 OS is installed on one, and all of your user data files are stored on another persistent medium, such as an additional SSD.

Of course, using a private Github.com repository for backup and archiving is not free. In addition, there are limits to the amount of data that you can store on Github. Therefore, this method of backup and archiving works best for an ordinary user, in a <u>public</u> repository at Github, with small user data storage requirements. Also, if you use another data storage model than what we recommend, the mechanics of doing Github archiving and backup would be dependent on that data storage model.

1.12.3.4 curl

What is **curl**? **curl** (Client URL) is a command-line tool used to transfer data between a local system and a remote server. It supports various protocols, including FTP, SFTP, HTTP, HTTPS, SCP, SMB, and more. It's commonly used for file transfers, backup automation, API requests, and web scraping. We showed another use of **curl** in Example 1.1.

*Installing **curl** on a Raspberry Pi 5*

> **curl** is usually pre-installed on Raspberry Pi 5 OS, but if it's missing or outdated, you can install or update it easily.

a. Check if **curl** is Installed
   Open a terminal and run:

```
$ curl --version
curl 7.88.1 (aarch64-unknown-linux-gnu) libcurl/7.88.1 OpenSSL/3.0.15 zlib/1.2.13
brotli/1.0.9 zstd/1.5.4 libidn2/2.3.3 libpsl/0.21.2 (+libidn2/2.3.3) libssh2/1.10.0
nghttp2/1.52.0 librtmp/2.3 Output truncated...
$
```

   If it prints the above output, you already have curl on your Raspberry Pi 5. If not, follow the steps below.

b. How to Install or Update **curl**

```
$ sudo apt update && sudo apt install curl -y
Output truncated...
```

   This installs curl or updates it to the latest version available in the repository.

c. Verify Installation
After installation, check again:

$ curl --version

You should see output like we got above in a. on our Raspberry Pi 5 OS

*How to Use **curl** for File Transfers on Raspberry Pi 5:*

1. Upload a File via FTP
To upload a file (backup.zip) to an FTP server:

$ curl -T backup.zip ftp://ftp.example.com/ --user username:password

where:

-T specifies the file to upload.

ftp://ftp.example.com/ is the remote server.

--user username:password provides login credentials.

Upload multiple files:

$ curl -T "{file1.txt,file2.txt}" ftp://ftp.example.com/ --user username:password

2. Download a File via FTP
To download backup.zip from an FTP server:

$ curl -O ftp://ftp.example.com/backup.zip --user username:password

where:

-O saves the file with the same name as on the server.

Download multiple files:

$ curl -O ftp://ftp.example.com/file1.txt -O ftp://ftp.example.com/file2.txt --user username:password

3. Mirror an Entire Directory
You can use curl to list and download an entire directory recursively (though lftp or wget is better for this).

$ curl -l ftp://ftp.example.com/directory/ --user username:password

For advanced recursive transfers, consider wget:

$ wget -m --ftp-user=username --ftp-password=password ftp://ftp.example.com/directory/

TABLE 1.8

curl vs. Other Backup Tools

Tool	Best For
curl	Simple file transfers, APIs, SFTP, FTP uploads/downloads
lftp	Better for mirroring/syncing entire directories
rsync	Best for SSH/SFTP-based backup automation
wget	Downloading large files & recursive website backup

4. Use **curl** for SFTP (Secure FTP)
   If you use SFTP (FTP over SSH) instead of FTP:

   $ **curl -T backup.zip sftp://youruser@yourserver.com/home/user/ --key ~/.ssh/id_rsa**

   where:

   sftp:// makes it secure.

   --key ~/.ssh/id_rsa allows authentication via SSH key.

5. Automating **curl** for Backups
   You can automate **curl** commands with cron. Here's an example daily FTP backup at 2 AM:

   $ **crontab -e**

   Add the following:

   0 2 * * * curl -T /home/pi/backup.zip ftp://ftp.example.com/ --user username:password

6. When to Use **curl** vs. Other Tools?

Table 1.8 provides a comparison of various Linux and UNIX backup tools.

1.13 Software Updates and Operating System Upgrades

We begin this section with two questions, which we try to answer for you to give you a better feel for why software updates and operating system updates are important.

Question: Why would the two most-significant, post-installation tasks that an ordinary user on a single-user Raspberry Pi 5 system needs to perform be as follows?

a. The addition, removal, or update of software applications as packages on the system.

b. The upgrade of the operating system itself to a newer, currently stable release

Answer:

a. The standard installation of the operating system does <u>not</u> include software that the user needs, given the use-cases she puts the system to. And also, changing conditions in use-cases require the removal of software packages as well. Finally, as newer and improved versions of installed packages become available, there must be a quick and easy way to update the packages to incorporate those improvements.

b. Purely from a performance and <u>security viewpoint</u>, upgrades of the Raspberry Pi 5 OS happen very regularly, and even an ordinary user should take advantage of these improvements via upgrades.

Question: What is the difference between "updating" and " upgrading" a Raspberry Pi 5 system?
   Answer: Generally, in the literature, the two terms are often confused with one another. But from our perspective in this section (and throughout this chapter), we define the two terms as follow:

Updating is the process of adding or replacing application software packages. For example, bringing the nginx web server application from an earlier-installed version to the latest stable release of it.

Upgrading is the process of replacing the entire operating system with a newer, hopefully stable release. The upgrade can be to a newer minor release or to a new major release. For example, upgrading from what was named Raspbian to the Raspberry Pi OS, an upgrade that was not just a naming convention change. Additionally, a change in the kernel from an earlier release to a later release constitutes a major upgrade of the operating system.

In this section, we show the basics of how these two fundamental tasks can be done on our representative Raspberry Pi 5 OS.
   For software application addition, removal, or updates, we limit the discussion to covering the Advanced Packaging Tool (APT), because that's the default package manager on the Raspberry Pi 5 OS. APT can be used very effectively in a text-based, CUI environment. That's how we approach it in this book. That doesn't preclude the use of GUI-based front ends to package managers, available via the Raspberry Pi menu Preferences > Add/Remove Software.

Additionally, we offer some information about Snaps here in this section. The Snap package manager is a software package management system developed by Canonical, the company supporting Ubuntu Linux. It is designed to work across different Linux distributions and provides a way to package and distribute software in a self-contained format called "Snaps".

Snaps are containerized software packages that include all the necessary dependencies and libraries required for the application to run, making them more isolated and secure. They aim to simplify software installation and updates by providing a consistent experience across different Linux distributions.

As for the Raspberry Pi 5 OS, the Snap package manager is <u>not</u> installed by default. However, it is possible to install Snap on Raspberry Pi 5 OS if desired. Canonical provides a version of the Snap package manager that is compatible with ARM-based systems like the Raspberry Pi 5 OS. Instructions for installing Snap on Raspberry Pi 5 OS can be found on the official Snapcraft website or through community resources.

Snap can be installed on a Raspberry Pi running the latest version of the Raspberry Pi 5 OS by opening a terminal and typing the following commands.

```
$ sudo apt update
$ sudo apt install snapd
Output truncated…
$
```

You will need to then reboot your system.

```
$ sudo reboot
```

Then install the core snap so you can get the latest snapd.

```
$ sudo snap install core22
Output truncated...
core22 20250110 from Canonical✓ installed
$
```

For upgrading the operating system itself, we show you a basic set of procedures in section 1.13.4 that suit the variable conditions of upgrading an operating system.

In-Chapter Exercise

26. In light of what we have said about updating and upgrading your Raspberry Pi 5 system, list applications that you want to install, given the use case(s) you undertake on your system. Then, as you

go through the rest of this section, use the APT package manager to install these.

The best way for you to get more basic help on the package management commands we show in this section is to read the man pages available for them on your system.

1.13.1 Preliminary Storage Model Suggestions

We previously provided an ordinary user with a suggested storage model, where the operating system is on a single medium (which we call the "boot/system disk"), and the user data is on one or more other media. One of the most useful and practical advantages this model gives an ordinary user is the ability to add or update software applications, and upgrade the operating system itself in a very reliable and time-efficient way. The software applications and operating system, since they exist on the boot/system disk, can be incrementally updated or upgraded independently of the user data. So for example, if you want to go from an earlier major release of the operating system to the latest release, you can detach and unmount the user data media, do a clean or fresh install of the new release onto the old, or even new, boot/system disk, and then simply reattach the user data to the system. We have found that this storage model, and this method of update/upgrade, is safest and most reliable, even for an ordinary user, i.e., it doesn't break the system, and thus lose user data.

If you choose to keep the older major release of the operating system, and just want to incrementally update software and upgrade the operating system, the sections below will give you a basic overview of how to do that.

There is a very wide selection of software programs available via the use of the facilities we show here. These programs are found in software archives known as "repositories". The repositories contain collections of "packages", and each package contains bundled-together software and dependencies that can all be automatically installed together. When downloaded and installed on your system by package management facilities such as APT or Snap (the two package management systems we mentioned earlier), that software becomes available to a user without the need to do anything else.

1.13.1.1 Default Repositories

The default repositories for the Raspberry Pi 5 OS are usually specified in the file /etc/apt/sources.list. This file contains a list of package repositories that are used by the APT package manager to install and update software.

By default, the Raspberry Pi 5 OS sources.list file on our Raspberry Pi 5, at the time this book was written, contained the following lines:

```
deb http://deb.debian.org/debian bookworm main contrib non-free non-free-firmware
deb http://deb.debian.org/debian-security/ bookworm-security main contrib non-free non-free-firmware
deb http://deb.debian.org/debian bookworm-updates main contrib non-free non-free-firmware
# Uncomment deb-src lines below then 'apt-get update' to enable 'apt-get source'
#deb-src http://deb.debian.org/debian bookworm main contrib non-free non-free-firmware
#deb-src http://deb.debian.org/debian-security/ bookworm-security main contrib non-free non-free-firmware
#deb-src http://deb.debian.org/debian bookworm-updates main contrib non-free non-free-firmware
```

In the above example listing, the repository URL is specified as http://deb.debian.org/debian*. This URL points to the official Raspberry Pi 5 OS repository server.

The repositories are divided into three components:

main: This component contains the core software packages officially supported by the Raspberry Pi 5 OS team.

contrib: This component contains packages that are not part of the core distribution but are still provided by the Raspberry Pi 5 OS team. These packages depend on software from the main component.

non-free: This component contains packages that are not free software and may have licensing restrictions. These packages depend on software from the main component.

Note

The contents of the sources.list file may change with updates to Raspberry Pi 5 OS, so it's always a good idea to check the file on your specific installation or consult the official Raspberry Pi 5 OS documentation for the most up-to-date information.

For software that provides a system service, such as sshd or a web server like nginx, the package manager not only downloads and installs all necessary components and their dependencies but also uses systemd facilities to start the service and ensure it automatically starts at every subsequent system boot.

In-Chapter Exercise

27. Determine exactly how your Raspberry Pi system deploys a storage model. For example, what are the paths to a user's home directory? How is the file system structure segregated on the storage media, if it is? How is this different from the storage model we suggest? How can you migrate the storage model that now exists on your Raspberry Pi system, so that it conforms

to our suggested model? Perhaps you are the person who has implemented the storage model as you installed the Raspberry Pi 5 OS. In that case, you can still answer this question for archival purposes and your own reference.

1.13.2 Using the Advanced Packaging Tool (APT)

For beginners, a Character User Interface(CUI) approach to package management at first might not seem to be the quickest and easiest way to accomplish one of the most significant post-installation tasks a system administrator must do. Graphical User Interface(GUI) approaches have some tremendous advantages, and not only in terms of saving time. But we feel the explicit control you get by using APT, on the command line, outweigh the initial advantages of a GUI. Of all of the tools available for APT, the **apt-get** command is the most useful for a beginner.

1.13.2.1 Using apt-get

The Advanced Packaging Tool (APT) is used for all aspects of managing packages. The most used (and useful) of its package management utilities is the CUI **apt-get** tool. Following is an abbreviated man page description of **apt-get**, taken from the man page for it on our Raspberry Pi 5 OS installation:

```
***********************************************************************
```
apt-get - APT package handling utility – CUI version

Syntax:
apt-get [-asqdyfmubV] [-o=config_string] [-c=config_file]
        [-t=target_release] [-a=architecture] {update | upgrade |
        dselect-upgrade | dist-upgrade |
        install pkg [{=pkg_version_number | /target_release}]... |
        remove pkg... | purge pkg... |
        source pkg [{=pkg_version_number | /target_release}]... |
        build-dep pkg [{=pkg_version_number | /target_release}]... |
        download pkg [{=pkg_version_number | /target_release}]... |
        check | clean | autoclean | autoremove | {-v | --version} |
        {-h | --help}}

Purpose: apt-get is the command-line tool for handling packages, and may be considered the user's "back-end" to other tools using the APT library. Several "front-end" interfaces exist.

Output: Added, removed, or updated software packages on the system.

Common Options and Commands:
Note: Unless the -h, or --help option is given, one of the commands below must be present.
Options-

-d, --download-only
> Download only; package files are only retrieved, not unpacked or
> installed. Configuration Item: APT::Get::Download-Only.

--only-upgrade
> Do not install new packages; when used in conjunction with install,
> only-upgrade will install upgrades for already installed packages
> only and ignore requests to install new packages.

-q, --quiet
> Quiet; produces output suitable for logging, omitting progress
> indicators.

-y, --yes, --assume-yes
> Automatic yes to prompts; assume "yes" as answer to all prompts and
> run non-interactively.

Commands-

install
> install is followed by one or more packages desired for
> installation or upgrading. The /etc/apt/sources.list file is used to locate the
> desired packages.

remove
> remove is identical to install except that packages are removed
> instead of installed. Removing a package leaves its
> configuration files on the system.

update
> update is used to resynchronize the package index files from their
> sources. The indexes of available packages are fetched from the
> location(s) specified in /etc/apt/sources.list.

upgrade
> upgrade is used to install the newest versions of all packages
> currently installed on the system from the sources enumerated in
> /etc/apt/sources.list.

****

We cover the following functions in APT for the Raspberry Pi 5 OS:
Installing, reinstalling, removing, and searching for packages.

Upgrading and updating packages.

In the Operations below, when we refer to **package_name**, this represents
any specific named package. Additionally, notice that we do these operations
as the root user!

Operation 1
> To use the apt-cache package query function as the root user, to list
> available packages on your system, use the following commands:

> ~# **sudo -i**
> **root@raspberrypi:~# apt-cache pkgnames**

Although this listing can be quite long, it is useful to find out if a package has been installed on your system. For example, in the nginx Example we show below, before you try to install a package named "nginx", it is a good idea to see if it has already been installed!

Operation 2

To install a package, use the following command:

root@raspberrypi:~# **apt-get install package_name**

At this point, install the nginx web server with the command **sudo apt-get install nginx**

Operation 3

To remove a package, or the package and its configuration files, use the following commands:

root@raspberrypi:~# **apt-get remove package_name**
root@raspberrypi:~# **apt-get purge package_name**

Operation 4

To update the package index files from the local sources.list directories (the metadata for packages), or upgrade all Debian packages to their latest versions, use the following commands:

root@raspberrypi:~# **apt-get update**
root@raspberrypi:~# **apt-get upgrade**

Operation 5

To individually update an installed package, by removing it and then reinstalling it, use the following command:

root@raspberrypi:~# **apt-get --reinstall install package_name**

Operation 6

To show metadata associated with an installed package on the system, use the following command:

root@raspberrypi:~# **apt-cache show package_name**

For example, on our Raspberry Pi system, the output of this command shows the nginx metadata information-

root@raspberrypi:~# **apt-cache show nginx**
Package: nginx
Version: 1.22.1-9
Installed-Size: 1342
Maintainer: Debian Nginx Maintainers <pkg-nginx-maintainers@alioth-lists.debian.net>
Architecture: arm64

Replaces: nginx-core (<< 1.22.1-6~), nginx-extras (<< 1.22.1-6~), nginx-light
(<< 1.22.1-6~)
Provides: httpd, httpd-cgi, nginx-abi-1.22.1-7
Depends: libc6 (>= 2.34), libcrypt1 (>= 1:4.1.0), libpcre2-8-0 (>= 10.22), libssl3
(>= 3.0.0), zlib1g (>= 1:1.1.4), iproute2, nginx-common (<< 1.22.1-9.1~), nginx-
common (>= 1.22.1-9)
Breaks: nginx-core (<< 1.22.1-6~), nginx-extras (<< 1.22.1-6~), nginx-light
(<< 1.22.1-6~)
Description-en: small, powerful, scalable web/proxy server
 Nginx ("engine X") is a high-performance web and reverse proxy server
 created by Igor Sysoev. It can be used both as a standalone web server
 and as a proxy to reduce the load on back-end HTTP or mail servers.
Description-md5: cb534cf82475d3e706f730549c99229f
Homepage: https://nginx.org
 Output truncated...

In-Chapter Exercises

28. First, install a single package on your system from the list you
    compiled in answer to In-Chapter Exercise 24, and as detailed in
    this section. Then, if they haven't already been installed by your-
    self or a system administrator, use APT on your Raspberry Pi 5
    system to install the following application packages if you haven't
    already done so:

    gnome-disk-utility 3.38.2, GIMP, openssh-server, and vsftpd.

    Finally, test each of these applications. Do these applications
    restart after a system reboot? How can you know if they would do
    that without actually rebooting the system?

29. Use APT on your Raspberry Pi 5 system to install application
    packages that fit your particular use-case(s). Go back to your
    answer to In-Chapter Exercise 24 for a preliminary listing of
    these.

1.13.3 Upgrading the Operating System

Similar to our recommendations for the exact, specific details of initially
installing your system, the minor or major release upgrades of the system
itself are very dependent on:

1. The specific system you are dealing with.
2. The versions of that system you are trying to upgrade between.

Although the Raspberry Pi 5 OS uses APT, there is enough variability
due to 2, that presenting the exact, specific details of upgrading the system

is best left to consulting relevant online sources at the time you want to do the upgrades. When we wrote this book, the upgrade procedure using APT could be summarized as follows:

1. The following APT commands, executed as the root user, worked for minor release upgrades:

   root@raspberrypi:~# **apt update**
   root@raspberrypi:~# **apt upgrade**
   root@raspberrypi:~# **apt dist-upgrade**

2. The major upgrade procedure is best done by consulting the online documentation at the time you want to do the upgrade, and of course, is constrained by 1 above.

In-Chapter Exercise

30. Create a document that details exactly what steps you must take to upgrade your Raspberry Pi 5 system, serving for both minor releases and major releases of the software. The scheduling of your procedural steps should reflect, for example, a weekly or monthly basis for minor release changes, or at some unspecified interval for major release changes. Then, implement the procedures that your document specifies.

1.14 System and Software Performance Monitoring and Adjustment

The most important considerations a Raspberry Pi 5 OS system administrator (and the ordinary, single user on her own computer) has to make, when dealing with system performance, revolve around CPU process management, memory management, disk usage/management, and network performance. Table 1.9 lists the controlling facilities and functions the Raspberry Pi 5 OS provides for system tuning and performance monitoring, most notably with the kernel-loadable ZFS component added, if that ever is the stable, and easily-implemented case.

The commands that implement and affect some of the functions from Table 1.9 are as follows. We also include commands that allow you to monitor these functions as well. We cover some of these commands in the sections below.

df, du, free, journalctl, nice, pgrep, ps, renice, systemctl, systemd-cgls, systemd-run, top

TABLE 1.9

Performance Tuning Functions

System Component	Control Facility
CPU	Nice numbers
	Process priorities
	Cgroup management
	Batch queues
	Scheduler parameters
Memory	Process resource limits
	Cgroup management
	Memory management parameters
	Paging space
ZFS vdevs, zpools and I/O (if installed)	ZFS pool and file system organization
	ZFS deduplication, efficiency, optimization
	I/O parameters
	Zvol creation and administration
Network I/O	Network memory buffers
	Network-related parameters
	Network infrastructure

1.14.1 Application-Level Process/Thread Resource Management

The basic reason for monitoring system resources, such as process CPU usage and system memory, in terms of how the system is performing given its designed for and intended use-case(s), is to allow you to observe, assess and then gain control, at the application level, of how programs important to you are effectively using major components of system resources.

For example, if a particular standard application (such as a web server which you have installed from an on-line repository) or even a user-written program's processes, are consuming too much of CPU or memory resources, according to criteria you determine given the use case(s) your system is designed or intended for, you can scale back that task's operation to better serve your user base. On the other hand, if those same processes are being under-served or starved for resources, for whatever reason, you can scale up that task's operation as well. There may be some situations where under-service may be caused by hardware malfunctions or illegal intrusion, but we do not cover those situations in this section.

A classic case of this, within the context of systemd control, is scaling back from the graphical.target state to the multi-user.target state. This is akin to using a server class install, rather than a full-blown desktop installation. We cover this change of system state, using the **isolate** command, in depth in Chapter 2.

The key is to be able to observe and assess the usage of system resources in a contemporary way on your Raspberry Pi 5, and then take some actions based on those observations and assessments. Those actions are, of course, guided by how you have strategically designed and implemented your administrative plan, given the use case(s) of your system.

Another way of assessing process activity, for example, in terms of scheduling processes and process groups through the CPU, is to examine the proc file system.

1.14.1.1 Traditional Process Control

Traditionally, the most important, complete, and readily available display of system process activity is given by the **ps** and **top** (or **htop**) commands, which allow you to monitor running processes.

1.14.2 Managing System Memory

systemd allows you to easily control and set limits on a unit's memory usage. This can be critical in cases where there is a smaller amount of installed memory on your Raspberry Pi 5 hardware. To see what percentage of memory a unit is consuming, use the **top** command and examine the column output for %MEM. Given the use-case(s) your system has been designed for, if an application or service is consuming too much memory, there are two ways you can limit its memory usage.

The limit specifies how much process and kernel memory can be used by tasks in this unit. The limit is a memory size in bytes. If the numerical value is followed by K, M, G, or T, the specified memory size is parsed as Kilobytes, Megabytes, Gigabytes, or Terabytes (with the base 1024), respectively. The special value "infinity" means that no memory limit is to be applied.

The simplest way to achieve this is to put the following directive in the [Service] section of the unit's configuration file:

MemoryLimit=value

Replace value with a limit on maximum memory usage of the processes executed in the cgroup. Use suffixes K, M, G, or T to identify Kilobyte, Megabyte, Gigabyte, or Terabyte as the unit of measurement. Also, the MemoryAccounting parameter has to be enabled for the unit.

The MemoryLimit parameter controls the memory.limit_in_bytes control group parameter.

To assign a 500 Megabyte memory limit to a service named test4 service, add a MemoryLimit setting in the /etc/systemd/system/test4.service file to include the following:

[Service]
MemoryLimit=500M

To apply the changes in either of the two ways, reload systemd's configuration and restart a service. In the two commands below, that service is named test4.service

$ sudo systemctl daemon-reload
$ sudo systemctl restart test4.service

In-Chapter Exercises

31. Set the MemoryLimit value for selected services on your Raspberry Pi 5 system, either higher or lower, depending upon specific use-case requirements.

32. Use the **free** command on your system and its options to gauge the distribution of system memory. Do the quantities you get agree with the amount of installed system memory you have?

From the output the **free** commands, what can you infer about the installed memory quantity on your system, in GB? See the man page for the **free** command on your system to get more information about its usage and options.

1.14.3 Assessment of System Disk Usage

Along with CPU usage and memory management, the ability to look at, then assess and possibly modify the resources of persistent storage media, particularly of a limited-capacity microSD card, is critical to a system administrator's task. Even for an ordinary user, storage space is a precious commodity, regardless of the availability and lower costs of terabyte-capacity externally-mounted media. Consider a Raspberry Pi 5 system that can only physically support a smaller capacity microSD card, for whatever reason. Or a system where an ordinary user is storing large files, such as video or other types of media files.

Traditionally, the **du** command allowed you to get a text-based summary of disk usage for files and directories, in a variety of formats. An administrator could then take action to trim storage usage according to the use case of the system. For more information on the **du** command, see the man page for **du** on your Raspberry Pi 5 system.

The **df** command (df is an abbreviation for disk free) allows you to display the amount of available storage space for file systems on which the invoking user has read access. **df** is typically invoked using the **-h** and **T** option, which gives a human-readable output format, which includes the file system types. For example, on our Raspberry Pi 5 system, whose boot/system medium is a microSD card, the following command gives information about storage and file system layout:

```
$ df -hT
```

Filesystem	Type	Size	Used	Avail	Use%	Mounted on
udev	devtmpfs	2.0G	0	2.0G	0%	/dev
tmpfs	tmpfs	405M	6.2M	399M	2%	/run
/dev/mmcblk0p2	ext4	28G	6.9G	20G	27%	/
tmpfs	tmpfs	2.0G	0	2.0G	0%	/dev/shm
tmpfs	tmpfs	5.0M	48K	5.0M	1%	/run/lock
/dev/mmcblk0p1	vfat	510M	67M	444M	14%	/boot/firmware
tmpfs	tmpfs	405M	192K	405M	1%	/run/user/1000
/dev/sda1	exfat	954G	8.1G	946G	1%	/media/bob/X31

```
$
```

More contemporary graphical methods can be used to view and assess disk usage on Raspberry Pi 5 systems. For example, you can use the gnome disk usage analyzer, named "Baobab". It displays either a bar or sector chart representation of relative disk usage for any attached persistent medium. This tool is very useful when you want to get a picture of where and what your disks are being used for. Figure 1.11 shows a typical disk capacity display of the root directory on the same Raspberry Pi 5 system. Similar tools are found on all Linux systems.

1.14.4 Network Configuration with the ip Command

The most important and useful command for the system administrator when doing a post-install network configuration is the **ip** command. The following sections illustrate the basic usage of this command, and give a use case example that illustrates how to assign more than one IP address to a Raspberry Pi 5 network interface.

With the new toolkit, it is easy to add new ip addresses, as follows:

```
$ ip addr add 192.168.1.1/24 dev eth0
```

1.14.4.1 Basic ip Command Syntax, Options, and Operations

An abbreviated version of the man page for the **ip** command is as follows:

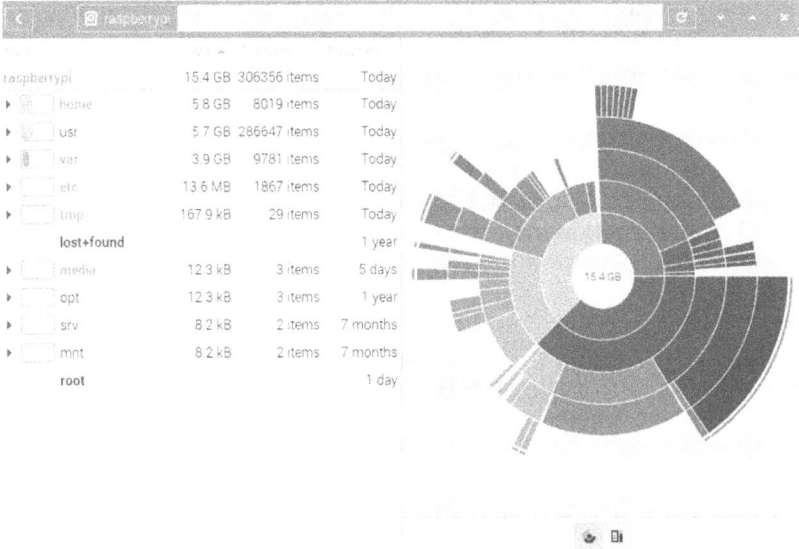

FIGURE 1.11
Disk usage analyzer display of the root directory.

****
ip

Syntax: **ip [Options] Object { Command | help }**
         ip [-force] -batch filename
where
    Object { link | addr | addrlabel | route | rule | neigh | ntable | tunnel | tuntap | mad-
          dress | mroute | mrule | monitor | xfrm | netns | l2tp | tcp_metrics }

    Options { -V[ersion] | -h[uman-readable] | -s[tatistics] | -r[esolve] | -f[amily] { inet |
          inet6 | ipx | dnet | link } | -o[neline] | -n[etns] name | -a[ll] | -c[olor] }

    Command
    Specifies the action to perform on the object. The set of possible actions depends
    on the object type.
    For most objects, the commands possible are **add**, **delete** and **show**. Some objects do
    not allow all of these operations, or have some additional commands. The help command
    is available for all objects. It prints out a list of available commands and argument
    syntax conventions.
    If no command is given, usually the **show** command is the default, if that option can be
    applied to the objects specified.

Purpose: Show or manipulate routing, devices, policy routing and tunnels.

Output: Output or modified routing, devices, policy routing, or tunnels.

Common Options, Objects, and Commands:
addr   IP address

To view an abbreviated syntax display of help on the ip route command, type the following:

$ ip addr help
Usage: ip address {add|change|replace} IFADDR dev IFNAME [LIFETIME]
                      [CONFFLAG-LIST]
   ip address del IFADDR dev IFNAME [mngtmpaddr]
   ip address {show|save|flush} [dev IFNAME] [scope SCOPE-ID]
             [to PREFIX] [FLAG-LIST] [label LABEL] [up]
   ip address {showdump|restore}
IFADDR := PREFIX | ADDR peer PREFIX
   [broadcast ADDR] [anycast ADDR]
   [label IFNAME] [scope SCOPE-ID]
Output truncated...

****

From the above abbreviated listing, you can see the Commands available to work on the Object route, i.e., add, change, replace, del(ete), show, save, flush, and showdump.

To see the status of the specific network interface named eth0, for example, type the following:

$ ip addr show eth0
2: eth0: <NO-CARRIER,BROADCAST,MULTICAST,UP> mtu 1500 qdisc pfifo_fast state DOWN group default qlen 1000
   link/ether 2c:cf:67:23:a9:43 brd ff:ff:ff:ff:ff:ff

This shows that there is no Ethernet cable connected.

To see the status of all network interfaces attached to, or defined on, the system, type the following:

$ ip addr show
1: lo: <LOOPBACK,UP,LOWER_UP> mtu 65536 qdisc noqueue state UNKNOWN group default qlen 1000
   link/loopback 00:00:00:00:00:00 brd 00:00:00:00:00:00
   inet 127.0.0.1/8 scope host lo
     valid_lft forever preferred_lft forever
   inet6 ::1/128 scope host noprefixroute
     valid_lft forever preferred_lft forever
2: eth0: <NO-CARRIER,BROADCAST,MULTICAST,UP> mtu 1500 qdisc pfifo_fast state DOWN group default qlen 1000
   link/ether 2c:cf:67:23:a9:43 brd ff:ff:ff:ff:ff:ff
3: wlan0: <BROADCAST,MULTICAST,UP,LOWER_UP> mtu 1500 qdisc pfifo_fast state UP group default qlen 1000
   link/ether 2c:cf:67:23:a9:44 brd ff:ff:ff:ff:ff:ff
   inet 192.168.1.14/24 brd 192.168.1.255 scope global dynamic noprefixroute wlan0
     valid_lft 85840sec preferred_lft 85840sec
   inet6 fe80::6950:e65e:eb76:1b0/64 scope link noprefixroute
     valid_lft forever preferred_lft forever

To display link characteristics of eth0, type the following:

$ ip link show dev wlan0
3: wlan0: <BROADCAST,MULTICAST,UP,LOWER_UP> mtu 1500 qdisc pfifo_fast state
UP mode DORMANT group default qlen 1000
    link/ether 2c:cf:67:23:a9:44 brd ff:ff:ff:ff:ff:ff
$

1.14.4.2 Use Case Example: Assigning Multiple IP Addresses to a Raspberry Pi 5

On Raspberry Pi 5 OS, Network Manager is the default tool for managing network connections. You can interact with it using both graphical and command-line interfaces-

Graphical Interface:

If you're using the Raspberry Pi 5 desktop environment, Network Manager provides a system tray icon – typically resembling a network or Wi-Fi symbol – located on the taskbar. Clicking this icon will display available network connections, allowing you to connect to Wi-Fi networks, manage Ethernet settings, and configure VPNs. For more advanced settings, you can access the "Edit Connections" option from this menu.

Command-Line Interface:

For terminal users, or when operating in a headless setup, Network Manager offers two primary tool:

> nmtui (Network Manager Text User Interface): This is a text-based interface that provides a user-friendly way to manage network connections without needing to remember complex commands. To launch it, simply open a terminal and type:
>
> **$ nmtui**
>
> From here, you can edit existing connections, activate or deactivate connections, and set the system hostname.
>   nmcli (Network Manager Command Line Interface): This is a powerful command-line tool for detailed network management. Some common commands include:
> * View the status of all interfaces:

$ nmcli dev status
DEVICE	TYPE	STATE	CONNECTION
wlan0	wifi	connected	NETGEAR58-5G
lo	loopback	connected (externally)	lo

```
p2p-dev-wlan0    wifi-p2p     disconnected       --
eth0             ethernet     unavailable        --
$
```

- List available Wi-Fi networks:

   $ **sudo nmcli device wifi connect "SSID" password "your_password"**

- Connect to a Wi-Fi network:

   $ **sudo nmcli device wifi** connect "**SSID**" password "**your_password**"

Replace "**SSID**" with the name of your Wi-Fi network and "**your_ password**" with the corresponding password.

Configuration Files:

Network Manager stores connection profiles in the /etc/ NetworkManager/system-connections/ directory. Each network connection has its own configuration file in this location. These files can be manually edited, if necessary, but it's crucial to ensure they have the correct permissions (typically 600) to be recognized and used by Network Manager.

This section and its Example show how to assign multiple IP addresses to your system, without using the deprecated **ifconfig** command, or its obsolete "alias" notation. If you prefer to manage your network interfaces with the interfaces file, you may need to disable dhcpcd:

$ **sudo systemctl disable dhcpcd**
$ **sudo systemctl stop dhcpcd**

This ensures that dhcpcd does not interfere with your manual network configuration.

Question: Why would you want to do this?

Answer: You want to have your now favorite web server, nginx, listen on several IP addresses on your LAN. You proceed with the following commands, and then modify the nginx configuration to do so.

****Note****

We do not show the nginx configuration changes here!

Example 1.12 Assigning Several IP Addresses to a Network Interface

Objectives: To use the **ip** command to assign several IP addresses to your system's network interface.

Pre-Requisites: Having superuser privileges on your system, using a wired network connection via an Ethernet cable.

Requirements: Do the following steps, in the order presented.

1. If you need an additional IP address temporarily, you can add it to any network interface by using the following general format command:

   $ sudo ip address add <ip-address>/<netmask> dev <interface>

   An actual example would be as follows:

   $ sudo ip address add 192.168.1.100/24 dev eth0

   $

   The above command would add an additional IP address to the network interface, using a 24-bit netmask, to whatever current IP addresses are already assigned to the nic eth0.
   You can check the result with the following command. Notice that the address 192.168.1.26 has already been assigned via the DHCP server on the network, by default :

   $ ip address show eth0
   2: eth0: <BROADCAST,MULTICAST,UP,LOWER_UP> mtu 1500 qdisc mq
   state UP group default qlen 1000
    link/ether e4:11:5b:12:c2:77 brd ff:ff:ff:ff:ff:ff
    inet 192.168.1.26/24 brd 192.168.1.255 scope global dynamic noprefixroute eth0
     valid_lft 14015sec preferred_lft 3215sec
    inet 192.168.1.100/24 scope global secondary eth0
     valid_lft forever preferred_lft forever
    inet6 fe80::9ef2:8f7f:e4c4:7ea2/64 scope link
     valid_lft forever preferred_lft forever

   You can delete this address again using the following command:

   $ sudo ip address del 192.168.1.100/24 dev eth0

   These changes are lost when you reboot your machine.
2. To make the additional IP address permanent, as superuser, you can edit the file /etc/network/interfaces as superuser, and add the above IP address at the bottom of the existing entries, while retaining the defaults found in that file. This is what the interfaces file must look like with the above assignment added to that file:

   # interfaces(5) file used by ifup(8) and ifdown(8)
   auto lo

```
iface lo inet loopback
# The primary network interface, the default which must be included in
this file!
auto eth0
iface eth0 inet dhcp
# The address added to the default
iface eth0 inet static
    address 192.168.1.100/24
```

The above file contents show you **must** explicitly retain the default settings for network interfaces, and add additional ones. If, in the above */etc*/network/interfaces file the primary network interface is <u>not</u> specified (the one assgned, in our case, by a DHCP server on our LAN), you must specify it as a DHCP-assigned address.

****Note**** assigned

If the file */etc*/network/interfaces file on your Raspberry Pi 5 OS doesn't exist, create it exactly as shown above.

Save the file, and reboot your Raspberry Pi 5 to make the new network settings permanent.

To return to the default network interface settings for eth0, simply edit the /etc/network/interfaces file again and remove the added IP address lines.

In-Chapter Exercises

33. In the above Example, what was the initial IP address assigned to eth0? How would you delete the assignment of the address 192.168.1.100 to eth0 during this session?

34. How would you ensure that the deletion persisted between system boots, after you have completed step 2 of the Example above?

35. How would you add more than just one new assignment of an IP address? Could you do this with the Network Manager via a GUI interface? How?

Conclusion: We assigned several IP addresses on our LAN for our Raspberry Pi 5 system.

1.15 System Security

There are two meanings of the word "security" relevant here, when referring to computers such as the Raspberry Pi 5. We will consider only one of them.

The first meaning denotes reliability. In other words, the files and data on the disks can be relied upon to be persistent over time. That is the objective of not only having persistent media but also of backing up the operating system itself, and the user files and data. For example, if the operating system crashes and cannot be brought back to the exact state it was before the crash, the user files and data are archived, secure, and can be recovered in total.

The second meaning denotes free from malicious intrusion by agents (such as robotic cracker programs) or objects (such as the processes that are the basis of program execution) that do <u>not</u> have the authority to access a specific part of the system, or any of its components, files, or data. The reasons for implementing system security in this second sense, both for an ordinary, single-user system and in a multi-user environment, should be very obvious to the beginner. Especially in the light of contemporary privacy issues, and the widespread hacking and system penetration forces prevalent on the Internet currently.

Since we've already dealt with the issues of persistent media in the previous sections, here in this section we deal primarily with the second meaning of computer security.

Fundamentally, according to this second meaning, there are at least four places where you can situate system security measures, as we show them in this section. They are as follows:

1. *At the Process Level*: You have to know and have a feel for the difference between "kernel space" and "user space". In a Linux system, **kernel space** is where the operating system's core functions execute with full access to hardware and system resources, ensuring security and stability. It includes drivers, process management, and memory handling. **User space**, on the other hand, is where applications run with restricted access, interacting with the kernel via system calls. This separation prevents user programs from directly affecting system stability and security. Therefore, the process model of the Raspberry Pi 5 OS makes this site most important. This model dictates security implemented on processes via authentication and credentialing techniques. Processes that are the basis for program execution and that bridge kernel and user spaces. Examples of these measures are:
   - Setting traditional UNIX permission bits (**rwx**), the special permission bits **SUID**, **SGID**, and the sticky bit. The setting of permission bits implies that the processes that shell commands create are the real objects that the permission bits files possess are aimed at or applied to. This is true of everything that creates processes in the Raspberry Pi 5 OS, which means user-written programs, and all other application programs and system programs as well.

- Deployment of ACL's, either extended POSIX1.e ACL's (which is the default implementation on the Raspberry Pi 5 OS) or NFSv4 ACL's.
- Use of Linux-specific "capabilities" applied to processes, as detailed in section 1.15.2.3.
- Namespace isolation of processes, using the Linux kernel namespace API, and the six major implementations of it.

2. *At the Physical Level*: When someone sits directly in front of the Raspberry Pi and tries to log in and use it. One of the ways that can be accomplished is through the use of password protection on user accounts. On a public computer system (which is kind of rare as far as we know for a Raspberry Pi 5!), this is the most valuable way to maintain general access security and user/account security. There are also many security techniques in this place that limit physical access to the hardware of the system, such as locking the door to the room where you keep the machine, or having protocols in place for limiting physical access to the machine.

3. *At the Network Level*: By placing safeguards on the computer's network connection. This is accomplished using various forms of not only monitoring with systemd **journalctl**, and using the many forms of intrusion detection, but also with intrusion prevention systems we illustrate below.

4. *At the Persistent Media Level*: On the persistent media attached, either physically or virtually, to the computer itself. These techniques are applied to the boot/system medium and other attached media, such as user data disks or mounted Network file systems(NFS). Examples of this are the use of virtualized "sandboxed" machines on traditional volumes, or on ZFS volumes, and the various domains of disk data encryption shown below.

Furthermore, the above sites use the following specific techniques. We will describe some of the important ones in the sections below. A further elaboration of some of these techniques is given in section 1.15.2.

- Password-based authentication
- Access control, either discretionary(DAC), mandatory(MAC), or role-based(RBAC)
- The **sudo** command
- Setting POSIX1.e ACL's and extended ACL's, and NFSv4 ACL's for files and directories
- Intrusion Detection and Intrusion Prevention
- Security Software
- ufw System Firewall

- Process Credentialing
- User namespace process isolation
- Whole disk, partition, directory, or file-level data encryption

1.15.1 Password-Based Authentication

The first line of defense in system security, and the technique employed almost universally across many types of computer systems, is password-based authentication. The Raspberry Pi 5 OS compares a user-entered password at login for a user's ID, compares the password to a previously established and stored one held in a password file for that user, and based on the comparison, either authenticates the user or denies access. The ID not only determines whether the user can gain access to the system itself, but also determines what privileges the user has. For example, superuser privilege. Also, the ID is used in Discretionary Access Control (DAC), as shown in section 1.15.2. The password file and a hash/salt scheme using a SHA256 hashing algorithm for encrypting the password work together to authenticate a user's ID. The password file on the system, in /etc/passwd, holds user information and works in conjunction with the /etc/shadow file to authenticate a user ID.

In-Chapter Exercise

36.   Examine the contents of the /etc/passwd file on your Raspberry Pi system. With reference to your username entry in that file, how many colon-delimited fields are there, and what are the meanings of those colon-delimited fields?

1.15.2 Access Control Credentials: Discretionary (DAC), Mandatory (MAC), and Role-Based (RBAC)

The terms we use in this section are important if you want to understand the different types of access control. When we talk about access control via security checks, here are the important terms:

Objects: A fundamental component of an executing kernel are the programs and processes it maintains. Objects are the entities that are targeted, or worked on, by the processes of a program. For example, processes themselves can be objects, or the processes that are generated by executing instances of a program.

Files/inodes are another form of object, particularly the executable form of file objects, and the data structure(s) holding their information. You shouldn't mix this up with file system objects, which we have referred to as either ordinary or directory.

Object Ownership: Indicates the owning, user, and group.

Object Context: Security checks are done when objects are acted on.

Subjects: An object that is acted upon by another object. Processes are active subjects, such as those processes that are created by an **exec()** or **fork()** system call from some originating process.

Subject Context: Security checks are done when an active subject performs its operations.

Action: What a subject does to an object. This includes reading, writing, creating, deleting files, or forking and signaling.

Permissions: Security checks when a subject acts upon an object. Taking the subject context, the object context, and the action, and searching one or more sets of permissions to see whether the subject is granted, or denied permission to act in the intended way on the object, given those contexts. In simple terms, match subject and object permissions, and let the subject act, or not, on the object.

There are three basic "classes" of permissions. These are:

1. Discretionary Access Control (DAC):
   Sometimes the object will include sets of rules as part of its description. This is an "Access Control List" or "ACL". A file may supply more than one ACL. A traditional Linux file, for example, includes a permissions mask that is an abbreviated ACL with three fixed classes of subject ("user", "group", and "other"), each of which may be granted certain privileges ("read", "write", and "execute" – or whatever those map to for the object in question). Linux file permissions do not allow the arbitrary specification of subjects, however, and so are of limited use.

   A Linux file might also support a POSIX1e ACL, or an NFSv4 ACL. These are a list of rules that grant various permissions to arbitrary subjects.

2. Mandatory access control (MAC):
   The system as a whole may have one or more sets of permissions that get applied to all subjects and objects, regardless of their source. Security Extended Linux (SELinux) is an example of this.

3. Role-Based Access Control (RBAC):
   Rather than use the user ID to find out what access rights users and groups have on the system, the Role-Based Access Control (RBAC) model gives access based on the role, or roles that a user assumes. The classic RBAC example is the use of the **su** or **sudo** commands to grant an unprivileged user root privileges, in a transient way. Another example can be found in ZFS, when you execute the **zfs** command, and your action is checked to see that the subject issuing the command has the role privilege, <u>even if the user is root</u>.

These classes of access control policies determine what action is allowed on what object, under what circumstances (DAC, MAC, or Role-Based Access Control (RBAC)), and by what subject. A permission in the traditional UNIX/ Linux sense, for example, is **rwx** (read, write, or execute privilege). A subject, for example, can be thought of as an executing process.

****Note****

Most importantly, an object can be thought of as a Linux process, since everything done on files and the data in them is done through active processes on the system.

In-Chapter Exercises

37. What major apparatus controls the execution of processes in the Raspberry Pi 5 OS?
38. Give other examples of DAC, MAC, and RBAC.

On the command line, an ordinary user or the system administrator is able to implement resource use restrictions and privileges by controlling process credential assignments, levied on subject executable image files, via the **chmod** command. An ordinary unprivileged user can be given the required privileged role with the **su** or **sudo** command. Then, as root, she can issue a privileged **chmod**, **chown**, and **chgrp** to grant, or modify file and directory access permissions, and use the DAC, MAC, or RBAC methods.

1.15.2.1 Types of Credentials

We are concerned with the three basic types of credentials that the Linux kernel supports. These are as follows.

Traditional UNIX Credentials

1. Real User ID
2. Real Group ID
   UID and GID are assigned to most objects. These mostly define the object context of that object, with processes included in this assignment.
3. Effective (EUID), Saved (SUID) and FS (FSID) User ID
4. Effective (EGID), Saved (SGID) and FS (FSGID) Group ID
5. Supplementary groups

The additional credentials used by processes are EUID/EGID/GROUPS, and are used as the subject context, and real UID/GID will be used as the object context.

1.15.2.2 ACL's (Access Control Lists)

ACLs provide the ordinary, unprivileged user with the ability to set finer access controls on directories and files than the traditional permissions, whether they are used on ext4, or ZFS file systems. Two different basic types of ACL apply to files and directories. An ACL that defines the current access permissions of files and directories is called an *access* ACL. An ACL, which can only logically be set on a directory, and that defines the permissions that a directory object inherits from its parent directory at the time of its creation, is called a *default* ACL. Additional basic types of ACL are *minimal* and *extended* ACLs. ACL permissions that can be equivalent to the traditional file mode permissions are called *minimal ACLs*. Minimal ACLs have three entries, which can be the same as the traditional file permissions. ACLs with more than three entries are called extended ACLs. Extended ACLs also contain a mask entry and may contain any number of named user and named group entries.

****Note****

Unfortunately, at the time of the writing of this book, the Raspberry Pi 5 OS and the POSIX.1e ACL model that it supports, does not easily allow for the interoperability, in terms of Network file system, version 4(NFSv4) ACLs, between Linux and non-Linux servers and clients.

For example, if a Linux user were to mount an NFSv4 ACL-compliant file system as an NFS shared resource, the default POSIX.1e implementation on Linux would not be able to take advantage of the NFSv4 ACL model of that file system. As noted above, that restriction is true even if a user were to install a special tool, **nfs4-acl-tools**, in addition to enabling NFS server facilities on the remote system, and client facilities on her Linux system. That is necessarily a more advanced application of ACLs. Another very practical limitation in this respect is virtualization with LXC/LXD containers. If you create LXC/LXD containers, on the Linux host for those containers, the NFSv4 ACLs could not be used on LXD container file objects.

Additionally, ACLs are <u>not</u> retained by the **tar** command.

1.15.2.3 Capabilities

Sets of capabilities are as follows:

1. Set of permitted capabilities
2. Set of inheritable capabilities
3. Set of effective capabilities
4. Capability bounding set

These are most pertinent when they apply to processes, which are the active elements in system operation. They are privileged permissions exercised in a "finer-grained" context. Finer-grained is used here to mean a more specific, targeted privilege. These are applied to a process, or processes that ordinarily, via the traditional model, could only be granted a blanket, all-or-nothing scheme of privileges. Putting a user in the sudoers file is an example of this traditional model's application.

Capabilities are controlled by changes in the traditional **rwx** permissions, but can also be set more finely and viewed directly by the **capset** and **getcap** system calls.

See the man page for capabilities on your system for further information about capabilities.

In-Chapter Exercise

39. How (and why) do you apply Linux capabilities on the command line? Provide an example of this, that you have implemented and tested on your Raspberry Pi 5 system.

1.15.3 sudo

In the Raspberry Pi 5 OS, programs, commands, and files are accessed through user and group permissions. Each user has a unique identifier, given as a username, or **UID**. Users belong to unique groups, given either as a group name or a **GID**. Specific users and groups have permission to access available programs, commands, and files.

The **sudo** program, or command, allows a single command to be run as the root user, or superuser, <u>or even as some other user</u>. Only the system administrator, or root user, can utilize a policy listing file (named *sudoers*) that contains commands that each user can execute. So the administrator controls what users have what privileges on the system. When any user needs to run a command that requires root permissions, that user types **sudo command** in a terminal window or console, allowing them to run **command** with root privileges. Then, **sudo** consults its permissions list in the policy listing file. If the user has permission to run that command, it runs the command. If the user does not have permission to run the command, **sudo** denies execution. Running **sudo** does not require knowing root's password, but by default requires entry of the user's own password to execute successfully.

An example of the use of the **sudo** command on our Raspberry Pi 5 system is as follows;

```
bob@raspberrypi:~ $ sudo -i
root@raspberrypi:~#
root@raspberrypi:~# exit
bob@raspberrypi:~ $
```

The **su** command (an abbreviation for "switch user") allows a user to switch roles and become the superuser on the system without logging off from their own account. You must know the password of the root account if you want to assume the role of root. On a Raspberry Pi 5 system, this command is restricted, and you are encouraged to include users that need to have higher levels of privilege on the system in the sudoers file. That way they can only execute privileged operations on a per-command basis.

In-Chapter Exercises

40. Are you included in the sudoers group and file on your Raspberry Pi 5 system? How did you find out if you are?

41. Enter some unprivileged user on your Raspberry Pi 5 system into the sudoers file. Then have them test the **sudo** command and its operation, as we have shown it in the above section.

42. Is the **su** command available for your use on your Raspberry Pi 5 system? Why or why not?

1.15.4 Intrusion Detection and Prevention Systems

A conceptual layout of how malicious activity from outside of the Raspberry Pi 5 OS interfaces through the components of a system is given in Figure 1.12. It is important to realize that Figure 1.12 does not specify the multitude of types of attack that can intrude upon your system from a LAN or the Internet, but does show the arrangement of system components that

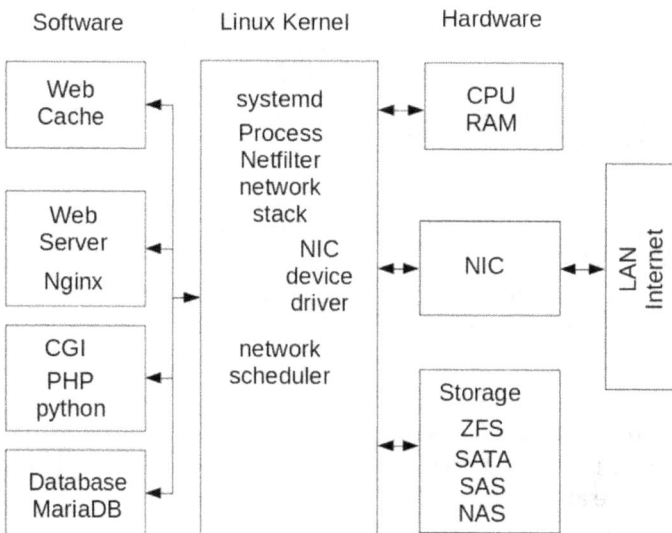

FIGURE 1.12
Routes of attack and system components.

these attacks can target. It also does not show where in the software, kernel, or hardware any defensive or preventative mechanisms are placed.

In-Chapter Exercises

43. Where would a Russian bot be situated in Figure 1.12?
44. What is the Red Team Field Manual (RTFM)? What is the Blue Team Field Manual (BTFM)? What is Pen testing? Why would you need to either or both of these manuals in the context of Pen testing?

An Intrusion Detection System (IDS) is a software application that monitors a network, or a single system, for unauthorized activity, or user protocol violations. It is situated on a software-specific interface, and its output is seen using log file monitoring. A wide variety of free or commercial IDS, from antivirus software to hierarchical systems that monitor the traffic of a backbone network, are available. They can be classified as Network Intrusion Detection Systems (NIDS), or as Host Intrusion Detection Systems (HIDS). An IDS that monitors operating system files is an example of a HIDS. An IDS that analyzes incoming network traffic is an example of a NIDS. Also, IDS can be classified by detection strategy. The most well-known types of detection strategies are signature-based detection (recognizing bad patterns, such as malware), and anomaly-based detection (detecting deviations from a predefined model of "good" traffic, which uses a form of Artificial Intelligence (AI). IDS that have some pre-determined and structured response protocol are referred to as Intrusion Prevention Systems (IPS).

A typical network intrusion detection system tries to detect malicious activity, such as a brute force attack, a denial of service attack, port scans, or attempts to crack into computers by monitoring network traffic.

Following is a partial listing of some free IDS available for installation, but not installed by default, on our Raspberry Pi system:

- AIDE is a HIDS that can monitor and analyze the internals of the operating system.
- Snort is a NIDS that performs packet logging and real-time traffic analysis on IP networks.
- fail2ban is an example of an IPS. One of the configurations it takes is based upon malicious activity coming into your system from a LAN, or the Internet, and locks out IP addresses that attempt to log in via ssh more than five times with the wrong password. This prevents brute force attacks through port 22.
- Wireshark is a network "sniffer", a tool that captures and analyzes packets off the wire. Wireshark can decode too many protocols to list here.

These four IDS are available via APT, or the Raspberry Pi 5 Menu Preferences > Add/Remove Software. The best way to find out more about the particulars of installing and configuring them is by reading their online documentation and tutorials.

In-Chapter Exercises

45. Install one or all of the above IDS packages on your system, using the package management system available. How do you deploy fail2ban, and how do you control its environment? For example, how do you "unblock" an IP address using fail2ban? Test this on your Raspberry Pi 5 system.

46. What are the capabilities and uses of Wireshark? Give a description of it in terms of the IDS's we describe above, and then install Wireshark and use it on your system.

1.15.5 Linux Security Software

All larger Linux computer server systems, as well as individual Raspberry Pi 5 desktop systems used by an ordinary user, can have several types of network-based and host-based security software available to detect malicious activity, protect systems and data, support intrusion detection, and the responses to them. They can be organized into the following categories:

- Intrusion Detection and Intrusion Prevention Systems
- Remote Access Software
- Web Proxies
- Vulnerability Management Software
- Authentication Servers
- Routers
- Firewalls
- Network Quarantine Servers

We covered some of the details of Intrusion Detection, and also gave a more complete description of Firewalls in the next section.

1.15.5.1 System Firewall

A firewall is a facility that prevents unauthorized access to or from a private network or a computer. Firewalls can be implemented in either hardware, software, or in both. Firewalls are mainly used to halt unauthorized access to a private network or intranet, from the Internet. All traffic entering or leaving a single computer, or intranet, passes through the firewall, which can look at each message packet stream, and block those that do not meet specific security requirements set by the system administrator. These requirements are codified in what are known as *firewall rules*.

In addition to limiting access to your computer and network, a firewall is also useful for allowing remote access to a private network through secure authentication certificates and logins. A common practice is to let a stand-alone computer serve as a single hardware firewall to a private network. Hardware firewalls can be purchased as a stand-alone product. They can also be found integral to broadband routers. Most hardware firewalls will have a minimum of four network connectors to link them to other computers, but for larger networks, there are business networking firewall solutions.

ufw (Uncomplicated Firewall) is <u>not</u> loaded by default on the Raspberry Pi 5 OS. However, you can easily install and enable it. To install and enable **ufw** on Raspberry Pi 5, do the following:

1. Install **ufw** with APT.
   Open a terminal and type the following command:

   $ sudo apt update && sudo apt install ufw -y
   Output truncated…
   $

2. Enable **ufw**.
   Start and enable ufw with:

   $ sudo ufw enable

3. Allow Essential Services.
   Before enabling, ensure ssh, and any other service you need to come through the firewall, are allowed (if using ssh to connect):

   $ sudo ufw allow from any to any port 22 proto tcp

4. Check Status
   Verify **ufw** is running with the following command:

   $ sudo ufw status verbose
   sudo ufw status verbose
   Status: active
   Logging: on (low)
   Default: deny (incoming), allow (outgoing), disabled (routed)
   New profiles: skip

To	Action	From
22/tcp	ALLOW IN	Anywhere
22/tcp (v6)	ALLOW IN	Anywhere (v6)
   $

5. (Optional) Enable **ufw** on Boot
To ensure **ufw** starts on boot:

$ sudo systemctl enable ufw

Now your Raspberry Pi 5 will have **ufw** running and protecting your network.

The Raspberry Pi 5 OS uses Uncomplicated Firewall, or **ufw**, to protect the system. The default configuration file for its rules is located in /etc/ufw/ufw.conf. The easiest way for you to find out more about text-based modifications to firewall rules is to see the **ufw** man page on your system.

It is not absolutely necessary to change the **ufw** firewall rules, unless your security model, and its impact on your particular use case, warrants firewall rule customization. We do provide a general overview of **ufw** in the next section.

In the Raspberry Pi 5 OS, if the firewall is *active* (enabled, or running), incoming traffic from the network is usually blocked until you specify a TCP or UDP port that traffic is allowed to come in on. Also, usually all outgoing traffic on all ports is allowed. In the next sections we describe the Uncomplicated FireWall (**ufw**).

To determine whether the firewall is active, use the following systemd command on your Raspberry Pi system:

$ systemctl status ufw
Status: active

To	Action	From
22/tcp	ALLOW	Anywhere
22/tcp (v6)	ALLOW	Anywhere (v6)
$		

Note

Be very careful when adding custom rules or modifying the firewall, it may endanger your system's security!

In-Chapter Exercise

47. Is **ufw** active on your system? Are there any firewall rules in effect by default, and what are they? How did you find this out?

1.15.5.2 ufw Basic Syntax

An abbreviated listing of the **ufw** man page is as follows:

****

ufw
Purpose:
> **ufw** is used to manage a Linux firewall, and provides an easy to use interface for the creation of firewall rules. The rules use a basic syntax as shown below.

Syntax:
> **ufw [option[s]] [command] [rule[s]]**

Output: New, modified, or deleted firewall rules to/from ports/ IP addresses, or devices.

Common Options:

--version	show program's version number and exit
-h, --help	show help message and exit
--dry-run	don't modify anything, just show the changes

Common Commands:

enable	reloads firewall and enables firewall on boot.
disable	unloads firewall and disables firewall on boot
reload	reloads firewall rules
default	change the default connection policy
logging	toggle and affect logging to journalctl
reset	disables and resets firewall to defaults
status	show status of firewall and rules
allow	add a valid allow rule
deny	add a valid deny rule
reject	add a valid reject rule
limit	add a valid limit rule
delete	deletes a valid by specification
insert	inserts a valid rule as a numbered rule

Common Rules:

ufw allow 22	allow tcp and udp port 22 to any IP address on a valid NIC
ufw deny proto tcp to any port 80	deny all connections to tcp port 80
ufw allow in on enp2s0 to 192.168.0.6 proto tcp	allow tcp connections through enp2s0 nic to IP address 192.168.0.6
ufw limit ssh/tcp	allow rate limiting on ssh to prevent brute-force attacks
ufw delete deny 80/tcp	delete the rule denying tcp connections on port 80
ufw delete 3	delete rule 3, number determined with the status command

****

1.15.6 Persistent Media Security

There are two basic strategies a system administrator can take to secure the persistent media, such as NMVe SSDs, or USB3-mounted media, and also to harden the file system structure on those media. The actual techniques of these two strategies overlap considerably with the other system administration tasks we have shown in the other sections of this chapter.

An example of an overlapping technique is found in the adding of additional media to the system, perhaps using ZFS to provide redundancy on the media per the recommended storage model that we have shown. This allows a system administrator to segregate the user files from other components of the system. That segregation provides a way of isolating those resources, and therefore allows them to be more securely accessed. And adding additional media addresses the administrator's responsibility to back up important data, most critically user data files.

The first strategy involves providing additional physical media, or additional partitions on existing media, to accommodate user data files or other components of your Raspberry Pi 5 OS file system.

The second strategy involves designing and implementing file and directory access permissions on those additional partitions or media, so that process authentication through the various forms of process credentialing can be achieved.

1.15.6.1 Persistent Media Allocations For /home

According to the recommended user data storage model we provided above, you should put the /home sub-directories, where all of your user directories are located, on its own physical medium. That is a traditional system administration technique for designing your file system structure. When you add mount options to a single formatted partition on this medium, you can do the following:

- Set the nosuid option to prevent SUID and SGID permission-enabled executable programs running from there. Programs that need SUID and SGID permissions should not be stored in /home, as a preventative measure.

- Set the nodev option so no device file located there will be recognized. Device files should be stored in /dev, not in /home.

- Optionally set the noexec option, so no executable programs which are stored in /home can be run.

In-Chapter Exercise

48. You are tasked by your boss to migrate all of the *home directories of all users on your system off their default location on a microSD-based boot*/system medium, to a NMVe SSD installation on the same Raspberry Pi 5. Sketch a detailed plan of exactly how you would do this, using the migration of a single user as an example. Show all commands you would use to achieve the migration, and successfully delete the old /home directory for that user's account.

1.15.7 Process Credentials

The multi-programming model requires that processes, whether they are generated by shell built-ins, external commands, user-written programs, or by any system programs that use the **fork**, **exec**, or **execve** system calls, have their credentials authenticated <u>before</u> they can make use of objects such as system resources, other processes, sockets, or files/inodes.

General Linux systems assign credentials to processes, which associate the process with a specific user and a specific group. These credentials are essential in a multi-user and multi-programming system because they determine what each process can or cannot do in user space and in kernel space, maintaining the autonomy and the security of each user's personal data, and by extension the stability of the system.

The use of credentials is applied in the process data structure and in the shared resources that the processes are trying to access. This is similar to a key and a set of tumblers in a lock. Files are the critical resource on the system. Thus, in the default ext4 file system, each file is owned by a specific user and belongs to a group of users. The owner of a file determines what kind of operations are allowed on that file, distinguishing among herself, the file's user group, and all other users on the system. When a process tries to make use of a file, the Linux Virtual File System (VFS) always validates whether the access is allowed or not, according to the permissions established by the file owner and the process credentials. Process credentials and file access permissions are integrated and inseparable. This authentication coupling is based upon the forms of file permissions we have detailed so far. We have shown that the **chmod** command is the instrument for granting these permissions to files and directories.

1.15.7.1 File Permission-based Mechanisms

In file-based permission mechanisms, those forms involve managing the basic permission bits on files and directories, and the SetUID (SUID), the SetGID (SGID), and sticky bit permissions. Examples include setting permissions using DAC on the /usr/bin/passwd, and /usr/bin/sudo commands. Each of these files should maintain their SUID permissions, as shown in the following output:

```
$ sudo ls -la /usr/bin/passwd
-rwsr-xr-x 1 root root 72048 Mar 23  2023 /usr/bin/passwd
$ sudo ls -la /usr/bin/sudo
-rwsr-xr-x 1 root root 269312 Jun 27  2023 /usr/bin/sudo
$
```

The commands **passwd** and **sudo** are SUID-capable programs. Even though those commands are ostensibly run with root user privilege, a non-privileged user can only change their own password with the **passwd** command, and can only assume root privileges with **sudo**. That is, if they are given privilege to do so in the /etc/sudoers file!

The **find** command allows you to search your system to see if there are any hidden or otherwise inappropriate SUID and SGID commands on your system. Following is an example:

```
$ sudo find / -perm /6000 -ls
131733    4 drwxrwsr-x  2 root   staff            4096 Oct 31 04:04 /var/local
131735    4 drwxrwsr-x  2 root   mail             4096 Nov 19 05:30 /var/mail
132592    4 drwxr-sr-x  3 root   systemd-journal  4096 Nov 19 05:43 /var/log/journal
280612    4 drwxr-sr-x  2 root   systemd-journal  4096 Mar  3 14:26 /var/log/journal/...
130355    4 drwxr-s---  2 root   dip              4096 Nov 19 05:33 /etc/ppp/peers
129824    4 drwxr-s---  2 root   dip              4096 Nov 19 05:33 /etc/chatscripts
Output truncated...
```

The **find** command reveals SetUID and SetGID commands that unprivileged users can run to assume the privileged role.

In-Chapter Exercise

49. Use the **find** command to list any hidden or inappropriate SUID and SGID commands on your Raspberry Pi 5 system.

1.15.8 Disk Encryption

When the ordinary user wants to do disk encryption for security purposes, the most critical thing is the scope of encryption she wants to implement. For example, she can encrypt the entire boot/system medium she is installing the Raspberry Pi 5 OS on, at the time she installs the system. Or she can do a post-installation encryption of an entire 1 TB NVMe SSD, selected partitions on it, selected directories, or individual files. What establishes the scope of encryption depends a great deal on the particular use case. It is critical to know why you want to do encryption when considering all of the possible strategies of encrypting your persistent media.

1.15.8.1 The Meaning of Encryption

Encryption uses a very developed science, known as *cryptography*, to implement data hiding. Cryptography is used on a Raspberry Pi 5 system to encode data to hide it from unprivileged users, and then decrypt, or decode the data for privileged users. On the Raspberry Pi 5 OS, the following are some of the objects that can be possible targets for encryption:

Individual files

Volumes or individual partitions

Web page connections

Network connections

Backup file objects on additional hard disks or other media

Compressed directories or files

Encryption/decryption basically uses a variety of mathematical algorithms to treat the above targets. These algorithms are called *cryptographic ciphers*. The important terms to know when dealing with cryptography are *plain text* and *cypher text*. Plain text is the unencrypted, or decrypted format, and cypher text is the encrypted format.

The details of encryption algorithms, their mathematics, and complexity are not as useful to the ordinary user as knowing where and when to apply them. That is, at the system, whole disk, partition, directory, or individual file levels. And also knowing why you want to use them, and carefully reasoning and designing your strategies for implementing these algorithms with the common command-line tools.

In-Chapter Exercise

50. Which of the encryption strategies, entire disk, selected partitions, selected directories, or individual files, would you deploy on your Raspberry Pi 5 system, and for what specific reasons? After deciding upon one, or even multiple encryption strategies on your system that you would want to use, implement those strategies.

1.16 Virtualization Methodologies

As stated earlier, the three governing functions that the Linux kernel performs in order to maintain the system in a steady state are Virtualization, Concurrency, and Secure Persistence.

At a certain level of abstraction, the kernel itself, and its global resources, are virtualized by systemd.

In this section, we introduce *namespaces* and LXC/ LXD, both of which also do forms of "virtualizing".

Historically speaking, to perform the kernel functions of Virtualization and Concurrency, the multiprogramming paradigm was established. Multiprogramming is a computer system model where the computer hardware and software are shared by several programs (and users) running and working on the system simultaneously. This led to the need for autonomy and sharing among programs. The needs of multiprogramming are closely tied to the concept of "virtual memory" in computers as well. In turn, this virtualization of memory is directly related to the virtualization of the entire operating system itself, as we describe it in this chapter.

Computer hardware virtualization is the simulation, to various degrees, of hardware platforms, parts of them, or only the functionality required to run one or more operating systems ("OS's"). It abstracts and effectively "hides" the physical characteristics of the hardware from the users. Traditionally, the software that controlled virtualized machines was known as the *hypervisor*. Currently, the hypervisor is often called a Virtual Machine Monitor (VMM).

Platform virtualization is accomplished on any given hardware by host software (the hypervisor), which creates a simulated computer environment, a VM, for its guest software. The guest software can be as small as a single user application or even as large as a complete OS. The guest software executes as if it were running directly on the physical hardware.

Virtualization comes with some performance disadvantages, both in resources required to run the hypervisor, and in reduced performance on the VM guest compared with running applications on a non-virtualized host physical machine. A VM can be more easily controlled and inspected from outside than a physical one, and its configuration is more flexible. This is very useful in kernel development and for teaching OS courses. A new VM can be implemented as needed without the need for an up-front hardware purchase. A VM can easily be moved from one physical machine to another as needed. An unrecoverable fault inside a VM guest does not harm the host system, so there is no risk of crashing the host OS.

Examples of virtualization implementations are as follows:

- Running one or more applications that are not supported by the host OS: A VM running the required guest OS could allow the desired applications to be run, without altering the host OS.

- Evaluating an alternate OS: The new OS could be run within a VM, without altering the host OS.

- Server virtualization: Multiple virtual servers, in what are often referred to as "containers", could be run on a single physical server to utilize more fully the hardware resources of the physical server. A cloud computing example of this is Amazon Web Services Elastic Cloud Computing (AWS EC2) virtual servers.

- Duplicating specific environments: A VM could, depending on the virtualization software used, be duplicated and installed on multiple hosts, or restored to a previously backed-up system state.

- Creating a protected environment: If a guest OS running on a VM becomes damaged in a way that is difficult to repair, such as may occur when testing, the VM can be discarded without harm to the host system, and a clean copy used next time.

Primary actual contemporary virtualization techniques are as follows:

- Full virtualization: In full virtualization, the VM simulates enough hardware to allow a complete "guest" OS, one designed for the same processor instruction set architecture (ISA) to be run in isolation. Examples for Linux systems running on X86 ISAs or ARM architectures include VirtualBox, Parallels Workstation, Oracle VM, Virtual Server, Hyper-V, VMware Workstation, and VMware.

- Hardware-assisted virtualization: In hardware-assisted virtualization, the hardware provides architectural support that facilitates building a VMM and allows guest OS's to be run in isolation. Examples of virtualization platforms adapted to such hardware include KVM, VMware Workstation, VMware Fusion, Hyper-V, Xen, Oracle VM server for SPARC, and VirtualBox.

- Partial virtualization: In partial virtualization, including address space virtualization, the VM simulates multiple instances of much of an underlying hardware environment, particularly address spaces.

- Paravirtualization: In paravirtualization, the VM does not necessarily simulate hardware, but instead (or in addition) offers a special application programmer's interface (API) that can only be used by modifying the "guest" OS. For this to be possible, the "guest" OS's source code must be available.

- OS-level virtualization: In OS-level virtualization, a physical server is virtualized at theOS level, enabling multiple isolated and secure virtualized servers to run on a single physical server. The "guest" OS environments share the same running instance of the OS as the host system. Thus, the same OS kernel is also used to implement the "guest" environments, and applications running in a given "guest" environment view it as a stand-alone system. In Linux, examples include LXC and LXD, and their derivative management system, Docker. Similar proprietary derived techniques are used by AWS EC2, Google Cloud, and iCloud.

A virtual environment for a computer program, and for an operating system, can be simply thought of as a shell within which the program functions autonomously. And as we have shown earlier, one of the parts of looking at an operating system at a certain level of abstraction is the ability of the operating system to present the illusion of virtual environments. A multitasking, multi-programming operating system, where all users are presented with this illusion that each individual user is working autonomously on her own discreet computer (when in fact many people might also be working on the same hardware platform), is a basic underlying aspect of operating system virtualization. In many respects, and at some other level of abstraction, systemd can be thought of as a virtualizing program. It virtualizes the

Linux kernel and gives you the illusion that you are working directly with it, when in fact you are working in the systemd environment. That way of looking at the systemd "super kernel", and the Linux kernel itself, most importantly assumes that the function of these two programs is to help maintain the steady state of the hardware and software as the power is turned on, the system is running, or it becomes necessary to have the power turned off. In Chapter 2, we give a complete and detailed description of systemd and its operation.

In LXC/LXD containers, any number of different kernels can be running simultaneously on one host machine. That means that for LXC/LXD containers, you can be running many different distributions of operating systems at the same time on one machine.

There are other similar virtualization facilities available for the Raspberry Pi 5 OS. Docker is another container application suite that allows you to "spin up" container instances that are lightweight, in terms of the disk space they occupy. A typical example of one of these lightweight Docker container instances is the web server software nginx. In terms of disk space occupied in general, the lightest weight facility is a Docker container, the middleweight is an LXC/LXD container, and the heavyweight is a VirtualBox guest.

Both LXC/LXD and Docker rely upon the namespaces system programming API and the **clone**(2) system call. We briefly mentioned namespaces above.

1.16.1 Virtualization Applications

The important application of LXC/LXD containers, in the context of system administration, is to provide a measure of system security. For example, it is possible, using LXC containers, to isolate a system service or application program in a guest operating environment, completely autonomous from the host operating system. A service like an SSH server can be run inside of an LXC/LXD container instance, and anything that intrudes upon that server and its system space does not intrude upon the host operating system space. If LAN or Internet traffic to and from the server is compromised in any way, the server can be stopped, restarted, or even deleted, without affecting the host operating system. Another example would be if a faulty, bug-ridden application program were run in an LXC/LXD container instance, it could bring the guest operating system kernel to a halt without in any way affecting the host operating system. Those two example cases are probably the most useful aspects of maintaining a virtual environment, but there are others.

In addition, another application of these methodologies is to allow you to use and experiment with different operating systems on a single piece of hardware. You can play with these other operating systems in a "sandbox", which is isolated from your host system and can access that host system *simultaneously* with the virtualized environments.

In-Chapter Exercise

51. What is KVM, and how does it compare to the virtualization applications we describe in this section? Which cloud-based system deploys KVM? Answer this question in terms of the type of virtualization, size of a virtual machine instances, ease of use, and speed of execution of virtual machine instances. Compare these KVM criteria to LXC/LXD containers, and Google Cloud and Amazon EC2 instances.

1.17 Summary

In this chapter, we use a "learning-by-doing" approach to accomplish the following common system administration tasks on the Raspberry Pi 5 OS:

1. Do various kinds of installations of a 64-bit version onto desktop systems, and do a preliminary configuration of those hardware systems and the OS.

2. Illustrate booting strategies and how to gracefully bring the system down.

3. Detail the basics of using systemd to manage system services.

4. Add additional users and groups to the system, and show how to design and maintain user accounts.

5. Adding persistent media to the system, in particular externally-mounted USB3 SSDs and NMVe SSDs. We also established a framework for connecting and maintaining the file system on that media, which classified the file system as either existing on a physical medium (physically connected to the computer) or a virtual medium (NFSv4, iSCSI).

6. Provide strategies using traditional and generic commands to backup and archive the system files and user files.

7. Update and maintain the operating system, and add/upgrade/remove user application package repository software to both increase functionality and upgrade existing packages.

8. Monitor the performance of the system and tune it for optimal performance characteristics.

9. Provide strategies for system security to harden the individual desktop computer.

10. Provide network connectivity strategies, both on a LAN and the Internet.

11. Give an overview of system virtualization, using LXD/LXC.

2

Applications of systemd for the Beginner

id -u, journalctl, ncat, nmap, systemctl, systemd-activate, systemd-cgls, systemd-socket-activate, who -r

2.0 Objectives and Introduction

1. Describe the systemd "superkernel", sub-commands, applications, and its development
2. Expose and emphasize the importance of systemd units and unit files
3. Dissect the anatomy of a unit file, with a specific example
4. Show how to create instance units from unit template files
5. Describe systemd targets, their variety, and their utility
6. Give a specific systemd target example – running a clock-time-based script
7. Add to the repertoire of unit management commands
8. Provide much additional practice with target units to the novice user
9. Illustrate how to switch the system between important target states
10. Expand our coverage of Linux cgroups, in the context of a systemd environment
11. Briefly mention the Linux kernel namespace concept
12. Define and expound upon the systemd journal daemon, journald
13. How to view system logs with the **journalctl** command
14. How to maintain the journal, and execute various boot process querying
15. Give further examples of systemd-controlled timers
16. Illustrate the activation behavior of "new-style" daemons
    To cover the Commands and Primitives:

    id -u, journalctl, ncat, nmap, systemctl, systemd-activate, systemd-cgls, systemd-socket-activate, who -r

DOI: 10.1201/9781003652427-3

2.1 Applications of systemd for the Beginner

In this chapter, we give a novice user a brief, but useful, introduction to the Linux "superkernel" known as systemd. Unless that novice user, or even a more seasoned system professional, has not only a basic but also a more complete knowledge of how systemd controls and oversees every process operation of the Raspberry Pi 5 OS, they will never be able to master administrating and implementing the kind of functionality that their use case(s) might ultimately require. Particularly for the user base on the system, and the demands that user base makes.

2.1.1 The Development of systemd and Its Integration into the Linux Ecosystem

The Linux operating system has undergone numerous changes since its inception in 1991. One of the most significant and controversial developments in recent years has been the introduction of systemd, an init system that replaces the traditional System V init and Upstart. One of the primary goals of systemd was to modernize and streamline system initialization and service management, but its adoption has sparked debate among developers and users alike. Here, we explore the development of systemd, its key features, integration into the Linux ecosystem, and the broader implications for the future of Linux.

2.1.1.1 The Background and Motivation for systemd

Before systemd, most Linux distributions relied on System V init, a system inherited from Unix that used *shell scripts* to start and manage services. While System V init was simple and well-understood, it had several limitations:

1. Sequential Startup: Services were started one after another, leading to long boot times.
2. Lack of Parallelization: With modern multi-core processors, the inability to start services in parallel meant inefficient resource utilization.
3. No Built-in Service Monitoring: If a service crashed, System V init had no mechanism to restart it automatically.
4. Complex Script-Based Configuration: Service management required shell scripting, making it difficult to maintain.

To address these shortcomings, some distributions experimented with alternative init systems. Upstart, developed by Canonical for Ubuntu, introduced event-driven service management but still relied on scripts and was not widely adopted outside Ubuntu. The need for a more efficient, feature-rich init system led to the development of systemd.

2.1.1.2 The Development of systemd

systemd was created by Lennart Poettering and Kay Sievers, developers at Red Hat, and was first released in 2010. It was designed from the ground up to take advantage of modern computing capabilities while providing robust service management. The name "system" follows the Unix naming convention, where "d" stands for "daemon".

The key design principles behind systemd include:

1. Parallelization: systemd starts services in parallel wherever possible, reducing boot time.
2. Socket and Bus Activation: Services are only started when they are needed, reducing resource consumption.
3. Service Supervision: systemd monitors services and restarts them if they fail.
4. Unified Configuration: Instead of shell scripts, systemd uses declarative unit files, which are simpler and easier to manage.
5. Integration with Linux Technologies: systemd incorporates features like cgroups (control groups) for resource management and journald for logging.

2.1.2 The Features and Functionality of systemd

As more fully explicated in the bulk of this chapter, here are the most important features and functions of systemd:

1. Unit Files
systemd replaces traditional init scripts with unit files, which define how services, mount points, devices, and other system components should be managed. These unit files are stored in:

/etc/stytemd/system and/usr/lib/systemd/system

Following is an example of a simple unit file for a service:

```ini
CopyEdit
[Unit]
Description=My Custom Service
After=network.target

[Service]
ExecStart=/usr/bin/myservice
```

```
Restart=always
User=nobody
```

```
[Install]
WantedBy=multi-user.target
```

This structured approach makes it easier to define dependencies and manage services.

2. Parallel and On-Demand Service Startup
Unlike System V init, which follows a rigid sequential process, systemd leverages dependency-based parallel startup. This means that if multiple services are independent of each other, they can start simultaneously. Additionally, socket-based activation allows systemd to start services only when they are first requested, improving efficiency.

3. Journald and Logging
systemd includes **journald**, a logging system that replaces the traditional syslog. It provides structured, indexed logs that allow for advanced filtering and searching.
   To view logs for a specific service:

```
$ journalctl -u myservice
```

   journald supports binary logs, which some users criticize for being harder to process with standard text-processing tools.

4. Cgroups Integration
systemd fully integrates with Linux control groups (cgroups), allowing fine-grained resource management for services. This ensures that runaway processes do not consume excessive system resources.
   For example, to limit a service's memory usage:

```
$ systemctl set-property myservice MemoryLimit=500M
```

5. Target-Based Boot Process
systemd replaces traditional runlevels with targets. Examples include:

- multi-user.target: Equivalent to runlevel 3 (text-based multi-user mode)
- graphical.target: Equivalent to runlevel 5 (GUI mode)
- rescue.target: Equivalent to single-user mode for system recovery

Switching between targets is easy:

```
$ systemctl isolate graphical.target
```

2.1.3 Integration of systemd into the Linux Ecosystem, and Its Adoption by Major Distributions

Since its release, systemd has been adopted by most major Linux distributions, including:

- Red Hat Enterprise Linux (RHEL)
- Fedora
- Debian Bookworm and Trixie, and downstream Raspberry Pi 5 OS
- Ubuntu
- Arch Linux
- openSUSE

The widespread adoption of systemd has led to a more consistent experience across different distributions. However, some projects, such as Devuan and Alpine Linux, have explicitly rejected systemd in favor of simpler init systems.

2.1.4 Integration with the Linux Kernel

While systemd is not part of the Linux kernel itself, it deeply integrates with kernel features. Some key integrations include:

- cgroups: systemd uses cgroups to manage service resources.
- namespaces: systemd leverages kernel namespaces for security and isolation.
- udev: The udev device manager, previously a separate project, is now part of systemd.

By tightly integrating with the kernel, systemd achieves a level of efficiency and control that was not possible with System V init.

2.1.5 The Future of systemd and the Raspberry Pi OS

Despite the controversy, systemd has established itself as the standard init system for most Linux distributions. Its active development continues to introduce new features, such as:

- systemd-homed: A feature for managing home directories in a portable way.
- systemd-oomd: A userspace out-of-memory daemon that proactively manages system memory.

The continued evolution of systemd suggests that it will remain central to Linux systems for years to come. While some distributions will continue to resist adoption, the efficiency and functionality of systemd make it difficult to ignore.

2.1.6 Advisory

Everything illustrated in this chapter, in the specific form (and the syntax of commands) found here, is explicitly applicable to the Raspberry Pi 5 OS.

The selective choices of subject matter are done according to the pedagogic needs of a beginner, as it follows from the system administration materials that precede it in the last chapter.

Anything that you are required to type on the command line is shown in **bold** type, always followed by pressing <Enter> on the keyboard.

2.2 Bootup in the Initial RAM Disk (initrd)

The initial RAM disk implementation (initrd) of the Raspberry Pi 5 OS can also be set up using systemd, and follows a prescribed structure. initrd is a scheme for loading a root file system, from a variety of possible sources, into memory, and it is used as part of the Raspberry Pi 5 OS startup process.

2.2.1 Querying the Boot Process

As shown in Section 2.6.2.6, the *systemd journald daemon* and journal give you the ability to view log records of how the system boots. In particular, it allows you to look at a log record of the current boot process and past boot processes with some specific command line tools, options, and their arguments. We refer you to Section 2.6.2.6 for a more complete treatment of the systemd journal and its capabilities with respect to booting logs.

2.3 systemd Units and Unit Files

systemd **unit files** are one of the most critical and ubiquitous features of systemd that a beginner needs to understand. In this section, we discuss more of the lower level functionality and application of systemd units and unit files.

2.3.1 Introduction to Units and Unit Files

In systemd, a unit refers to an object that changes the characteristics of the steady state of the Raspberry Pi 5 OS, or its normal operating condition. Units and unit files are the primary objects that systemd creates and manipulates with user commands such as **systemctl**. These objects are configured with files called unit files. We will introduce you to the different units that systemd can handle. We will also be covering some of the many "directives" that can be put in unit files in order to configure the way these objects handle resources on your system.

2.3.2 Roles systemd Units Play

Units and unit files take on a very standardized format, which we describe in detail because they are the primary instrument of user functionality and control in systemd. They enable you to manage system resources using the daemons, services, and utility commands, as shown in Figure 2.1. They are found schematically on the first two top levels of this figure.

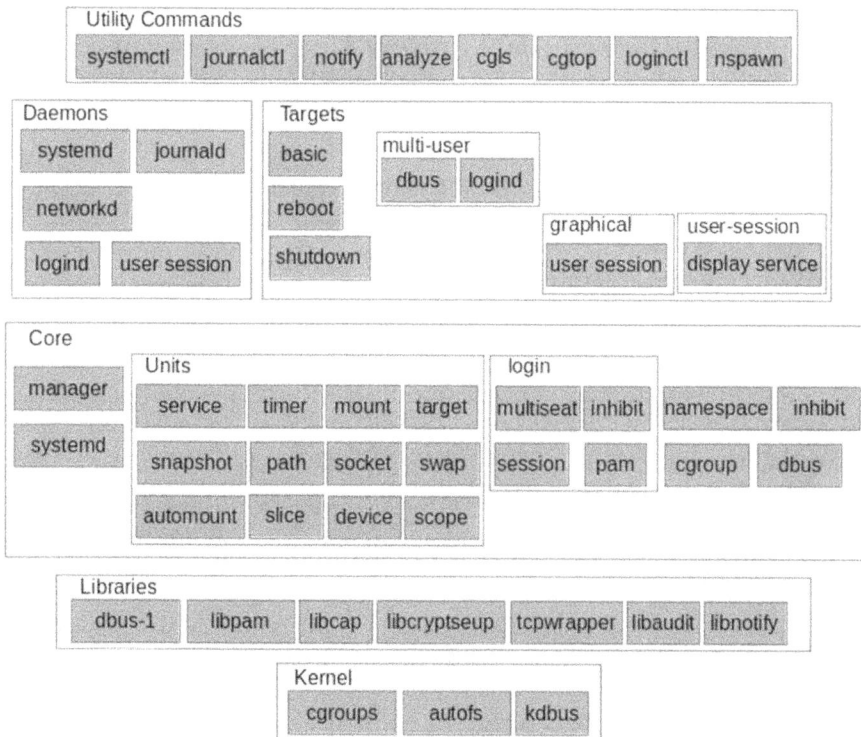

FIGURE 2.1
systemd Architecture.

A unit works with and affects traditional system services, network resources, devices, file system mounts, resource pools known as *Control Groups*, or *cgroups;* even very transient tasks such as single Raspberry Pi 5 OS terminal-executed commands, as shown in Chapter 0, and throughout this book!

Some of the key advantageous features that units have are:

1. Socket-based activation: The delay of the start of a service until activation of its socket(s). This feature is very crucial in making the system run faster, and the startup process itself much faster.

2. D-bus-based activation: Units can be started when an associated bus is published.

3. Path-based activation: A unit can be started based on activity on, or the availability of, certain filesystem paths.

4. udev device-based activation: The start of units can also be delayed until the first time a piece of hardware becomes available. This feature is also very crucial in making the system run faster and start up much faster.

5. Implicit dependency mapping: Most of the dependence between units, during their start time, can be built by systemd itself, although by editing and changing the dependencies between units, this can be modified by the user.

6. Instances and templates: Template unit files can be used to create multiple instances of the same general unit. This is very critical and efficient in operating system virtualization via containers and virtual machines!

7. Security: Units can implement security features via the use of directives in the unit file.

8. Drop-ins and snippets extensibility: Units can easily be extended by providing modifiers that will override parts of the system's unit files.

We address many of the above features in the following sections.

2.3.3 Unit File Locations in the Filesystem, and Editing or Modifying Them

Unit files are located in basically three different, very standardized locations in the Raspberry Pi 5 OS file system structure, depending on how important the unit file is.

Table 2.1 lists these default locations and gives a brief description of their utility.

Adding, or modifying a unit by editing it to modify the way that the unit functions, should be done by creating it in the /etc/systemd/system

TABLE 2.1

Unit File Locations

/etc/systemd/system	Place where unit files used to override default ones are stored.
/run/systemd/system	Middle-priority unit file location, the systemd process itself uses this location for dynamically created unit files created at runtime.
/lib/systemd/system	System copy where software using the unit file is installed. Also locates the default controlling unit file for the software.

directory. Unit files found in this directory location take precedence over any of the other locations.

If you need to modify the system's copy of a unit file, putting a replacement in this directory is the most reliable, safest, and flexible way to do this.

To override specific directives from the system's generic unit file, you create unit file "snippets", i.e., smaller versions, within a very standard and specific subdirectory. This will add to or modify the directives of the system's copy, allowing you to specify only the behavior of the unit you want to change. These systemd directives are what specify explicitly how the unit behaves.

To do this, you create a directory named after the unit file with **.d** appended to the name. For a unit called example.service, you create a subdirectory called example.service.d. Within this directory, a file ending with. conf can be used to override or add to the directives of the system's default unit file.

2.3.3.1 Editing Unit Files

Editing unit files is secondarily important to actually creating one from scratch, for a service that you want to create and run on the Raspberry Pi 5 system. We show how to create a unit file below. The premier systemd command, **systemctl**, provides options for editing and modifying unit files if you need to make adjustments. The **systemctl edit** command, by default, will open a unit file snippet for the unit in question.

For example, to further customize an nginx web server service, which has a unit file automatically created by the Aptitude package manager (APT) when nginx is installed on the Raspberry Pi 5 OS, you can use the following command:

$ **sudo systemctl edit nginx.service**

This will be a blank file that can be used to override or add directives on top of the existing service unit definition. A directory will be created within the /etc/systemd/system directory, which contains the name of the unit with .d appended. For instance, for the nginx.service, a directory called nginx. service.d will be created.

Within this directory, a snippet will be created called **override.conf**. When the unit is loaded, systemd will merge the override snippet with the full unit file. The snippet's directives will take precedence over those found in the original unit file.

To edit the full unit file, instead of creating a snippet, use the **--full** option:

```
$ sudo systemctl edit --full nginx.service
```

This will load the current unit file into the default editor, where it can be changed. When you exit the editor, the changed file will be written to /etc/systemd/system, which will take precedence over the system's unit definition found in /lib/systemd/system.

To remove any additions you have made, either delete the unit's .d configuration directory, or the modified service file from /etc/systemd/system. To remove a snippet, use the following command:

```
$ sudo rm -r /etc/systemd/system/nginx.service.d
```

To remove a full modified unit file, type:

```
$ sudo rm /etc/systemd/system/nginx.service
```

After deleting the file or directory, you should reload the systemd process so that it no longer attempts to reference these files and reverts back to using the system default copies.

You can do this with the following <u>very ubiquitous and critical command</u>:

```
$ sudo systemctl daemon-reload
```

In-Chapter Exercise

1. When you install the nginx web server, where does the installer locate the default copy of the service unit file? How did you find this out? If you haven't done the installation of nginx, either do that now, or answer this exercise with another service that you have installed.

2.3.4 Types of Units

systemd units, and the files that define them, are the primary mechanism that systemd uses to keep control of the system state. If you look at the suffix attached to a unit file, you can determine which of the 12 types of unit it is. The following list describes the types of units available to systemd:

1. .service: A service unit, which we detail most extensively below, describes how to manage a service or application on the system. Important things like what the path is to the executable code, how

the service starts or stops, when and how it should be automatically started, and dependencies and "order-of-starting" information are found here. These are also part of cgroup categories, as we detail in Section 2.6.1.

2. .socket: This defines network, IPC socket, or an FIFO buffer that is used for a socket-based activation. Socket-based activation means starting a service when the socket receives incoming traffic. This allows the starting of services in parallel, a very critical speedup procedure different from what has traditionally been available to init systems. We will provide examples of this below.

3. .device: Describes a device that requires systemd management by udev, or the sysfs filesystem. udev is a device manager for the Linux kernel, and manages device nodes in the /dev directory. It also manages user space events and hardware devices that are added into the system or removed from it.

4. .mount: Defines mountpoints on the system. These are assigned names after the mount path, with slashes changed to dashes in those names.

5. .automount: Defines a mountpoint that is automatically assigned. These must be named after the mount point they refer to, and have a matching .mount unit to define the actual details of the mount.

6. .swap: Defines swap space on the Raspberry Pi 5 OS. The name of these units comes from the device name or file pathname of the swap space.

7. .target: Provides a way of coordinating other units' operations when the system starts up or when there are changes in the system's state. A good example, that we describe in Section 2.5.3, is going from the multi-user.target state to the graphical.target state, and vice versa. We cover much of what can be done with targets in this chapter.

8. .path: Defines a path that can be used for path-based activation. Path-based activation allows the operating system to take actions if a particular file, group of files, or directory gets modified or changed somehow.

9. .timer: We illustrate these in detail in Section 2.6.3. They define timing controls that systemd uses when controlling system state.

10. .snapshot: Created automatically by the **systemctl snapshot** command. There is no unit file associated with snapshots. It allows you to reconstruct portions of the current state of the system after making changes. It's important to note that snapshots do <u>not</u> survive across reboots or restarts of the system, and are used essentially to roll back to temporary system states during the current boot.

11. .slice: Defined by Linux cgroup nodes, allowing system resources to be given to any processes associated with the named slice. These are also a crucial cgroup feature, detailed in Section 2.6.1.

12. .scope: Created automatically by systemd, using information from its bus interfaces. These are also a crucial cgroup feature, detailed in Section 2.6.1.

We will mainly be focusing on .service unit files, and their editing and creation, for the ordinary user of the Raspberry Pi 5 OS. This is due to the fact that they are most useful for an ordinary user, and the use cases she might put the system to. We will also detail, to some extent, their use by an appointed system administrator to manage the state of the system in general. Aside from .service unit files, all of the other unit file types are basically coordinating and synchronization tools that link services to hardware, cgroups, IPC sockets, timing constraints, etc. This coordination and synchronization is the hallmark and greatest advantage systemd has, and its major advantage over any older UNIX or Linux init systems.

2.3.5 Anatomy of a Unit File

The internal structure of unit files is segregated into sections. Sections are delimited by a pair of square brackets "[" and "]", with the section name enclosed in the brackets. Each section extends until the beginning of the next section or until the end of the file.

2.3.5.1 An Example Service Unit File – ssh.service

It would be very instructive at this point to show the structure and the exact contents of a typical service unit file. Figure 2.2 shows the contents of the ssh unit file on our Raspberry Pi 5 OS, found in /lib/systemd/system. You should carefully look at this figure while reading an actual service unit file(perhaps the ssh service file on your system) for comparison.

2.3.5.2 The General Format of Unit Files

As shown in Figure 2.2, the sample file is divided into sections. Section names are case-sensitive and enclosed in square brackets []. Within each section, the way the unit works and stores data is done using standard, simple directives, with allowed values assigned as follows:

In any section:

```
[Section]
Directive=value
Directive=value
```

```
[Unit]
Description=OpenBSD Secure Shell server
Documentation=man:sshd(8) man:sshd_config(5)
After=network.target auditd.service
ConditionPathExists=!/etc/ssh/sshd_not_to_be_run

[Service]
EnvironmentFile=-/etc/default/ssh
ExecStartPre=/usr/sbin/sshd -t
ExecStart=/usr/sbin/sshd -D $SSHD_OPTS
ExecReload=/usr/sbin/sshd -t
ExecReload=/bin/kill -HUP $MAINPID
KillMode=process
Restart=on-failure
RestartPreventExitStatus=255
Type=notify
RuntimeDirectory=sshd
RuntimeDirectoryMode=0755

[Install]
WantedBy=multi-user.target
Alias=sshd.service
```

FIGURE 2.2
ssh Unit File example.

If you use an override file, as is explained when editing the unit file in Section 2.3.3, directives are reset by assigning them to an empty string or null string. For example, the system's copy of a unit file could have a directive set to a value as follows:

Directive=default_value

The default_value can be eliminated in an override file by referencing the directive without a value, like this:

Directive=

2.3.5.3 ssh Example Unit, Service, and Install Sections Directives

This section details the specific directives for the three sections of the ssh example unit file, as shown in Figure 2.2.

[Unit] Section Directives

The first section found in the ssh.service unit file is the [Unit] section. This is generally used for defining metadata for the unit and configuring the relationship of the unit to other units.

Although section order does not matter to systemd when reading the file, this section is traditionally placed at the top because it provides an overview of the unit. The particular directives that are in the [Unit] section are:

1. Description=**OpenBSD Secure Shell server**
    Describes the name and basic functioning of the unit. It's used by various systemd tools.

1.a. Documentation=**man:sshd(8) man:sshd_config(5)**
    This directive names existing man pages that describe **ssh**, and the **sshd** daemon.

2. After=network.target auditd.service
    Units that will be started <u>before</u> starting the current unit.

3. ConditionPathExists=**!/etc/ssh/sshd_not_to_be_run**
    This can be used to provide a generic unit file that will only be run on appropriate systems. If the condition is not met, the unit is skipped.

[Service] Section Directives
The [Service] section provides a configuration that is only applicable for services.

The basic thing that should be specified in the [Service] section is the Type= of the service. This categorizes services by their process and behavior as a daemon. This is important because it tells systemd how to correctly manage the service and find out its state.

1. EnvironmentFile=**-/etc/default/ssh**
    Reads the environment variables for the unit from a text file. The text file should contain new-line-separated variable assignments. Lines without a "=" separator, or lines starting with ; or # will be ignored as comments. A line ending with a backslash will be continued on the following one.

2.a. ExecStartPre=/**usr/sbin/sshd -t**
    Additional commands that are executed before or after the command in ExecStart=, respectively. Syntax is the same as for ExecStart=, except that multiple command lines are allowed and the commands are executed one after the other, serially.

2.b. ExecStart=**/usr/bin/sshd –D $SSHD_OPTS**
    Probably the most critical directive! It designates the full path and the possible arguments of the command to be executed to start the process. This may only be specified once (except for "oneshot" services).

3. ExecReload=**/bin/kill –HUP $MAINPID**
    This optional directive indicates the command necessary to reload the configuration of the service if available. One additional,

special environment variable is set: if known, $MAINPID is set to the main process of the daemon, and may be used for command lines.

4. KillMode=**process**
Designates how processes associated with this unit shall be killed.

5. Restart=**on-failure**
Indicates how systemd will attempt to automatically restart the service. Allowable values are "always", "on-success", "on-failure", "on-abnormal", "on-abort", or "on-watchdog".

6. RestartPreventExitStatus=**255**
Lists exit status definitions, when returned by the main service process, prevent automatic service restarts, no matter what the restart setting configured, with Restart=. Exit status definitions are numeric exit codes, or termination signal names, separated by spaces.

7. Type=**notify**
Establishes the process start-up type for this service unit, within certain constraints. That type can be: simple, forking, oneshot, dbus, notify, or idle.

8. RuntimeDirectory=**sshd**
Take as argument(s) a space character-separated list of directory names. The directory names are relative and may not include the designation of parent directory (..).

9. RuntimeDirectoryMode=**0755**
Designates the access mode of the directories specified in RuntimeDirectory=, StateDirectory=,
    CacheDirectory=, LogsDirectory=, or ConfigurationDirectory=, as an octal number. Defaults to 0755.

[Install] Section Directives
The last section found in the ssh.service unit file is the [Install] section. This section is optional. It is used to configure extra features of a unit that will either enable or disable it. <u>A unit can be automatically started at boot with directives in this section.</u>

1. WantedBy=**multi-user.target**
The WantedBy= directive is the most common way to specify how a unit is enabled. It is similar to the Wants= directive in the [Unit] section. When a unit with this directive is enabled, a directory is created within /etc/systemd/system named after the specified unit with **.wants** appended to the name. A symbolic link to the current unit is created, creating the dependency. If the current unit has WantedBy=multi-user.target, a directory called multi-user.target.

wants is created within /etc/systemd/system (if it's not already there) and a symbolic link to the current unit is placed within that directory. Disabling this unit removes the link and the dependency relationship.

2. Alias=**sshd.service**
Allows the unit to be enabled under another name or alias.

2.3.5.4 Additional Unit File Sections and Their Unit-Specific Section Directives

As can be seen in our ssh service unit file example in Section 2.3.5.1, the Service Section is found between the Unit Section and the Install Section.

In a more complex unit file, the following sections are found between the Unit and Install Sections. Note that among the 12 unit types, most contain directives that only apply to their type.

The following brief listings provide references for additional critical values assigned to directives in those sections:

The [Socket] Section
Socket unit files are configured because, as seen in many sections and problems we present below, many services implement socket-based activation to achieve system parallelization and speed.

Note that each socket unit must have a matching service unit that will be activated when the socket receives activity.

Perhaps the hallmark of systemd control, the methods of socket control simplify and enhance an administrator's ability to oversee everything that is happening on the Raspberry Pi 5. By default, the socket name will attempt to start the service of the same name upon receiving a connection. When the service is initialized, the socket will be passed to it, allowing it to begin processing any requests.

To specify the actual socket, the premier directive is ListenStream=, which defines an address for a stream socket, and which supports socket IPC communication. Services that use TCP generally use this unit type.

The [Timer] Section
This section is used to schedule system events at some specific time, either measured on a clock, on the calendar, or after a certain delay. This unit file type is meant to replace the traditional function of the cron daemon. A unit file, such as a service unit, must be created to be activated when the timer is "triggers"!

The [Timer] section of a unit file contains the directive "Unit=", which specifies the unit that should be activated when the timer signals the event.

2.3.6 Creating Instance Units from Template Unit Files

For an ordinary user, template unit files let you reproduce a unit file several times, to get multiple copies of it (which you can slightly modify for each copy).

The primary commercial, or even non-commercial, reason for using template unit files, and their mechanisms, is to run multiple virtualized containers on a server.

For example, when you want to have many services listen on many sockets or ports at the same time, you could run multiple instances of the service as separate isolated virtual machine or container environments, each with a different name, and each using different ephemeral ports they're listening on.

You must map these virtual machines or containers' ports to network-facing IP addresses.

These could be public-facing network addresses assigned by a DHCP server, rather than private addresses, as is used primarily by container software such as Docker.

2.3.6.1 Template and Instance Unit Names for Services

A template unit file contains an @ symbol after the name and before the type.

In-Chapter Exercise

2. Find an example of a template unit file on your Raspberry Pi 5 OS system.

2.4 Targets

Targets, or target units, are the same as all other systemd unit types. They collect units together using dependencies (for changes in state, such as booting or shutdown), and create standard, or user-defined names, for synchronization of dependencies between units.

As an example of their use, the processes that start up the system and shut it down are used by systemd with the sequential (not hard-wired!) use of target units.

2.4.1 Basic Target Concepts

systemd can boot, do system service management, and perform other functions for the Raspberry Pi 5 OS by using standard and named target units. For example, the target graphical.target provides a multiuser system with

TABLE 2.2

systemd Important targets

default.target	The target that is booted by default. Not a real target, but a symbolic link to another target like graphical.target.
emergency.target	Starts an emergency shell on the console. Only used at the boot prompt as systemd.unit=emergency.target.
graphical.target	The default target in a desktop system GUI installation. Starts a system with network, multiuser support, and a display manager.
halt.target	Shuts down the system.
multi-user.target	Starts a multiuser system with network.
reboot.target	Reboots the system.
rescue.target	Starts a single-user system without network.

network connectivity <u>and</u> a graphical display manager. An interdependent set of units with unit dependencies can group controls related to system state, and provides a way of establishing custom system state controls.

Table 2.2 shows some critical systemd target units.

The following are listings and descriptions of some other special system target units. For a full list, refer to the man page on your system for systemd. special. Incidentally, these target states are the equivalents of "run levels" found in the older legacy Linux init system(s).

basic.target

A special target unit that does the basic boot-up operation. systemd automatically adds dependencies of the types Requires= and After= for this target unit. This starts all local mount points plus /var, /tmp and /var/tmp, swap devices, sockets, timers, path units, and other initialization processes necessary for daemons.

ctrl-alt-del.target

This target starts whenever **<Control>+<Alt>+<Del>** is pressed on the terminal keyboard. It's aliased through a symbolic link to reboot.target.

default.target

The bootup default systemd unit. It's aliased through a symbolic link to multi-user.target or graphical.target.

emergency.target

The special target unit that starts an emergency shell on the main console. Similar to with rescue.target, but which also starts the most basic services and mounts all file systems.

exit.target
  The special service unit for shutting down the system, or the user
  service manager.

final.target
  Target that is used during system shutdown and may be used to start
  late services after all normal services are already terminated, and all
  mounts unmounted.

graphical.target
  A special target unit for graphical login and operation, the
  default target on Raspberry Pi 5 OS systems that use a GUI-based
  desktop.

****Note**** This target requires multi-user.target as a dependency.

halt.target
  Target unit for shutting down and halting the system.

kexec.target
  Target unit for shutting down and rebooting the system via kexec.

multi-user.target
  Target unit for setting up a multi-user system with a text-only
  console interface.
    Primarily used in server machines. This target is a dependency
  required by graphical.target.

poweroff.target
  Target unit for shutting down and powering off the system.

reboot.target
  Target unit for shutting down and rebooting the system.

rescue.target
  Target unit that starts the base system processes (including the system mount points.) and starts a rescue shell.

shutdown.target
  Target unit that stops all services upon system shutdown.

slices.target
  Target unit that establishes all slice units that become active after
  booting.

sockets.target
 Target unit that configures all socket units that become active after booting.

sysinit.target
 Target that starts the services needed for system initialization.

system-update.target
 Target unit that manages off-line system updates.

timers.target
 Target unit that manages all timers that become active after booting.

umount.target
 Target unit that unmounts all mount points and automount points upon system shutdown.

2.4.2 A Target Example: Clock-Time-Based Running of a Script File

Question: Why would you want to do this, as an ordinary user?

 Answer: One particular useful reason for the ordinary user would be because at some particular time of the day, you want the system to automatically backup critical directories and files on designated media, via some automating shell script, like Bash, or perhaps a Python3 script file. There are numerous other events you might want to schedule aside from backups as well.

 "Monotonic Scheduling" of events can be thought of as basing an event happening on the system in clock time. Clock time is designated in minutes, hours, days, weeks, etc. The following example creates a timer unit that relies on a specific target unit to execute a script file on a daily basis. The service that needs to be run daily can be designated as a dependency of this target.

 The script file, which is named **your_script**, is made into a service via the creation of a service unit file. your_script can have arguments when it is run, as shown below. Also, you must set the permissions on **your_script**, with **chmod 755**, so that it will execute properly when it is a service!

 To get more information about how systemd specifies time, see the man page for **systemd.time**.

1. Use the following command to create a directory that will hold the calendar-based timer unit:

```
$ sudo mkdir /etc/systemd/system/timer_daily.target.wants
```

2. The following timer unit file will need to be created, using the nano text editor, in the path specified below:

$ **sudo nano /etc/systemd/system/timer_daily.timer**

to add the following unit-

[Unit]
Description=Daily Timer for Events

[Timer]
OnBootSec=5min
OnUnitActiveSec=1d
Unit=timer_daily.target

[Install]
WantedBy=basic.target

3. Create the target unit, with the nano text editor, in the specified directory:

$ **sudo nano /etc/systemd/system/timer_daily.target**

as follows:

[Unit]
Description=Daily Timer Target
StopWhenUnneeded=yes

4. Now that we have a timer unit and timer target file created, adding events to this target involves placing an event into the **/etc/systemd/ system/timer_daily.target.wants** folder.

For any particular event to take place daily, create a service unit file for the particular event in the **/etc/systemd/system/timer_daily. target.wants** folder.

For example, if you wish to run **your_script.service** daily (which, for example, runs a Bash script named **your_script**), create the following file with the nano text editor:

$ **sudo nano /etc/systemd/system/timer_daily.target.wants/your_script.service**

[Unit]
Description=Whatever your script file does

[Service]
User=bob
Type=Simple

Nice=19
IOSchedulingClass=2
IOSchedulingPriority=7
ExecStart=/home/bob/your_script –arg1 –arg2

Use more **ExecStart** lines in the above file if you want to start more than one event daily.

5. Start and enable the daily timer:

```
$ sudo systemctl start timer_daily.timer
$ sudo systemctl enable timer_daily.timer
```

In-Chapter Exercise

3. Using the five steps above, take a Bash script of your own, and have systemd execute it daily.

2.4.3 Unit Management with Additional Commands

So far, we have been working with services and displaying information about the unit and unit files that systemd is maintaining. However, we can find out more specific information about units using some additional commands. The following topics provide that specific information by using the commands shown.

Displaying a Unit File
To display the unit file that systemd has loaded into its system, you can use the cat command. For example, to see the unit file for the sshd daemon, type the following:

```
$ sudo systemctl cat sshd
# /lib/systemd/system/ssh.service
[Unit]
Description=OpenBSD Secure Shell server
Documentation=man:sshd(8) man:sshd_config(5)
After=network.target auditd.service
ConditionPathExists=!/etc/ssh/sshd_not_to_be_run

[Service]
EnvironmentFile=-/etc/default/ssh
ExecStartPre=/usr/sbin/sshd -t
ExecStart=/usr/sbin/sshd -D $SSHD_OPTS
ExecReload=/usr/sbin/sshd -t
ExecReload=/bin/kill -HUP $MAINPID
KillMode=process
Restart=on-failure
RestartPreventExitStatus=255
```

```
Type=notify
RuntimeDirectory=sshd
RuntimeDirectoryMode=0755

[Install]
WantedBy=multi-user.target
Alias=sshd.service
$
```

The output is the unit file as available to the currently running systemd process. This can be critical if you have modified unit files recently, or if you are overriding certain options in a unit file that was installed and built by the package management system.

Displaying Dependencies
To see a unit's dependency tree, you can use the list-dependencies command:

$sudo systemctl list-dependencies sshd.service

This will display a hierarchy mapping the dependencies that must be dealt with in order to start the unit in question. Dependencies, in this context, include those units that are either required by or wanted by the units above them.

```
sshd.service
● ├──.mount
● ├─system.slice
● └─sysinit.target
● ├─apparmor.service
● ├─dev-hugepages.mount
● ├─dev-mqueue.mount
● ├─fake-hwclock.service
● ├─keyboard-setup.service
● ├─kmod-static-nodes.service
● ├─plymouth-read-write.service
● ├─plymouth-start.service
● ├─proc-sys-fs-binfmt_misc.automount
● ├─sys-fs-fuse-connections.mount
● ├─sys-kernel-config.mount
● ├─sys-kernel-debug.mount
● ├─sys-kernel-tracing.mount
● ├─systemd-ask-password-console.path
● ├─systemd-binfmt.service
Output truncated...
```

The recursive dependencies are only displayed for .target units, which indicate system states. To recursively list all dependencies, include the --all flag.

To show reverse dependencies (units that depend on the specified unit), you can add the --reverse flag to the command. Other flags that are useful are the --before and --after flags, which can be used to show units that depend on the specified unit starting before and after themselves, respectively.

Checking Unit Properties

To see the low-level properties of a unit, you can use the show command. This will display a list of properties that are set for the specified unit using a key=value format:

```
$ sudo systemctl show sshd.service
Type=notify
Restart=on-failure
NotifyAccess=main
RestartUSec=100ms
TimeoutStartUSec=1min 30s
TimeoutStopUSec=1min 30s
RuntimeMaxUSec=infinity
WatchdogUSec=0
WatchdogTimestamp=Mon 2016-08-08 15:51:56 PDT
WatchdogTimestampMonotonic=8131498
FailureAction=none
PermissionsStartOnly=no
RootDirectoryStartOnly=no
RemainAfterExit=no
GuessMainPID=yes
MainPID=914

Output truncated...
```

If you want to display a single property, you can use the **-p** option with the property name. For example, to see the conflicts that the sshd.service unit has, you can type:

```
$ sudo systemctl show sshd.service -p Conflicts
Conflicts=shutdown.target
$
```

Masking and Unmasking Units

systemd has the ability to mark a unit as completely unstartable, automatically or manually, by linking it to /dev/null. This is called "masking" the unit, and is done with the mask command:

```
$ sudo systemctl mask nginx.service
```

This will prevent the nginx service from being started, automatically or manually, for as long as it is masked. If you check the list-unit-files, you will see the service is now listed as masked:

```
$ sudo systemctl list-unit-files
```

If you attempt to start the service, you will see a message like this:

$ **sudo systemctl start nginx.service**
Failed to start nginx.service: Unit nginx.service is masked.
$

To unmask a unit, making it available for use again, simply use the unmask command:

$ **sudo systemctl unmask nginx.service**

This will return the unit to its previous state, allowing it to be started or enabled.

Editing Unit Files
While the specific format for all unit files is outside of the scope of this chapter, systemctl provides several built-in mechanisms for editing and modifying unit files if you need to change them. The edit command, by default, will open a unit file snippet for the unit in question:

$ **sudo systemctl edit nginx.service**

This will be a blank file that can be used to override or add directives to the unit definition. A directory will be created within the **/etc/systemd/ system** directory, which contains the name of the unit with .d appended. For instance, for the nginx.service, a directory called nginx.service.d will be created.

Within this directory, a snippet will be created called **override.conf**. When the unit is loaded, systemd will, in memory, merge the override snippet with the full unit file. The snippet's directives will take precedence over those found in the original unit file.

If you wish to edit the full unit file instead of creating a snippet, you can pass the --full flag:

$ **sudo systemctl edit --full nginx.service**

This will load the current unit file into the default editor, where it can be modified. On our Raspberry Pi 5 OS system, the default editor was nano. When you save and exit the editor, the saved file will be written to **/etc/ systemd/system**, which will take precedence over the system's unit definition, found in/**lib/systemd/system**.

To remove any changes you made, either delete the unit's .d configuration directory or the modified service file from **/etc/systemd/system**. For example, to remove a snippet, we could type:

$ **sudo rm -r /etc/systemd/system/nginx.service.d**

To remove a full modified unit file, we would type:

```
$ sudo rm /etc/systemd/system/nginx.service
```

After deleting the file or directory, you should reload the systemd process so that it no longer tries to reference these files and reverts back to using the system copies. The following command does this:

```
$ sudo systemctl daemon-reload
```

In-Chapter Exercise

4. To get practice with the service management commands presented in the above section, execute them on your system, using the nginx service rather than sshd.

2.5 Practicing on Target Units

systemd "target" states are instanced by target unit text files. Target units' filenames end with the **.target** file extension, and are used to basically collect and create other systemd units through dependencies.

The graphical.target unit, which is used to instantiate or create a GUI session as a Raspberry Pi OS desktop system, starts many other system services on our Raspberry Pi 5 OS system. It also starts the multi-user.target unit, because that target is a dependency of graphical.target. The multi-user.target unit starts many other critical system services, such as NetworkManager (NetworkManager.service,) or D-Bus (dbus.service), and is, or becomes, a milestone target unit.

2.5.1 Viewing the Default Target

To find out which target unit is the final target that determines the operating state of the system, you can use the following command:

```
$ sudo systemctl get-default
graphical.target
$
```

This executes the symbolic link located at/**etc/systemd/system/default.target**, and displays the result.

****Note****

The default target unit can be different from the current target that defines the current state of the system!

2.5.2 Viewing All Targets

To list all currently loaded target units, use the following:

$ sudo systemctl list-units --type target

For each target unit, this command displays its full name (UNIT) followed by a note whether the unit has been loaded (LOAD), its high-level (ACTIVE) and low-level (SUB) unit activation state, and a short description (DESCRIPTION). By default, the systemctl list-units command displays only active units. If you want to list all loaded units regardless of their state, run this command with the **--all** or **-a** command line option:

$ sudo systemctl list-units --type target --all

When we executed this command on our Raspberry Pi OS system when the GUI interface was active, we got the following output:

```
$ systemctl list-units --type target --all
```

UNIT	LOAD	ACTIVE	SUB	DESCRIPTION
basic.target	loaded	active	active	Bas>
blockdev@dev-disk-by...	loaded	inactive	dead	...
blockdev@dev-disk-by\...	loaded	inactive	dead	...
blockdev@dev-mmcblk0p1	loaded	inactive	dead	...
blockdev@dev-nvme0n1p1	loaded	inactive	dead	Blo>
blockdev@dev-sda1.target	loaded	inactive	dead	Blo>
bluetooth.target	loaded	active	active	Bluetooth Support
cryptsetup-pre.target	loaded	inactive	dead	Local Encrypted Volu>
cryptsetup.target	loaded	active	active	Local Encrypted Volu>
emergency.target	loaded	inactive	dead	Emergency Mode
first-boot-complete.target	loaded	inactive	dead	First Boot Complete
getty-pre.target	loaded	active	active	Preparation for Logi>
getty.target	loaded	active	active	Login Prompts
graphical.target	loaded	active	active	Graphical Interface

Output truncated...
LOAD = Reflects whether the unit definition was properly loaded.
ACTIVE = The high-level unit activation state, i.e. generalization of SUB.
SUB   = The low-level unit activation state, values depend on unit type.

52 loaded units listed.
To show all installed unit files, use "systemctl list-unit-files".

$

2.5.2.1 Viewing the Currently Loaded Targets

To list all currently loaded target units, use the following command:

$ sudo systemctl list-units --type target

The following command illustrates the systemd logging facility (which has effectively replaced older, more traditional logging mechanisms) known as *journald*. The command that displays various aspects of systemd-style logging is the **journalctl** command. We describe journalctl in detail in Section 2.6.2. To use journalctl, along with the **grep** command, to list the current target, type the following:

$ sudo journalctl | grep Reached | tail -3
Mar 15 05:13:24 raspberrypi systemd[1]: Reached target network-online.target - Network is Online.
Mar 15 05:13:26 raspberrypi systemd[1]: Reached target multi-user.target - Multi-User System.
Mar 15 05:13:26 raspberrypi systemd[1]: Reached target graphical.target - Graphical Interface.
$

The output of the above command shows the current target unit and the two previous to it.

2.5.3 Changing the Current Target by Isolating Targets

It is possible to start all of the units associated with a target at once and stop all units that are not part of the dependency tree for that target. This is similar to changing the run level in older, legacy init systems.

For instance, if you are operating in a GUI environment, with **graphical.target** currently defining the system state, you can shut down the graphical system, and put the system into a multi-user state, which is a Character User Interface(CUI) state by what is termed "isolating" the **multi-user.target**. This is achieved with the **isolate** command. Since graphical.target (lower down on the dependency tree, as shown in Figure 2.2) depends on **multi-user.target**, all of the graphical units below **multi-user.target** will be terminated.

But you need to look very carefully at the dependencies of the target you are isolating before doing this, to make sure that you are not stopping vital system services, which would make the system unusable. To do this, use the following command:

$ sudo systemctl list-dependencies multi-user.target

To switch over to a different target unit in the current session, type the following command:

$ sudo systemctl isolate name.target

Replace **name** with the name of the target unit you want to use (for example, multi-user). This command starts the target unit named multi-user.target, and all dependent units, and immediately terminates all other units. To turn off the graphical user interface and change to the multi-user.target unit in the current session, type the following command:

$ sudo systemctl isolate multi-user.target

****Note and Caveat****

When you execute this command, make sure that you don't have running programs, such as an opened document in LibreOffice! Switching target states will terminate those running programs ungracefully, and, in the case of LibreOffice, will require you to recover those documents.

Caveat: After executing the above command on our Raspberry Pi 5 OS, at the time of the writing of this book, it was necessary to change the virtual terminal to another virtual terminal (tty1 through tty7 were the possibilities), such as tty1 by holding down the following keystroke sequence at one time:

<Ctrl>+<Alt>+F1

where **F1** represents the function key **F1** on your keyboard.

You are then logged into the system, now running in the **multi-user.target** state, in a text-only, Character User Interface(CUI). This caveat was necessary because the active graphical display manager and the normal virtual terminal for display of Wayland and Wayfire programs on our desktop, hooked up to tty7 (the default screen display in a **graphical.target** state), to the display screen, which was blank because that's where the GUI is displayed! So we simply switched our virtual display to tty2 with the keystroke sequence above to facilitate the target isolation using **<Ctrl>+<Alt>+F2**.

After we tried the next command:

$ sudo systemctl isolate graphical.target

on our system in tty2, the display switched to **graphical.target** automatically after a few seconds.

So, to switch back to a **graphical.target** state, type the following command:

$ sudo systemctl isolate graphical.target

Question: If you hold down **<Ctrl>+<Alt>+F2** while the **graphical.target** is active (i.e., you have a desktop environment on-screen) and switch to a virtual terminal (tty 2), have you switched to the **multi-user.target** as well? And what command or commands would show you the savings in system resources by shifting to a **multi-user.target** state versus being in the **graphical.target** state?

Answer: No, the way to conserve system resources is to use:

sudo systemctl isolate multi-user.target.

Just switching to another tty, and even logging in there, doesn't affect the target state the system is in, or the number of resources used by services in that target state. And of the commands like **ps -aux | less**, **htop**, **top**, our favorite is the **pstree** command. It shows the significant differences in running processes for the **multi-user.target** and graphical.target states. Of course, Webmin also achieves that.

2.5.3.1 Changing the Default Target

To have the system use a different default target unit when it starts up, type the following command:

```
$ sudo systemctl set-default name.target
```

Substitute **name** with the name of the target unit you want to be the new default (such as multi-user). This replaces the **/etc/systemd/system/default.target** file with a symbolic link to **/usr/lib/systemd/system/name.target**, where **name** is the name of the target unit you want to have the new default.

To configure the system to use the **multi-user.target** unit by default, type the following command:

```
$ sudo systemctl set-default multi-user.target
```

After a restart of the system, you will exclusively be able to log in via a text-only, CUI. To permanently change back to a **graphical.target** state at restart, type the following command:

```
$ sudo systemctl set-default graphical.target
```

2.5.4 Changing to Rescue Mode

An ordinary, unprivileged user of a Raspberry Pi 5 OS would not have recourse to use the commands found in this section and the following section. Most of the time, the system is operating normally, and it also starts up normally.

Rescue mode allows a valuable, single-user environment to be in place to repair the system when it is unable to complete the regular Boot and Startup processes. In rescue mode, the system attempts to mount all local file systems and start some important system services, but it does <u>not</u> activate any network interfaces or allow multiple users to be logged into the system at the same time.

To change the current target and enter rescue mode in the current session, type the following command:

```
$ sudo systemctl rescue
Welcome to rescue mode! After logging in, type-
journalctl -xb to view system logs,
systemctl reboot to reboot,
systemctl default or the key combination <Ctrl>+D to boot into default mode:
Give root password for maintenance (or press <Ctrl>+D to continue):
```

This command is similar to **systemctl isolate rescue.target**, but it also sends a warning message to all users who are currently logged into the system. To prevent systemd from sending this message, type this command with the --no-wall command option:

$ **sudo systemctl --no-wall rescue**

2.5.5 Changing to Emergency Mode

Emergency mode is exactly the state it sounds like, the most minimal environment possible that allows for the repair of the system. Even, believe it or not, in instances when the system is unable to enter rescue mode itself! In emergency mode, the system mounts the root file system in read-only mode and does not attempt to mount any other local file systems. Like rescue mode, it does not activate network interfaces and only starts a few essential services.

To change the away from the current target, and enter emergency mode, type the following command:

$ **sudo systemctl emergency**
Welcome to emergency mode!
After logging in, type journalctl -xb to view system logs,
systemctl reboot to reboot,
systemctl default or <Ctrl>+<D> to boot into default mode.
Give root password for maintenance (or press Control-D to continue):

This command is similar to **systemctl isolate emergency.target**, but it can also send an informative message to all users who are currently logged into the system. To prevent systemd from sending this message, run this command with the **--no-wall** command line option:

$ **sudo systemctl --no-wall emergency**

The above two sections, which allow you to change the system state to rescue or emergency modes, are most likely to be used when the system is not working correctly or when there is a performance-oriented problem. But then what does an ordinary user do when a normal boot into either **multi-user.target** or **graphical.target** cannot be done at all, for whatever reason? There are several options, which we do not cover here in detail, to interrupt the boot process or boot into previous kernel versions. A listing of these situations is as follows:

a. Power or hardware-related issues.

b. Entering GRUB2 recovery mode.

c. Booting into previous "boot environments".

d. If using the Zettabyte File System(ZFS) on zpools, use ZFS Recovery Mode.

2.5.6 Practice in Working with Targets

Following is a short command line practice session that allows you to work with the **systemctl** command and the important options shown in the preceding sections to effect systemd target states.

1. Check the default systemd.target-

```
$ sudo systemctl get-default
graphical.target
$
```

2. List the target units, and determine the current systemd target with the Linux multiple command conjoining **who -r** with options, and **grep**:

```
$ sudo systemctl list-units --type=target |grep active |egrep "graphical|multi|rescue|emergency"
graphical.target      loaded active active Graphical Interface
multi-user.target     loaded active active Multi-User System
$
```

The following command checks the target state we are currently in:

```
$ sudo who -r
      run-level 5  2017-08-10 13:50
$
```

****Note****

The legacy run-level 5 designation corresponds to the graphical.target state.

3. Now we can change the systemd target to **multi-user.target**, use the multiple command **systemctl list-units**, conjoining **grep** and **egrep** to check units availability and status, and finally the who -r command to find the run level:

```
$ sudo systemctl set-default multi-user.target
Removed symlink /etc/systemd/system/default.target.
Created symlink from /etc/systemd/system/default.target to /lib/systemd/system/multi-user.target.
$
$ sudo systemctl list-units --type=target | grep active | egrep "graphical|multi|rescue|emergency"

graphical.target    loaded active active Graphical Interface
multi-user.target   loaded active active Multi-User System
$
```

```
$ sudo who -r
     run-level 5  2022-11-15 06:37
$
```

Dependencies between targets imply that one systemd target can be part of another systemd target. Both graphical. target includes **multi-user.target**, and **multi-user.target** depend on various other targets. Now, check the systemd target dependencies using the following **systemctl list-dependencies** command, which checks the dependencies for systemd **multi-user.target**:

```
$ sudo systemctl list-dependencies multi-user.target |grep target
multi-user.target
●  ├─basic.target
●  │ ├─paths.target
●  │ ├─slices.target
●  │ ├─sockets.target
●  │ ├─sysinit.target
●  │ │ ├─cryptsetup.target
●  │ │ ├─local-fs.target
●  │ │ └─swap.target
●  │ └─timers.target
●  ├─getty.target
●  ├─nfs-client.target
●  │ └─remote-fs-pre.target
●  ├─remote-fs.target
●  │ └─nfs-client.target
●  │   └─remote-fs-pre.target
●  └─zfs.target
●    ├─zfs-import.target
●    └─zfs-volumes.target
$
```

To list the available systemd targets on the system, use the following command:

```
$ sudo systemctl list-units --type=target
```

UNIT	LOAD	ACTIVE	SUB	DESCRIPTION
basic.target	loaded	active	active	Basic System
cryptsetup.target	loaded	active	active	Local Encrypted Volumes
getty.target	loaded	active	active	Login Prompts
graphical.target	loaded	active	active	Graphical Interface
local-fs-pre.target	loaded	active	active	Local File Systems (Pre)
local-fs.target	loaded	active	active	Local File Systems
multi-user.target	loaded	active	active	Multi-User System
network-online.target	loaded	active	active	Network is Online
network.target	loaded	active	active	Network

nfs-client.target	loaded	active	active	NFS client services
paths.target	loaded	active	active	Paths
remote-fs-pre.target	loaded	active	active	Remote File Systems (Pre)
remote-fs.target	loaded	active	active	Remote File Systems
slices.target	loaded	active	active	Slices
sockets.target	loaded	active	active	Sockets
swap.target	loaded	active	active	Swap
sysinit.target	loaded	active	active	System Initialization
time-set.target	loaded	active	active	System Time Set
time-sync.target	loaded	active	active	System Time Synchronized
timers.target	loaded	active	active	Timers
zfs-import.target	loaded	active	active	ZFS pool import target
zfs-volumes.target	loaded	active	active	ZFS volumes are ready
zfs.target	loaded	active	active	ZFS startup target

LOAD   = Reflects whether the unit definition was properly loaded.
ACTIVE = The high-level unit activation state, i.e. generalization of SUB.
SUB   = The low-level unit activation state, values depend on unit type.
23 loaded units listed. Pass --all to see loaded but inactive units, too.
To show all installed unit files use 'systemctl list-unit-files'.

4. Reboot the system using the **systemctl reboot** command. Since we set the default systemd target to multi-user.target, the system will restart into that target state.

$ sudo systemctl reboot

Output truncated…

5. Once the system has restarted, check the systemd target units and the current active target state.

$ sudo systemctl list-units --type=target |grep active |egrep "graphical|multi|rescue|emergency"

basic.target	loaded active active Basic System
cryptsetup.target	loaded active active Encrypted Volumes
getty.target	loaded active active Login Prompts
local-fs-pre.target	loaded active active Local File Systems (Pre)
local-fs.target	loaded active active Local File Systems
mail-transport-agent.target	loaded active active Mail Transport Agent
multi-user.target	loaded active active Multi-User System
network-online.target	loaded active active Network is Online
network-pre.target	loaded active active Network (Pre)
network.target	loaded active active Network
paths.target	loaded active active Paths
remote-fs-pre.target	loaded active active Remote File Systems (Pre)
remote-fs.target	loaded active active Remote File Systems
slices.target	loaded active active Slices
sockets.target	loaded active active Sockets
swap.target	loaded active active Swap

```
sysinit.target              loaded active active System Initialization
time-sync.target            loaded active active System Time Synchronized
timers.target               loaded active active Timers
zfs.target                  loaded active active ZFS startup target
20 loaded units listed. Pass --all to see loaded but inactive units, too.
$ sudo who -r
         run-level 3  2022-11-15 07:37
```

Since we are now in the **multi-user.target** state, **multi-user.target** is highlighted in the above output. Also, the **sudo who -r** command shows us we are in runlevel 3, the legacy equivalent of the **multi-user.target** state.

If you wish to return to the GUI interface on your Raspberry Pi 5, undo step 3 with the command:

$ sudo systemctl set-default graphical.target

and then reboot.

2.5.7 Other systemctl Options that Work with Target Units

Targets, as defined and illustrated above, are unit files that describe the system state, or points of synchronization. Like other units, they can be identified by the file extension .target.

Targets are used to coordinate and group units together.

This brings the system to some desired states, which then allows use case-dictated functionality. For example, the Raspberry Pi 5 OS on hardware that is configured as a server, with a text-only CUI, doesn't have the performance overhead, which is essentially wasted resource, of a graphical display manager, or desktop environment.

Targets are used as a coordination point, which makes desired functionality available, allowing the system administrator to designate the "milestone" state (which might consist of many inter-dependent targets) rather than designating individual units to start to produce that state.

Target unit files specify, in their content configuration, that they are WantedBy=, or RequiredBy= some individual unit file, thus establishing dependency relationships. Units that must be made available can specify this condition using the Wants=, Requires=, and After= designations to indicate that particular dependency relationship.

2.5.8 Using Target Shortcuts

There are target units available for critical events, such as powering off the system or rebooting. The **systemctl** command has options that give you faster and better methods to allow the execution of those critical events.

To halt the system, you can use the halt command:

$ sudo systemctl halt

To initiate a full shutdown, you can use the poweroff command:

$ sudo systemctl poweroff

A restart can be started with the reboot command:

$ sudo systemctl reboot

The above three commands notify logged-in users that the critical event is about to occur (that's very important in a multi-user system, where many users might be in the middle of critical operations!,) something that running, or isolating a particular target will <u>not</u> do.

****Note****

Ordinary Raspberry Pi 5 OS system commands will tie together the necessary operations to accomplish the above state changes on the system, so that they will work properly with systemd-controlled state changes.

For example, an ordinary Raspberry Pi 5 OS command that will do this, to reboot the system, you can simply type:

$ sudo reboot

In-Chapter Exercise

5. You want to ssh into a newly-installed Raspberry Pi 5 system from another machine on your LAN or intranet. When you attempt that, you get some obscure error message that denies you access via ssh to the new machine. Out of the multitude of debugging scenarios you could go through to find out why you are getting the error, you could use a single systemd command while sitting at the new machine to find out whether the sshd daemon is running, or even installed. Then proceed to solve your problem quickly and easily from there. What systemd command from the above sections gives you that expedient procedure?

2.6 Other Important systemd Commands

As can be seen above, the **systemctl** command affects Units and Targets. But systemd has other important commands that provide control of many system functions. The following sub-sections detail the use of some of these other important systemd commands.

2.6.1 Cgroups

A systemd *cgroup* (*control group*) is a Linux kernel feature managed by systemd that organizes and limits system resources (CPU, memory, I/O, etc.) for processes. systemd uses cgroups to track, isolate, and control processes efficiently within service units.

cgroups, included as part of systemd in the Linux kernel, allow you to create prioritized and structured groups of processes running on your system. They are invoked by the systemd **systemctl** command. Considering the various ways of using cgroups, the most important one is to monitor and control Raspberry Pi 5 OS resources.

Cgroup monitoring, assessment, and control are used via systemd unit files. It can be transient or persistent.

The **systemd-run** command is used to create and start a transient unit as its own cgroup self-contained module, and then run a Raspberry Pi 5 OS command in that unit.

To create persistent cgroups, it is necessary to build service unit files for them in the **/etc/systemd/system** directory. That directory is the standard location for user-installed and user-defined services in systemd.

The objective of this section is to provide a pictorial description of the cgroup "tree", give some basic definitions, further describe the structure of cgroup unit types, and illustrate their standard arrangement. We also define Linux *namespaces*, point you to a system programming example of namespace creation, and provide sources of further documentation for you to explore.

2.6.1.1 Default Cgroup Hierarchies for System Resource Control

To start, we show an instructive diagram, one which you can obtain on your own Raspberry Pi 5 OS system with the **systemd-cgls** command. The following are the truncated results of that command on our Raspberry Pi 5 system:

```
$ systemd-cgls
Control group /:
Control group /:
-.slice
├─user.slice
│ └─user-1000.slice
│   ├─user@1000.service
│   │ ├─app.slice
│   │ │ ├─gvfs-goa-volume-monitor.service
│   │ │ │ └─1046 /usr/libexec/gvfs-goa-volume-monitor
│   │ │ ├─pulseaudio.service
│   │ │ │ └─781 /usr/bin/pulseaudio --daemonize=no --log-target=journal
```

```
    │ │ │    ├─gvfs-daemon.service
    │ │ │    │    ├─  879 /usr/libexec/gvfsd
    │ │ │    │    ├─  885 /usr/libexec/gvfsd-fuse /run/user/1000/gvfs -f
    │ │ │    │    ├─ 1066 /usr/libexec/gvfsd-trash --spawner :1.8 /org/gtk/gvfs/exec_spaw/0
    │ │ │    │    ├─63616 /usr/libexec/gvfsd-network --spawner :1.8 /org/gtk/gvfs/exec_spaw/2
    │ │ │    │    └─63630 /usr/libexec/gvfsd-dnssd --spawner :1.8 /org/gtk/gvfs/exec_spaw/4
   ...
    └─init.scope
    │    │    ├─765 /lib/systemd/systemd --user
    │    │    └─766 (sd-pam)
    │    ├─session-3.scope
    │    │ ├─1219 /bin/login -f
    │    │ └─1492 -bash
    │    └─session-1.scope
    │      ├─  760 lightdm --session-child 14 17
   ...
    ├─systemd-timesyncd.service
    │ └─446 /lib/systemd/systemd-timesyncd
    ├─avahi-daemon.service
    │ ├─481 avahi-daemon: running [raspberrypi.local]
    │ └─485 avahi-daemon: chroot helper
    └─systemd-logind.service
      └─518 /lib/systemd/systemd-logind
```

In-Chapter Exercises

6. Compare the output of the above **systemd-cgls** command with the
    pstree command output. How are they similar in both structure and
    content? How are they different? Execute the **pstree** command and
    the **systemd-cgls** command on your Raspberry Pi 5 system,
    and compare the output you get to the output we show, in terms of
    fine-grained similarities and differences. What options of the **pstree**
    command can give displays of PIDs (Process Identifiers), similar to
    the output of the **systemd-cgls** command?

    ****Extra For Experts****

7. Are PID and cgroup number the same for all processes and threads?
    Write a system program that creates multiple persistent threads
    with the fork() system call, and then examine the cgroup numbers
    assigned to those threads.
        Next, we give you some basic definitions that more fully describe
    the objects found in the **systemd-cgls** command's output graphics.

    Slice – A group of units that organizes them in some way.

    Service – A process, or a group of processes, which is started using a
        service unit configuration file.
        For example, **systemd-logins.service** is a service.

Scope – Processes that are started and stopped by transient processes that use the fork() system call, and are registered by systemd at runtime. All user sessions are a good example of this.

In the command output text above, init.scope, and session-c1.scope are examples.

Slices, services, and scopes are most importantly created by the system administrator or by system programs. By default, systemd and the operating system start up mandatory and essential services automatically at system startup, dictated by the final target state that the system will run in.

Three slices are created by default:

- -.slice — the root slice;
- system.slice — the default path location for all system services;
- user.slice — the default path location for all user sessions;

In-Chapter Exercise

****For Experts****

8. Are the threads you created for In-Chapter Exercise 7 slices, services, or scope units? Why?

To summarize, looking at the output of the **systemd-cgls** commands above, the root of the cgroup tree is the root slice, -.slice. The first major branch, aside from the system.slice, is the user.slice, with a number of scopes under that for user sessions. Proceeding down the tree, there are a number of other slices grouped under the major "branch" known as the system.slice, for example, avahi-daemon.service, cron.service, cups.service, ssh.service, etc. That is a capsule overview of the tree.

It is useful to list loaded slice unit types by using the following command:

```
$ systemctl list-units --type=slice
```

UNIT	LOAD	ACTIVE	SUB	DESCRIPTION
-.slice	loaded	active	active	Root Slice
system-configure\x2dprinter.slice	loaded	active	active	system-configure\x2dprinter.slice
system-bthelper.slice	loaded	active	active	system-bthelper.slice
system-getty.slice	loaded	active	active	system-getty.slice
system-modprobe.slice	loaded	active	active	system-modprobe.slice
system-systemd\x2dfsck.slice	loaded	active	active	system-systemd\x2dfsck.slice
system.slice	loaded	active	active	System Slice
user-1000.slice	loaded	active	active	User Slice of UID 1000
user.slice	loaded	active	active	User and Session Slice

LOAD   = Reflects whether the unit definition was properly loaded.
ACTIVE = The high-level unit activation state, i.e. generalization of SUB.

SUB   = The low-level unit activation state, values depend on unit type.
9 loaded units listed. Pass --all to see loaded but inactive units, too.
To show all installed unit files use 'systemctl list-unit-files'.
$

2.6.1.2 *Additional cgroup Reference Resources*

To find more information about resource control under systemd, the unit
hierarchy, as well as the kernel resource controllers, refer to the materials
listed below.

Cgroup-Related systemd Documentation
The following man pages give you more information on systemd
cgroups:

systemd.resource-control - describes the configuration options for resource control shared by
system units.
systemd.unit - describes common options of all unit configuration files.
systemd.slice - provides general information about .slice units.
systemd.scope - provides general information about .scope units.
systemd.service - provides general information about .service units.

Additionally, you can install the kernel documentation on cgroups by
using the following command on your Raspberry Pi 5 OS system:

$ sudo apt install linux-doc
 Reading package lists... Done
Building dependency tree... Done
Reading state information... Done
The following packages were automatically installed and are no longer required:
 libcamera0.3 libwlroots12 lxplug-network
Use 'sudo apt autoremove' to remove them.
The following additional packages will be installed:
 linux-doc-6.6
The following NEW packages will be installed:
 linux-doc linux-doc-6.6
0 upgraded, 2 newly installed, 0 to remove and 0 not upgraded.
Need to get 36.2 MB of archives.
After this operation, 191 MB of additional disk space will be used.
Do you want to continue? [Y/n]**Y**
Output truncated…
$

Once the documentation for the kernel has been downloaded, you can
access and view the cgroups-specific content by viewing the **cgroups** man
page on your system.

2.6.1.3 Linux Namespaces

There is a kernel-level construct in Raspberry Pi 5 OS Linux, appropriately called "namespaces", which segregates and isolates the cgroup processes seen in Section 2.6.1, also and their system resources, in a separate and protected environment. This allows them to operate in their own process environments on the system. A very close analogy of namespaces, which you might be familiar with, is the concept of a variable's *scope* in a high-level computer programming language, such as C or Python3.

Namespaces use the **clone** system call to accomplish this process isolation. The biggest and most important use of namespaces is in the system-level creation and maintenance of Linux containers, such as LXD/LXC. For complete reference information on namespaces, consult the man pages on your Raspberry Pi 5 system for **namespaces**, and **user_namespaces** – particularly the EXAMPLES on the **user_namespaces** man page, which gives an excellent and instructive C language system programming implementation of the clone system call used to create a child process that executes a shell command in a new namespace.

2.6.2 Journal Logging

System logging using log files is extremely useful for system administration, for finding out what might have gone wrong with your software or hardware. The logs record activity and events on the Raspberry Pi 5 OS. Journal logging with systemd is very similar to the traditional methods available for logging. They are created so that you can carefully, systematically, and periodically audit the general operation of the system, especially with regard to performance enhancements that perhaps you've made, and to maintain system security.

2.6.2.1 systemd journal Log Messages

The systemd journal is created and managed by a special daemon, named journald, which channels all of the messages produced by the facilities and programs such as the kernel, initrd, systemd services, etc. into a database record structure. The systemd journal is a single, centralized management program for collecting together logs, regardless of where the log messages themselves are generated.

****Note****

A critical, as well as controversial aspect of systemd journal logging, is that the log files are stored as binary data, and can be searched by a process deploying a specialized database traversal program. They are not plain text files. Previous legacy system logs were plain text files that could be viewed easily as such, or even edited in a text editor such as nano, Vi, or emacs.

Storing the log information in a binary format mandate that the log information be displayed in useful output formats specific to proprietary database management technologies. Simply stated, using that proprietary technology is the major drawback.

But logs can be displayed using the **journalctl** command that we show in the next section.

2.6.2.2 Using the journalctl Command to Query the Journal

The **journalctl** command is a convenient way of querying entries in the journal database. Following is a synopsis of the command, extracted from the **journalctl** man page:

```
*********************************************************************
journalctl - Query the systemd journal


Syntax:
    journalctl [options...] [matches...]

Purpose:
    journalctl may be used to query the contents of the systemd journal as written by
systemd-journald.service.

If called without options or arguments, it will show the full contents of the journal, starting
with the oldest entry collected.

All users are granted access to their private per-user journals. However, by default, only root
and users who are members of a few special groups are granted access to the system journal
and the journals of other users.

Commonly Used Features:
-a, --all    Show all fields in full, even if they include unprintable characters or are very long.
-f, --follow    Show only the most recent journal entries, and continuously print new entries as
                they are appended to the journal.
-r, --reverse    Reverse output so that the newest entries are displayed first.
-u, --unit=UNIT|PATTERN    Show messages for the specified systemd unit UNIT
                           (such as a service unit), or for any of the units matched by
PATTERN.
-S, --since=, -U, --until=    Start showing entries on or newer than the specified date, or on or
                              older than the specified date, respectively. Date specifications
                              should be of the format "2012-10-30 18:17:16".
*********************************************************************
```

To get more information about the use of the **journalctl** command, particularly about the structure that the command uses to query the journal, examine the **man journalctl** command contents as necessary on your system.

2.6.2.3 *Journal Logging Basics, and Applied to the Webserver2 Program*

In this section, we show how to use the **journalctl** command and its options and arguments to do some basic systemd-style journal query operations. We then apply a set of those commands and options to a program named "webserver2". That program generates systemd-style journal log output. Our use of the **journalctl** command applied to that program's journal output is relevant in this section, so as to better and more practically illustrate the use of **journalctl** options and arguments to a real application.

2.6.2.3.1 *Basic Log Viewing*

To see the logs that the journald daemon has collected, use the **journalctl** command.

When used without any options or arguments, every journal entry that is in the system will be displayed. The oldest entries will be first in the listing:

$ journalctl
Oct 10 10:40:53 raspberrypi kernel: Booting Linux on physical CPU 0x0000000000 [0x414fd0b1]
Oct 10 10:40:53 raspberrypi kernel: Linux version 6.6.51+rpt-rpi-2712 (serge@raspberrypi.com) (gcc-12 (Debian 12.2.0-14) 12.2.0, GNU ld>
Oct 10 10:40:53 raspberrypi kernel: KASLR enabled
Oct 10 10:40:53 raspberrypi kernel: random: crng init done
Oct 10 10:40:53 raspberrypi kernel: Machine model: Raspberry Pi 5 Model B Rev 1.0
Output truncated…

But what if you want to see the journal with the newest entry first? Use the **–r** (reverse) option on the basic **journalctl** command.

$ journalctl -r
Oct 10 10:40:53 raspberrypi kernel: Booting Linux on physical CPU 0x0000000000 [0x414fd0b1]
Oct 10 10:40:53 raspberrypi kernel: Linux version 6.6.51+rpt-rpi-2712 (serge@raspberrypi.com) (gcc-12 (Debian 12.2.0-14) 12.2.0, GNU ld>
Oct 10 10:40:53 raspberrypi kernel: KASLR enabled
Oct 10 10:40:53 raspberrypi kernel: random: crng init done
Oct 10 10:40:53 raspberrypi kernel: Machine model: Raspberry Pi 5 Model B Rev 1.0
Oct 10 10:40:53 raspberrypi kernel: efi: UEFI not found.
Oct 10 10:40:53 raspberrypi kernel: Reserved memory: created CMA memory pool at 0x0000000002000000, size 320 MiB
Output truncated…

In-Chapter Exercise

9. From the output of the above two commands executed on your Raspberry Pi 5 system, what can you tell about the most recent current boot time and the current time?

2.6.2.3.2 Journal Query Structures

The main purpose of collecting the log information together from many sources, thus centralizing them in one place, such as in the journal, is to be able to quickly and easily look at and take action based on the entries in the log that are important to you for some reason. That reason could be because you have security concerns, or because a newly-installed program is misbehaving, and causing the system to crash. That could be true of an ordinary desktop user or a server system administrator.

Because of this, the most important use features of the **journalctl** command's options and arguments are its methods of ordering, and making inquiries into the journal, or separating out more useful, understandable, and compact information from it. The following are some of the ways these searches through the log can be done.

For example, the journal has many "field headings" that can be used for inquiry. Each of these fields acts as an index, or key, into specific kinds or sets of entries in the journal. Some of those fields are passed to it from the process being logged, and some are applied by the daemon journald, with data it gathers from the system at the time the log is from.

A leading underscore indicates that a field is of the latter type. The journal automatically records and indexes logging for that type of query. You can get more information about all of the available journal fields by typing:

$ **man systemd.journal-fields**

2.6.2.3.3 Querying by Time

You can also see parts of the log in a "from-to" display. You would most likely want to do this when the system has been operating for a long time without a reboot. You can do an inquiry by using the **--since** and **--until** options, which limit the entries displayed to those after, or before some specified given times.

The time parameters are in a variety of formats. For absolute time values, you should use the following format:
YYYY-MM-DD HH:MM:SS

For example, we can see all of the entries since 2025-04-04 07:52:30 PDT using this command:

$ **journalctl --since "2025-04-04 07:52:30 PDT"**

If parts of the above time specification argument are left off, standard defaults are used instead. For example, if the date is omitted, the current date will be used. If the time component is missing, "00:00:00" (midnight) will be used. The seconds field can be left off to default to "00":

$ **journalctl --since "2025-04-04 " --until "2025-04-04 08:30 PDT"**

The journal also accepts some relative values, and English-language shortcuts. For example, you can use the words "yesterday", "today", "tomorrow", or "now". You do relative times by placing these symbols before arguments: "-" or "+" to a numbered value or using words like "ago".

To get the data from yesterday, use this command:

$ journalctl --since yesterday

If you used another system monitoring tool, and it gave information about a service interruption starting at 11:00 PM and continuing until an hour ago, you could type:

$ journalctl --since 11:00 --until "1 hour ago"

2.6.2.3.4 *Querying by Unit*

The most useful and practical way of querying is by designating the service unit's name you are interested in. You use the **-u** option to query by unit.

For example, to see all of the logs from the **web server2** unit on your system, use the following command:

$ journalctl -u webserver2.service

You can perform compound queries by adding arguments to the above unit query by unit name. To query by time and name, to check the status of the service you are interested in, use the following command:

$ journalctl -u webserver2.service --since today

Compound querying is useful when you want to compare log entries from related units running on the system. For example, if you want to compare log entries from your **web server2** service to the status of another unit, you can view the entries from both in chronological order by using the following compound query statement:

$ journalctl -u webserver2.service -u systemd-logind.service --since yesterday

This allows you to study the interactions between different programs and debug targets and the interaction of dependencies, instead of just individual, isolated units.

2.6.2.3.5 *Querying by Process, User, or Group ID*

Several services may fork many child processes to accomplish their purposes. If you know the exact PID of a process you are interested in, you can perform a **journalctl** query by PID. To do this, execute the query by specifying the _**PID** field. For example, if the PID we're interested in is 1, use the following command:

$ journalctl _PID=1

You can also show all of the entries logged from a specific user or group. This is done with the **_UID** or **_GID** filters. For example, if **webserver2** is being run by the user bob, you can find the user ID with the following command:

```
$ id -u bob
1000
$
```

Then, you can use the **id** that was returned to structure a query command based on the results, as follows:

```
$ journalctl _UID=1000 --since today
```

The **-F** option of the **journalctl** command is used to show all of the available values for a given journal field. To see which group IDs the systemd journal has entries for, use the following command:

```
$ journalctl -F _GID
0
1000
112
110
106
996
109
997
121
7
65534
$
```

The above output shows all of the values that the journal has stored for the group ID field. This can help you construct your queries with the Group ID field.

2.6.2.3.6 *Querying by Component Path*

You can apply a filter to the query by providing a pathname. If the pathname leads to an executable image, **journalctl** will display all of the entries that are related to that particular executable image. For example, to find log entries that involve the **web server2** executable program, use the following command:

```
$ journalctl /home/bob/webserver2
```

where the path to the executable image is /**home/bob**, and the name of the executable program is **webserver2**.

Usually, if a unit file is available for the executable, this method is more understandable, and gives useful information to someone trying to achieve system administration tasks, such as security intrusions (entries from associated child processes, etc.). However, this does not always yield useful information.

2.6.2.3.7 Querying by Priority

One query filter that system administrators are very interested in is the message priority. While it is useful to log information at a very verbose level, when actually trying to read and interpret the observed and available information, listing of low-priority logs can be obscure and useless.

You can use **journalctl** to display only messages of a specified priority or above by using the **-p** option. This allows you to filter out lower-priority messages. For instance, to show only entries logged at the error level or above, you can type:

$ journalctl --b -p err
Mar 07 16:02:38 raspberrypi bluetoothd[682]: src/plugin.c:plugin_init() Failed to init vcp plugin
Mar 07 16:02:38 raspberrypi bluetoothd[682]: src/plugin.c:plugin_init() Failed to init mcp plugin
Mar 07 16:02:38 raspberrypi bluetoothd[682]: src/plugin.c:plugin_init() Failed to init bap plugin
Mar 07 16:02:38 raspberrypi bluetoothd[682]: profiles/sap/server.c:sap_server_register() Sap driver initialization failed.
Mar 07 16:02:38 raspberrypi bluetoothd[682]: sap-server: Operation not permitted (1)
Mar 07 16:02:39 raspberrypi wpa_supplicant[845]: nl80211: kernel reports: Registration to specific type not supported
Output truncated ...

This will display all messages marked as error, critical, alert, or emergency. The journal implements the legacy UNIX/Linux syslog message levels. You can use either the priority name or its corresponding numeric value. The order of highest to lowest priority are shown in Table 2.3.

The above numbers or names can be used interchangeably with the **-p** option. Selecting a priority will display messages marked at the specified level and those above it.

In-Chapter Exercise

10. What does the **--b** directive in the previous command do, as far as a compound query goes?

2.6.2.4 Query Output Display

The above queries showed particular kinds of log entry outputs. There are other ways we can add options and addendums to the queries.

TABLE 2.3

systemd Error Priorities

Priority	Name	Description and Possible Action(s) to be Taken
0	emerg	Emergency- A "panic" condition – notify system administration.
1	alert	Alert – Notify system administrator who can fix the problem. Example: loss of backup ISP connection.
2	crit	Critical – Failure in a primary system. Fix crit problems before alert problems. Example: loss of disk subsystem.
3	err	Error – Non-urgent failures, should be sent to developers or development admins.
4	warning	Warning – Not an error, but shows that an error will occur if action is not taken, e.g., file system nearly full.
5	notice	Notice – Unusual events, but not error conditions. No immediate action required.
6	info	Information- Normal operating messages – No action required.
7	debug	Debug – Info useful for developers for debugging the app, not useful during operations.

The **journalctl** output is a more condensed and legible, thus more readable display. Organized in a way that is more understandable if you want to cull certain information from it.

****Note****

In certain output displays below, exiting or stopping the display of journal entries can be done by typing **q** on the command line.

To display a certain number of log entries, you can use the **-n** option. By default, it will display the most recent 10 entries:

$ **journalctl -n**

You can also specify the number of entries you'd like to see, with a number after the **-n**:

$ **journalctl -n 15**

2.6.2.4.1 Displaying Log Entries in Real Time

To show the content of the journal in real time, and see the logs as they are being written, use the **-f** option

$ **journalctl -f**

Adjusting how journalctl displays log data, shrinking or expanding, can be achieved by using the following option. By default, **journalctl** will show the entire entry in the pager, left-to-right, allowing the entries to trail off to the right of the screen. This rightward-extensive display data can be seen by pressing the right arrow key. If you'd rather have the output truncated, inserting an ellipsis where information has been removed, you can use the **--no-full** option:

```
$ journalctl - -no-full
Oct 10 10:40:53 raspberrypi kernel: Booting Linux on physical CPU 0x0000000000 [0x414fd0b1]
Oct 10 10:40:53 raspberrypi kernel: Linux version 6.6.51+rpt-rpi-2712 (serge@raspberrypi.com)
(gcc-12 (Debian 12.2.0-14) 12.2...024-10-08)
Oct 10 10:40:53 raspberrypi kernel: KASLR enabled
Oct 10 10:40:53 raspberrypi kernel: random: crng init done
Oct 10 10:40:53 raspberrypi kernel: Machine model: Raspberry Pi 5 Model B Rev 1.0
Oct 10 10:40:53 raspberrypi kernel: efi: UEFI not found.
Oct 10 10:40:53 raspberrypi kernel: Reserved memory: created CMA memory pool at
0x0000000002000000, size 320 MiB
Output truncated ...
```

You can also specify **journalctl** to display all of its information, no matter whether it includes unprintable characters or not. We can do this with the **-a** option:

```
$ journalctl -a
```

By default, **journalctl** displays the output of a query in a "paged" manner, one screenful at a time. To be able to process the data with text manipulation tools, such as a text editor, or LibreOffice Writer, for example, you can output to standard output, redirecting it into a post-processing program, or to a disk file. You can do this with the **--no-pager** option. In the following example, we redirect the pager output to a file named "page1":

```
$ journalctl --no-pager > page1
```

2.6.2.4.2 *Query Output Formats*

If you are post-processing journal log entries with some particular program, as mentioned above, you will have an easier time parsing the data into that program if it is in a more amenable format. The journal can display its output in a variety of formats. You can do this using the **-o**, option with a format specifier.

For example, you can output the journal entries in JSON format with the following command:

```
$ journalctl -b -u webserver2 -o json
```

This is useful for parsing with certain utility programs. You could use the **json-pretty** format to get a better handle on the data structure before passing it off to the JSON consumer:

```
$ journalctl -b -u webserver2 -o json-pretty
```

TABLE 2.4

journalctl Output Formats

cat	Displays only the message field itself.
export	A binary format suitable for transferring or backing up.
json	Standard JSON with one entry per line.
json-pretty	JSON formatted for better human-readability
json-sse	JSON formatted output wrapped to make add server-sent event compatible
short	The default syslog style output
short-iso	The default format augmented to show ISO 8601 wallclock timestamps.
short-monotonic	The default format with monotonic timestamps.
short-precise	The default format with microsecond precision
verbose	Shows every journal field available for the entry, including those usually hidden internally.

Table 2.4 shows the formats that might be used for such a display:

These options allow you to display the journal entries in whatever format best suits how you want to do the post-processing treatment of the content of the journal.

2.6.2.5 Journal Maintenance

It may become necessary to not only look through older boot environments, and correlate the logs found in them with the most current boot logs, but also to delete older, obsolete log entries. Log and journal maintenance is an important aspect of system administration.

****Note****

At the time this book was written, "vacuuming", or cleaning out journal log files, only works on archived files and corrupted files, and does not work on active log files!

You can find out the amount of space that the active and archived journals are currently occupying on disk by using the --disk-usage option of the **journalctl** command:

```
$ journalctl --disk-usage
Archived and active journals take up 48.0M in the file system.
$
```

The active journal logs cannot be pruned.

When this facility becomes available for active journal logs, there are basically two different ways you will be able to do that.

1. If you use the **--vacuum-size** option, you can shrink your journal by indicating a size. This will remove only old archived entries that are corrupted or empty, until the total journal space taken up on disk is at the requested size:

$ sudo journalctl --vacuum-size=1M
Deleted archived journal /var/log/journal/42ef46612dc64ec2bf13b9704a661ec8/
user-1000@0005fa1821e06e36-c096421281b7ec8d.journal~ (8.0M).
Deleted archived journal /var/log/journal/42ef46612dc64ec2bf13b9704a661ec8/
system@0005fa1821194676-6ee6ae817589e0dc.journal~ (16.0M).
Vacuuming done, freed 24.0M of archived journals from /var/log/journal/42ef46612dc
64ec2bf13b9704a661ec8.
Vacuuming done, freed 0B of archived journals from /run/log/journal.
Vacuuming done, freed 0B of archived journals from /var/log/journal.
$

2. Another way that you can prune the archived journal log is by specifying a cutoff time with the **--vacuum-time** option. Any entries beyond that time are deleted. This allows you to keep the entries that have been created after a specific time.

    For instance, to keep entries from the last year, you can type:

$ sudo journalctl --vacuum-time=1years

Limiting Journal Expansion
You can limit how much persistent storage on disk the journal can take up. This can be done by editing the **/etc/systemd/journald.conf** file. The following items in that file can be used to limit the journal growth:

SystemMaxUse=: The maximum disk space that can be used by the journal in persistent storage.
SystemKeepFree=: The amount of space that the journal should leave free when adding journal entries to persistent storage.
SystemMaxFileSize=: How large individual journal files can grow to in persistent storage before being rotated.
RuntimeMaxUse=: The maximum disk space that can be used in volatile storage (within the /run filesystem).
RuntimeKeepFree=: The amount of space to be set aside for other uses when writing data to volatile storage (within the /run filesystem).
RuntimeMaxFileSize=: The amount of space that an individual journal file can take up in volatile storage (within the /run filesystem) before being rotated.

2.6.2.6 Boot Process Querying

Using the journal, you can examine logs of the present boot record and its progress, and past boot records. This is useful from a system administration perspective when something goes wrong with the boot process or when software or hardware on the system fails to start or operate properly after the system boots and is in the steady state condition.

2.6.2.6.1 Querying Past Boots

To display the information from the current boot, there are times when past boot sequence records would be helpful to examine and compare to the current one. The journal can save information from many previous boots, and the **journalctl** command can be made to display that information in an effective and concise comparative way. Note that in order for you to retain journal information from past boots, you must complete the procedures shown in this section first.

To enable persistent boot information, you can do the following:

1. Create the directory to store the journal with the following command:

   $ **sudo mkdir -p /var/log/journal**

2. Edit the journal configuration file with the editor of your choice:

   $ **sudo nano /etc/systemd/journald.conf**

   Under the [journal] section, uncomment (remove the # sign) the Storage= option, and set it to "persistent" to enable persistent logging:

   /etc/systemd/journald.conf
   . . .
   [Journal]
   Storage=persistent

   When retaining previous boots via persistence is enabled on your system, the **journalctl** command provides some options for working with boots as a unit. To see the boots that journald knows about, use the **--list-boots** option with **journalctl**:

   ```
   $ journalctl --list-boots
   IDX BOOT ID                              FIRST ENTRY              LAST ENTRY   >
    0   6d54cb09c6134fe7ace8f98c86bb3b9e Fri 2025-03-07 16:02:35 PST Sun 2025-03-09>
   $
   ```

   The above command will display a line for each boot, as shown in Table 2.5.

To display more verbose information from these boots, you can use information from either the first or second column. To see the journal from the previous boot, use the -1 relative pointer with the -b flag:

$ **journalctl -b 0**

You can also use the boot ID to call back the same data from boot 0:

$ **journalctl -b 6d54cb09c6134fe7ace8f98c86bb3b9e**

TABLE 2.5

systemctl Boot Information

0	The first column is the offset for the boot from 0, the current boot environment.
6d54cb09c6134fe7ace8f98c86bb3b9e	An absolute reference, the boot ID is in the second column.
Fri 2025-03-07 16:02:35 PST Sun 2025-03-09	The time that the boot session spans, with two time specifications (from-to).

2.6.2.6.2 The Current Boot

To display journal logs from the current boot, use the following command:

$ journalctl -b

   This will show you all of the journal entries that have been collected since the most recent reboot, particularly if you have done the procedures in the previous section and then rebooted a number of times. You can then monitor information about your current environment.

2.6.2.6.3 Displaying Kernel Messages

Kernel messages related to booting, those usually found in dmesg output, can be retrieved from the journal as well. To display only these messages, we can add the **-k** or **--dmesg** flags to the **journalctl** command:

$ journalctl -k

   By default, this will display the kernel messages from the current boot. You can specify an alternative boot environment using the normal boot selection specifications above, being sure that a persistent boot environment was enabled. For instance, to get the messages from five boots ago (if they exist in the journal!), you could type:

$ journalctl -k -b -5

In-Chapter Exercises

11. A new app you have installed refuses to run on your Raspberry Pi 5 OS system. Out of the multitude of debugging scenarios you could go through to find out why that app is misbehaving, you could use a single systemd command to check the most recent record of system activity, and then solve the problem with the app quickly and easily from there.

     Which specific command in the previous sections most compactly provides you with the procedure to expedite your viewing of recent system activity?

12. To get practice with the **journalctl** commands from the previous section, query the boot record from the 3 previous system boots (if there are that many!) from the current boot environment.

2.6.3 systemd timers

systemd takes on many of the functions and facilities that legacy Cron did, via support for clock-time-based and calendar-time-based events.

From a system administrator's perspective, systemd can do Cron-like scheduling of system events. We give examples below of clock-time-based running of a single script and calendar-based scheduling of events.

In order to get a complete description of how systemd deals with time-based specifications and operations, see the man page for **systemd.time**.

2.6.3.1 An Example of Clock-Time-Based Running of a Script

If you have a script **/usr/local/bin/myscript** that you want to run every hour, do the following steps:

1. Create a service unit file, named **myscript.service**, with your favorite text editor. Save it in **/etc/systemd/system/**, with the following content:

   [Unit]
   Description=Whatever MyScript Does

   [Service]
   Type=simple
   ExecStart=/home/bob/myscript

   Note that it is important to set the Type variable to be "simple", not "oneshot". If you specify "oneshot", the script will be run the first time, and then systemd will not run it again, and will turn off the timer.

2. Create the following timer unit file in the same directory as the service unit file above.

   [Unit]
   Description=Runs myscript every hour

   [Timer]
   # Time to wait after booting before we run first time
   OnBootSec=10min
   # Time between running each consecutive time

```
OnUnitActiveSec=1h
Unit=myscript.service

[Install]
WantedBy=multi-user.target
```

3. To start and enable the service:

```
$ sudo systemctl start myscript.timer
```

and to enable it for every subsequent boot:

```
$ sudo systemctl enable myscript.timer
```

In-Chapter Exercises

13.
```
#!/bin/bash
# My first script converted into a service
echo "Hello World!"
```

If the above script file in your home directory on your Raspberry Pi 5 system (which you have named **myscript.bash**) is made into a service with the three steps shown above, how can you get the message "Hello World!" to display every 10 minutes on the stdout of a terminal?

14. a) What command do you use to stop the service? b) What command do you use to ensure the service does not run on every subsequent boot?

2.6.3.2 Example of Calendar-Based Running of the above Script File

If you want to start the service shown in Section 2.6.3.1 according to a calendar event, and not a clock-based interval specification, create a new timer unit, and link the service unit file from that example to that new timer unit.

1. Create the timer unit with your favorite text editor (or nano if that's your favorite), using the following command:

```
$ sudo nano /etc/systemd/system/cal.timer
```

Then put this text into that file:

```
[Unit]
Description=Calendar-based timer

[Timer]
OnCalendar=Mon-Fri *-*-* 00:00:00
Unit=myscript.service
```

```
[Install]
WantedBy=basic.target
```

   The service file and the timer unit file are put in the **/etc/systemd/ system/** folder.

2. To start the calendar timer:

```
$ sudo systemctl start cal.timer
```

and to enable it for every subsequent boot:

```
$ sudo systemctl enable cal.timer
```

In-Chapter Exercise

   15.   What does the time stamp Mon-Fri *-*-* 00:00:00 in the above example specify for the running of the script file?

2.7 A Python3-Based Web Server as a "New-Style Daemon"

For our purposes here in these sections of the chapter, a *new-style daemon,* program, app, or method is one that is systemd-controlled. This example deploys a special Python3 module that easily creates a web server daemon, and puts this module under the control of systemd as a new-style daemon. You don't absolutely need to have any Python knowledge, just to follow along with the steps shown below:

   1. Place a valid index.html file in your home directory.

                        ****Note****

   Our home directory in the steps below is /home/bob.
      Additionally, our very simple index.html file is this:

```
<!DOCTYPE HTML PUBLIC "-//W3C//DTD HTML 4.0 Transitional//EN">
<html>
<head>
        <meta http-equiv="content-type" content="text/html; charset=utf-8"/>
        <title></title>
        <meta name="generator" content="LibreOffice 7.4.7.2 (FreeBSD)"/>
        <meta name="created" content="2025-04-25T18:47:03.316903354"/>
        <meta name="changed" content="2055-04-25T18:48:11.213818830"/>
     <link href="/home/bob/favicon.ico" rel="icon" type="image/x-icon" />
</head>
<body lang="en-US" dir="ltr" style="background: transparent">
<p>Under Construction</p>
</body>
</html>
```

2. Create a service unit file for the web server in **/etc/systemd/system**, named **simp.service**, with the following content. We used the command **sudo nano simp.service** to achieve this:

[Service]
ExecStart=/usr/bin/python3 -m http.server -d /home/bob 8000

3. To start the service, use the following command:

$ **sudo systemctl start simp.service**

4. To view the status of the service, type the following:

$ **systemctl status simp.service**
● simp.service
  Loaded: loaded (/etc/systemd/system/simp.service; static)
  Active: active (running) since Sat 2025-3-22 06:48:00 PST; 25s ago
 Main PID: 141711 (python3)
   Tasks: 1 (limit: 4164)
    CPU: 191ms
  CGroup: /system.slice/simp.service
          └─141711 python3 -m http.server -d /home/bob 8000

Mar 22 06:48:25 raspberrypi systemd[1]: Started simp.service.
$

5. To view the web page this service provides, in a web browser on your local machine, type in the **URL 127.0.0.1:8000**
   The **index.html** file is now displayed in your browser.

6. To stop the service, type the following command:

$ **sudo systemctl stop simp.service**

In-Chapter Exercise

16.   a) Modify the service file for simp.service, so that the Python3 built-in web server is exposed on port 8001. Also, modify the contents of the index.html file code so that it is customized to your liking. Add things like more text, images, links to other pages, etc. Name the service simp2, and complete the 6 steps shown above to make it into a systemd-controlled service. Then run the services simp and simp2 simultaneously, and with your favorite Web browser, browse to the ports 8000 and 8001. What do you see there?

b) How can you expose the ports 8000 and 8001 to the Internet safely, so that from a remote site, you can see the web pages you've created for this Exercise?

The above three examples illustrated how simple Bourne shell script files and a Python built-in can be made into daemon services under the control and monitoring of systemd. The first and second examples illustrated how to make a shell script a daemon by adding a service unit file for it in /etc/systemd/system. The third example illustrated how to make a simple Python built-in, which runs a Python-based web server application, into a systemd service.

2.7.1 systemd Methods of Changing the Activation Behavior of a New-Style Daemon

There are several other "new-style" techniques and methods that can be applied instead of, or to replace an old-style daemon (a traditional UNIX or Linux daemon), to update it to be systemd-compliant and more effectively and efficiently controlled by systemd.

These include the following general ways of achieving that:

Boot-Based Activation
"Old-style" daemons are started when the system boots, and/or by individual script files on a per-service basis, using UNIX BSD or SysV initialization. This is the traditional method of service activation, used before systemd's installation in the kernel. systemd uses a modernized version of activation, both when the system boots and at runtime, using minimal service description files that we have described in the sections above.

Socket-Based Activation
The chief advantage of socket-based activation of daemons is, most importantly, the simplification of configuration and the program development process. In socket-based activation, the creation and binding of listening sockets happen in systemd. Using initialization and service unit files for daemon configuration, systemd installs the sockets and then assigns them to the systemd-started process when some triggering event occurs.

Bus-Based Activation
When the D-Bus InterProcess Communication (IPC) system is used, new-style daemons deploy bus activation so that they are automatically activated when a client application accesses their IPC interfaces or channels.

Device-Based Activation
New-style daemons that manage a particular type or class of hardware, like disk volumes or ZFS datasets, are activated only when the hardware of the respective kind is plugged in, or otherwise becomes available.

Path-Based Activation
systemd provides a way to bind service activation to file system changes. This is implemented using path-based activation configured in path unit files, as illustrated and described in the man page for systemd.path.

Timer-Based Activation
New-style daemons can implement clean-up jobs that are intended to be executed in regular intervals. In systemd, this is implemented via timer unit files as shown in the examples above, as described in the man page for systemd.timer.

It is possible, and preferable, for services to be activated by more than one of the above methods.

Examples of this are Wi-Fi, Bluetooth, and CUPS printer services, which can be made active when their respective devices are plugged in, or when activity is first seen on a particular port.

We provide a simple example of socket-based activation in Section 2.7.1.1.

2.7.1.1 A Simple Sockets-Based Activation Example

****Note****

Part of the efficiency and speed advantage systemd gives the Raspberry Pi 5 OS is the ability to delay the start of services and daemons until they are actually needed, instead of running all of them when the system boots and enters the steady operating state.

Sockets-based activation for a daemon, such as a web server, means that when a request is made on a specified port that the web server is hooked to, the web server then starts as a daemon. It then services all requests made on that port.

In this example, we use the special **systemd-activate** command, which is usually used to test sockets-based activation, to achieve our objectives. **systemd-activate** "listens" on a port.

The following are steps you can easily take to make a web server application start when an HTTP request is made on a particular port of your choosing. You can change the port numbers shown in the example steps below to any ephemeral ports you want.

1. ****Optional**** Place a valid index.html file in your home directory on your Raspberry Pi 5 OS system, if you haven't already done so for the example above in Section 2.7.

****Note**** Our home directory in the steps below is /home/bob.

Additionally, our very simple index.html file is the following:

```
<!DOCTYPE HTML PUBLIC "-//W3C//DTD HTML 4.0 Transitional//EN">
<html>
<head>
        <meta http-equiv="content-type" content="text/html; charset=utf-8"/>
        <title></title>
        <meta name="generator" content="LibreOffice 4.3.5.2.0 (FreeBSD)"/>
        <meta name="created" content="2025-04-25T18:47:03.316903354"/>
        <meta name="changed" content="2025-04-25T18:48:11.213818830"/>
     <link href="/home/bob/favicon.ico" rel="icon" type="image/x-icon" />
</head>
<body lang="en-US" dir="ltr" style="background: transparent">
<p>Under Construction</p>
</body>
</html>
```

2. Type the following command (where instead of the path /home/ bob), you substitute the path to the directory where you placed the index.html file:

```
$ systemd-socket-activate -l 2000 -a python3 -m  http.server -d /home/bob 8096
Listening on [::]:2000 as 3.
```

This command awaits a request on port 2000, and then when one comes in (from a web browser, for example), it executes the command shown after the -a option to activate the Python3 http.server web server built-in application. So basically, you are using the **systemd-socket-activate** command to activate port 2000, and then coupling Python3 to this activation to run the http.server built-in application on port 8096.

3. To test this activation, with your favorite web browser, set the URL to

http://your_ip_address:2000

Our local network web address was 192.168.1.14

> ****Note**** You will get an error in the browser, or
> the browser will spin for a while. No worries!

In the terminal window you typed the command into, this will be displayed:

```
Listening on [::]:2000 as 3.
Communication attempt on fd 3.
Connection from 192.168.1.14:50418 to [::ffff:192.168.1.14]:2000
Spawned python3 (python3 -m http.server -d /home/bob 8096) as PID 19747.
Execing python3 (python3 -m http.server -d /home/bob 8096)
Serving HTTP on 0.0.0.0 port 8096 (http://0.0.0.0:8096/) ...
```

You just "primed" the systemd-socket-activate program, and it has spawned the Python3 http.server application! You can check this by using the **ps -aux** command in another terminal window at this point.

4. Set your browser's URL to http://your_ip_address:8096, and press Enter. You have accessed the Python3 http.server on port 8096. To check this, use the **ps -aux** command again. It should now show two processes running: the systemd-socket-activate process, and the Python3 http.server process, which was socket-activated. Plus, perhaps a couple of web browser processes as well.

5. Something similar to this will now show in the terminal window from Step 2:

192.168.1.14 - - [09/Mar/2025 10:25:47] "GET / HTTP/1.1" 200 -
192.168.1.14 - - [09/Mar/2025 10:25:47] code 404, message File not found
192.168.1.14 - - [09/Mar/2025 10:25:47] "GET /home/bob/favicon.ico HTTP/1.1" 404 -

Whatever is in the directory you set in Step 1 above will be displayed. If the directory contains files, it will show you a listing of the files in the directory. And if there is a valid HTTP-formatted index. html file in that directory, as optionally shown in Step, your web browser will show its valid HTML contents in the browser window.

6. To terminate the Python3 built-in http.server, hold down <Ctrl> + <C> on the keyboard in the terminal window you typed the command from Step 2. You'll get a Keyboard interrupt received, exiting message.

One of the obvious drawbacks of this example is that the Python3 built-in http.server web server does not stop running after requests have stopped coming into it on port 8096. It's not socket-deactivated! Building a timeout into this simple example would be an interesting exercise, so that the web server is not always running. And, as you can see, the Simple Sockets-Based Activation Example is not a rigorous and thorough explication of socket-based activation, but it gives you the idea behind it using a single, and very simple, systemd command.

In-Chapter Exercises

17. a) How would you terminate the simple sockets-based activation example you created in Section 2.7.1. from the command line? b) If you reload the webpage URL from step 4 above, what is displayed in your browser window?

18. Use the **ncat** command (from the nmap tools) to achieve the same results as the systemd-socket- activate program example above, except instead of a Python3 web server program, launch a bash shell.

(Hint: On a server, use **ncat** to both listen on a port, and then start the bash shell when a request comes in on that port, and on a client connect to the server on that port)

2.8 Chapter Summary

In this chapter, we provided a complete overview of the superkernel known as systemd, which essentially controls everything on the Raspberry Pi 5 OS system, including the Linux kernel itself. We covered the following basic systemd, and other Linux commands:

id -u, journalctl, ncat, nmap, systemctl, systemd-activate, systemd-cgls, systemd-socket-activate, who -r.

3

Python 3

3.0 Objectives and Introduction

1. To illustrate the history of the development of the Python 3 programming language
2. To give a quick start into programming with Python 3 using Thonny on the Raspberry Pi 5 OS
3. To give an overview of the Python 3 programming language
4. To cover the basic syntax of Python 3
5. To show how to install and run Python 3 on a Raspberry Pi 5 system
6. To provide several basic practical examples of using Python 3
7. To cover the commands and primitives:

python3, **Thonny**

3.0.1 The History of the Development of the Python Programming Language

The Python programming language has grown from a niche scripting language into one of the most widely used and influential programming languages in the world. Its development has been shaped by a focus on simplicity, readability, and versatility. From its humble beginnings in the late 1980s to its current status as a dominant force in software development, Python has undergone significant evolution.

Origins and Early Development
Python was conceived in the late 1980s by Dutch programmer *Guido van Rossum* while he was working at the Centrum Wiskunde & Informatica (CWI) in the Netherlands. Van Rossum had been involved with the development of the ABC programming language, which was designed for teaching and prototyping. ABC emphasized ease of use, but it had limitations, particularly in extensibility. Inspired by ABC but eager to improve upon it, van Rossum sought to create a language that was both powerful and user-friendly.

DOI: 10.1201/9781003652427-4

In December 1989, van Rossum began working on Python during his holiday break. He wanted to develop a language that was easy to learn, allowed for rapid development, and had a strong emphasis on readability. He also wanted it to support both procedural and object-oriented programming paradigms. Python was named after the British comedy group *Monty Python*, reflecting van Rossum's desire to make programming fun and accessible.

The Release of Python 1.0
On February 20, 1991, van Rossum released Python 1.0 to the public. This initial release included many of the core features that still define Python today, such as exception handling, modules, functions, and dynamic typing. Python's clear and concise syntax immediately set it apart from other languages, making it particularly attractive for beginners and experienced programmers alike.

Python 1.x releases continued throughout the 1990s, gradually adding more features such as support for lambda functions, map/filter/reduce functions, and an improved exception-handling model. The language gained a small but devoted following, particularly among those in academia and research who valued its ease of use for scripting and automation.

The Evolution of Python 2.x
In 2000, Python 2.0 was released, introducing several important features, including list comprehensions and garbage collection based on reference counting and cycle detection. This version aimed to improve performance and maintainability while keeping the core philosophy of Python intact.

However, Python 2.x also introduced some inconsistencies, particularly in handling Unicode and integer division. These issues, combined with the need for backward compatibility, led to challenges in future development. Over the years, the Python community realized that significant changes were needed, but making these changes within the Python 2.x version was impractical.

The Transition to Python 3.x
Recognizing the need for a more forward-looking approach, van Rossum and the Python community decided to create Python 3.0, which was released in December 2008. This version introduced several major changes, including better Unicode support, a more consistent standard library, and improvements to syntax and performance.

One of the most controversial aspects of Python 3 was its incompatibility with Python 2.x. While the changes were necessary for long-term growth, the transition period was challenging. Many organizations were reluctant to move to Python 3 due to the vast amount of legacy Python 2 code in use. As a result, Python 2.7, the last release in the Python 2 series, continued to be supported until January 1, 2020.

Python's Rise to Prominence

Throughout the 2010s, Python experienced an explosion in popularity. Several factors contributed to its growth:

1. Data Science and Machine Learning – Python became the dominant language in data science, artificial intelligence, and machine learning, thanks to libraries like NumPy, Pandas, TensorFlow, and scikit-learn.

2. Web Development – Frameworks like Django and Flask made Python a strong choice for web development.

3. Automation and Scripting – Python's simplicity made it ideal for automating tasks, scripting, and DevOps.

4. Education – Many universities adopted Python as the primary teaching language due to its readability and ease of learning.

By the late 2010s, Python had become one of the most widely used programming languages in the world. Its community-driven development model, extensive libraries, and versatility cemented its position across multiple domains.

Modern Python and Future Directions

As of the 2020s, Python continues to evolve under the guidance of the Python Software Foundation (PSF). Recent releases, such as Python 3.10 and 3.11, have introduced pattern matching, performance optimizations, and enhanced type hinting. The language has also become more efficient, with Just-In-Time (JIT) compilation efforts aimed at improving execution speed.

Python's future remains bright, with ongoing improvements in concurrency, security, and developer experience. The language continues to adapt to new technological trends while staying true to its core principles of readability and simplicity.

Python 3 has a central role in AI and large language models (LLMs), for several key reasons:

1. Primary Language for AI Development
   Python 3 is the de facto standard language for building and using AI systems, including large language models. Its syntax is clean, readable, and expressive, which makes prototyping and experimentation faster and easier.

2. Foundation of ML & DL Libraries
   Python 3 is the base for nearly all major machine learning (ML) and deep learning (DL) libraries:
   • TensorFlow and PyTorch (core frameworks for training LLMs)

- Transformers (Hugging Face) (for using and fine-tuning pre-trained LLMs)
- NumPy, SciPy, Pandas (for data handling and scientific computing)
- scikit-learn (for classical ML algorithms)

These tools are used to train, fine-tune, serve, and evaluate language models.

3. Used to Build and Control LLMs
   The entire lifecycle of an LLM is handled in Python 3:
   - Data preprocessing (tokenization, cleaning, formatting)
   - Model training (via GPU/TPU-enabled frameworks)
   - Inference and deployment (e.g., with Flask/FastAPI, or Hugging Face pipelines)
   - Evaluation (metrics, error analysis, etc.)

   Python scripts are also often used to glue together distributed training jobs running across multiple machines or GPUs.

4. Open-Source Community & Ecosystem
   Python 3's vast ecosystem makes it easy to integrate:
   - Datasets
   - Visualization tools (e.g., Matplotlib, Seaborn)
   - NLP tools (e.g., spaCy, NLTK)
   - Model sharing platforms (e.g., Hugging Face Hub)

5. Running LLMs in Python
   You can interact with LLMs (like GPT) directly using Python code:

```
from transformers import pipeline
llm = pipeline("text-generation", model="gpt2")
print(llm("Once upon a time, there was a fox", max_length=30))
```

Python 3 is not AI itself, but it's the primary tool used to create, train, and deploy AI, including large language models. Without Python, the development of modern LLMs like GPT, BERT, or Claude would be far more cumbersome and slower.

Conclusion

Python's journey from a personal project to a global programming powerhouse is a testament to its design philosophy and strong community support. Guido van Rossum's vision of a language that emphasizes simplicity, readability, and productivity has been realized and expanded upon by countless developers worldwide. Whether in web development, AI, or automation, Python remains a vital tool for programmers across industries, and its influence shows no signs of waning.

In this chapter, we give a broad introduction to the Python programming language, using Python version 3. For the beginner Python 3 programmer, we illustrate all of its important programming capabilities and syntactic structures, in the context of the three predominant computer programming paradigms:

Virtualization, Concurrency, and Persistence.

We first give a brief introduction to Thonny, the Python 3 Integrated Development Environment (IDE), and then use it throughout the rest of the chapter. We show all of Python 3's critical and basic syntax, including numbers and expressions, variables, statements, getting input from the user, functions, OOP in Python, modules, saving and executing Python 3 scripts, string and sequence operations, and error handling. We also give many basic and practical examples, such as:

a. another way of writing shell script files,

b. rewriting Bash and tcsh scripts,

c. basic user file maintenance, backing up files,

d. remote copying with the **rsync** command, and

e. graphics using **tkinter**.

Finally, we show how thread execution is achieved in Python 3 and how OOP can be deployed to accomplish it.

The major sections of this chapter are as follows:

3.1 A Quickstart into Python 3 with the Thonny Integrated Development Environment

3.2 An Overview of the Python 3 Language

3.3 Python 3 Syntax

3.4 Practical Examples

3.1 A Quickstart into Python 3 with the Thonny Integrated Development Environment

The easiest and quickest way to use Python 3 on the Raspberry Pi 5 is to deploy a GUI, the Thonny Integrated Development Environment (IDE), to interact with Python 3 and construct and run program code. This IDE comes pre-installed on the Raspberry Pi 5 OS, as does the latest version of Python 3 that accompanies your version of the Raspberry Pi 5 OS. Thonny is a graphical front end to Python 3, and as such allows the use of toolbar icons to execute many useful operations expediently and very effectively. This is a somewhat different way of interacting with the Raspberry Pi 5 than what we've shown previously. By and large, we've used text-based, command-line interface operations to perform our system administration tasks.

Which is <u>not</u> to say that in developing Python 3 program code with Thonny, you don't use text!

The Python language implementation has a highly structured text syntax and grammar, as you shall see in the sections below.

Everything we do in this chapter is either done with Thonny or done on the Bash command line. But in most of our work below, we only show the areas of the Thonny window known as the "Script Area" and the "Shell Area". And be aware that Thonny has two modes, Regular and Simple. Since our work here is for beginners, we show the Simple Mode of operation. That's the default when you launch Thonny. If you want to switch to "Regular Mode", there's a text link on the right side of the Thonny window that would allow you to change Thonny to a necessarily more complex display, with more pull-down menu choices that go beyond what the Simple Mode gives you.

If you want to change your style of interaction to that necessarily more complex, but verbose, way of interacting with Python 3 via Thonny Regular Mode, we give step-by-step instructions that show how to do that.

There are other IDEs available on the Raspberry Pi 5 OS that you can use with Python 3. From the Raspberry Pi menu, Programming > Geany is one of them. We've found that the Geany IDE is necessarily more complex, and useful for the development of C programs, for example, and that language's program systems, but feel free to experiment with Geany for Python 3 scripts and program code development. We don't show Geany here, and leave that experimentation up to you.

3.1.1 Launching Thonny, and the Thonny Window

To launch Thonny, from the Raspberry Pi menu, make the choice Programming > Thonny. The Thonny window opens onscreen, as shown in Figure 3.1.

At the top of the window is a row of *Toolbar Area* icons that allow you to do various operations, such as debug or test, load, save, and execute Python 3 program code.

Next, below the row of Toolbar icons, is the *Script Area*, where you can type in multiple lines of Python 3 code, or input an already completed program from a file. Notice that line numbers for your program are illustrated in the left margin of the Script Area, and above that area in the upper left is a tab naming the current program being worked on. In Figure 3.1, it reads **<untitled>**.

And finally, below that is the *Python 3 Shell Area*, where the command line prompt **>>>** from Python is found. Here, you can type in one line of Python 3 code, and have it executed, or "interpreted" when you press the **<Enter>** key on the keyboard of the Raspberry Pi 5. Also, error messages or other

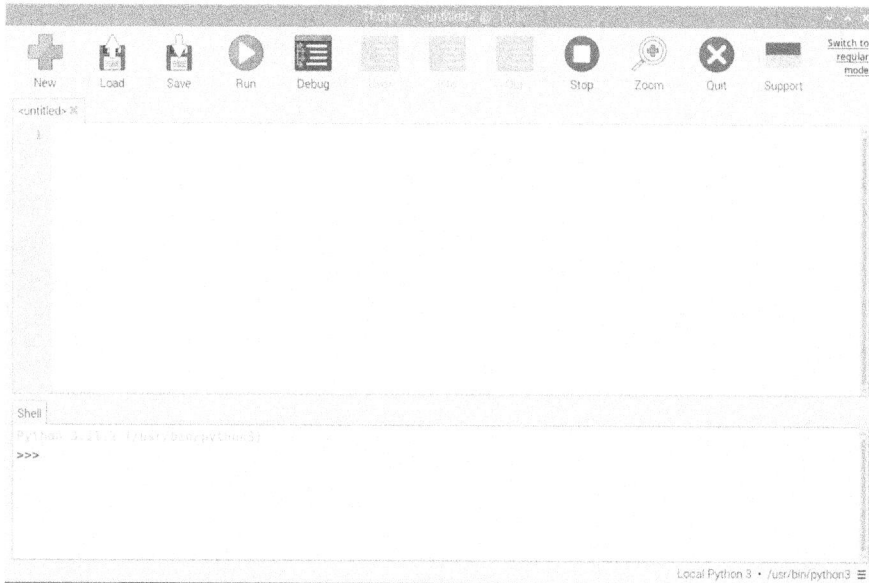

FIGURE 3.1
Thonny window.

feedback from Python 3 are displayed in this area. Figure 3.1 shows we're running Python 3.11.2, found in */usr*/bin/python3. This version of Python, and Thonny as well, is dependent upon what release of the Raspberry Pi 5 OS you've installed on your system. These versions of Python 3 and Thonny are the defaults on the Raspberry Pi 5 OS we're using.

3.1.2 Creating and Running a Simple Python 3 Program from within Thonny

Let's create and execute a simple Python 3 program, which has a determinate repetition structure in it (as opposed to an indeterminate structure), and prints some output to the Python 3 Shell Area. Launch Thonny on your Raspberry Pi 5, and type the following lines into the Python 3 Script Area (making sure to press the Enter key on the keyboard after each line):

```
print("Count for me, Python!")
for n in range (5):
    print("I'm counting!", n)
print("I'm done counting!")
```

Notice that after the 2nd line, Thonny <u>automatically</u> inserts a mandatory 4 space indentation for the 3rd line! That mechanism, of automatic indentation, is critical to the technique of *structured programming*, where flow-of-control programming structures are delineated by proper indentation.

****Note****

Thonny achieves that automatic indentation for you, because most beginners commit either indentation errors in their programs, or syntax errors due to typos.

Thonny also automatically indents the 4th line, but you can override this indentation by pressing the **<Delete>** key on your keyboard to type the 4th line flush left, like the 1st and 2nd lines.

Now, click on the Run Toolbar icon in the Toolbar Area. In the Shell Area, the following should be displayed:

```
Count for me, Python!
I'm counting! 0
I'm counting! 1
I'm counting! 2
I'm counting! 3
I'm counting! 4
I'm done counting!
>>>
```

How come the count started at zero(0)? That's because Python is a zero-indexed system, where counts start at 0, not 1.

Now, click on the Save icon in the Toolbar Area. In the Save dialog window that appears, name this Python 3 program **looper.py**, making sure to add the file extension **.py** as shown, and designate a folder on your system where you want the program to be saved. Then click Save. Once the save is completed, notice that the title bar of the Thonny window shows the path to, plus the name of this program you just saved, and that the tab at the top of the Script Area now shows the name **looper.py**.

****Note****

If you want to run that program in "Interactive Mode", outside of the Thonny IDE, you can by launching Python 3 as we show in a few places below in this chapter.

In-Chapter Exercises

1. How can you make Python count from 1 to 5, using the above program structure?
2. How can you clear the program from the Script area?

You're done with this first Python 3 program! In the sections below, we'll cover much more of the syntax and structure of a Python 3 program. But for now, play around with Thonny and this program, and then you can click on the Quit Toolbar icon. The next time you run Thonny, this same program will be loaded, unless, of course, you cleared it according to your answer to In-Chapter Exercise 2!

3.2 An Overview of the Python 3 Language

Computer programs execute and accomplish their objectives in a particular order, from start to finish. They may "branch" within that order, perhaps to only execute some of their instructions, based on certain logical tests or conditions. They may also repeat segments of their operation, either for some predetermined number of times or indefinitely, based on changing conditions. Python conforms to this model and operates using the following scheme of levels:

Level 1. *Everything* in Python 3 programs, or scripts, is composed of modular components.

Level 2. These modular components contain syntactically correct Python statements.

Level 3. These statements contain expressions.

Level 4. The expressions create and manipulate objects.

The Python 3 code development process starts by formulating syntactically correct elements at Level 1, and proceeds downwards through the levels sequentially until Level 4 is achieved.

In the Raspberry Pi 5 OS environment, if you are presented with a task that requires you to do either script writing or programming, the first thing you have to decide is which overall guiding programming model you are going to adopt to accomplish the task. In simple terms, this means using one of three predominant programming models, or maybe even a combination of them:

a. the procedural/imperative programming model,

b. the Object Oriented Programming (OOP) model, or

c. the logic programming model.

Of course, how well you accomplish the task, or tasks you set for yourself, depends on how much script writing or programming experience you have, using any, or all of those models. And perhaps, if you are doing this with a group of people, their experiences and preferences count for a great deal as well. But, how you formulate the task(s) in terms of any of the models is related, most importantly, to your experience in using these models. There are no simple guidelines for applying any of the models to the vast number of possible script-writing or programming tasks that exist in the realm of computer programming.

However, the bottom line in the accomplishment of your goals is how familiar you are with the syntax of the languages that implement the model you choose.

That's why we explain Python 3 syntax in detail in this chapter. Python 3 can utilize all of these programming models, and can, in fact, mix the techniques used in the models. We make some commentary on this here and illustrate some simple uses of the models in the next few sections.

Python 3 is fundamentally a *high-level*, *structured* (in this case, meaning built of regular structured components, like determinate or indeterminate repetition, for example), and an *interpreted* programming (or scripting) language, as opposed to a low-level, compiled language like C or Java. That doesn't exclude the fact that it can be compiled as well. As stated, it is also a *multi-paradigm* programming language, which allows you to use data abstractions from the three predominant paradigms. For our purposes, "scripting" and "programming" can be thought of as the same thing.

So why use a "pure" OOP approach?

Instead of totally defining the most fundamental aspects and parts of OOP (which you can find descriptions of easily in the extensive literature on Python 3 and several other computer programming languages), we choose to contrast and compare it to the more traditional procedural programming method, to give you a more intuitive feel for the approach OOP uses.

Procedural/imperative, non-OOP programs, as we have noted, can run through their structured, flow-of-control operation using the Python 3 syntax we show in the sections below. Non-trivial programs can possibly be made up of groupings of flow-of-control operations, known as procedures, modules, or subroutines. This way of using Python 3 syntax, since the language "accommodates" the procedural/imperative model, can put together a program that emphasizes more traditional algorithms and Abstract Data Types (ADT). Simple examples of these two things are the algorithm (or mathematical plan) for computing the greatest common factor of two integers, or the definition of integers themselves as a certain kind of numerical value, along with the prescribed set of possible operations on them.

One of the biggest problems with this approach is that if variables take on a global *scope*, in a global *namespace* outside of the "container" it's defined in, the assignment of values to it can be conflicting and cause errors. That is, in part, why using namespaces, as we showed in Chapter 1, to essentially isolate processes, is so effective. Variables (which are active in any particular process namespace) are exclusively and *locally* defined and used.

In Python 3 OOP, this is basically done using what is known as "encapsulation". The idea is that the data and the functions that manipulate the data <u>are one entity</u>. This keeps both objects safe from unwanted changes to them from any environment outside the entity. This fundamental component of OOP, which combines data with a set of *methods* for accessing and managing the data, is called an *object*. Its data treatment model is completely different from the procedural/imperative program model previously described.

Of course, it is possible with the rich set of syntax available in Python 3 to combine both non-OOP and OOP styles in one program.

****Note****

Python 3 does not faithfully implement the functional, or logic, programming structure known as *tail recursion*, as does a language such as MIT Scheme. But it is capable of recursion, as we also show below.

3.2.1 Objects and Classes

If you haven't discovered this yet, our coverage of topics here in this book revolves around a little bit of "Why?", and a lot more "How?" It would be prudent to first cover, in an introductory fashion, the "How?" aspect of the data model (and also the "Why?") that Python 3 programming uses. In particular, as that applies to OOP. OOP is a programming model that represents concepts as *objects* that have fields (which are basically attributes that describe the object) and associated processes, or if you will, functions, known as *methods,* which are basically known as "messaging" operations on those attributes. Objects, which are established as instances of what are known as "classes", are constructed to interact with one another using the messaging system, to design applications and computer programs. Some examples of modern OOP languages are Smalltalk, C++, C#, Java, Perl, Ruby, PHP, and Python 3.

Below are some common terms used in OOP:

Class: A user-defined model for an object that defines characteristics of any object in that class. The characteristics are data members (class variables and instance variables) and methods, accessed via what's called dot(.) notation.

Class variable: A variable that is shared by all instances of a class. Class variables are defined within a class, but outside any of the class's methods.

Data member: A class variable or instance variable that holds data associated with a class and its objects.

Instance variable: A variable that is defined inside a method and belongs only to the current instance of a class.

Inheritance: The transfer of the characteristics of a class to other classes that are derived from it.

Instance: An individual object of a certain class. An object that belongs to a class named Circle, for example, is an instance of the class Circle.

Instantiation: The creation of an instance of a class.

Method: A special kind of function that is defined in a class definition.

Object: A unique instance of a data structure defined by its class. An object can comprise both data members (class variables and instance variables) and methods.

The general form of a class definition is:

```
class ClassName:
    'Optional class documentation string'
    class_suite
```

The class has a documentation string, which can be accessed via **ClassName.__doc__**.

The **class_suite** consists of all the component statements defining class members, data attributes, and methods.

The following lines of interactive code very simply illustrate the inheritance model of OOP classes, and in particular, their hierarchical nature. Launch Thonny on your Raspberry Pi 5 OS system, and execute the code below in the Thonny Shell Area. Be sure to press the **<Enter>** key at the end of Line 2 of the code. (There is no need to type in the comment line numbers, which we provide here for reference only.)

```
>>> class tab: pass               #Line 1
...                               #Line 2
>>> tab.name = 'Bob Koretsky'     #Line 3
>>> tab.age = 85                  #Line 4
>>> print (tab.name,tab.age)      #Line 5
Bob Koretsky 85
>>> x = tab()                     #Line 6
>>> y = tab()                     #Line 7
>>> x.name                        #Line 8
Bob Koretsky
>>> y.name = 'Alan Turing'        #Line 9
>>> tab.name, x.name, y.name      #Line 10
('Bob Koretsky', 'Bob Koretsky', 'Alan Turing')
>>>
```

A line-by-line analysis and description of this code is as follows:

Line 1: Starting with the keyword **class**, you name a class **tab**. You use the keyword **pass** to assign the class to an empty namespace object, that is, *it has no class members, attributes, or methods yet.* A class is a model of an object!

Line 2: Continue by pressing **<Enter>**.

Line 3: You now add an attribute called **name** to the class named **tab**. The class **tab** has no instances yet!

Line 4: You assign another attribute called **age** to the class tab.

Line 5: You print out the attributes of **tab**.

Line 6: You now assign an instance, named **x**, to the class **tab**, which is now an empty instance.

Line 7: You now assign another instance, named **y**, to the class **tab**, which is another empty instance.

Line 8: The instance **x** inherits the attribute **name** from **tab**. You use the dot (.) operator to connect or refer to the instance **x** with name "Bob Koretsky" in the class tab.

Line 9: You now explicitly assign the instance **y**, with an attribute **name**, the value "Alan Turing". You use the dot (.) operator to connect the instance **y** with name "Alan Turing".

Line 10: You print out the name in **tab**, the name referred to in **x** inherited from tab, and the explicitly assigned name in **y**. Attribute references work through the mechanisms of inheritance, and attribute assignments work on the objects to which the assignment is done.

The following is a more involved example of creating a class and then using some methods to manipulate the objects in that class. Type the following code into a file named **firstclass.py** using your favorite text editor, and save it in the directory that is Thonny's current working directory:

Example 3.1

```
#!/usr/bin/python3
class Structure:
    'Common base class for all Python Structures'
    StrucCount = 0

    def __init__(s, name, number):
        s.name = name
        s.number= number
        Structure.StrucCount += 1

    def displayCount(s):
        print ("Total Structures %d" % Structure.StrucCount)

    def displayStructure(s):
        print ("Name : ", s.name,  ", Number : ", s.number)
```

Then, in Thonny, use Way 3 (Import Script mode), which we define more fully below, to run **firstclass.py**

In the Thonny Shell Area, type the following (you can, again, leave out the comments):

```
>>> import firstclass
>>> Stru1 = firstclass.Structure("Arithmetic Operators", 17)   #creates the first object
>>> Stru2 = firstclass.Structure("Logical Operators", 10)      #creates the second object
>>> Stru1.displayStructure()
Name : Arithmetic Operators,  Number : 17                      #displays the first object
>>> Stru2.displayStructure()                                   #displays the second object
Name : Logical Operators,, Number : 10
>>> print ("Total Structures %d" % firstclass.Structure.StrucCount) #prints total structures
Total Structures 2
>>> Stru1.inst = 7                                             #creates a new attribute of Stru1
>>> hasattr(Stru1, 'inst')                                     #checks object for attribute
True
>>> getattr(Stru1, 'inst')                                     #gets the value of the attribute
7
>>> getattr(Stru1, 'name')                                     #gets the value of the attribute
'Arithmetic Operators'
>>>
```

There are three important things to notice about this OOP Example:

1. The variable **StrucCount** is a class variable whose value is shared among all instances of this class. This variable can be accessed as **Structure.StrucCount** from inside the class or as **firstclass.Structure.StrucCount** outside the class.

2. The first class method, **__init__()**, is a special method, which is called a *class constructor* or *initialization* method. Python 3 calls this method when you create a new instance of this class.

3. You declare other class methods like normal Python 3 functions, with the exception that the first argument to each method is **s**. Python 3 adds the **s** argument to the list for you; you do <u>not</u> need to include it when you call, or invoke the methods.

3.2.2 Python 3 Program Data Model

Following are some statements about the Python 3 model of data that might help you organize your concepts and thoughts about what the "nuts and bolts" of Python 3 are:

1. Even though Python 3 incorporates many of the features of a multi-paradigm programming ensemble, its actual and fundamental basis is shown in the following 5 statements::

2. Everything in the Python 3 program can be referred to as an *object*, with the same exact meaning of the word *object* used in OOP. These objects have three parts: an *identifier*, a *type*, and a *value*.

   For example, when you assign x = 62.25 interactively in the Python 3 interpreter, or in a Python 3 module, script file, or library of modules, a real number object type is created; it has a value of 62.25, and it is identified as an object with a pointer to its location in memory. x is the identifier that refers to its specific location in memory. The equal sign (=) is essentially the reference between an identifier and a value.

3. In OOP languages, such as Python 3 and Java, the type that an object assumes gives it membership in a particular set, called its *class*. The class of the object limits, and also defines what are known as the *methods*, or operations, which can be performed on or with it.

4. When a particular object of some type is created, that particular object is called an *instance* of that type. In general, an object's identity and type cannot be changed. They are known as *immutable*. If an object's value can be modified, the object is said to be *mutable*. An object that refers to other objects to obtain value and type is known as a *container*.

5. Objects can also define their own *attributes*, or characteristics, of the data they are comprised of, and even the *methods* used on them. An attribute is a property or value associated with an object. A method is a function internal to a class of objects that performs some sort of operation on those objects when the method is used or invoked.

6. Attributes and methods are accessed using the dot(.) operator, as shown in the following examples:

```
x = 2 + 4j        creates a complex number x.
A = a.real        uses a method known as real to extract the real part (an attribute) of a.
c = [1, 2, 3]     creates an instance of type list identified as c of the integers 1, −2, and −3.
c.append(7)       adds a new element to c using the append method.
```

3.2.3 Python References and Releases

Before you begin this section, and as you proceed through the rest of this chapter, it would be helpful for you to reference, and read for understanding in a "top-down" manner, the following references (the versions and editions of which were available at the time this book was written). The Python 3 online documentation and the printed book we used are as follows:

The Python Language Reference -- https://docs.python.org/3/reference/

Use the latest versions and editions of the above references, and if necessary, and perhaps even have a printed form of them. Whatever top-down principles you can carry with you from these references throughout your Python 3 programming experience, both in this chapter and beyond, are very important and will enable you to see the complex details in a much larger context.

At the time this book was written, Python 3.13 was the latest stable version of the Python language available for the Raspberry Pi 5 OS, but its installation from packages is not something that a beginner would need to do for everything we present here in this chapter. As you can see from Figure 3.1, for our release of the Raspberry Pi 5 OS on our Raspberry Pi 5, Python 3.11.2 is used here.

We also provide an abbreviated Python 3 command syntax reference for Python 3.11.2 in Table 3.1. You can refer to this whenever you need a handy reference for syntactic components of the language. In addition to the command syntax reference, we present a glossary of Python 3 terms at the end of the chapter as well.

TABLE 3.1

Python 3 Syntax and Command Summary

Command	What it Does
__init__	Initializes an object instance.
__main__	Indicates the main script execution entry point.
__name__	Stores the name of the module.
__repr__	Defines a detailed string representation of an object.
__str__	Defines a string representation of an object.
abs()	Returns the absolute value of a number.
all()	Returns True if all elements in an iterable are true.
any()	Returns True if any element in an iterable is true.
assert	Checks a condition and raises an exception if false.
async def	Defines an asynchronous function.
asyncio.run()	Runs an asynchronous function.
await	Waits for an asynchronous operation to complete.
bin()	Converts an integer to a binary string.
bool()	Converts a value to a boolean.
break	Exits a loop early.
chr()	Returns a string representing a character from its Unicode code.
class	Defines a class.
classmethod	Defines a class method.
close()	Closes a file.
collections.Counter()	Counts occurrences of elements in an iterable.
collections.defaultdict()	Creates a dictionary with a default value type.
collections.namedtuple()	Creates a lightweight object similar to a tuple.
continue	Skips the current iteration of a loop.
datetime.datetime.now()	Gets the current date and time.
def	Defines a function.
del	Deletes an object or attribute.

(Continued)

TABLE 3.1 (*Continued*)

Python 3 Syntax and Command Summary

Command	What it Does
dict()	Creates a dictionary.
dir()	Returns a list of attributes and methods of an object.
elif	Defines an else-if condition.
else	Defines an alternative execution path.
enumerate()	Adds an index to an iterable and returns it as an enumerate object.
filter()	Filters elements of an iterable based on a function.
float()	Converts an object to a floating-point number.
for	Defines a loop that iterates over an iterable.
from-import	Imports specific functions or attributes from a module.
hash()	Returns the hash value of an object.
help()	Displays help information about a function or object.
hex()	Converts an integer to a hexadecimal string.
id()	Returns the memory address of an object.
if	Defines a conditional statement.
import	Imports a module.
input()	Takes user input from the console.
int()	Converts an object to an integer.
isinstance()	Checks if an object is an instance of a class.
issubclass()	Checks if a class is a subclass of another class.
itertools.combinations()	Returns combinations of elements from an iterable.
itertools.permutations()	Returns permutations of elements from an iterable.
json.dumps()	Converts a Python object into a JSON string.
json.loads()	Parses a JSON string into a Python object.
lambda	Defines an anonymous function.
len()	Returns the length of an object (list, string, etc.).
list()	Creates a list.
map()	Applies a function to all items in an iterable.
math.pow()	Raises a number to a power.
math.sqrt()	Returns the square root of a number.
max()	Returns the largest value in an iterable.
min()	Returns the smallest value in an iterable.
oct()	Converts an integer to an octal string.
open()	Opens a file and returns a file object.
ord()	Returns an integer representing the Unicode code of a character.
os.getcwd()	Gets the current working directory.
os.listdir()	Lists files and directories in a specified path.

(Continued)

TABLE 3.1 (*Continued*)

Python 3 Syntax and Command Summary

Command	What it Does
os.path.join()	Joins path components.
pass	Placeholder statement that does nothing.
print()	Outputs text or variables to the console.
property	Defines a property for a class.
raise	Raises an exception.
random.choice()	Selects a random item from a list.
random.randint()	Generates a random integer between two numbers.
random.shuffle()	Shuffles a list in place.
range()	Generates a range of numbers.
re.findall()	Finds all occurrences of a pattern in a string.
re.match()	Checks if a string matches a pattern.
re.search()	Searches for a pattern in a string.
re.sub()	Replaces occurrences of a pattern in a string.
read()	Reads content from a file.
reversed()	Returns an iterator that yields values in reverse order.
round()	Rounds a number to a given precision.
self	Represents the instance of a class.
set()	Creates a set.
sorted()	Returns a sorted list from an iterable.
staticmethod	Defines a static method in a class.
str()	Converts an object to a string.
sum()	Returns the sum of elements in an iterable.
super()	Calls a method from a parent class.
sys.argv	Returns command-line arguments as a list.
sys.exit()	Exits the program.
threading.Thread()	Creates a new thread.
time.sleep()	Pauses execution for a given time.
try-except	Handles exceptions.
try-finally	Executes cleanup code regardless of an exception.
tuple()	Creates a tuple.
type()	Returns the type of an object.
while	Defines a loop that runs while a condition is true.
with open()	Opens a file using a context manager.
write()	Writes content to a file.
yield	Pauses and resumes a generator function.
zip()	Combines multiple iterables into tuples.

3.2.4 Python 3 Standard Type Hierarchy

The *type* of an object describes the Python data structure representation of the object as well as the methods and operations that can be carried out on that object. Table 3.2 is a listing of the type categories, and following it is a brief description of some of the categories in the table.

TABLE 3.2

Python 3 Type Categories

Category	Name	Description
None	None	Null object
Numbers	int	Plain integer
	Long	Arbitrary-precision integer
	Float	Floating point number
	Complex	Complex number
	Bool	Boolean (True or False)
Sequences (immutable)	str	Character string
	Unicode	Unicode character string
	tuple	Tuple
Sequences (mutable)	list	List
	bytearray	Returned by bytearray()
Mapping	dict	Dictionary
Sets	set	Mutable set
	Frozenset	Immutable set
Callable	BuiltinFunctionType	Built-in functions
	BuiltinMethodType	Built-in methods
	type	Type of built-in types and classes
	object	Ancestor of all types and classes
	FunctionType	User-defined function
	InstanceType	Class object instance
	MethodType	Bound class method
	UnboundMethodType	Unbound class method
" Modules	ModuleType	Module
" Classes	object	Ancestor of all types and classes
" Types	type	Type of built-in types and classes
" Files	file	File
" Internal	CodeType	Byte-compiled code

(Continued)

TABLE 3.2 (*Continued*)

Python 3 Type Categories

Category	Name	Description
	FrameType	Execution frame
	GeneratorType	Generator object
	TracebackType	Stacks traceback of an exception
	Slice	Generated by extended slices
	Ellipsis	Used in extended slices
" Classic	Classes ClassType	Legacy class definition
	InstanceType	Legacy class instance

The None type has a single value that contains a null object (an object with no value). Its truth value is False.

Numeric types: Booleans, integers, long integers, floating point numbers, and complex numbers.

Sequence types: *Sequences* represent ordered sets of objects indexed by nonnegative integers and include strings, Unicode strings, lists, and tuples.

Mapping types: A *mapping object* represents an arbitrary collection of objects that are indexed by another collection of nearly arbitrary key values. Unlike a sequence, a mapping object is unordered and can be indexed by numbers, strings, and other objects. *Dictionaries* are the only built-in mapping type and are similar to a *hash*.

Set types: A *set* is an unordered collection of unique items. Unlike sequences, sets provide no indexing or slicing operations. They are also unlike dictionaries in that there are no key values associated with the objects. In addition, the items placed into a set must be immutable.

Callable types: These represent objects that support the function call operation. There are several kinds of objects with this property, including user-defined functions, built-in functions, instance methods, and classes.

Classes and types: When you define a class, the class definition normally produces an object of type *type*.

Modules: The *module* type is a container that holds objects loaded with the **import** statement.

Files: The *file* object represents an open file and is returned by the built-in **open()** function.

Internal types: Objects used by the interpreter are exposed to the user, such as *traceback objects, code objects, frame objects, generator objects, slice objects*, and the *ellipsis object*.

Code objects: These represent raw byte-compiled executable code, or *bytecode*, and are typically returned by the built-in *compile()* function.

Frame objects: These are used to represent execution frames and most frequently occur in traceback objects.

Traceback objects: These are created when an exception occurs and contain *stack trace information*.

Generator objects: These are created when a *generator* function is invoked. A generator function is defined whenever a function makes use of the special yield keyword.

Slice objects: These are used to represent slices given in extended slice syntax, such as:

a[i:j:stride], a[i:j, n:m], or a[..., i:j]

Ellipsis object: The ellipsis object is used to indicate the presence of an ellipsis (...) in a slice. There is a single object of this type, accessed through the built-in name Ellipsis. It has no attributes and evaluates as True.

Classic classes: In versions of Python prior to version 2.2, classes and objects were implemented using an entirely different mechanism, which is now deprecated. For backward compatibility, however, these classes, called *classic classes* or *old-style classes*, are still supported.

3.2.5 Basic Assumptions We Make

The four basic and important assumptions we make in this chapter are:

1. You have the default Python 3.X installed on your Raspberry Pi 5 system. Python 3.11.2, for example, was already installed as part of the installation of our Raspberry Pi 5 OS itself.

   If you type in the following command (as we did on our Raspberry Pi 5 system), you will see where Python 3 and its components (and what versions) are installed on your system:

```
$ whereis python3
python3: /usr/bin/python3 /usr/lib/python3 /etc/python3 /usr/share/python3 /usr/share/man/man1/python3.1.gz
$
```

2. The path of execution to the Python 3 program and the path of execution to all the Python scripts you create in this chapter include the current working directory where you want to do Python in!

   If you don't know, given the particular shell you are using (we use the default Bash shell, with the $ prompt), what your path of execution is set to, examine your path and set it properly. For example, in the Bash shell, you can see your path of execution by typing **echo $PATH** at the shell prompt. On our Raspberry Pi 5 OS system, Python 3 is installed by default in /usr/bin, as seen from the **whereis python3** command output of 1 above.

3. For a majority of the Examples below, you are doing Python 3 in the Thonny IDE.

   The basic procedures you'll follow in this chapter, to execute either single Python 3 interactive commands or multi-line programs, are as follows:

   a. You execute single-line Python 3 commands interactively, by typing them carefully and faithfully into the Thonny Shell Area. We call this *"Way 1 (Interactive Mode)"*, and give an illustrative example of it in Section 3.2.6.

   b. You carefully, and faithfully, type short, or even long, multi-line Python 3 scripts that are presented below into the Thonny Script Area, click the Run Toolbar icon, and observe the results. You then save those scripts for later use in a convenient directory on your Raspberry Pi 5, if necessary. We call this *"Way 2 (Script Mode Mode)"*, and give an illustrative example of it in Section 3.2.6.

   ****Note****

   Of course, since all of the code for the Examples below can be found at the book website, you can download them to a convenient location on your Raspberry Pi 5, and then use the Thonny Load Toolbar icon to bring them into Thonny and Run them. But we encourage you (in the beginning at least) to type in the commands shown in the Examples, to get practice producing syntactically-correct code!

   c. You create a multi-line Python 3 script in your favorite text editor (such as nano), and import that file into Thonny's Script Area using the **import** Python 3 command. We call this *"Way 3 (Import Script Mode)"*, and give an illustrative example of it in Section 3.2.6.

   d. Alternately, you type **python3** on the command line of a Raspberry Pi 5 terminal window, which launches and then allows you to use Python 3 interactively in the terminal window. We don't deploy this method very frequently, but you need to know about it as an interactive interpreter mode of doing Python 3. Remember, Python 3 is basically an interpretive language, and ostensibly on the surface at least, it's running an interpreter, rather than a compiler, to execute your code.

4. In general, whenever we want you to type something on the Python 3 interactive command line, or in the Thonny Script Area, we will indicate what is to be typed in **bold** text. In addition, output from Python 3 will be shown in unbolded text.

3.2.6 Running Python 3 Using Our Standard Ways

The following sub-sections illustrate the ways that we use Thonny to run Python 3 on our Raspberry Pi 5 system.

Way 0 (Command Line Mode)
Type **Python** or **Python 3** on the Bash command line, and then commands one line at a time, followed by pressing **Enter**.

****Note****

The three greater-than symbols (>>>) are the Python 3 interpreter prompt, letting you know you are in Python 3! To exit back to the Bash command line prompt in the terminal window, press **<Ctrl> + <D>** after the **>>>**.

Way 1 (Interactive Mode)
In the Shell Area of Thonny, you type a single line of Python 3 code on the Python 3 command line (>>>), or maybe multiple lines of Python 3, and see the results immediately. A good reason to use this mode is that you can test small fragments of Python 3 code, one line, or a couple of lines at a time, directly in the current Python 3 interpreter. A simple example of this (seen in the Thonny Shell Area) would be as follows:

```
>>>print ("How about some more?")
How about some more?
>>>
```

Remember, to submit a line of Python code to its interpreter, at the end of the line, press **<Enter>** on the keyboard.

Way 2 (Script Mode)
You type possibly multiple, properly formatted, and syntactically correct Python 3 commands into the Thonny Script Area. This is traditionally called a *script file* (perhaps even saved using the Toolbar Save Icon in Thonny, and named **first.py**). Then you click on the Thonny Run Toolbar icon, and the results of the execution of the Python 3 commands are seen. Generally, those results scroll by in the Shell Area of Thonny, but they also may generate other forms of output, like graphics in other windows that Python 3 opens.

A good reason to use this mode is if you have scripts with more than a few lines of code in them, and you do <u>not</u> want to type that code in every time you want to run it. A simple example of this would be as follows:

Example 3.2

```
print("Count for me, Python!")
for n in range (5):
    print("I'm counting!", n)
print("I'm done counting!")
```

```
>>> %Run -c $EDITOR_CONTENT
Count for me, Python!
I'm counting! 0
I'm counting! 1
I'm counting! 2
I'm counting! 3
I'm counting! 4
I'm done counting!
>>>
```

If the commands contain any output directed to the screen, such as using print statements as shown in Example 3.2, the shell prompt will immediately reappear at the termination of execution, <u>if the script file terminates without error!</u>

Of course, if you use the Thonny Toolbar Save Icon, you can save the multi-line Python 3 code into a file in Python 3's current working directory, and then at some later time, use Thonny's Load Toolbar Icon to bring that file back into the Script Area.

Way 3 (Import Script Mode)
Similarly to Way2 (Script Mode), you use a text editor of your choice to create and save multiple Python commands in a script file, perhaps named **first.py**, in the current working directory that has been set in Thonny.

In the Thonny Shell Area, and at the Python 3 command prompt there, you bring the script file into Python with the Python 3 **import** command. A good reason to use this mode is if your script files contain function definitions. A simple example of this is as follows:

Example 3.3

```
>>>import first
Count for me, Python!
I'm counting! 0
I'm counting! 1
I'm counting! 2
I'm counting! 3
I'm counting! 4
```

I'm done counting!
>>>

where **first** is the file without the **.py** extension. It should contain syntactically correct Python 3 commands and be in the Python 3 current working directory. Now, the objects, statements, expressions, and modules (like Python functions) in **first.py** are available to you in Thonny. A good reason to use this mode is to bring those structures and functions into the current interactive Thonny Python session environment, or namespace.

****Note****

Once you leave Thonny by clicking on the Toolbar icon Quit, the current interactive session is ended, and the environment you have created in Python is lost.

How do you know what the Thonny current working directory is?

It's set to a default and can be changed to any directory you want in the file system of your Raspberry Pi 5 OS, to retrieve or save Python 3 script files from or to. To find out and be able to reset the current working directory in Thonny, in the Thonny Shell Area, type the following commands:

```
>>> import os
>>> os.getcwd()
'/home/bob/Public'
>>>
```

We see from the above output that the current working directory, where Thonny retrieves and saves script files from the Script Area, is */home*/bob/ Public

The name of Python 3's current working directory may be different than this on your Raspberry Pi 5.

To change the current working directory to */home*/bob/Documents, for example, type the following command on the command line in the Thonny Shell Area, after you've typed in the previous two commands-

```
>>>os.chdir("/home/bob/Documents")
```

Way 4 (Bash Mode)

We don't use this Mode very much in the sections below, but there is an alternative way of executing Python 3 scripts that depends upon the working environment within which you are executing Python 3.

That alternative, very similar to the way of executing a Bash, or other script file, is to include the following line as the first line in the Python script file (which you've created in your favorite text editor; we used nano, and have named the nano-created file **first.py** in this example case):

Example 3.4

#! /usr/bin/env python3

You must also be sure that you have execute privilege on **first.py**, using the **chmod u+x first.py** command. Then, to execute the **first.py** script file, on the Bash command line, type the following:

$./first.py

This method uses Python 3 to execute the script file.

The main advantage of the method is that, depending on which version of Python you want to run, you can place the command name for that version in the first line of the script file. For example, if you want to use Python Version 3.13 (if you've gone through the necessary more advanced steps of installing that, or the latest version!) to run the script file, you could modify the first line in the script file to read-

#! /usr/bin/env python3.13

There are portability issues with this method, for example, when the working environment is in conflict with what version of Python 3 you want to execute the script file code with. But for beginners, you can ignore those issues for now.

This method of executing the Python code is sometimes called running it as a *user-written library module*.

There is another way of running a Python script, which we do not use in this Chapter, but which is useful, and we illustrate it in the next section.

3.2.6.1 *Compiling a Script File into Bytecode for Bash Execution*

It is possible to run a Python 3 script file that you have used the interpreter to compile into a portable form of executable code, to execute from the Bash command line. It's called the *bytecode form*. Here's how to do it:

In Python 3, the process of converting a script into bytecode is handled by the Python 3 interpreter itself. Normally, and under the hood, when you run a Python 3 script, the Python 3 interpreter first compiles it into bytecode before executing it. This bytecode is then executed by the Python Virtual Machine (PVM).

If you want to explicitly generate bytecode from an already-created Python script, without using Thonny, or running Python 3 itself in a terminal, you can use either the **py_compile** module from the Python 3 command line, or on the Bash command line, with the **-m py_compile** command-line option, to generate the bytecode.

Do the following things to accomplish this:

0. As specified and explained above at the end of Example 3.3, how do you know what the current working directory that Thonny is using to look for script files in? You can find out and set it to be whatever you want, by using the following Python 3 commands in the Thonny Shell Area-

```
>>> import os
>>> current_directory = os.getcwd()
>>> print("Current working directory:", current_directory)
Current working directory: /home/bob
>>>
>>> os.chdir("/home/bob/Public")
```

So, for the steps below, we want to change the current working directory <u>for Thonny</u> to where we're keeping our Python 3 script files for this example, i.e., in */home*/bob/Public!

****Note****

And you want to make sure that you've used the bash **mv** command to move the file **first.py** into the directory /home/bob/Public, or wherever in your Raspberry Pi directory structure you are doing this work.

1. Using the **py_compile** module-
   In the Thonny Shell Area, to create a bytecode version of the script file **first.py**, type:

```
>>> import py_compile
>>> py_compile.compile('first.py')
'__pycache__/first.cpython-311.pyc'
>>>
```

This will generate a bytecode file named something like first. cpython-311.pyc, in a subdirectory of the directory that the original script file was located in(/home/bob/Public, in our case). This sub-directory will be named __pycache__
   The generated bytecode file (first.cpython-311.pyc,) can be executed directly by the Python interpreter as shown in step 3 below, without the need for recompilation. It contains the compiled bytecode instructions ready for execution by the PVM. Descend to the sub-directory __pycache__, and make sure you give yourself execute privilege on the bytecode file with the **chmod u+x first.cpython-311.pyc** command.

```
>>>
```

2. Or using the **-m py_compile** switch-
   Open a terminal, to get a Bash command prompt, and set the current working directory to the directory where your Python script is located. Then run the following command:

```
$ python3 -m py_compile first.py
```

This will generate the bytecode file named something like **first.cpython-311.pyc**, in a subdirectory of the directory that the

original script file was located in. This subdirectory will be named
__pycache__

The generated bytecode file (first.cpython-311.pyc) can be executed directly by the Python interpreter without the need for recompilation. It contains the compiled bytecode instructions ready for execution by the PVM.

Descend to the sub-directory __pycache__, and make sure you give yourself execute privilege on the bytecode file with the **chmod u+x first.cpython-311.pyc** command.

3. Then type the following to execute the bytecode file, in a bash terminal outside of Thonny:

$ python3 first.cpython-311.pyc
Count for me, Python!
I'm counting! 0
I'm counting! 1
I'm counting! 2
I'm counting! 3
I'm counting! 4
I'm done counting!

****Note****

The bytecode generated by the Python interpreter is specific to the version of Python you are using, as seen by the appended **311** to the bytecode filename. So, bytecode generated for a particular version of Python 3 may not be compatible with earlier versions of Python.

3.2.7 Uses of Python 3

Python 3 can accomplish several kinds of programming tasks, which might be broken down into the following sample categories:

Shell scripting

Systems programming

Network and Internet scripting

Database programming

Systems administration scripting

Graphical User Interface(GUI) scripting

Scientific and math programming

Data mining

In this chapter, we predominantly use Ways 1–4 when running Python 3, shown in all of the Examples, plus Way 0 whenever it's convenient, and we give a beginners' introduction to the Python 3 language. We also follow the model of level schemes as shown at the beginning of Section 3.2, going roughly from the top of the scheme to the bottom.

3.2.8 Information on the Installation of Python

Version 3.11.2 of Python was already installed and usable by us on the Raspberry Pi 5 OS we had deployed on our Pi 5. But, you may need to, or want to, install a more recent version of Python 3 on your system, or if you want to install a later version of the software alongside, or to even replace the version your system already has preinstalled on it. Be aware that because of variations in the way your system has been installed by you, or the system administrator, and exactly what version of the Raspberry Pi 5 OS has been installed, the installation procedure for the latest available Python 3 may have to be already done by a system administrator for you! A good example of a similar situation would be that you do not have a C compiler available, or you want to upgrade to the latest *gcc* compiler, and don't know how to do that with or without a package manager!

We give installation instructions for the installation of the latest Thonny (available at the time we wrote this book) below.

3.2.8.1 Switching Thonny to the Latest Python

To change the version of Python used by Thonny on your Raspberry Pi, you need to be using Thonny in Regular Mode. To switch back to Simple Mode later, use the Tools > Options> General > UI mode > simple menu choice when you are in Regular Mode. Be aware that you will have to click OK in the Thonny Options dialog box, and then restart Thonny to get back to Simple Mode!

Follow these steps in Regular Mode to switch to the latest Python you downloaded and installed in the last section:

1. Open Thonny on your Raspberry Pi. Switch to Regular Mode by clicking on the "Switch to regular mode" message in the extreme right corner of the Thonny Toolbar. You get a message box that opens saying that the Configuration has been updated, and to restart Thonny to start working in Regular Mode. Click OK.

2. After you restart Thonny, in the menu bar at the top, click on "Tools" and then select "Options".

3. In the "Options" dialog box, navigate to the "Interpreter" tab.

4. Under the "Interpreter" tab, you'll see a list of available Python interpreters. This list includes the Python versions installed on your Raspberry Pi.

5. Select the desired Python version from the list. You can choose from the available versions or click on the "Browse" button to specify a custom Python interpreter.

6. After selecting the desired Python version, click on the "OK" button to save the changes.

Thonny will now use the selected Python version as the default interpreter for running and executing your Python code.

Note

You need to have the desired Python 3 version already installed on your Raspberry Pi 5 for it to appear in the list of available interpreters in Thonny.

If the desired Python version is <u>not</u> listed in Thonny's interpreter options, you need to install it on your Raspberry Pi 5 <u>before</u> it can be selected.

3.2.8.2 Finding Out What Version of Python 3.X is Installed on Your Raspberry Pi 5 System

The easiest way of knowing what versions of Python are already installed on the Raspberry Pi 5 you are using is to use <u>*Mode 0 Command/Mode*</u> and simply type **python** or **python3** and press **<Enter>** at the Bash shell prompt ($) in a console or terminal window.

When we typed **python3** and pressed **<Enter>** at the Bash shell prompt ($) in a console or terminal window, we got the following output on our Raspberry Pi system:

~$ **python3**
Python 3.11.2 (main, Nov 30 2024, 21:22:50) [GCC 12.2.0] on linux
Type "help", "copyright", "credits" or "license" for more information.
>>>

The three greater-than symbols (>>>) are the Python interpreter prompt, letting you know you are in Python! To exit to the command line prompt in the terminal window, press **<Ctrl-D>** after the >>>.

The first line of responses from our system shows that Python 3.11.2 is installed and running on this system.

If you get an error message on the Bash command line in the terminal window, such as command not found, either Python 3 has not been installed on your system, or you do not have access to it. You would need to then contact your system administrator to install the program or set up your working environment to give you privileges to execute it. Or if you are the system administrator, for example, on your own single-user Raspberry Pi 5 OS computer, you would need to install the appropriate versions of Python and set up your working environment so that you have access to those versions of the program.

Of course, in Thonny, the version of Python 3 it's using is shown at the top of the Shell Area, as seen in Figure 3.1.

Every single line of Python 3 code, or every script file or program shown in this chapter, can be done, by default, in Python 3.

3.2.8.3 Getting Help

If you need help on a particular module, keyword, or topic in Python 3, in the Shell Area of Thonny, at the command prompt >>>, you can always type in the function call to help as follows to get into the help system:

>>> **help ( )**
Welcome to python3.11's help utility!
If this is your first time using Python, you should definitely check out this excellent tutorial on the Internet at https://docs.python.org/3.11/tutorial/.
Enter the name of any module, keyword, or topic to get help on writing Python 3 programs and using Python 3 modules. To quit this help utility and return to the interpreter, just type "quit".
To get a list of available modules, keywords, symbols, or topics, type "modules", "keywords", "symbols", or "topics". Each module also comes with a one-line summary of what it does; to list the modules whose name or summary contain a given string such as "spam", type "modules spam".

help> **quit**
You are now leaving help and returning to the Python 3 interpreter.
If you want to ask for help on a particular object directly from the interpreter, you can type "help(object)". Executing "help('string')" has the same effect as typing a particular string at the help> prompt.
>>>

3.3 Python 3 Syntax

Python 3 has a rich and useful syntactic repertoire you can draw from in order to successfully complete the programming tasks you set out to do. In this section, we give an overview of that syntax, with several examples.

3.3.1 Printing Text, Comments, Numbers, Grouping Operators, and Expressions

To use Python 3 in practical examples, as shown later in this chapter, it's absolutely necessary to first become familiar with the syntax of the language. For example, how it's used as a calculator, in "interpretative mode", to execute single lines of Python code to accomplish short, meaningful operations and tasks.

One of the first things you must know about how a calculator works is how to enter numbers and mathematical expressions on the calculator. So, with Python 3, instead of listing all the syntactic rules, we will execute a number of examples as illustrations, and have you work with some of the most important of those rules.

Here are a couple of the important considerations you need to be aware of before you enter any Python 3 code on the Python 3 command line or into a file.

1. The rule of four: The *indentation* spaces that you place on each line of Python 3 code are very important!

   This is done automatically for you in the Script Area of Thonny, when you are entering several lines of Python 3 code.

   Since Python 3 is a structured programming language that uses specific structures in blocks, those blocks are delimited, or defined by the indentation you give them on each line (unlike in other languages that use specific printing characters to delimit blocks). This means you must line up your blocks of Python 3 structures vertically, starting from the left-hand side, and for our purposes, use four spaces for each indented block. For example, the following sample shows this four-space indentation constraint:

```
Block 1 head
    xxxxxxxxx
    xxxxxxxxx
        Block 2 head
            xxxxxxxxx
            xxxxxxxxx
                Block 3 head
                    xxxxxxxxx
                    xxxxxxxxx
                    end of Block 3
                end of Block 2
            end of Block 1
```

   where Blocks 1, 2, 3, and so on, and their statements xxxxxxxxx, line up vertically with an indentation of four spaces before each block, from left to right.

2. Normal order and applicative order evaluation: The order of execution of a mathematical expression used by Python 3 is PEMDAS: Parentheses(from inner to outer) (from left to right), Exponents, Multiplication, Division, Addition, and Subtraction. See Table 3.3 for even more details of operator precedence in Python 3 expressions.

The first thing we want Python 3 to do is to print, or echo, a line of text we type at the keyboard. This is done by typing the following at the Python 3 command prompt in the Thonny Shell Area:

TABLE 3.3

Python 3 Order of Evaluations

Operator	Description
()	Parentheses (grouping)
f(args...)	Function call
x[index:index]	Slicing
x[index]	Subscription
x.attribute	Attribute reference
**	Exponentiation
~x	Bitwise not
+x, -x	Positive, negative
*, /, %	Multiplication, division, remainder
+, -	Addition, subtraction
<<, >>	Bitwise shifts
&	Bitwise AND
^	Bitwise XOR
|	Bitwise OR
in, not in, is, is not, <, <=, >, >=, <>, !=, ==	Comparisons, membership, identity
not x	Boolean NOT
and	Boolean AND
or	Boolean OR
lambda	Lambda expression

```
>>>print ("This is the number of fingers I am holding up:")
This is the number of fingers I am holding up:
>>>
```

To add comments to a script file of Python 3 commands, you place the pound sign(#) before (and possibly after) everything on the line you want commented. For example, in interactive mode:

```
>>> #This is a comment, which you can use to annotate your script file code.
...
>>> #Anything after the # is ignored by python.
...
>>> print "You could have comments appear like this:" # this comment is ignored.
```

You could have comments appear like this:

```
>>> #You can also use the pound sign to comment out a piece of code:
...
>>> #print "This won't run."
```

```
...
>>> print "This will run."
This will run.
>>>
```

In the interactive session above, just press **<Enter>** on the Python 3 command line when the ... appears.

Quotation marks (straight up-and-down ones) are used for "string literals", or characters of text you want to include "literally" as they are in the output of an executed Python 3 script file. To include a single quotation mark in a string literal, enclose it inside of double quotation marks. For example:

```
>>> '"Don\'t," he said.'
'"Don\'t," he said.'
>>> print('"Don\'t," he said.')
"Don't," he said.
>>> s = 'First place.\nSecond place.'# \n means newline
>>> s                      # without print(),\n is included in the output
'First line.\nSecond line.'
>>> print(s)          # with print(), \n produces a new line
First place.
Second place.
>>>
```

Triple quotation marks are used to enclose long lines of string literals.

****Note****

Of the two types of quotation marks, Python 3 uses **Straight Quotation Marks (" and ')** – These are simple, vertical marks that do not change shape. They are often used in programming and basic text formatting. If you use **Curly (or Smart) Quotation Marks (" " and ' ')**, you'll get a syntax error. That's true on the Linux command-line and in other programming and scripting languages as well.

Next, we want to combine some text with an arithmetic expression that Python evaluates for us:

```
>>> print ("Not Ring Fingers", 7 − (1 + 1))
Not Ring Fingers 5
>>>
```

Notice that in evaluating the mathematical expression, Python 3 evaluates what is in parentheses first by doing the addition of $1 + 1$, then, from left to right, subtracts 2 from 7.

In-Chapter Exercises

3. Have Python 3 evaluate the following expressions, and list what Python 3 prints:
   $((7 + 5) * (3 + 2))/(6/18)$

4. How can you change the previous expression so that it yields a numeric answer, and why?

5. $3 + 2 + 1 - 5 + 4 \% 2 - 1 / 4 + 6$

6. What kind of operator is the percent sign (%)?

We can also use relational operators in arithmetic expressions, such as less than (<), greater than (>), greater than or equal to (>=), and less than or equal to (<=). For example:

```
>>> print ("Is it true that 3 + 1 < 5 - 7?")
Is it true that 3 + 1 < 5 - 7?
>>> print (3 + 1 < 5 - 7)
False
>>> print ("Is it greater?", 4 > -2)
Is it greater? True
>>> print ("Is it greater or equal?", 4 >= -2)
Is it greater or equal? True
>>> print ("Is it less or equal?", 4 <= -2)
Is it less or equal? False
>>>
```

In-Chapter Exercise

7. What are the results of typing in the following Python statements, and why?

```
>>> 5 + 7>= 6 <= 78 - 9
>>> 5 + 7>= 6 >= 78 - 9
>>> (5 + 7>= 6 >= 78 - 9)/8
>>> (5 + 7>= 6 >= 78 - 9)/-8
```

3.3.2 Variables and Naming Conventions

An important feature of a high-level programming language like Python 3 is providing names that allow you to refer to computational objects. The name represents, or stands for, in any particular computational environment of interest, the value or values which the object can take on; thus it is called a "variable".

Python 3 variable names, and the names of script files as well, can contain both letters, numbers, and the underscore (_) character, but must begin with a letter. If you get an error message about the use of a variable name, it may be a reserved word or keyword in Python 3. Table 3.4 lists the 31 keywords that may not be used as variable or script file names in a Python 3 statement.

TABLE 3.4

Python 3 Keywords

and	del	from	not	while
as	elif	global	or	with
assert	else	if	pass	yield
break	except	import	print	
class	nonlocal	in	raise	
continue	finally	is	return	
def	for	lambda	try	

To get a list of keywords in your current version, type the following at the Python 3 prompt. In our version of Python 3.11.2, we got the output shown:

```
>>> import keyword
>>> print(keyword.kwlist)

['False', 'None', 'True', 'and', 'as', 'assert', 'async', 'await', 'break', 'class', 'continue', 'def', 'del', 'elif', 'else', 'except', 'finally', 'for', 'from', 'global', 'if', 'import', 'in', 'is', 'lambda', 'nonlocal', 'not', 'or', 'pass', 'raise', 'return', 'try', 'while', 'with', 'yield']
>>>
```

The **(keyword.kwlist)** target of the print command is an illustration of a Python 3 method application. In the following simple example, we define some variables and use them:

```
>>> pie = 3.14159
>>> radius = 10
>>> pie * (radius * radius)
314.159
>>> circumference = 2 * pie * radius
>>> circumference
62.8318
>>>
```

3.3.3 Functions

Python 3 provides a programming construct called a *function*, which allows you to define your own named procedures, and lets you reuse those procedures in a modular fashion in your code. You can think of a function as a black box machine that takes named objects present before the function call or invocation as inputs, processes them inside the black box with names that are only seen inside the black box, and then spits them out as named objects available to the Python 3 program via an assignment statement.

The general form of a function definition is:

```
def name (formal parameters):
    body of the function
    return (returned parameters)
```

where **name** is the name you give the function (make sure you are <u>not</u> using a Python 3 keyword!), **formal parameters** are the named objects that are passed to the function so it can carry out some operations on them and, optionally, **returned parameters** are named objects that are used by your program.

There are two basic ways you can execute a function:

1. Use Way 1 (Interactive Mode), and by typing or copying and pasting each line of code that is the function definition into the Thonny Script Area.

2. Use Way 3 (Import Script Mode), and create the function definition in a file with a **.py** extension. Then import the file into Thonny in the Shell Area, with the **import** command.

A simple example of the first way to use a function definition in Python 3 is as follows. Type the following six lines of Python 3 code into the Script Area of Thonny, and then click on the Run Toolbar icon. Remember to let Thonny indent the lines shown!

```
w = 7
x = 12
def add(a, b):
    c = a + b
    return (c)
z = add(w, x)
```

Then type the following in the Thonny Shell Area:

```
>>>z
19
>>>
```

If you want to, you can use the Thonny Save Toolbar Icon to save the above code in Thonny's current working directory.

From this example, we can call **w** and **x** the actual parameters passed to the function definition, **a** and **b** the formal parameters used in the body of the function definition, and **c** a returned parameter.

Notice that, for the returned parameter to be used in the remainder of your Python 3 session after the function definition, you must assign a named variable on the left-hand side of the equals sign to the function call or invocation on the right-hand side of the equals sign.

A simple example of using Way 3 (Import Script Mode) to bring a function definition into Python 3 is as follows:

Use the text editor of your choice (We like nano) to create and save the following file, named **math1.py**, in the current working directory that is set in Thonny. Remember the Rule of Four!

Example 3.5

```
def add(a, b):
    c = a + b
    return(c)
def subtract(a, b):
    c = b - a
    return(c)
def multiply(a, b):
    c = a * b
    return(c)
def divide(a, b):
    c = a / b
    return(c)
```

Then, run Thonny, and in the Thonny Shell Area, type the following three lines of Python 3 code:

```
>>> import math1
>>> z = math1.add(3, 4)
>>> z
7
>>>
```

The first line you typed into the Thonny Shell Area made the named objects in the **math1.py** module available in the current session of Python 3. The second line allowed you to address the **add** function from that module as **math1.add**. This is another example of the use of a Python 3 **method** and its invocation. The assignment statement on the second line in the Thonny Shell Area also allowed you to add 3 and 4 together, and assign the returned value to a variable named **z**. We will cover more about Python 3 methods, modules, and global and local scopes in functions in the sections below.

3.3.4 Conditional Execution

As mentioned in Section 3.2, the order in which computer programs execute includes a "branching", or conditional execution structure. Python 3 uses the truth value of certain test conditions to determine whether prescribed blocks of code will be executed or not. This is implemented in Python 3 with the **if** statement. The general form of the **if** statement construct is:

```
if cond1 is true:
    initial statement(s)
elif cond2 is true:
```

>   **additional statement(s)**
> **else:**
>   **final statement(s)**

where:

cond1 is a test condition whose truth value determines whether the initial statement(s) block gets executed,

cond2 is a test condition whose truth value determines whether the additional statement(s) block gets executed, and

else is the default, which executes final statement(s).

A simple example of the use of this structure using Way 2 (Script Mode) in the Thonny Script Area is as follows.

Remember to press **<Enter>** on the keyboard after each line you type into the Script Area in Thonny. Notice that Thonny properly indents lines in the Script Area, the requisite number of spaces, according to its structured programming rules.

Example 3.6

```
x = 1
if x == 0:  # the == is a logical, or Boolean operator
    print ("x equal 0")
elif x == 1: #one or more of these optional blocks are allowed
    print ("x equal 1")
else:    #the optional block
    print ("x is something else")
```

When done correctly typing the above in, click on the Run Icon in the Thonny Toolbar.

```
>>> %Run -c $EDITOR_CONTENT
x equal 1
>>>
```

In-Chapter Exercises

8. If you leave out the **elif** block in Example 3.6, what prints out?

9. If you change the first line to read x = 3, and leave out the **else** line in Example 3.6, what prints out?

10. If you change the first line to read x = 1.8 in Example 3.6, what prints out?

It is also possible to nest conditional execution blocks inside one another.

For example, we'll use a variation of Way 3 (Import Script Mode) for the code execution below. Enter the following code correctly into a file named **two7.py**. Remember to indent according to the Rule of Four!

Then, in Thonny click on the Load Toolbar icon, and load the file from the default directory you created **two7.py** in, into the Thonny Script Area:

Example 3.7

```
w = 36
y = 13
z = 20
if w < 37:
    print ("w is less than 37")
    if y > 13:
      print ("y is greater than 13")
    elif y == 13:
      print ("y is equal to 13")
    else:
      print ("y is less than 13")
    if z > 21:
      print ("z is greater than 21")
    elif z == 21:
      print ("z is equal to 21")
    else:
      print ("z is less than 21")
else:
    print ("w is greater than or equal to 37")
```

Finally, click the Run Thonny Toolbar Icon. The following is what should appear on your display in the Thonny Shell Area:

```
>>> %Run two7.py
w is less than 37
y is equal to 13
z is less than 21
>>>
```

3.3.5 Determinate and Indeterminate Repetition Structures and Recursion

Using the procedural/imperative model, Python 3 can repeat segments of program or script file structures in two basic ways: via *determinate repetition structures* or *indeterminate repetition structures*. Traditionally, a determinate repetition structure is called *counting repetition*, and an indeterminate repetition structure is called *logical repetition*. These two methods are implemented with the **for** procedural statement and the **while** procedural statement. Generally, if you know ahead of time (for example, at the time you are writing the code) how many repetitions of a block of code you want to execute, you use the **for** statement, and if you do <u>not</u> know (when, for example, you allow the user to input the number of repetitions as the script file is run), you use the **while** statement.

Of course, it is possible to implement the same two ways of repetition by <u>not</u> using a specific structured programming approach; for example, by using conditional execution and unstructured switching to obtain the same results. This is not acceptably good practice, and we choose to show the structured approach in Python 3.

Make sure that, in the body of statements included in the indeterminate repetition block that **while** is executing, the test condition for continued execution becomes false. Otherwise, this will result in *infinite repetition*! To halt infinite repetition in an executing script file, hold down the **<Ctrl>** and **C** keys on the keyboard at the same time.

****Note****

An explanation of Python 3 style is in order at this point.

Pythonic
Proceeding from Guido van Rossum's definition of *Pythonic* in the Python Language Reference, a common technique in Python 3 is to loop over all elements of an *iterable* object using a **for** statement. Many other languages do not have this type of construct, so people unfamiliar with Python 3 sometimes use a numerical counter instead, such as:

```
>>>for i in range(len(money)):
...  print money[i]
```

The Pythonic way is:

```
>>>for bills in money:
...  print (bills)
```

The Pythonic way can be characterized as *iteration*, whereas the traditional language construct can be characterized as *counting*.

The **for** structure can repeat a block of operations on any *iterable* sequence data, such as strings, lists, tuples, or user-defined iterable objects in classes.

The general Pythonic form of the **for** statement structure is as follows:

```
for a certain number of times
   repeat these statements
```

The **while** structure can repeat a block of operations as long as a test condition is true.

The general Pythonic form of the **while** statement structure is:

```
while a certain condition is true
   repeat these statements
```

An object, K, is iterable if it can be successfully run with the following code in Way 2 (Script Mode). This code also shows that a counting form of iteration, such as the traditional **for** loop structure, can be implemented with a

while structure. No need to type the comments into the Thonny Script Area. To run the code, click on the Toolbar Run Icon-

```
K = [22,33,44,55]              #Lists are iterable.
c = K.__iter__()               #c is the counter
while 1:                       #execute while true
    try:
        item = next(c)         #get the next one
        print (item)           # Do operations on each item as you count through
    except StopIteration:      #Nothing left
        break
```

```
>>> %Run -c $EDITOR_CONTENT
22
33
44
55
>>>
```

The following are two simple examples of both forms of repetition. We use Way 2 (Script Mode) to run them:

Type the following three lines of code into the Thonny Script Area. Notice that the keywords in the Python 3 script file are in **bold** type for didactic purposes here:

Example 3.8

```
limit = [1, 2, 3, 4, 5]
for number in limit:
    print ("number of repeats %d" % number)
```

Then click on the Run Toolbar icon. Your output in the Shell area should be:

```
>>> %Run -c $EDITOR_CONTENT
number of repeats 1
number of repeats 2
number of repeats 3
number of repeats 4
number of repeats 5
```

Type the following seven lines of Python 3 into the Thonny Script Area. Notice that the keywords in the Python script file are again shown in **bold** type:

Example 3.9

```
s= int(input("Enter an Integer"))
i = 0
numbers = []
while i < s:
    numbers.append(i)
    i = i + 1
    print ("numbers now: ", numbers)
```

Then click on the Thonny Run Toolbar Icon. Your output in the Shell area should be as follows. When prompted for an integer, type in **6** and then press **<Enter>** on the keyboard. Your output should be:

```
>>> %Run -c $EDITOR_CONTENT
Enter an Integer 6
numbers now:  [0]
numbers now:  [0, 1]
numbers now:  [0, 1, 2]
numbers now:  [0, 1, 2, 3]
numbers now:  [0, 1, 2, 3, 4]
numbers now:  [0, 1, 2, 3, 4, 5]
>>>
```

Try this same script file using different input integers each time you run it, to confirm that indeterminate repetition is happening.

Another interesting and extremely useful indeterminate repetition method that Python 3 can implement is known as *recursion*.

Basically, recursion is the repetition of a body of calculations to accumulate intermediate results, until some basic state is reached, and at that point, the calculations yield the final results.

The following is an example of a recursive process that calculates the factorial of an integer, implemented in Python 3 as a function that calls, or invokes, itself an indeterminate number of times (the Python 3 keywords are shown in **bold** type, and we are using Way 3 [Import Script Mode] to execute the script):

Example 3.10

```
def factR(n):
    if n == 1:
        return n
    else:
        return n*factR(n – 1)
```

If you create this function definition in a file named **FactR.py** in Thonny's current working directory, then typing the following into Thonny's Shell Area will yield the factorial of the input argument 7 as shown:

```
>>> import FactR
>>> FactR.factR(7)
5040
>>>
```

In-Chapter Exercises

11. What error message do you get if you supply a real number, such as 9.76, when you run the code of Example 3.9? Why do you get this error message?

12. How can you find the factorial of a real number in Python? Such as the factorial of 3.72, for example.

3.3.6 File Input and Output

If you look back to Section 3.2.7, at the programming tasks that Python 3 is capable of (such as systems programming, network and Internet scripting, database programming, systems administration scripting, GUI scripting, scientific statistical math programming, and AI scripting), the common thread which runs through all of those tasks is the ability to interface with the Raspberry Pi 5 OS via utilities that work with Linux files. For example, you may be programming a statistical analysis script in Python 3 that perhaps has its data generated from some other program or utility stored in a file somewhere in the file structure of your Raspberry Pi system. These files can be text, Unicode text, or binary, raw 8-bit bytes.

The general form of a file operation in Python 3 is:

```
name = open(filename, mode)
name.method(argument(s))
name.close()
```

where:

name is a file object name in the current procedure,

open is the keyword that opens Python 3's connection to an external file,

filename is the name of the external file, which may include directory paths, and so on,

mode is a way of accessing the file, like reading from it, or writing to it,

method is one of several operations that are allowed to be performed on the open external file,

argument(s) is(are) one or more qualifiers on the operation specified in method, and

close is the termination of connection to the external file.

The mode can be **r**, **w**, or **a**, for reading (the default, meaning you do <u>not</u> need to specify this to open with read), writing, or appending to the file, respectively. The file will be created if it doesn't exist, and opened for writing or appending if it does exist. It will be truncated when opened for writing. Add **b** to the mode for binary files. Add + to the mode to allow simultaneous reading and writing.

The preferred way to open a file is with the built-in **open()** function. Add **u** to the mode to open the file for input with universal newline support.

In the following Examples, we illustrate some simple operations on files, such as how to open, write/read from, and close them.

In the first Example, we input a string of text into a named file. In the Thonny Shell Area, type the following three lines of code:

Example 3.11

```
>>> file = open('sometext', 'w')
>>> file.write('This is a line of text.')
23
>>> file.close()
>>>
```

Then, when you are in the same current directory set by Thonny, type the following line at the Bash shell prompt (shown as $):

```
$ more sometext
This is a line of text.
$
```

In the next Example, we input some integer data into an external file using your favorite text editor, and then do some Python 3 operations on that data. In the current directory set by Thonny, run your favorite text editor, and in a file you name **somedata.txt**, type the following four integers (one integer per line):

23
33
43
54

Then, in the Thonny Shell Area, execute the following lines of code. The variable named **x1** is a *list*, which we will discuss in more detail in Section 3.3.7. So, the list element **x1[0]** is the first element of the list that has been read from the first line in the external file. The **float** and **int** functions convert the text strings in the file to real numbers and integers:

Example 3.12

```
>>> file = open('somedata.txt')     #the default mode is reading
>>> x1 = file.readlines()
>>> x1
['23\n', '33\n', '43\n', '54\n']
>>> s = float(x1[0])
>>> s
23.0
>>> r = int(x1[0])
>>> r
23
>>> s + r
46.0
>>> file.close()
>>>
```

We can also write list elements, such as numbers, to an external file. For example, type or paste the following Python 3 code into the Thonny Script Area. It uses the write method to place three lists into a file named **listw.txt.** Then, click on the Run Toolbar Icon in Thonny:

Example 3.13

```
L = [1, 2, 3]
M = [4, 5, 6]
N = [7, 8, 9]
F = open('listw.txt','w')
F.write(str(L) + '\n')
F.write(str(M) + '\n')
F.write(str(N) + '\n')
F.close()
```

In the Thonny Shell area, the following appears:

```
>>> %Run -c $EDITOR_CONTENT
>>>
```

On the Bash shell command line, <u>where the current directory is Thonny's default directory</u>, in a Raspberry Pi 5 terminal window, view the contents of **listw.txt** with the following command:

```
$ more listw.txt
[1, 2, 3]
[4, 5, 6]
[7, 8, 9]
$
```

In-Chapter Exercises

13. What commands do you use to add the first three elements of the list x1 of Example 3.12, and print that sum?

14. What are the \n characters shown on line 4 of Example 3.12?

15. What happens if you edit the file **somedata.txt**, and enter the numbers 23,33,43, and 54 on a single line in your text editor instead of on four different lines, save the file, and try to perform the same action in Example 3.12 on the new file **somedata.txt**?

16. After you close the file thus created, can you still access the values 43 and 54 in any way?

17. How would you specify the third element of the list x1?

3.3.7 Lists and the List Function

On the lowest level of the organizational scheme for Python 3, the *list* is an object that can contain multiple elements of possibly different types.

Just like a shopping list can contain different kinds of things from a store, such as food, household goods, automotive supplies, and so on, a Python 3 list can be made up of different types of elements, like integers, real numbers, strings, and so on; in fact, a list can contain any type of Python 3 object. For example:

```
>>> A = [ 34, 'Bob', 54.76, [4,7,9]]
```

is an expression that assigns the integer **34**, the string "**Bob**", the real number **54.76**, and another list comprised of the numbers **4, 7,** and **9** to a variable named **A**. List indices are integers, starting with 0. So, the following statements in Python 3 yield the results:

```
>>> A[2]
54.76
>>>A[0]
34
>>>A[3][2]
9
>>>
```

A 2 × 2 matrix (or array) can be specified as:

B = [[x, x],[y, y]]

Here is Python 3 code to create a 3 × 3 matrix (or array) named **x**, of random numbers, using the list function that works on objects (please notice that your results will differ from the output shown here, since the numbers shown in the example are randomly generated!):

Example 3.14

```
>>> import random      # random is a function from the Standard Library
>>> x = list(list (random.random() for i in range(3)) for j in range(3))
>>> x
[[0.1455440585876967, 0.7525092872509719, 0.30168961326498955],
[0.6967960669374997, 0.8715621457012694, 0.24960628313623423],
[0.891389814359208, 0.9591605275600708, 0.5240885874508074]]
>>>
```

3.3.8 Strings, String Formatting Conversions, and Sequence Operations

In Python 3, strings and sequences are fundamental data types that are widely used for representing and manipulating collections of characters or other values.

A string is a sequence of characters enclosed in either single quotes (' ') or double quotes (" "). It can contain letters, numbers, symbols, and spaces. Strings are *immutable*, which means that once a string is created, it can't be changed!

Following are a few examples: (No need to type in the comments on these examples).

```
greeting = "Hello, World!"
print(greeting) # Output: Hello, World!

name = 'Alice'
print("Hello, " + name) # Output: Hello, Alice

first_letter = greeting[0]
print(first_letter) # Output: H

sliced = greeting[7:12]
print(sliced) # Output: World
```

Sequences are ordered collections of elements, where each element has an assigned index. Python 3 provides several sequence types, including strings, lists, and tuples. Sequences can contain elements of different data types, and they can be mutable or immutable depending on the type. Some common operations on sequences include indexing (accessing elements by their position), slicing (extracting portions of the sequence), concatenation (combining two or more sequences), and repetition (creating a new sequence by repeating an existing one). The following are a few examples:

```
nums = [1, 2, 3, 4, 5]
print(nums[2]) # Output: 3

fruits = ('apple', 'banana', 'cherry')
print(fruits[1]) # Output: banana

combined = nums + list(fruits)
print(combined) # Output: [1, 2, 3, 4, 5, 'apple', 'banana', 'cherry']

repeated = nums * 3
print(repeated) # Output: [1, 2, 3, 4, 5, 1, 2, 3, 4, 5, 1, 2, 3, 4, 5]
```

Strings of characters can also be treated as sequences, so you can use sequence operations on strings as well. Both strings and sequences are versatile data types in Python 3, and understanding their properties and operations allows you to work effectively with text and collections of data.

3.3.8.1 Strings

As stated above, strings are a class of objects in Python 3 that can represent text, and are basically seen in their single-quoted and double-quoted form, which are interchangeable. For example:

```
>>> 'program', "program's"
('program',"program's")
>>>
```

To format strings in an expression, you can use the % binary operator to format values as strings according to a specific format definition. On a line of code, on the left of the % operator, put in a format string that has one or more code types. On the right of the % sign, put in objects you want to substitute in for the types.

The operator **(s % k)** produces a formatted string, given a format string *s* and a collection of objects in a tuple or mapping object (dictionary).The string *s* may be a standard or Unicode string. The format string contains two types of objects: ordinary characters (which are left unmodified) and conversion specifiers, each of which is replaced with a formatted string representing an element of the associated tuple or mapping.

If k is a tuple, the number of conversion specifiers must exactly match the number of objects in k. If k is a mapping, each conversion specifier must be associated with a valid key name in the mapping, using parentheses. Each conversion specifier starts with the % character and ends with one of the conversion characters shown in Table 3.5.

TABLE 3.5

String Formatting Conversions

Character	Output Format
d, I	Decimal integer or long integer
u	Unsigned integer or long integer
o	Octal integer or long integer
x	Hexadecimal integer or long integer
X	Hexadecimal integer (uppercase letters)
f	Floating point as [−]m.dddddd
e	Floating point as [−]m.dddddde±xx
E	Floating point as [−]m.ddddddE±xx
g, G	Use %e or %E for exponents less than −4 or greater than the precision
s	String or any object. The formatting code uses str() to generate strings
r	Produces the same string as produced by repr()
c	Single character
%	Literal %

The following Example allows you to perform some basic operations on strings, such as *concatenating* them (adding their characters together), embedding escape sequences in them (to include special characters), finding their lengths (an integer representing their length), or *slicing* them (extracting smaller sub-string parts of them).

Example 3.15

```
>>> a = 'programming'
>>> b = 'programmer\n'
>>> c = 'programs'
>>> print (a + ' ' + b + c)
programming programmer
programs
>>> len(a+b+c)                    #len is the length operator
30
>>> d = a[0:3] + b[3:7] + c[7]    #b[3:7] is gram
>>> d
'programs'
>>> b[3:]
'grammer\n'
>>> print (b[3:])
grammer
>>> q = c[:]
>>> q
'programs'
>>>
```

In-Chapter Exercises

18. Instead of printing the concatenated strings in line 4 of Example 3.15, what do you get echoed to you on the Shell Area command line if you just type **a + b + c**?

19. The variable c has 12 characters in it. Why are there 30 characters returned for the length of the concatenation of a, b, and c?

20. What is the first index value used to extract sub-strings from a string?

21. What is the last index value used to extract sub-strings from a string?

22. What does the indexing operation [:] shown in Example 3.15 accomplish?

23. What does a[1:3] return, and why?

3.3.8.2 Sequence Operations

Three important, and quite useful operations you can perform on sequence types of objects are *indexing*, *slicing*, and *extended slicing*. Objects such as

TABLE 3.6

Indexing, Slicing, and Extended Slicing Operations

Operation	Description
s[n]	Returns nth element of s
s[i] = x	Index assignment
s[i:j] = r	Slice assignment
s[i:j:stride] = r	Extended slice assignment
del s[i]	Deletes an element
del s[i:j]	Deletes a slice
del s[i:j:stride]	Deletes an extended slice

strings and tuples are immutable and cannot be modified after creation. But lists can be modified with the following operators, as shown in Table 3.6.

The following section describes and gives examples of some sequence operations on mutable objects.

Indexing into the sequence:
Gets components using offsets, where the first element indexed is at zero (0) offset.
Negative indices count backward from the end, where the last element is at offset –1.

s[0] gets the first element, s[1] gets the second element, and so on.

s[–2] gets the second from last element.

Slicing the sequence:
Extracts contiguous sections of a sequence, from i to j-i.
Slice boundaries i and j default to 0 and sequence length len(s).

s[1:4] retrieves elements from offset 1–3.

s[1:] retrieves from offset 1 until the end of the sequence object.

s[:–1] retrieves from offset 0 to the next to last element.

s[:] makes a copy of the sequence object.

Extended slicing of the sequence:
The third element is a *stride*, which defaults to 1, added to the offset of each element extracted.

s[::2] is every other item in the sequence.

s[::–1] is the reverse of the sequence.

s[4:1:–1]retrieves from offset 4, up to but not including 1, in reverse.

<u>Slice assignments:</u>
On mutable objects, deleting elements of the sequence and then reinserting new ones.
Iterable objects assigned to slices s[i:j] do not have to be the same size.
Iterable objects assigned to extended slices s[i:j:k] must match in size.

Here are several interactive code examples of sequence object operations on a list of integers, typed into the Thonny Shell area:

```
>>>m = [0, 1, 2, 3, 4, 5, 6, 7, 8, 9]
>>>n = m[::2]
>>>m
[2, 6, 10, 14, 18 ]
>>>p = m[::-2]
>>>p
[20, 16, 12, 8, 4]
>>>q = m[0:5:2]
>>>q
[2, 6, 10]
>>>r = m[5:0:-2]
>>>r
[12, 8, 4]
>>>s = m[:5:1]
>>>s
[2, 4, 6, 8, 10]
>>>t = m[:5:-1]
>>>t
[20, 18, 16, 14]
>>>u = m[6::1]
>>>u
[14, 16, 18, 20]
>>>v = m[5::-1]
>>>v
[12, 10, 8, 6, 4, 2]
>>>w = m[5:0:-1]
>>>w
[12, 10, 8, 6, 4]
>>>
```

Here are several more code examples, again typed into the Thonny Shell Area, of some further uses of formatting expressions on different objects.

Example 3.16

```
>>>x = 400
>>>y = 75.142783
>>>z = "master"
>>>d = {'x':13, 'y':1.54321, 'z':'unive'}
```

```
>>>q = 1234567812345678
>>>print ('x is %d' % x)
 x is 400
>>>print ('%10d %f' % (x,y))
400 75.142783
>>>print ('%+010d %E' % (x,y))
+0000000400 7.514278E+01
>>>print ('%(x)-10d %(y)0.3g' % d)
13 1.54
>>>print ('%0.4s %s' % (z, d['z']))
mast unive
>>>print ('%*.*f' % (5,3,y))
75.143
>>>print ('q = %d' % q)
q = 1234567812345678
>>>
```

Here are even more interactive code examples showing slicing operations on a list of integers:

```
>>>x = [1,2,3,4,5]
>>>x[1] = 6
>>>x
[1,6,3,4,5]
>>>x[2:4] = [10,11]
>>>x
[1,6,10,11,5]
>>>x[3:4] = [-1,-2,-3]
>>>x
[1,6,10,-1,-2,-3,5]
>>>x[2:] = [0]
>>>x
[1,6,0]
>>>
```

A slicing assignment may be supplied with an optional *stride* argument. The argument on the right side of the assignment statement must have exactly the same number of elements as the slice that is being replaced. Here are a few code examples of this, typed into the Thonny Shell Area:

```
>>>y = [1,2,3,4,5]
>>>y[1::2] = [10,11]
>>>y
[1,10,3,11,5]
>>>y[1::2] = [30,40,50]
Traceback (most recent call last):
  File "<stdin>", line 1, in <module>
ValueError: attempt to assign sequence of size 3 to extended slice of size 2
>>>
```

3.3.9 Tuples

Similar to the list object described in Section 3.3.7, the Python 3 *tuple* is a simple object that creates data structures using any other object type. Tuples support most of the same operations as lists, such as indexing, slicing, and concatenation. But you cannot modify the contents of a tuple after creation, as you can with a list.

This is a tuple's most important feature, as a sequence object used in data structures:

It cannot be changed.

The following Example uses Way 2 (Script Mode) to execute the code, and shows the creation, querying, and manipulation of tuples in a database.

Example 3.17

With your favorite text editor, create the following file of six lines (named **data.txt**) in Thonny's current working directory, making sure that after you save it in the editor, you use the Bash shell command **chmod u+x data.txt**:

```
Conditions,23,45.8
Methods,12,11.75
Objects,40,17.1
Modules,1023,1.4
Dictionaries,45,120.71
Comprehensions,5,234.75
```

Next, type in or paste the following code into the Thonny Script Area:

```
filename = "data.txt"
collection=[]
for line in open(filename):
    fields = line.split(",")        #splits line by commas
    name = fields[0]                #create the fields
    uses = int(fields[1])
    value = float(fields[2])
    card = (name,uses,value)        #create the tuple
    collection.append(card)
print (collection[0])
print (collection[3][2])
sum = 0.0
for name, uses, value in collection:
    sum += uses / value
print (sum)
```

Then, click on the Thonny Run Toolbar Icon.
You should see the following output in the Thonny Shell Area:

```
>>> %Run -c $EDITOR_CONTENT
('Conditions', 23, 45.8)
1.4
734.9710205576091
>>>
```

3.3.10 Sets

Another elementary object type in Python 3 is the *set*, which is an *unordered* collection of objects that have no duplicate elements. The distinguishing feature of a set as an unordered sequence is that you cannot address or index into the set using the index operations on sequences we illustrated for lists and tuples. To create sets and do some operations on them, do the following example (you can omit typing in the comments shown!):

Example 3.18

```
>>> x = set([1.0, 2.0, 3.0, 4.0])
>>> x
{1.0, 2.0, 3.0, 4.0}
>>> z = set([10,11,12,13,14])
>>> z
{10, 11, 12, 13, 14}
>>> q = set("Hello")
>>> q
 {'H', 'e', 'l', 'o'}                #no repeated elements
>>> a = z | q                       #union of z and q
>>> a
{'l', 10, 11, 12, 13, 14, 'H', 'o', 'e'}  #ordered ascending
>>> r = set([9, 8, 7, 6])
>>> b = q | r
>>> b
{'l', 6, 7, 8, 9, 'H', 'o', 'e'}        #ordered ascending even
                                        #though r is descending!
>>> c = r | a
>>> c
{'l', 6, 7, 8, 9, 10, 11, 12, 13, 14, 'H', 'o', 'e'}
>>> c = r & a                       #intersection of r and a
>>> c
set()                               #the empty set
>>> x.add(5.0)                      #add an element
>>> x
{1.0, 2.0, 3.0, 4.0, 5.0}
>>> x.remove(4.0)                   #remove an element
>>> x
{1.0, 2.0, 3.0, 5.0}
>>> x.update([6.0, 7.0, 8.0])       #add multiple elements
>>> x
{1.0, 2.0, 3.0, 5.0, 6.0, 7.0, 8.0}
>>>
```

In-Chapter Exercises

24.　In Example 3.18, why is c finally the empty set?

25.　What would the set x contain if you added three number 5.0's with only one **x.add** command? What would the set x contain if you added three number 5.0's with the **x.update** command?

26.　Can you use slice assignment statements to reassign new values to elements of a tuple?

3.3.11 Dictionaries

A Python 3 *dictionary* is a data structure, or "container", that acts like a table of objects that can be indexed into, where parts of it can be addressed by what are known as *keys*. The keys can be strings or one of several distinct other Python 3 objects. The container is not a sequence object, in the way that a list is. An example of dictionary creation commands, created and run in the Thonny Script Area, that uses strings as keys, is as follows:

> **Example 3.19**
> ```
> function = {
>     "name":"operator",
>     "class" :"arithmetic",
>     "number": 12
>     }
> ```
> Then, when you type the following in the Thonny Shell Area, you get:
>
> ```
> >>> function
> {'number': 12, 'name': 'operator', 'class': 'arithmetic'}
> >>>
> ```
>
>   The keys are the strings "name", "class", and "number", the field data are "operator", "arithmetic", and 12, and the curly braces { } are the syntax that allows you to define the dictionary.

Notice that the order of how the keys and their field data are presented on output by Python 3 may <u>not</u> necessarily be the same order in which you defined them!

Here is a way of extracting a value from the table **function** we created in Example 3.19, and then changing one of the data values in it. In the Thonny Shell Area, type the following:

```
>>> n = function.get("number")
>>> n
12
>>> function["class"]="logical"
>>> function
{'number': 12, 'name': 'operator', 'class': 'logical'}
>>>
```

Here is a way that lets you sort the keys in a **for** loop using the **sorted** function. Python 3 has two basic ways of sorting. The **sorted** function sorts any iterable object, such as entries in a Python dictionary. The **sort** method is a **list** method that works on Python 3 lists (there is no need to type in the comments shown next to the commands you input into the Thonny Shell Area. Remember, ellipses(…) indicate you've pressed the **<Enter>** key on the previous line in the Thonny Shell Area:

```
>>> K = {'x':1, 'y':2, 'z':3}        #creates the dictionary
>>> K
{'x': 1, 'y': 2, 'z': 3}             #not a sequence, thus comes back in any order
>>> for key in sorted(K):
...      print (key, '=', K[key])    #auto-indent by Thonny, and press Enter twice here!
...
x = 1
y = 2
z = 3
>>>
```

3.3.12 Generators

A Python 3 functional technique of program execution, which uses the advanced programming methodologies of data flows, streams, and process pipelines, and preserves the state of the "propagation" of output as it executes in a "stepwise" fashion, is called a *generator*. A generator produces a collection of output results only when a method named **next()** in Python 3 is called. The **next()** method is executed by the Python 3 **yield** statement. When a collection of data needs to be created on the fly, perhaps in single steps("stepwise"), at a particular time during program execution, the generator function is called. The **next()** built-in function steps you through and generates the output.

****Note****

The techniques shown in this and the following section are necessarily for more advanced programming applications.

Example 3.20 shows how to create and invoke a generator function. It's helpful to dissect this Example into its component parts, as shown on the Thonny Shell Area, as follows:

a. Propagation, or generation, then

b. Invocation with a seed value of 4, then

c. Invocation again with a seed value of 6, then

d. Output

Example 3.20

```
>>> def generadd(Q):
...     for i in range(Q):
...         yield i      #generates the next value
...         i += 1
...
>>> for i in generadd(4): #whenever function is called, #the values are generated
...     print (i)
...
0
```

```
1
2
3
>>> z = generadd(6)     #this passes 6 to generadd
>>> z                   #this will show you the compiled generator object
<generator object generated at 0x284f60f4>
>>> next(z)             #the next built-in steps you through and generates the value
0
>>> next(z)
1
>>> next(z)
2
>>> next(z)
3
>>> next(z)
4
>>> next(z)
5
>>> next(z)
Traceback(most recent call last):
 File "<stdin?", line 1. in <module>
StopIteration
>>>
```

As a further application of generator use, the code of Example 3.21 shows how to implement generator functions, in a file named **regen.py** that you create with your favorite text editor. First, create the file **regen.py** as shown in the current directory that Thonny is using, and then use Way3 (Import Script Mode) to do In-Chapter Exercises 27–29:

Example 3.21

```
def abc():
    a = deff()
    for i in a:
        yield i
    yield 'abc'
def deff():
    a = ijk()
    for i in a:
        yield i
    yield 'deff'
def ijk():
    for i in (1,2,3):
        yield i
    yield 'ijk'
```

In-Chapter Exercises

27. Give the exact Thonny operations that would bring the three functions from Example 3.21 into the Python 3 interpreter, given that you have used Way 3 (Import Script Mode).

28. Give the exact Python 3 code that would invoke the three functions from Example 3.21 on the Thonny Shell Area command line.

29. Give the exact Python 3 code that would allow you to step through the invocation of the three functions from Example 3.21, to generate its output results until you reach the **StopIteration** message. List the output generated at each step through the recursion.

3.3.12.1 Generator Recursion

Recursion, which is the delay of computation until some target final state is reached, can be implemented using Python 3 generator functions by defining a generator function that <u>calls itself within the body of its own definition</u>. Here's an example of that kind of a recursive generator function in Python 3:

```
def recursive_generator(n):
    if n == 0:
        return
    yield n
    yield from recursive_generator(n - 1)
for num in recursive_generator(5):
    print(num)
```

Save the above code in a file named **recursive.py**, in Thonny's current working directory. In this descriptive example, the **recursive_generator** function takes an integer **n** as its parameter. If **n** is 0, the function simply returns, indicating the final state of the recursion has been reached. Otherwise, it yields the current value of **n** and then calls itself again, recursively with **n - 1**, using the **yield from** statement to assign the iteration to the recursive call. But **n** is assigned the value of 5.

Using Way 3 (Import Script Mode), here's how you can use the **recursive_generator** function to generate a sequence of numbers. When you import the above code into the Thonny Shell Area, the output is as follows:

```
>>>import recursive
5
4
3
2
1
```

In this descriptive example, calling **recursive_generator(5)** generates a sequence of numbers from 5 down to 1, using recursion. The **for** loop iterates over the generated values and prints them one by one.

Note that the use of a generator function for recursion allows you to iterate over the generated values *lazily*, i.e., one value at a time, which can be memory-efficient compared to generating the entire sequence upfront.

3.3.13 Coroutines

So, perhaps to end your suspense, here's how we answered the last three In-Chapter Exercises in the Thonny Shell Area:

```
>>>import regen
>>>x = regen.abc()
>>>next(x)
1
>>>next(x)
2
>>>next(x)
3
>>>next(x)
'ijk'
>>>next(x)
'deff'
>>>next(x)
'abc'
>>>next(x)
Traceback(most recent call last)
File "<stdin>", line 1, in <module>
StopIteration
>>>
```

In the previous section, we introduced the advanced programming technique of using generator functions, which use **yield** to give output results. Python 3 generator functions can also "consume" results using a **yield** statement. In addition, two new methods applied to generator objects, **send()** and **close()**, create a "framework" for objects, that consume and produce values. Generator functions that define these objects are called *coroutines*. Coroutines consume values using a **yield** statement on the right side of an expression, as follows:

value = (yield)

Using this syntax, execution pauses at this here until the object's **send** method is invoked with an argument:

coroutine.send(data)

Then, execution resumes, with **value** being assigned or referenced to the value of data. To signal the end of a computation, we shut down a coroutine using the **close()** method. This raises a GeneratorExit exception inside the coroutine, which we can catch with a **try/except** clause.

The next example illustrates these concepts. It is a coroutine that prints strings that match a provided template pattern. Use Way 2 (Script Mode), and the Thonny Run Toolbar icon to implement this in Thonny:

Example 3.22

```
def grepper(template):
    print ('Searching for ' + template)
    try:
        while True:
            x = (yield)
            if template in x:
                print (x)
    except GeneratorExit:
        print ("Done")
```

In the Thonny Shell Area, type the following:

```
>>> q = grepper("Pythonista")
>>> next(q)
Pythonista
>>> q.send("After doing this section, you will be known as a Pythonista")
After doing this section, you will be known as a Pythonista
>>> q.send("Not a very Pythonic answer")
>>> q.send("Python makes C look high maintenance and too complex")
>>> q.close()
Done
>>>
```

When we call **q.send** with a value, evaluation resumes inside the coroutine **q** at the statement line **= (yield)**, where the sent value is assigned to the variable line. Evaluation continues inside **q**, printing out the line if it matches, going through the loop until it encounters the line **= (yield)** again. Then, evaluation pauses inside **q** and resumes where **q.send** was called.

We can chain functions that **send()** and functions that **yield** together to achieve complex behaviors, similar to streaming or pipelining. In the following code, the function **read** splits a string named "text" into words and sends each word to another coroutine. Continuing in the Thonny Shell Area, with grepper still defined:

```
>>> def read(text, next_coroutine):
...     for line in text.split():
...         next_coroutine.send(line)
...     next_coroutine.close()
...
```

Each word is sent to the coroutine bound to **next_coroutine**, causing **next_coroutine** to start executing, and this function to pause and wait. It waits until **next_coroutine** pauses, at which point the function resumes by sending the next word, or exiting with the message Done.

By continuing in the Thonny Shell area as follows, we're joining the **read** function together in a pipeline with the function **grepper**, thus creating a program that allows us to print out only the words that match a particular word.

```
>>> text = "0110 1100 0101 1000 1010 0111 1111 0001 0110"
>>> found = grepper('01')
>>> next(found)
Looking for 01
>>> read(text, found)
0110
0101
1010
0111
0001
0110
Done
>>>
```

The **read** function sends each word to the coroutine **grepper**, which prints out any input that matches its template pattern. Within the **grepper** coroutine, the line x = **(yield)** waits for each word sent, and it transfers control back to **read** when it is reached.

In-Chapter Exercises

30. a. Put the code from Example 3.22 into a file (if you have not done so already), and using Thonny and Way 3 (Import Script Mode), invoke the coroutines **grepper** and **read** on the template "1201".

     b. Then search the following string using that template: "0120 1201 1020", "3012 3013 3212", "12010203101213012".

     c. What prints out on your screen when you use the proper commands, similarly to what is shown in the follow-up code to the **read** function?

31. a. Put the code from Example 3.22 in a file (if you have not done so already), and using Thonny and Way 3 (Import Script Mode), invoke the coroutine **read** on the template "Python is the most Pythonic enterprise a Pythonista can practice".

     b. Then search for the string "Python" in that template using the coroutines **grepper** and **read**.

     c. What prints out on your screen when you use the proper commands, similarly to what is shown in the follow-up code to the **read** function?

3.3.14 Exceptions

It's worth noting that there are some very useful facilities in Thonny that can help you to debug your program or script in a "trial run", step-by-step fashion. Usually, these facilities are a part of a Python 3 IDE like Thonny, or any high-level language capable IDE.

A good example of one of these facilities that we've seen in Thonny is automatic indentation. Another is Thonny's interactive step-by-step debugging tools, which are seen as icons in the Toolbar. We don't show the use of the debugging icons, but encourage you to play around with them while any of the script files in this chapter are active in Thonny's Script Area.

With that said, within the language itself and its syntactic structures, an exception, or unexpected end to a program or a block of code, is a Python 3 object that represents an error. To terminate the flow of execution of such things because of some exception the interpreter has found, Python 3 has two kinds of exception-handling structure that can end the program or block of code. These structures are:

1. Exception handling that uses, for example, **try:...except:...else:** as shown in Example 3.23, and the standard exception, for example, **StopIteration**.
2. Assertions, for example, using the **assert** statement.

The general form of **try:...except:...else:** is:

try:
   Some operations...
   ...
except ExceptionI:
   If there is an Exception, do this...
else:
   If there is no Exception then, do this...

The following is a simple exception test example of the **try:...except:...else:** construct, which, when run in the Thonny Script Area by clicking on the Run Toolbar Icon, opens a new file in the current working directory, writes some content to the file, and then exits normally.

Example 3.23

```
try:
    handler = open("datafile", "w")
    handler.write("This is a data file for testing exception handling!!")
except IOError:
    print ("Error: Can\'t find file or write data")
else:
    print ("File write successful")
    handler.close()

>>> %Run -c $EDITOR_CONTENT
File write successful
>>>
```

In-Chapter Exercises

32. List five other standard exceptions, what general class of exception they signal, and what source you used to obtain their names.

33. Modify the code of Example 3.23 so that it writes the integers 1, 2, 3, 4, 5, 6, 7, 8, 9, and 10 as a string list to the file named **datafile2**.

3.3.15 Modules, Global and Local Scope in Functions

At a certain level of abstraction, everything in Python 3 is a module, even Python 3 itself!

A Python 3 module is a container, or package, which holds all the hierarchical objects, statements, expressions, and other modular components we spoke about in the beginning of this chapter, that are necessary to accomplish an intended task, or sub-task. Modules may contain function definitions, class operations, and variable assignments. Basically, there are only two types of Python 3 modules: a module written by you, or a module from some external library, like the Python 3 standard library. The standard library that is built into Python 3 contains over 200 modules, and there are many other module resources available online that a programmer can use, so that she does not have to "reinvent the wheel", so to speak.

A schematic diagram of the modular construction of a possible Python program is as follows:

Python shell --->
    First Module.py --->
        Second Module.py, etc. --->
            Standard Library >>> commands
                    <---objects --->results

Example 3.24, using the code in Example 3.5, shows the composition and use of a module, which happens to be a function, that you create.

If you have not already done so, type the code from it into a file named **arith1.py** using your favorite text editor (or use the Raspberry Pi 5 OS **mv** command rename **math1.py** as **arith1.py**). Make sure you rename the file math1.py to arith1.py so that it's in the same directory! Then type the following lines of Python 3 code at the Python command line using Way 0 (Command Line Mode):

Example 3.24

```
$ python3
Python 3.11.2 (main, Nov 30 2024, 21:22:50) [GCC 12.2.0] on linux
Type "help", "copyright", "credits" or "license" for more information.
```

```
>>> import arith1
>>> A = arith1.add(3.5,4.2)
>>> B = A + arith1.subtract(14.78,20.45)
>>> C = arith1.multiply(B,5.0)
>>> D = arith1.divide(A,C)
>>> D
0.11518324607329841
>>>
```

Notice these things about Example 3.24's code:

1. You use **import**, rather than **from…import**.
2. The methods in **arith1** are addressed, or "touched", by referencing the general syntactic form **arith1.function_name**. For example, by applying the method **arith1.add**.

In-Chapter Exercises

34.   After doing Example 3.24, what result do you get if you type **b** on the Python 3 command line, and why?

35.   After doing Example 3.24 using Way 0 (Command Line Mode), redo it in the Thonny Shell Area. Type **del arith1** on the Thonny Shell Area command line. Then type **D = arith1.divide(A,C)** and press **<Enter>** on the keyboard. What result do you get, and why?

36.   Edit the file **arith1.py**, and comment out all of the return statements in the functions. Then, redo the commands shown in Example 3.24 in the Thonny Shell Area. What is **D** equal to then, and why?

A simple example of a library module from the standard library that you can import and use to execute Raspberry Pi 5 OS commands is given next. Type in the commands shown on the Thonny Shell Area command line (the output results given in the example may differ from what you see on your screen, depending on the specific content in the targeted directory of your system):

Example 3.25

```
>>> import os
>>> File = os.popen('pwd')
>>> File.read(50)
'/home/bob\n'
>>> for line in os.popen('ls -la m*'): print(line.rstrip()) #Press Enter twice!
...
-rw-r--r-- 1 bob 201 Mar 10 15:47 math1.py

>>>
```

3.4 Practical Examples

To begin this section, it would be helpful for you to read and try to become somewhat familiar with the following two references in the Python 3 online documentation for the release of Python 3 you are using. With the purpose of getting a better "top-down" overview of how Python 3 is structured.

1. *The Python Language Reference -- https://docs.python.org/3/reference/*
2. Python standard library, particularly the **sys** and **os** modules.

In the previous sections of this chapter, we provided an overview of the Python 3 language and its syntax via the writing and execution of small (1–25 line) script files and functions. In this section, we will detail some of Python3's practical applications in real-world computer programming with larger (25–50 line) user-written modules, functions, and scripts.

As mentioned in Section 3.2.7, Python 3 can be used to accomplish tasks revolving around shell scripting, systems programming, network and Internet scripting, database programming, systems administration scripting, GUI scripting, scientific and math programming, and AI scripting.

We will begin by writing script files in Python 3 that accomplish what Raspberry Pi 5 OS shell scripts accomplish, with the goal of familiarizing you with some simple practical applications of Python 3.

3.4.1 Another Way of Writing Shell Script Files

In this section, we do not go over the basics of shell scripting, but provide methods and practical examples (including the rewriting of shell scripts) of how to accomplish what shell scripting accomplishes, using Python 3 language syntax and structure. The advantages of using Python 3 are that it is a more robust and extensible language, with many more features and capabilities than any of the usual scripting languages, like Bash, Tcsh, or csh. One of these features is Python 3 OOP, which Bash and Tcsh scripts are not capable of.

3.4.1.1 Rewriting Bash and Tcsh scripts

We start with a simple example of a Bash shell script rewritten in Python 3. The Bash shell script to print out whether a certain directory path exists on our file system or not is given first, and then its Python 3 equivalent is shown in Example 3.26. You should run both, using Way 4 (Bash Mode) for the Python 3 code, and run the Bash script on the Raspberry Pi command line in a terminal. Shown below are these code samples. You should note the comparative output on your system.

Example 3.26

<u>Bash script code</u>

```bash
#!/bin/bash
if [ -d "/usr/bin" ] ; then
   echo "/usr/bin is a directory"
else
   echo "/usr/bin is not a directory"
fi
```

<u>Equivalent Python 3 code</u>

```python
#!/usr/bin/python3
import os
if os.path.isdir("/usr/bin"):
   print ("/usr/bin is a directory")
else:
   print ("/usr/bin is not a directory")
```

On our Raspberry Pi 5 system, using Python 3.11.2, we executed the Python 3 code equivalent using a variation of the alternative method of Way 4 (Bash Mode). In our nano text editor, we created and named the Python 3 equivalent **ex26.py**. We obtained the following output of running both the Python 3 Equivalent and **ex26.bash** (remember to make the bash script and the Python 3 Equivalent executable using the **chmod u+x** command!):

```
$ ./ex26.py
/usr/bin is a directory
$
```

The important thing to notice about the above Python 3 code, and its execution, is that:

1. A standard library module named **os** is imported at the top of the script file.

2. **os.path** is a nested module that provides directory and pathname tools, in addition to those tools in the **os** standard library module.

In-Chapter Exercises

37. Give the exact syntax you used on the Bash command line to run the Bash shell script shown in Example 3.26.

38. Referring to the online documentation, what other **os** module from the standard library can be used to achieve the same thing as the Python 3 code in Example 3.26?

39. Edit the Python 3 code for Example 3.26, and substitute the path **/usr/bin/yyy** for **/usr/bin**. What output from the program do you get when you run it after making this change?

Another simple example of a Bash shell script converted to Python is as follows. Again, we ran the Python 3 script using Way 4 (Bash Mode).

Example 3.27

Bash script code

```
#!/bin/bash
echo "Enter input: \c"
read line
echo "You entered: $line"
echo "Enter another line: \c"
read word1 word2 word3
echo "The first word is: $word1:"
echo "The second word is: $word2:"
echo "The rest of the line is: $word3:"
exit 0
```

Equivalent Python code

```
#!/usr/bin/python3
import sys
s = input("Enter input:")
print ("You entered:", s)
r = input("Enter another line:")
words = r.split()
print ("The first word is:", words[0])
print ("The second word is:", words[1])
rest = (r.join(words[2:]))
print ("The rest of the line is:", rest)
sys.exit() #normal exit status
```

On our Raspberry Pi 5 system, using Python 3.11.2, we ran the Python code equivalent, using Way 4 (Bash Mode). We named the Python 3 equivalent **ex27.py**. We obtained the following output, with the supplied text shown (remember to make the bash script and the Python 3 Equivalent executable using the **chmod u+x** command!):

```
$ ./ex27.py
Enter input: Linux rules!
You entered: Linux rules!
Enter another line: Raspberry Pi rules!
The first word is: Raspberry
The second word is: Pi
The rest of the line is: rules!
Process ended with exit code 0.
$
```

In-Chapter Exercises

40. Give two examples of list indexing or slicing used in Example 3.27.

41. Give two examples of string methods from Example 3.27.

The following is another illustration of taking a Bash shell script and converting it to Python 3.

Example 3.28

Bash script code

```
#!/bin/bash
echo "The command name is: $0."
echo "The value of the command line arguments are: $1 $2 $3 $4 $5 $6 $7 $8 $9."
echo "Another way to display values of all the arguments: $@."
echo "Yet another way is: $*."
exit 0
```

Python code

```
#!/usr/bin/python3
import sys
x = (sys.argv)
print ("The command name is: ", sys.argv[0])
print ("The value of the command line arguments are: ", x[1:10])
print ("Another way to display values of all the arguments: ", sys.argv[1:])
print ("Yet another way is: ", sys.argv[slice(1,15)])
sys.exit ()
```

On our Raspberry Pi 5 system, using the default Bash shell and Python 3.11.2, we ran both the Example 3.28 Bash script code and its Python 3 code equivalent (using Way 4 (Bash Mode). We named the Bash version **ex28. bash**, and the Python 3 equivalent **ex28.py**. We obtained the following output, with the argument lists shown (remember to make the Bash script file and its Python equivalent executable using the **chmod u+x** command before you run these commands!):

```
$ ./ex28.bash a b c d e f g h i j k l m n
The command name is: ./ex28.bash.
The value of the command line arguments are: a b c d e f g h i.
Another way to display values of all the arguments: a b c d e f g h i j k l m n.
Yet another way is: a b c d e f g h i j k l m n.
$
```

```
$ ./ex28.py a b c d e f g h i j k l m n
The command name is: ./ex28.py
The value of the command line arguments are:  ['a', 'b', 'c', 'd', 'e', 'f', 'g', 'h', 'i']
Another way to display values of all the arguments:  ['a', 'b', 'c', 'd', 'e', 'f', 'g', 'h', 'i', 'j', 'k', 'l', 'm', 'n']
Yet another way is:  ['a', 'b', 'c', 'd', 'e', 'f', 'g', 'h', 'i', 'j', 'k', 'l', 'm', 'n']
$
```

Similar to the Bash shell in syntax and structure, the tcsh shell has functional capabilities that can be implemented easily in Python 3. The following is a tcsh script file, whose syntactic structure and program functionality are converted to a Python 3 script file that you should run using Way 4 (Bash Mode), similar to the above Examples in this section:

Example 3.29

tcsh shell code

```
#!/bin/tcsh
if ( ( $#argv == 0 ) || ( $#argv > 1 ) ) then
   echo "Usage: $0:t ordinary_file"
   exit 1
endif

if ( -f $1 ) then
   set filename = $argv[1]
   set inode = `stat -c "%i" $filename`
   set size = `stat -c "%s" $filename`

   echo "File Name:      $filename"
   echo "Inode Number:   $inode"
   echo "Size (bytes):   $size"
   exit 0
else
   echo "Error: File $1 does not exist or is not a regular file."
   exit 1
endif
```

Python code

```
#!/usr/bin/python3
import os
import sys
if len(sys.argv) == 1 or len(sys.argv) > 2: #check for no/too many args
   print ("Usage: ", sys.argv[0], " ordinary file")
   sys.exit(1)
if os.path.isfile(sys.argv[1]):    #bingo, get stats
   filename = sys.argv[1]
   fileinfo = os.stat(filename)
   print ("Filename  inode  size")
   print (" ")
   print (filename, fileinfo.st_ino, fileinfo.st_size)
   sys.exit(0)
else:                         # argument must something else!
   print (sys.argv[1], " argument must be an ordinary file")
   sys.exit(1)
```

Running the tcsh script

****Note****

In executing ex29.tcsh, we chose to use as an argument file names (ex26.py, Music), which we knew were in the current working directory. The filenames you choose as an argument to test the tcsh script will, of course, be different. Also, you have to install tcsh on your Raspberry Pi5 with the command:

```
$ sudo apt install tcsh
Output truncated…
$
```

To switch to the tc shell, type **tcsh on the Bash command line,** then we tested the two files as follows:

```
$ tcsh <Enter>
raspberrypi:~> ./ex29.tcsh ex26.py
File Name:     ex26.py
Inode Number:    1278
Size (bytes):   147
raspberrypi:~> ./ex29.tcsh Music
Error: File Music does not exist or is not a regular file.
raspberrypi:~>
```

To leave tcsh, and return to the Bash shell, type **exit** and then press **<Enter>**.

Running the Python 3 script
On our Raspberry Pi 5 system, we ran the Python 3 code equivalent using Way 4 (Bash Mode). We named the Python 3 equivalent **ex29.py**. We obtained the following output, where there was a file named **ex29.py** in the current working directory, but <u>no</u> file named **lab1** (remember to make the Tcsh script and the Python 3 Equivalent executable using the **chmod u+x** command!):

```
$ chmod u+x ex29.py
$ ./ex29.py
Usage: ./ex29.py ordinary file
$ ./ex29.py lab1
lab1  argument must be an ordinary file
$ ./ex29.py ex29.py
Filename  inode   size

ex29.py 12452180 572
$
```

3.4.2 A Basic Web Server and User File Maintenance

A very useful and practical example of using built-in Python 3 capabilities on your Raspberry Pi 5 system is the **http.server** module, which comes standard with Python 3. The value of using this module, at least for an ordinary user of a Raspberry Pi 5 system, is that you can quickly and easily implement a system service that can be programmed, configured, and controlled by that ordinary user.

Another very useful and important aspect of an ordinary user's interaction with a Raspberry Pi 5 system, which we cover in Section 3.4.2.2, is how effectively you can maintain the files on your system. The Python 3 standard library, and many user-written libraries and modules, can help you do this efficiently on the Raspberry Pi 5 OS. You can utilize the extensive syntax and the multi-paradigm programming capabilities of Python 3 to go far beyond the capabilities of doing operating system and file maintenance that are available in any of the shell script-creation programs.

User file maintenance consists of creating, saving, organizing, and deleting files on your system, in your own account, or globally for the entire system and its users.

3.4.2.1 Web Server Example

In this section, we show an ordinary user how to create and use a web server, using a built-in Python 3 module.

Example 3.30

A Simple Web Server Implemented in Python 3
   The **http.server** module that comes with Python 3 is a simple HTTP server that provides standard GET and HEAD request handlers. An advantage of using the Python 3 built-in HTTP server is that you don't have to install and configure anything! The only thing that you need is to have Python 3 installed on your system, which is by default on our Raspberry Pi 5 OS. And your Raspberry Pi 5 needs to be connected to a Local Area Network (LAN), such as your home network or the Internet.

   Step 1. To start an HTTP server on port 8000 (which is the default port), type this command in a terminal window:

```
$ python3 -m http.server
Serving HTTP on 0.0.0.0 port 8000 (http://0.0.0.0:8000/) ...
```

This will begin to serve files and directories in a browser, whose URL is set to your IP address (in the case of the above command, this is 0.0.0.0) and port 8000, where the files and directories are located in the current working directory when you typed the above command.

You could have also changed the port to some other valid port number, for instance 8096, by typing this command instead:

```
$ python3 -m http.server 8096
```

   Step 2. To share other files and directories on your LAN, or the Internet, in a terminal, change the current directory with the **cd** command to whichever directory you wish to have accessible via browsers and HTTP. For example:

```
$ cd /home/bob/Desktop
```

```
$ python3 -m http.server
Serving HTTP on 0.0.0.0 port 8000 (http://0.0.0.0:8000/) ...
192.168.1.14 - - [17/Mar/2025 05:47:26] "GET / HTTP/1.1" 200 -
```

192.168.1.14 - - [17/Mar/2025 05:47:26] code 404, message File not found
192.168.1.14 - - [17/Mar/2025 05:47:26] "GET /favicon.ico HTTP/1.1" 404 -
Output truncated ...

Step 3. Then, in a web browser on your Raspberry Pi system, put in either of the following two addresses:

http://your_ip_address:8000

or to the localhost:

http://127.0.0.1:8000

If you don't have a valid index.html file in the current working directory, then all files and directories in /home/bob/ Desktop, or whatever your current working directory was when you issued the command, will be listed. If there's a valid index. html file in the Desktop above (which, in our case, there wasn't), you will see the content of that index.html page displayed in the web browser. As long as the Python 3 HTTP server is running, the terminal will update with messages as they are loaded from the server. These messages will be standard http logging information (GET and PUSH), 404 errors, IP addresses, dates, times, and a subset of **journald** messages.

To terminate the Python HTTP server, in the terminal you launched it from, type **<Ctrl>+<C>**

^C

Keyboard interrupt received, exiting.

$

In-Chapter Exercise

42. Use the steps shown in Example 3.30 to implement and test a basic web server on your Raspberry Pi 5 system. What security issues might arise if you have not deployed firewalls or taken other preventative measures on your Internet-connected Raspberry Pi 5?

3.4.2.2 *Backing up Your Files*

We will not go into the general necessity of backing up your files on your Raspberry Pi 5 system, as a part of maintaining that computer system, because the reasons for doing that should be pretty obvious to even novice users. According to Linux system professionals, there is an easy-to-remember and important set of considerations you have to make when backing up the system as an ordinary user, and perhaps even as the system administrator. This set of considerations can be posed in simple question form as "How,

What, Why, When, Where, and Who?" Some of the answers to these simple questions can be dovetailed together, and we give a selected list of example answers as follows:

"How" means on the boot/system medium, to Dropbox, to a USB thumb drive manually, to another computer on your home network, automatically by *cron, systemd or ZFS*, to an NVMe-connected medium (manually or automatically,) totally, incrementally, via RAID or NFSv4, or any variant and combination of all of these.

"What" means just some of your personal files, all of them, only certain kinds of documents, your entire home directory, the whole boot/system medium, multiple external media, and so on.

"Why" means deciding on the relative importance of "What" you are backing up.

"When" means every five minutes, hourly, once a day, once a week, once a month, every time you save a particular file, and at what time exactly, like AM.

"Where" means very much the same thing as "How".

"Who" means you personally, automatically by cron, systemd, or ZFS, the designated system administrator, Dropbox.com, or some other commercial backup agent.

To give you a notion of a prudent strategy to deploy in backing up your own user files, the file that contains the words you are reading right now was archived in the following manner:

1. Saved at regular intervals to an attached USB3 -mounted SSD.

2. Saved incrementally and periodically to my gmail.com account in specifically-named archival folders.

We will use the **rsync** command to accomplish our backup strategies in this section. This command is similar to the **cp**, and **rcp**, commands, except that it is more efficient and faster.

Most importantly, **rsync** "synchronizes" two files or directory structures so that changes in one are reflected in the **rsync** duplicate, either locally between mounted media, or remotely over a local area network (LAN) or the Internet.

It can copy locally or to/from another host over any remote shell, particularly **ssh**. It has a large number of options that control every aspect of its behavior and permit very flexible specification of the set of files to be copied. The **rsync** command finds files that need to be transferred using a "quick check" algorithm (by default) that looks for files that have changed in size or in last-modified time. We encourage you to consult the **rsync** man page for more information.

The general forms of the **rsync** command are:

Local:

rsync [OPTION(S)...] SRC... [DEST]

Across a network:

Pull: rsync [OPTION(S)...] [USER@]HOST:SRC... [DEST]
Push: rsync [OPTION(S)...] SRC... [USER@]HOST:DEST

where **OPTION(S)** are the valid options for the **rsync** command, **SRC** is the source file or directory, and **DEST** is the destination path.

The next four examples will use Python 3 standard library modules, and embed Bash shell commands in a Python "wrapper" (Raspberry Pi 5 shell command(s) embedded in Python code). The examples primarily use the Python 3 **os.system** module to:

1. Back up a single file on the system medium to a mounted USB drive.
2. Back up a single directory beneath your home directory on the system medium to a directory on a mounted USB3 drive.
3. Back up a single directory beneath your home directory on the system medium to another network location on your LAN in **Push** mode.
4. Back up a directory on the system medium to a mounted USB3 thumb drive in a rolling, incremental scheme, that creates "snapshots" of the source directory anytime the Python 3 script is run.
5. Customize a system command to show permissions of files in the current working directory that match a certain pattern.

Example 3.31 shows you how to use Thonny, in the Shell Area, and Python 3 to back up a single file on your system medium to a USB3 thumb drive you mounted and attached to your file system. It assumes you have an ordinary file in the current working directory named **ex28.bash**, and that the destination path on the USB3 drive is **/media/bob/7C87-8F1D**.

> ****Note**** That path to the thumb drive on your
> Raspberry Pi 5 system will be different!

Example 3.31

```
>>>import os
>>>os.system('rsync -av ex28.bash /media/bob/7C87-8F1D')
sending incremental file list
ex28.bash

sent 331 bytes  received 35 bytes  104.57 bytes/sec
total size is 225  speedup is 0.61
0
>>>
```

The following example shows you how to use Thonny and Python 3 to back up an entire directory on your system medium to the USB drive you have mounted and attached to your system. It assumes that Thonny's current working directory has a subdirectory named __pycache__, and that the destination path on the USB drive is **/media/bob/7C87-8F1D**.

****Note**** That path to the thumb drive on your
Raspberry Pi 5 system will be different!

Example 3.32

```
>>>import os
>>>os.system('rsync -av __pycache__ /media/bob/7C87-8F1D')
sending incremental file list
__pycache__/
__pycache__/grepper.cpython-39.pyc
__pycache__/looper.cpython-39.pyc
__pycache__/looper2.cpython-39.pyc

sent 1,103 bytes  received 77 bytes  2,360.00 bytes/sec
total size is 782  speedup is 0.66
0
>>>
```

The following example shows you how to use Way 0 (Command Line Mode) to back up an entire directory on your boot/system medium to a remote location on your local area network. It assumes:

0. You will execute Python 3 on the Bash command line.
1. You have the **ssh** daemon running on both your local and remote host, and that you have successfully logged into the remote host and previously exchanged keys between local and remote host.
2. You have a directory under the current working directory named **__pycache__**, with some files in it
3. Where a password is asked for, you type in your password on the remote host
4. That the destination path to the remote host is **bob@192.168.1.7:/home/bob**

****Note**** That path to the thumb drive on your
Raspberry Pi 5 system will be different!

Example 3.33

```
$ python3
Python 3.11.2 (main, Nov 30 2024, 21:22:50) [GCC 12.2.0] on linux
Type "help", "copyright", "credits" or "license" for more information.
>>>
>>>import os
>>>os.system('rsync -av __pycache__ bob@192.168.1.7:/home/bob')
```

```
bob@192.168.1.7's password: zzz
sending incremental file list
__pycache__/
__pycache__/grepper.cpython-39.pyc
__pycache__/looper.cpython-39.pyc
__pycache__/looper2.cpython-39.pyc

sent 1,103 bytes  received 77 bytes  214.55 bytes/sec
total size is 782  speedup is 0.66
>>>
```

In-Chapter Exercise

43.   Repeat the operations shown in Examples 3.31–3.33, substituting
      file names and directory paths on your computer system and local
      network for those shown in the examples. When backing up files
      to a USB3 drive is finished, be sure to **unmount** that drive before
      removing it from the USB connector on your machine. Unless you
      want to use it again in Example 3.34.

The following Example shows you how to create a rolling backup scheme
of "snapshots" of a directory on an SSD medium, and archive the contents of
the directory to multiple (five) backup directories on a USB3 thumb drive you
mounted and attached to your Raspberry Pi 5 system. It is assumed that the
source directory, containing some files, already exists. Every time you execute this Python 3 script, it recycles (in other words, deletes) the oldest (fifth)
archived directory, and creates a new full backup, using the **rsync** command.
You should use a text editor to create the file below, and then to execute it,
run Python 3 on the Bash command line, with Way 0 (Command Line Mode,
as you did in Example 3.33 above). The destination path on our USB3 drive is
seen in the code for this Example as **/media/bob/7C87-8F1D**:

****Note**** That paths on your Raspberry Pi 5 system will be different!

Example 3.34

```
#!/usr/bin/python3
import os
import shutil
target = "/media/bob/7C87-8F1D/"
i = 1
while i <= 5:
    temp_path = target + str(i) + "/"
    if not os.path.exists (temp_path):
        try:
            os.makedirs (temp_path)
            print ("Created  " + temp_path)
        except:
            print (" Could not create  " + temp_path)
    i = i + 1
print ("Deleting the oldest archive")
```

```
shutil.rmtree (target + "5")
print ("Recycle the backups")
os.rename (target + "4", target + "5")
os.rename (target + "3", target + "4")
os.rename (target + "2", target + "3")

os.system('cp -a ' + target + "1" + " " + target + "2")
os.system('rsync -av __pycache__' + " " + target + "1")
```

When we ran the code from Example 3.34 on our Raspberry Pi 5 system <u>for</u> <u>the first time</u>, using the pathnames to the source directory for the backup and the USB drive, as shown in the code, we got the following output:

$ python3 ex34.py
Created /media/bob/7C87-8F1D/1/
Created /media/bob/7C87-8F1D/2/
Created /media/bob/7C87-8F1D/3/
Created /media/bob/7C87-8F1D/4/
Created /media/bob/7C87-8F1D/5/
Deleting the oldest archive
Recycle the backups
sending incremental file list
__pycache__/
__pycache__/grepper.cpython-39.pyc
__pycache__/looper.cpython-39.pyc
__pycache__/looper2.cpython-39.pyc

sent 1,103 bytes received 77 bytes 2,360.00 bytes/sec
total size is 782 speedup is 0.66
$

In summary, we used the **rsync** command to backup a file and directories from the system medium to a USB3 drive, to a remote host on the local network, and in a rolling scheme to a USB3 drive.

3.4.3 Graphical User Interfaces with Python 3 and tkinter Widgets

Up until this point in the chapter, we have interacted with Python 3 via a graphical IDE, although basically in a text-based manner, where we typed commands into Thonny's Script and Shell Areas, into a text editor, or at the command line, and executed Python 3.11.2 to view the output results as text. In this section, we will build a "widget"-based (widget is short for window gadget) GUI with Python 3, where we still create and execute the Python 3 code as text, but see the resulting output of the Python 3 script in the form of widget graphics. We use **tkinter** as the GUI interface, or toolkit. tkinter is an abbreviation for the *TK interface*. And *TK*, which is short for *toolkit*, is a platform-independent, customizable, and configurable GUI library. The Python module **tkinter** allows Python 3 programs to interface with the TK libraries, to produce pictures, and other forms of graphics, on the display of the Raspberry Pi 5.

To accomplish this, we assume the following:

1. That you are using a GUI, desktop environment to interact with your Raspberry Pi 5 system, <u>and the graphical system is based upon the X Window System</u>. After all, that's what Thonny is! A graphical IDE. Therefore, we also have a GUI capability when we program with **tkinter** to create Python 3 GUI's.

****Note****

If you've switched your graphical system for the Raspberry Pi 5 OS to be the X Window System, the output of the **inxi** command, as shown in Chapter 1, would yield the following line describing the display system:

Display: x11 server: X.Org v: 1.21.1.7 with: Xwayland v: 22.1.9 driver: X:loaded:

Most **tkinter** applications will work as long as XWayland is enabled. If you're running a pure Wayland session without XWayland, **tkinter** may not function properly unless **Tk** has been compiled with full Wayland support. If you encounter issues, using XWayland as a fall-back will help. Again, you may, or may not, get the same results as we do, or any results at all, if you've switched to pure Wayland.

2. That you have version Python 3.11X or higher on your Raspberry Pi 5 system. The command line sessions, In-Chapter Exercises, Examples, and Questions and Problems found in this and in the following sections, all require that you have at least this version of Python 3 installed on your Raspberry Pi 5 system.

Our coverage of GUI construction with **tkinter** uses Python 3.11.2, and the appropriate **tkinter** module for that version of Python 3. Depending upon the default Python 3 you are using, and given the specific Raspberry Pi 5 OS distribution you are executing it on, the **tkinter** installation instructions may vary slightly from what is shown in Section 3.4.3.1, but basically it will be the same.

3.4.3.1 Installing tkinter

The standard widget GUI package that works with Python 3 is named **tkinter** in Python 3.11.2.

****Note**** For you to add widget GUI components and functionality to Python 3, you must be able to import this component package into your Python 3 session.

In this section, as much as is possible and practical given the Python 3 GUI scripts we show, we add widgets from a "styled" widget set. These were available since TK version 8.5, and are named **ttk** widgets.

You can easily test to see if your default Python system has **tkinter** available. On the Python command line, type:

>>> **import tkinter**

If you get an error message that the module does not exist, or some similar error message, then you must install the **tkinter** package. To accomplish this, use the **apt** command on the Bash command line as follows:

$ **sudo apt-get install python3-tk**

You may also have to install the required Tcl/Tk development packages with the following command:

$ **sudo apt-get install tk-dev**
Output truncated...
$

3.4.3.2 *tkinter Toolkit Graphical User Interfaces*

A GUI allows you to use a mouse, or other pointing device (such as your finger on a tablet), rather than just the keyboard, to interact with programs that are running. Generally, when you use a CUI, such as during a Bash shell session, and you execute a command, the tasks that command accomplishes do so in some structured order, either in a determinate (counting-wise) or indeterminate (logic-wise) manner. Then the command eventually terminates. But the Python 3 GUI programs we show in the sections below create screen widgets that are displayed on screen, and then the Python 3 script that generates the icons and widgets "waits" for the user to do something with them.

This kind of programming structure is event-driven. *GUI programs, particularly in X windows graphics systems, are event-driven.* We emphasize that kind of programming structure in the Examples and descriptions we provide below.

A meaningful and useful Python 3-scripted GUI program generally always has some form of this basic content and structure:

1. Data of some sort is produced, or already exists, for example, in the form of numbers, or database text on the Raspberry Pi 5. This data itself can be generated in a variety of ways. It could be generated by Python 3 user-written modules placed before the GUI-constructing components in a Python 3 script, which is the style of Python 3 GUI programming shown in all of our examples. It could also be input

interactively while the Python 3 GUI script is running. It could use preexisting data generated beforehand by some other application, or it could even use a C program that generates data within the Python 3 environment, while the Python 3 script is executing!

2. Widgets are created and are organized within some encompassing window frame, and then displayed on screen to the user. These widget objects are instances of master widget classes in **tkinter**, and contain GUI functions that are selected for, and specify particular kinds of responses to user input, and possible data-generating application events.

3. There is a "hooking", or tying together, of the instances from Step 2 that utilize "callback" GUI functions to access the data you want to display, or otherwise modify. For example, you can use any *callable* Python 3 object as a callback. These might be ordinary Python 3 functions, bound methods, lambda expressions, and any other callable object.

> ****Note**** This above is the most critical, and therefore the most useful aspect, of Python 3 GUI programming.

4. Steps 2 and 3 exist inside an infinite event-driven loop that processes user events. When a user event, such as a mouse button press, occurs, the event-driven loop invokes the function associated with a specific event.

5. Data is modified or produced with no apparent visible change on screen, or with graphical changes occurring on screen. This is the "request" step.

6. The loop continues to wait for events, and process them, until a possible termination event happens.

As we present in Section 3.4.3.3, **tkinter** widgets can be chosen and constructed to display and be hooked up to data using OOP, where the widgets are object instances of master classes of **tkinter** widgets. But the style and execution of the Python 3 GUI script file itself can take on a procedural/imperative programming model approach. We choose, as much as possible, to show the procedural/imperative approach because we feel it's easier for beginners to understand and figure out; particularly people who are <u>not</u> familiar with the OOP model of programming. Python 3 does <u>not</u> have core modules that implement GUI, event-driven-programming. GUI programming is implemented using imported modules, such as those from the **tkinter** toolkit.

To summarize the above steps, a user presses a mouse button to signify a graphical "pick" in a widget, within an encompassing **tkinter**-produced frame shown on-screen. That choice, or "event", is recognized by and acted upon by the **tkinter** function controlling that widget. This event may generate a "request" for graphical service, and this request displays the data or graphics within the **tkinter** frame. A very similar situation is present in the X Window System Event-Request Model.

3.4.3.2.1 *Non-Event Driven tkinter*

That brings up some interesting questions: What kind of graphics is <u>not</u> event driven, and what apps or programs accomplish this way of displaying data? Basically static, non-interactive forms of computer graphics. Can you name any of those? And, is **tkinter** able to do this form of non-event driven processing, and exactly how?

Well, here's an answer to that last question.

As we've noted, **tkinter** is primarily designed for event-driven graphics programming, where the program responds to user input or system events. However, you can also create non-event driven graphics using **tkinter** by using a technique called "animation loops".

In a non-event driven program, you need to create your own loop that continuously updates the graphical elements.

Here's a basic example of how you can create a non-event driven graphical program using **tkinter**:

Example 3.35

```
import tkinter as tk
def update_graphics():
    # Update your graphical elements here
    # This function will be called repeatedly in the main loop
    # Example: Move a shape on a canvas
    canvas.move(shape, 1, 0)
    # Schedule the next update
    root.after(10, update_graphics)  # Update every 10 milliseconds
root = tk.Tk()
canvas = tk.Canvas(root, width=400, height=400)
canvas.pack()
# Create a shape on the canvas
shape = canvas.create_rectangle(50, 50, 100, 100, fill='red')
# Start the update loop
update_graphics()
root.mainloop()
```

In the above example, the **update_graphics()** function is called repeatedly using the **root.after()** method, which schedules a function to be called after a specified delay (in milliseconds). Inside the **update_graphics()** function, you can update your graphical elements as needed. In this case, the example moves a rectangle on a canvas by calling the **canvas. move()** method.

By adjusting the delay passed to **root.after()**, you can control the speed of the updates. Smaller delays result in faster updates and smoother animation, but they can also consume more system resources.

Keep in mind that **tkinter** is not optimized for high-performance graphics or animations! For more complex or demanding graphics, you might consider using specialized libraries or frameworks such as Pygame or OpenGL.

3.4.3.3 Basic Widget Construction Techniques

Widgets are constructed images on the screen display, and they have a unique "style", depending on the details of what information, and the kind of interactivity you want them to participate in. The "style" of a widget is controlled by many complex graphical components. For example, the X Window System, the display manager used, and the operating system itself. The **tkinter** module contains two versions of widgets: a default, or "generic version", which makes widgets look the same regardless of what windowing system, operating system, or display manager is running. **tkinter** also implements widgets that emulate a particular windowing system, operating system, or display manager's "style". Which **tkinter** modules you import determines which widget sets are available to generate events and "callbacks". The standard way of doing this uses the module tk to access the "generic" widgets, and the module ttk to access the "styled" widgets. You <u>must</u> import the tk module, because it allows you to create a "root", or outer-most frame window. You optionally import the ttk module if you want the "styled" widgets.

Note

As is done in some of the following examples, you can use both the tk and ttk widgets in a GUI Python 3 script file.

To use the "generic" widgets, include the following **import** statement at the top of the Python 3 script file-

import tkinter as tk
or-
import tkinter

To use the "styled" widgets, include the following **import** statement at the top of the Python 3 script file:

from tkinter import ttk

The following two tables list the standard, pre-defined widgets in the **tkinter** module.

The listing of widgets in Table 3.7 is used for user input. You can choose between the tk and ttk widgets. But sometimes you must use the tk version because the equivalent ttk versions don't exist.

Table 3.8 shows widgets display information, but don't allow any user interaction.

TABLE 3.7

tkinter, tk and ttk Input Widgets

Widget Name in tk and ttk	Function
tk.Button, ttk.Button	Display a button to execute some operation.
tk.Menu	Produce a top level pulldown or popup menu.
ttk.Menubutton	Display a popup or pulldown menu of buttons.
tk.OptionMenu	Display a popup menu, and a button to activate it.
tk.Entry, ttk.Entry	Enter one line of text in an object.
tk.Text	Display and edit formatted multi-line text.
tk.Checkbutton, ttk.Checkbutton	Display on-off, or True-False selections in an object.
tk.Radiobutton, ttk.Radiobutton	Display on-off selections in an object.
tk.Listbox	Display one or more alternatives from a list of choices.
ttk.Combobox	Display a text field with a pulldown list of values.
ttk.Notebook	Manages a collection of windows and displays a single one at a time.
tk.Scale, ttk.Scale	Allows selection a numerical value via a "slider" on a scale.

TABLE 3.8

tkinter, tk, and ttk Information Display Widgets

Widget Name in tk and ttk	Function
tk.Label, ttk.Label	Display a fixed text string, or image.
tk.Message	Display a fixed multi-line text string.
ttk.Separator	Display a horizontal or vertical separator line.
ttk.Progressbar	Shows the relative progress of some operation.
ttk.Treeview	Display a hierarchy of items as a tree.

When we wrote this book, we found out the version of the Tk toolkit by using the following commands in Python Version 3.11.2 running on our Raspberry Pi 5 system:

```
$ python3
Python 3.11.2 (main, Nov 30 2024, 21:22:50) [GCC 12.2.0] on linux
Type "help", "copyright", "credits" or "license" for more information.
>>> import tkinter
>>> tkinter.TkVersion
8.6
>>>
```

At the time we wrote this book, the best source of documentation for **tkinter** can be found at the following URL:

https://docs.python.org/3/library/tk.html

3.4.3.4 General Form of a Widget Call, and a Primary Example

As shown in Section 3.4.3.2, there are several parts to **tkinter** widget GUI script file construction, but the basic parts follow this outline:

1. Generating data.
2. Constructing your widgets, using a set of universal constructor tools and the **tkinter** widget method set.
3. "Hooking" the data of the first part to the widget constructors of the second part, all within the context of an infinite(but indeterminately interrupted) event-loop.

In this section, we show the general form of widget instancing. We then show an outline of **tkinter** GUI scripting, and also a primary example of one.

tkinter widgets can be constructed to display and be hooked up to your Python 3 application code, either using purely an OOP approach, or they can be constructed using a procedural/imperative programming approach.

As stated in Section 3.4.3.2, we choose the latter approach because it's easier for beginners. By the time you do all the examples we present here, you should be able to see that OOP is an essential, but not <u>mandatory</u>, part of **tkinter** GUI programming.

The general form of using a **tkinter** widget is as follows:

```
>>> widget = Widget.method (master, option=value, option=value,...)
```

where:

widget is the name assigned in your Python 3 script to the particular instance you are creating and using

Widget is the master instance of a widget class in the **tkinter** module

method is the "operation" of instancing some master instance of the widget

master is the "container", or frame, to which our instance of the widget belongs, or is attached to

option is a graphical entity or modifier that gives attributes to your particular instance

value is one of the characteristics that the option can take on

After importing the **tkinter** module, the first thing you need to do is create an object, which is a surrounding frame or window, for the display of your information and/or data. This is done by creating a TK object with the following generic line of Python 3 code:

window_object_name = tkinter.Tk()

Then you create widgets you've selected for their suitability to your purposes, and add them to the frames widget hierarchy.

For example, to create a button widget instance, you would call either the tk or ttk Button method. You need to specify the window_object_name as the first argument, as follows:

cmd_button = tk.Button(window_object_name, text="Some text.")

or

cmd_button = ttk.Button(application_window, text="Some text.")

The arguments needed to create each kind of widget vary, so you should refer to the Python 3 documentation we specified in Section 3.4.3.2 for each specific widget type shown in brief in Table 3.7.

The following simple example shows a complete **tkinter** Python 3 script and the widget it creates. You should create and then execute these six lines of code in Thonny's Script Area, and run it with the Toolbar Run icon, using Way 2 (Script mode). Line numbers are shown <u>for reference only</u> in the following code.

Example 3.36

```
1 import tkinter
2 from tkinter import ttk
3 w = tkinter.Tk()
4 w.title("Python GUI")
5 ttk.Label(w,text="My first tkinter gui window").grid(column=0, row=0)
6 w.mainloop()
```

When this widget was generated on our Raspberry Pi 5 OS display, it appeared in the extreme upper-left corner of the display screen, just below the Raspberry in the Raspberry Pi menu, but we could manually move it wherever we wanted on the screen display.

To close the widget, just click on the "destroy window" button (shown in Figure 3.2 as the X in the upper right-hand corner of the widget) in your

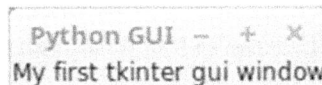

FIGURE 3.2
First Python GUI display.

style of GUI window in which the widget was created. You may have to expand the window to see all of the window manipulation buttons, but we didn't need to do that on our Raspberry Pi 5. The following universal traits of a **tkinter** widget GUI script file, which are illustrated in Example 3.36 and Figure 3.2, are as follows:

1. As specified in Section 3.4.3.2, **tkinter** programming is event driven, meaning you invoke **tkinter** and put it in a *wait state*, where it waits for an event like a mouse button click on the destroy window button, or a keyboard entry, and so forth. The widgets you create, and which remain on screen, generally only do so while **tkinter** is waiting for an event to happen, or until you destroy the window. You can also construct exit handling events in your script to close the widget and its window.

2. Lines 1 and 2 import all **tkinter** modules and the ttk styled widgets into the current session.

3. Line 3 creates the frame within which all widgets will exist, and assigns it a name **w**.

4. Line 4 gives a title, "Python GUI", to the frame.

5. Line 5 instantiates the ttk *Label method*, assigns it a title "My first **tkinter** gui window", and then uses the grid geometry manager to position the label in the frame **w**. There are three geometry managers available in **tkinter**: "pack", "grid", and "place". The grid geometry manager, which treats every window or frame as a table of rows and columns, gives you the greatest control over where widgets and their components are placed.

6. Line 6 starts off the event-driven loop that **tkinter** enters, and constructs the *Label widget*, with your modifying options, on screen.

In-Chapter Exercise

44. If necessary, install **tkinter** on your Raspberry Pi system, and do Example 3.36. Then modify it to execute any other simple widget display you find interesting and useful on your system. How can you control exactly where it's placed on the screen display when the widget is instanced?

3.4.3.5 Hooking tkinter Widgets to Applications in Python: Examples

Provided with the widget method set of available core widgets in **tkinter**, and armed with your knowledge of Python 3 programming up to this point in the chapter, you are ready to do the following Examples. The next simple Example allows a user to add two real numbers as text, which has been entered interactively, on lines inside the widget. Line numbers and comments are for reference only and are <u>not</u> executed. We again describe and explain in simple terms what each line in the code does. And, as in Example 3.36, you can enter the code in Thonny's Script Area and use the Toolbar Run Icon to launch it.

Example 3.37

```
 1  import tkinter as tk
 2  from tkinter import ttk
 3  from functools import partial
    # This is the data generating module, which computes the sum.
 4  def add_it(label_result, n1, n2):
 5      num1 = (n1.get())
 6      num2 = (n2.get())
 7      result = float(num1)+float(num2)
 8      label_result.config(text="Sum = %f" % result)
 9      return
    # This "grids" the widget object where indicated, then returns it.
10  def mkgrid(r, c, w):
11      w.grid(row=r, column=c, sticky='news')
12      return w
13  root = tk.Tk()
14  root.title('Real Number Adder')
    # The rest hooks the adder into the grid manager widgets.
15  add1_lab = mkgrid(0, 0, ttk.Label(root, text="addend 1",anchor='e'))
16  add2_lab = mkgrid(1, 0, ttk.Label(root, text="addend 2",anchor='e'))
17  add1= mkgrid(0, 1, ttk.Entry(root))
18  add2= mkgrid(1, 1, ttk.Entry(root))
19  spacer = mkgrid(0, 2, ttk.Label(root, text="))
20  labelResult = ttk.Label(root)
21  labelResult.grid(row=7, column=2)
22  add_it = partial(add_it, labelResult, add1, add2)
23  add_but = mkgrid(1, 2, ttk.Button(root, text="Add them",command=add_it))
    # Starts the root main event loop
24  root.mainloop()
```

A line-by-line description/explanation of Example 3.37 is as follows:

Lines 1 and 2. Import all **tkinter** modules and the ttk styled widgets into the current session.

Line 3. Imports the **partial functools** function module.

Lines 4–9. Defines the function **add_it**, that computes the real number sum.

Lines 10–12. Defines a function that will specify grid locations for the grid manager.

Line 13. Creates the frame within which all widgets will exist, and assigns it a name- "root".

Line 14. Adds a title, "Real Number Adder", to the frame "root".

Lines 15 and 16. Constructs 2 Label widgets to designate the input locations for the addends.

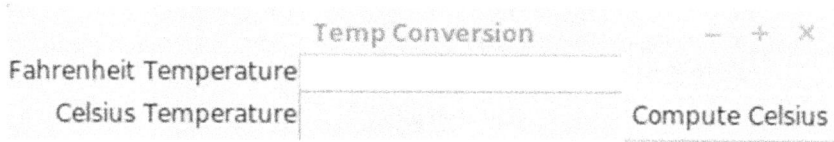

Temp Conversion   – + ×

Fahrenheit Temperature

Celsius Temperature   Compute Celsius

FIGURE 3.3
Tk Temp conversion display.

Line 17 and 18. Allows input of both addends and constructs them using the Entry widget.

Line 19. Places a spacer at grid position 0,2.

Lines 20 and 21. Establish a ttk label in the root window for the sum.

Line 22. Uses the Python 3 **partial** function to call the **add_it** function, with values of **add1** and **add2**.

Line 23. Defines a ttk button at grid location 1,2, that calls the function **add_it** to find the sum when the button is "pressed" to generate an event.

Line 24. Starts the event loop, creating the root window and all widgets defined above.

Even though Example 3.37 uses the procedural/imperative programming paradigm, syntax, and data abstraction, after having examined the line-by-line description and explanation of it above, you should begin to see that **tkinter** GUI scripts are basically composed of OOP class instance objects. All of the methods applied to those instances come from the methods applied to the core widgets in **tkinter**.

The following example will construct a Fahrenheit-to-Celsius temperature conversion GUI with **tkinter**. A line-by-line description/explanation of the script follows the code (see Figure 3.3). Line numbers and comments are for reference only and are <u>not</u> executed. And, as in Examples 3.36 and 3.37, you can enter the code in Thonny's Script Area and use the Toolbar Run Icon to launch it.

Example 3.38

```
1 import tkinter as tk
2 from tkinter import ttk
# This function computes the Celsius temperature from the Fahrenheit.
3 def findcel():
4     famt = ftmp.get()
5     if famt == '':                          #not double quote, 2 single quotes
6             cent.configure(text='')
7     else:
8             famt = float(famt)
9     camt = (famt - 32) / 1.8
```

```
# A method (configure) applied to cent to convert camt to a string (str(camt)).
10      cent.configure(text=str(camt))
# This grids the widget object where indicated, then returns it.
11 def mkgrid(r, c, w):
12      w.grid(row=r, column=c, sticky='news')
13      return w
14 root = tk.Tk()
15 root.title('Temp Conversion')
# The rest hooks the Temperatures into the grid manager widgets.
16 flab = mkgrid(0, 0, ttk.Label(root, text="Fahrenheit Temperature",anchor='e'))
17 clab = mkgrid(1, 0, ttk.Label(root, text="Celsius Temperature",anchor='e'))
18 ftmp = mkgrid(0, 1, ttk.Entry(root))
19 cent = mkgrid(1, 1, ttk.Label(root, text="", relief='sunken',anchor='w'))
20 elab = mkgrid(0, 2, ttk.Label(root, text="))
21 fbut = mkgrid(1, 2, ttk.Button(root, text="Compute Celsius",command=findcel))
# Starts the root main event loop
22 root.mainloop()
```

Here is a line-by-line description/explanation of the code of Example 3.38.

Lines 1 and 2. Imports all **tkinter** modules and the ttk styled widgets into the current session.

Lines 3–10. Defines the function **findcel**, that does the temperature conversion from F to C. Note that lines 5 and 6 ensure that if an empty string is entered for **famt**, then **cent** is empty as well. Line 10 converts **cent** to text.

Lines 11–13. Defines a function that will specify grid locations for the grid manager.

Line 14. Creates the frame within which all widgets will exist, and assigns it a name "**root**".

Line 15. Adds a title, "**Temp Conversion**", to the frame "**root**".

Lines 16–21. Define the labels and buttons necessary for the event generation and callbacks.

Line 22. Starts the main root event loop.

Again, even though the previous example is a procedural/imperative model program design, you should be able to recognize from this line-by-line description and explanation that the underlying core widgets from **tkinter** are OOP classes that we have instanced as objects.

The example used methods applied to those classes, but the structure of our script file was still functional and declarative in nature.

In-Chapter Exercises

45.   What functional and declarative control structure is most similar to the event loops used in the above three Examples?

46. Do Examples 3.37 and 3.38 on your Raspberry Pi 5 system. Then modify them to accomplish interesting calculations, of your own choosing, that take input in a Tk GUI, and show output results in a similar fashion to the Examples.

47. What is the difference between a Python 3 method and a Python 3 function?

48. In the grid geometry manager, where does the numbering of cells that widgets can be placed in begin, and how do the numbering indices evolve? For instance, in Example 3.38, what does grid position 0,2 mean?

49. What code would put a "quit" button in the grid cell 0,2 instead of a blank label?

3.4.4 Multi-threaded Concurrency with Python

The first question you must ask yourself about how and why the Raspberry Pi 5 OS functions the way it does is: Given the limited resources and very prodigious nature of modern computer hardware, how does an operating system maximize performance and efficiency for all users of the system? And furthermore, how can user programs, such as Python 3 scripts, reflect this technique?

The answer to that question for the Raspberry Pi 5 OS is:

First, by separating the hardware, that is, the SoC CPU and its cores, main memory, and peripheral memory, into multiple virtual machinery: in short, via *virtualization*.

Then, by executing instructions *concurrently* on this virtualized machinery – this means not in any particular sequence, and perhaps even all at once.

Finally, by making sure that the data generated and stored in the file system is *persistent* over time.

Python 3, as a Raspberry Pi 5 software tool that creates user programs and scripts, can achieve concurrency with a mechanism called *threads*, and the concurrent execution of instructions by threads. This is very similar to UNIX and Linux system programming with threads.

Similar to the Linux system programming concurrency facility, Python 3 threads give you the ability to run several programs concurrently, in a single process. When you create one or more threads in your Python 3 program, they are executed concurrently, independently of each other, and they can share information among them because they are using the same resources of a single process. These features make Python 3 threads useful in creating Python 3 applications for such things as network programming and the creation of GUI programs.

Python 3 supports threads on the Raspberry Pi 5 OS, and any other systems that use the *POSIX threads library (pthreads)*.

In terms of Python 3 performance, threads *cannot* ordinarily take advantage of multiprocessor or multicore processor architectures, even with the ARM architecture used in the Raspberry Pi 5's CPU. Thread switching can only occur between the execution of individual bytecodes in the Python 3 interpreter. The frequency with which the interpreter checks for thread switching is set by the **sys.setcheckinterval()** function. By default, the interpreter checks for thread switching after a limited, but prescribed number of bytecode instructions.

One of the many ways around this impasse is to use various Python 3 extension modules. The coverage of these is beyond the scope of what we can illustrate here for beginners, and what is necessary for a beginner to have at her command. But being somewhat familiar with Python 3 threads is useful, even for the beginner.

3.4.4.1 Python Thread Examples Using Procedural/Imperative Programming

We show both the **_thread** and **threading** modules in Python 3.11.2, in the examples we present in this section.

Unless you absolutely need OOP tools and capabilities for Python 3, in general, and specifically in the threading module, the choice is largely a matter of programmer and programming team preference, and their programming design goals/methodologies. We also cover some of the functions offered in the **threading** module in Section 3.4.5.

> ****Note**** The basic **_thread** module does <u>not</u>
> necessarily require that you program with OOP!

It's very easy to use if you are accustomed to, and desire to, exclusively structure your programs with the procedural/imperative programming model. The procedural/imperative model is used by programming languages such as C.

The **_thread** module provides low-level primitives for working with multiple threads of control (also called *lightweight processes* or *tasks*) that share their global data space. For synchronization, simple *locks* (also called *mutexes*) are provided within the classes and methods of this module.

3.4.4.1.1 _thread Functions Reference

Since the basic **_thread** module is a bit simpler than the more advanced **threading** module covered later in the next subsection, we give examples of that first. This module provides a portable interface to whatever threading system is available on your platform: its interfaces work in the same way on any system with an installed pthreads POSIX threads implementation (including Linux systems and others). Python 3 scripts that use the Python 3 **_thread** module work on all of these platforms without changing their source code.

3.4.4.1.2 *Examples*

Our first Example allows you to experiment with a script that deploys the main **_thread** interfaces.

The script in Example 3.39 uses Way 2 (Script Mode) to enter the code into Thonny's Script Area and is run with the Toolbar Run Icon. It starts successive, one-at-a-time-only threads. Each new thread creation is triggered by a key typed at the Python 3 command line in Thonny's Shell Area, followed by pressing **<Enter>**, until you type an **x** at that console, followed by pressing a final **<Enter>**. Following is the code, and its execution in Python 3.11.2 on our representative Raspberry Pi systems.

Example 3.39

```
import _thread
def child(tid):
    print ('Started thread', tid)
def parent():
    i = 0
    while 1:
        i += 1
        _thread.start_new_thread(child, (i,))
        if input() == 'x': break
parent()

>>> %Run -c $EDITOR_CONTENT
Started thread 1
k
Started thread 2
o
Started thread 3
r
Started thread 4
x
>>>
```

What exactly is going on in Example 3.39? A single thread is being started, and then it immediately dies, and the program loops indeterminately, allowing you to create successive new threads by pressing a key on the keyboard, followed by pressing **<Enter>**. Only two thread calls are made in this example: the import of the **_thread** module, and the call to its method, **start_new_thread**, that creates a new thread. This call takes a function (or other callable) object as a tuple argument, and starts a new thread to execute a call to the passed function with the passed arguments. It's that simple!

Following is the code of another Example, which you can again use Way 2 (Script Mode) to enter the code into Thonny's Script Area, and run with the Toolbar Run Icon. Its command line execution in the Thonny Shell Area is done in Python 3.11.2 on our representative Raspberry Pi systems. It iterates to create new threads that exist simultaneously, in parallel:

Example 3.40

```
import _thread, time
def counter(myId, count):        # function that will run in each thread
  for i in range(count):
    time.sleep(1)                # simulate useful code here? why here?
    print ('[%s] => %s' % (myId, i))
  for i in range(5):             # call start_new_thread 5 times
  _thread.start_new_thread(counter, (i, 3)) # loop the newest thread 3 times
  time.sleep(5)                  # prevents exit from parent too early
  print ('Main thread exiting.') # all threads are destroyed by default
```

When we execute this script file with the Thonny Toolbar Run icon, we get:

```
>>> %Run -c $EDITOR_CONTENT
[1] => 0[0] => 0[2] => 0[3] => 0[4] => 0

[1] => 1[3] => 1
[0] => 1
[2] => 1
[4] => 1

[3] => 2
[1] => 2
[2] => 2
[4] => 2
[0] => 2
Main thread exiting.
>>>
```

What exactly is happening in Example 3.40? Five threads are being created and run simultaneously. Within each thread, the counter value, which is displayed from 0 to 4, is being printed in the Thonny Shell Area. The **time.sleep(1)** method in the function **counter** is used to "simulate" code that might be used to do some system programming task(s) at that point in the code.

In-Chapter Exercises

50. If each of the threads you start in Example 3.39 were to perform some operations, after what line in the given code would you put the lines of code that performed that work?

51. In the output of Example 3.40, you will notice that the order in which the value of the **myId** variable is printed is not always the same. Why is this true?

52. If you run Example 3.40 a few times, is the order of the printed value of **myId** the same on each successive run of the program? Why or why not?

3.4.4.2 Python Thread Example Using the OOP Model

The **threading** module builds higher-level threading interfaces on top of the lower-level **_thread** module. If you want your applications to take advantage of the computational power of the multi-core Broadcom CPU in your Raspberry Pi 5, you should use the multi-processing **threading** module. However, **threading** is still an appropriate model to deploy if you want to run multiple I/O-bound tasks.

3.4.4.3 OOP GUIs and Producer–Consumer Model Threads

Threads are an extremely integral part of the Tk GUI toolkit, which we illustrated in Section 3.4.3. This also applies in general to GUI libraries, such as Qt. Since many of the functions of a GUI use synchronous I/O, any operation that can block or take a long time to complete must be spawned to run in parallel so that the central GUI module (the main thread) is always running. Although such spawned children can be run as multiple processes, the efficiency and shared environment model of threads make them ideal for this role, since they are run in the namespace of a single process. Most GUI toolkits do <u>not</u> allow multiple threads to update the main thread in parallel-updates are usually restricted to the main thread.

The two important points to be made about Python 3 threads in a GUI are that the main thread handles all screen graphics updates, and that GUI threads must obey the synchronization rules established for general thread concurrency according to standardized models.

All threads in a GUI generally follow what is called the *producer–consumer model*. Simply put, that's where one or more objects (the producers) are responsible for placing data into some storage pool, and one or more objects (the consumers) are responsible for removing data from that pool.

The drawbacks to the producer-consumer model are as follows:

The producer(s) cannot add more data than the storage pool can hold.

The consumers(s) cannot take from an empty pool.

The actions of all objects *must* be synchronized.

We address more of the issues of the producer–consumer model in Section 3.4.5, and give an example Python 3 program in that section to illustrate the solution implemented by the model, using what are known as *condition variables*.

3.4.4.4 OOP Threads Example

The following is an example illustrating the basic methodology of using OOP and Python 3 threads. We first describe, in blocks of code, what's happening in the Python 3 code of the Example. Then, we present the actual Example code in its entirety. Finally, we show sample output when the code is run in Thonny.

It would be very instructive for a beginner to compare what the basic methodology and structure of the following OOP example is, compared with the previous Python 3 thread code examples presented.

The components of Example 3.41 are shown as blocks of code as follows (the blocks are indicated as comments on the line of code that begins the block):

Block 1.

Import the Thread class from the threading module. Why do it this way? The **Thread** class of the **threading** module contains many useful methods that allow you to construct and manipulate threads. Using it avoids having to define your own functions or methods to do the same operations. Not doing it this way would mean you would have to write lower-level system programming functions to accomplish thread creation and synchronization, and then, somehow, stitch that code together with higher-level Python 3 functional programming code.

Block 2.

Subclass your own thread, named **Threader**, by defining it as a child class based on the **Thread** class, and also define the constructor properties of it as function definitions.

Block 3.

Define a **.run** method in the **Threader** class. This run method is always executed when we call the **start** method of any object in our **Threader** class. The **sleep** function makes the thread inactive for a definite amount of time. This randomly-timed sleep will ensure that the code will <u>not</u> be executed so quickly that we will not be able to notice any changes.

Block 4.

<u>The critical block.</u> Create three objects. Apply the **.start** method to each object, which, in turn, executes the **.run** method for each object. You need to call the **.join** method built into the **Thread** class, and apply it to each object, or the program will terminate before the threads complete their execution!

Place the following code in the Thonny Script Area, and use the Run Toolbar Icon to execute it:

Example 3.41

```
from threading import Thread        #Block 1.
from random import randint
import time
```

```
class Threader(Thread):                  #Block 2.
    def __init__(self, val):
        # The Constructor
        Thread.__init__(self)
        self.val = val
    def run(self):                       #Block 3.
        for i in range(1, self.val):
            print('Value %d in thread %s' % (i, self.getName()))
            # Sleep for random time
            GoToSleep = randint(1, 5)
            print('%s sleeping for %d seconds...' % (self.getName(), GoToSleep))
            time.sleep(GoToSleep)

if __name__ == '__main__':               #Block 4.
    # Declare Threader class
    Threader_Object1 = Threader(4)
    Threader_Object1.setName('Thread 1')
    Threader_Object2 = Threader(4)
    Threader_Object2.setName('Thread 2')
    Threader_Object3 = Threader(4)
    Threader_Object3.setName('Thread 3')
    # Run the threads!
    Threader_Object1.start()
    Threader_Object2.start()
    Threader_Object3.start()
# Wait. . .
    Threader_Object1.join()
    Threader_Object2.join()
    Threader_Object3.join()
#Exit. . .
    print('Main Terminating...')
```

The output from the program is as follows, as shown in the Thonny Shell Area:

```
>>> %Run ex41.py
Value 1 in thread Thread 1
Thread 1 sleeping for 5 seconds...Value 1 in thread Thread 2

Value 1 in thread Thread 3Thread 2 sleeping for 4 seconds...

Thread 3 sleeping for 1 seconds...
Value 2 in thread Thread 3
Thread 3 sleeping for 4 seconds...
Value 2 in thread Thread 2
Thread 2 sleeping for 3 seconds...
Value 2 in thread Thread 1
Thread 1 sleeping for 1 seconds...
Value 3 in thread Thread 3
Thread 3 sleeping for 4 seconds...
Value 3 in thread Thread 1
Thread 1 sleeping for 2 seconds...
Value 3 in thread Thread 2
```

Thread 2 sleeping for 4 seconds...
Main Terminating...
>>>

Note

When we ran this script file in Python 3.11.3, we got the following DeprecationWarning messages:

/home/bob/Public/ex41.py:21: DeprecationWarning: setName() is deprecated, set the name attribute instead **Threader_Object1.setName('Thread 1')**
/home/bob/Public/ex41.py:23: DeprecationWarning: setName() is deprecated, set the name attribute instead **Threader_Object2.setName('Thread 2')**
/home/bob/Public/ex41.py:25: DeprecationWarning: setName() is deprecated, set the name attribute instead **Threader_Object3.setName('Thread 3')**
/home/bob/Public/ex41.py:12: DeprecationWarning: getName() is deprecated, get the name attribute instead **print('Value %d in thread %s' % (i, self.getName()))**
Value 1 in thread Thread 1Value 1 in thread Thread 2
Value 1 in thread Thread 3
/home/bob/Public/ex41.py:15: DeprecationWarning: getName() is deprecated, get the name attribute instead **print('%s sleeping for %d seconds...' % (self.getName(), GoToSleep))**

So if you're running Python 3.11.3 or later, you can substitute the "instead" code shown above in the DeprecationWarning messages into your script file, and be in conformance with the latest release of Python 3 at the time you're running the script file.

In-Chapter Exercise

53. If you wanted the threads to do some actual work, in what block of Example 3.41, and exactly where in that block, would you put the Python 3 code to accomplish that work?

3.4.5 Talking Threads: The Producer–Consumer Problem Using the queue Module

In computing, the *producer–consumer problem* (sometimes called the *bounded-buffer problem*) is a classic example of the use of various approaches to the synchronization of the execution of multiple threads, or processes. We addressed some of the issues involved with the producer–consumer model in Section 3.4.4. In this section, we give more details and a worked example to further illustrate this important computer science concept using Python 3.

The problem concerns two tasks, the "producer" process and the "consumer" process, that share a common, fixed-size queue, or storage pool. The producer "produces" a piece of data, puts it into the queue, and starts producing more data. Simultaneously, the consumer is "consuming" the data, i.e., removing it from the queue.

The solution to the problem, as we present it here, is to make sure that the producer will not add data into the queue when it's full, and that the consumer will not try to remove data when the queue is empty. The next time the consumer removes an item from the queue, it notifies the producer, which starts to fill the queue again. In the same way, the consumer can become idle if it finds the queue is empty. The next time the producer puts data into the queue, it activates the idled consumer.

There are a variety of approaches to the solution in Python 3, for example, using locks, semaphores, event synchronization, condition objects or variables, barriers, and the **queue** module. The Python 3 **queue** module has three classes that facilitate threading, and these are only different in terms of retrieval order from the queue: **Queue**, **LifoQueue**, and **PriorityQueue**. It also uses a number of Python 3 methods, which have within them the "locking/releasing" mechanisms that can be applied in order for you to work very efficiently with multi-threaded process applications. We choose to implement our example solution in Section 3.4.5.2 using the **queue** module, with its **Queue** class, and its accompanying Python 3 methods. Section 3.4.5.1 gives a basic overview of the **queue** module, along with its classes and methods.

In all of the approaches to a solution in Python 3, the threads, as executing processes, "talk" to each other, or have *interprocess communication (IPC)*, while they are actively producing or consuming data.

A summary of the solution is illustrated in Figure 3.4.

3.4.5.1 The queue Module, Its Classes and Methods

The **queue** module in Python 3 implements three OOP classes of queue, which differ only in the order in which the entries are retrieved. In a *First In First Out* (FIFO) queue, the first tasks put into the queue are the first taken out. In a *Last In First Out* (LIFO) queue, the most recently added entry is the first retrieved (similar to a "push-down" stack). In a priority queue, the entries are sorted, and the lowest-valued entry is retrieved first.

The critical feature of the **queue** module is that locks, and release mechanisms, that temporarily block or free competing threads are implemented in the OOP "public" methods for the classes, <u>without the programmer having to do it</u>!

For your convenience, we present the **queue** module definitions, taken from the Python documentation, of the following Queue classes, and their exception handling methods:

class queue.Queue(maxsize=0)
This is the FIFO constructor for a queue. The argument for **maxsize** is an integer that defines the largest number of items that can be placed in the queue. Placement of items on the queue will be blocked if the **maxsize** has been reached; queued items must be consumed to unblock. The queue size default is infinite.

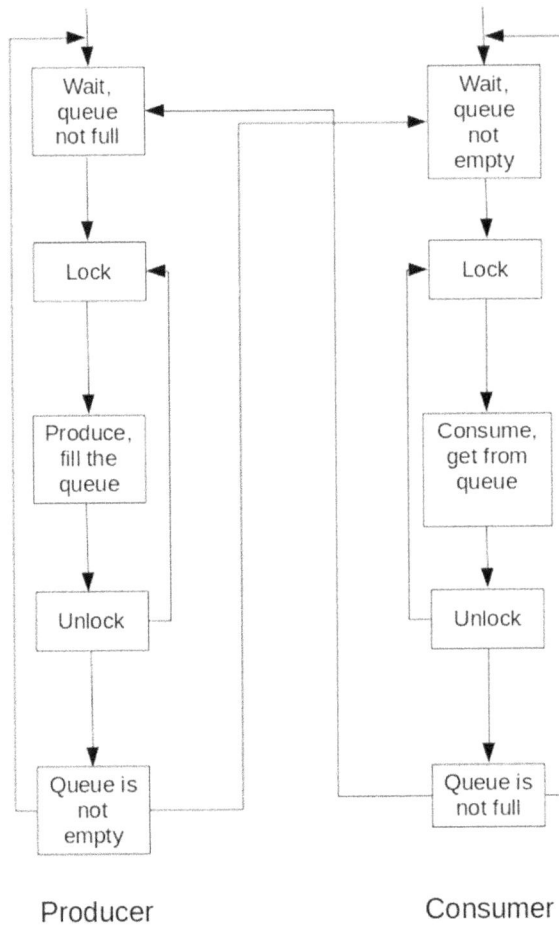

FIGURE 3.4
Producer/consumer model solution.

class queue.LifoQueue(maxsize=0)
This is the LIFO constructor for a queue. The argument for **maxsize** is an integer that defines the largest number of items that can be placed in the queue. Placement of items on the queue will be blocked if the size has been reached; queued items must be consumed to unblock. The queue size default is infinite.

class queue.PriorityQueue(maxsize=0)
This is the constructor for a prioritized queue. Placement of items on the queue will be blocked if the **maxsize** has been reached; queued items must be consumed to unblock. The queue size default is infinite. Note that the lowest valued entries in the queue are retrieved first (the lowest valued entry

is the one returned by sorted(list(entries))[0]). Typically, entries are tuples of the form- (priority_number, data).

exception queue.Empty

An exception raised when non-blocking .get() or .get_nowait() is called on a Queue object which is empty.

exception queue.Full

An exception raised when non-blocking .put() or .put_nowait() is called on a Queue object which is full.

The three Queue classes provide the public methods described in Table 3.9, which have also been taken from the Python 3 documentation. Remember that a public method is accessible anywhere outside of the class.

TABLE 3.9

queue Class Public Methods

Methods and Arguments	Description
Queue.qsize()	Obtain the approximate size of the queue. No assurance that put() or get() will not block.
Queue.empty()	Tests the truth value of an empty queue. No assurance that put() or get() will not block.
Queue.full()	Tests the truth value of a full queue. No assurance that put() or get() will not block.
Queue.put(item, block=True, timeout=None)	Adds item to the queue. If block is true and timeout is None, blocking occurs. If timeout is a positive number, block occurs at that number of seconds, and the Full exception is raised. If block is false, put item on the queue if a space is available. If no space is available, raise a Full exception, and ignore the timeout.
Queue.put_nowait(item)	Same as .put, with arguments item and block=false.
Queue.get(block=True, timeout=None)	Delete and return an item from the queue. If block is true and timeout is None, block until an item is available. If timeout is a positive number, it blocks at most timeout seconds and raises the Empty exception if no item is available within that time. Otherwise (block is false), return an item if one is immediately available, else raise the Empty exception (timeout is ignored in that case).
Queue.get_nowait()	Equal to .get(False)
Queue.task_done()	Signals that an enqueued task is finished.
Queue.join()	Blocks until all items in the queue have been retrieved and processed. The count of unfinished tasks goes up or down depending on whether an item is added or taken off the queue.

3.4.5.2 *Examples of Using the Queue Module Queue Classes*

The three Examples we present in this section illustrate **queue** module classes and methods, and are used to construct a queue in a very simple and basic way. Example 3.42 uses the LifoQueue class to implement a LIFO queue, similar to a stack. Example 3.43 uses the PriorityQueue class to implement a queue in which the order of retrieving the elements has to do with some characteristic of each element. Example 3.44 uses the Queue class to implement a FIFO queue. They can each be executed in Thonny, using the Script Area and the Run Toolbar Icon.

Example 3.42

```
import queue

q = queue.LifoQueue()
for i in range(7):
    q.put(i)
while not q.empty():
    print(q.get(), end=' ')

>>> %Run -c $EDITOR_CONTENT
6 5 4 3 2 1 0
>>>
```

Example 3.43

```
import queue as Q

q = Q.PriorityQueue()
q.put(15)
q.put(18)
q.put(4)
q.put(9)
while not q.empty():
        print (q.get(),)

>>> %Run -c $EDITOR_CONTENT
4
9
15
18
>>>
```

Example 3.44

```
import queue

q = queue.Queue()
for i in range(8):
    q.put(i)
while not q.empty():
```

```
      print(q.get(), end=' ')
      print()
>>> %Run -c $EDITOR_CONTENT
0
1
2
3
4
5
6
7
>>>
```

3.4.5.3 An Example of the Queue Class Solution
to the Producer–Consumer Model

The following Python 3 code brings together much of the syntax and structure from this chapter. This final Example illustrates a Python 3 solution to
the producer-consumer problem, using a FIFO queue with the **queue.Queue**
class, in a multi-threaded program. It uses OOP, the threading module and
its methods, to start two threads – Producer and Consumer.

An overview of how we use the Queue class to obtain a solution to the
producer–consumer problem, taken from the reference material, is as follows:

> "The Producer places a piece of data on the queue using the **.put** method.
> The utility and advantage the queue module is most visible here- **.put**
> locks the queue, checks to see if the queue is full, and calls an internal
> **.wait()** to pause the producer if the queue is full. The Consumer then
> uses the **.get** method to acquire the lock before removing data from the
> queue, and **.get** checks for an empty queue. If the queue is empty, the
> consumer is put in a wait state.
>
>   **.get()** and **.put()** also implement the notification logic to allow "talk-
> ing" between Producer and Consumer threads."

What exactly is happening, step-by-step, in the code of Example 3.45
below? A brief explanation of the layout of the program, in major summary
blocks, and a description of the operational heart of the code is as follows:

Block 1:
>   This is the initialization part of the program, where the **thread-
> ing** module, sub-module **Thread**, and modules **queue, time,** and
> **random** are imported. In this block, we also instance a class of the
> **queue.Queue** class, and name it **q_buffer.**

Block 2:
>   This defines the function **Producer** as a class derived from the
> **Thread** module, and runs it as self. It specifies the range of integers

that will be used as data "numbering", using the variable numbers. It specifies, in a determinate, or logical repetition loop, how we will add data, as an "actual_number", to the queue. The Producer is put to sleep for a random amount of time.

The shared namespace for **q_buffer** is established here using the **global** keyword.

Block 3:

Very similar to Block 2, this defines the function **Consumer** as a class derived from the **Thread** module, and runs it as self. It specifies, in a determinate, or logical repetition loop, how we will retrieve data, in the form of an "actual_number_gotten", from the queue. The **Consumer** is put to sleep for a random amount of time.

The shared namespace for **q_buffer** is used here via the **global** keyword.

Block 4:

Producer is started first, and then Consumer is started. The threads continue to be produced and consumed until a **<Ctrl> + <Z>** interrupt is sent to the running process from the keyboard.

Trace the steps through the Blocks of code we present next in Example 3.45, in preparation for completion of the In-Chapter Exercises and Problems that follow. Also, in this final Python 3 Example, create the code in a file named **ex45.py** with your favorite text editor, and run it (and also terminate it, and the Python 3 process it spawns), according to our Way4 (Bash Mode) from the Bash command line as shown below :

Example 3.45

```
from threading import Thread        #Block 1
import time
import random
import queue

q_buffer = queue.Queue()

class Producer(Thread):             #Block 2
  def run(self):
    numbers = range(5)
    global q_buffer
    while True:
      actual_number = random.choice(numbers)
      q_buffer.put(actual_number)
      print ("Produced thread", actual_number)
      time.sleep(random.random())
```

```
class Consumer(Thread):                #Block 3
  def run(self):
    global q_buffer
    while True:
      actual_number_gotten = q_buffer.get()
      q_buffer.task_done()
      print ("Consumed thread", actual_number_gotten)
      time.sleep(random.random())

Producer().start()                     #Block 4
Consumer().start()
```

The output from the above example is as follows:

```
$ python3 ex45.py
Produced thread 1
Consumed thread 1
Produced thread 0
Produced thread 4
Consumed thread 0
Consumed thread 4
Produced thread 3
Consumed thread 3
Produced thread 0
Consumed thread 0
Produced thread 4
Consumed thread 4
Produced thread 4
Consumed thread 4
Produced thread 2
Produced thread 1
Consumed thread 2
Produced thread 1
^Z
[1]+  Stopped           python3 ex45.py
$ ps
   PID TTY        TIME CMD
 50443 pts/0   00:00:00 bash
 50611 pts/0   00:00:00 python3
 50615 pts/0   00:00:00 ps
$ kill -9 50611
$
```

In-Chapter Exercise (refer to Example 3.45)

54. As the output of running this program one time shows, the pro-
     duction and consumption of data to and from the buffer are spo-
     radic. That is, sometimes data is produced and then immediately
     consumed, and sometimes data is produced and not immediately
     consumed. Also, you will notice that if you do several runs of the
     program, each run may yield different patterns of production and
     consumption. Why is this so?

3.5 Summary

We gave a broad introduction to the Python 3 programming language, using Python 3.11.2. For the beginner Python 3 programmer, we illustrated all of its important programming capabilities and syntactic structures in the context of the three predominant computer programming paradigms: *virtualization, concurrency, and persistence.* We gave a brief introduction to Thonny, the Python 3 IDE. We showed all of Python 3's important basic syntax, including numbers and expressions, variables, statements, getting input from the user, functions, the procedural/imperative OOP programming models in Python 3, functions, modules, saving and executing Python 3 scripts, string and sequence operations, and error handling. We also gave many basic and practical examples, such as another way of writing shell script files, rewriting Bash and tcsh scripts, basic user file maintenance, backing up files, remote copying with the **rsync** command, and graphics using **tkinter**. Finally, we showed how various forms of thread execution are achieved in Python 3, and how OOP can be deployed to accomplish them.

3.6 Ultimate Reference Glossary

A simplified and abbreviated glossary of some of the terms we have abstracted from the references in Section 3.4 are as follows:

Class: A template for creating user-defined objects. Class definitions normally contain method definitions which operate on instances of the class.

Expression: A piece of syntax which can be evaluated to some value. In other words, an expression is an accumulation of expression elements like literals, names, attribute access, operators, or function calls, which all return a value.

In contrast to many other languages, not all language constructs are expressions. There are also statements which cannot be used as expressions, such as print or if. Assignments are also statements, not expressions.

Immutable: An object with a fixed value. Immutable objects include numbers, strings, and tuples. Such objects cannot be altered. A new object has to be created if a different value has to be stored; for example, a key in a dictionary.

Iterable: An object capable of returning its members one at a time. Examples of iterables include all sequence types (such as a list, string, and tuple) and some nonsequence types like dict and file and objects of any classes you define with an __iter__() or __getitem__() method. Iterables can be used in a for loop and in many other places where a sequence is needed. When an iterable object is passed as an argument to the built-in function iter(), it returns an iterator for the object. This iterator is good for one pass over the set of values. When using iterables, it is usually not necessary to call iter() or deal with iterator objects yourself. The for statement does that automatically for you, creating a temporary unnamed variable to hold the iterator for the duration of the loop.

Lambda: An anonymous inline function consisting of a single expression, which is evaluated when the function is called. The syntax to create a lambda function is lambda [arguments]: expression.

Method: A function which is defined inside a class body. If called as an attribute of an instance of that class, the method will get the instance object as its first argument (which is usually called self).

mutable: Mutable objects can change their value but keep their class identity.

Pythonic: An idea or piece of code which closely follows the most common usages of the Python language, rather than implementing code using structures common to other languages. For example, a common usage in Python is to loop over all elements of an iterable using a for statement. Many other languages do not have this type of construct, so people unfamiliar with Python sometimes use a numerical counter instead:

```
for i in range(len(money)):
    print (money[i])
```

The Pythonic way:

```
for bills in money:
    print (bills)
```

Sequence: An iterable which supports efficient element access using integer indices via the __getitem__() special method and defines a len() method that returns the length of the sequence. Some built-in sequence types are list, str, tuple, and unicode. Note that dict also supports __getitem__() and __len__(), but is considered a mapping rather than a sequence because the lookups use arbitrary immutable keys rather than integers.

type: The kind of object, such as integers or character strings.

Index

Note: Locators in *italics* represent figures and **bold** indicate tables in the text.

For Product Safety Concerns and Information please contact our EU
representative GPSR@taylorandfrancis.com
Taylor & Francis Verlag GmbH, Kaufingerstraße 24, 80331 München, Germany

www.ingramcontent.com/pod-product-compliance
Lightning Source LLC
Chambersburg PA
CBHW060759220326
41598CB00022B/2484